Eastern Europe Unmapped

Eastern Europe Unmapped
Beyond Borders and Peripheries

Edited by
Irene Kacandes and Yuliya Komska

First published in 2018 by
Berghahn Books
www.berghahnbooks.com

© 2018, 2020 Irene Kacandes and Yuliya Komska
First paperback edition published in 2020

All rights reserved. Except for the quotation of short passages
for the purposes of criticism and review, no part of this book
may be reproduced in any form or by any means, electronic or
mechanical, including photocopying, recording, or any information
storage and retrieval system now known or to be invented,
without written permission of the publisher.

Library of Congress Cataloging-in-Publication Data

Names: Kacandes, Irene, 1958– editor. | Komska, Yuliya, editor.
Title: Eastern Europe unmapped : beyond borders and peripheries / edited by
 Irene Kacandes and Yuliya Komska.
Description: First edition. | New York : Berghahn Books, 2018. | Includes
 bibliographical references and index.
Identifiers: LCCN 2017037764 (print) | LCCN 2017041803 (ebook) |
 ISBN 9781785336867 (ebook) | ISBN 9781785336850 (hardback : alk. paper)
Subjects: LCSH: Europe, Eastern—Boundaries—History—20th century. |
 Europe, Eastern—Geography. | Europe, Eastern—Civilization—20th century. |
 Transnationalism.
Classification: LCC DJK48.5 (ebook) | LCC DJK48.5 .E27 2018 (print) |
 DDC 327.47—dc23
LC record available at https://lccn.loc.gov/2017037764

British Library Cataloguing in Publication Data

A catalogue record for this book is available from the British Library

ISBN 978-1-78533-685-0 hardback
ISBN 978-1-78920-530-5 paperback
ISBN 978-1-78533-686-7 ebook

Contents

List of Maps and Figures	vii
Introduction: A Discontiguous Eastern Europe *Yuliya Komska*	1
Part I. Re-placed Religion	29
1. The "Jewish Pope" in the 1940s: On Jewish Cultural and Ethnic Plasticity *Miriam Udel*	31
2. Unmapping Islam in Eastern Europe: Periodization and Muslim Subjectivities in the Balkans *Piro Rexhepi*	53
Part II. Dislodged Dissent	79
3. Located on the Archipelago: Toward a New Definition of Belarusian Intellectuals *Tatsiana Astrouskaya*	81
4. Re-reading *Kultura* from a Distance *Jessie Labov*	104
Part III. Fictional Cartographies and Temporalities	131
5. Troubles with History: The Anecdote, History, and the Petty Hero in Central Europe *Daniel Pratt*	133
6. The Transnational Matrix of Post-Communist Spaces *Ioana Luca*	151

Part IV. Appropriated Afterlives 173

   7. Appropriations of the Past: The New Synagogue in Poznań
      and Olsztyn's Bet Tahara 175
      Sarah M. Schlachetzki

   8. Bruno Schulz's Murals, *Oyneg Shabes,* and the Migration
      of Forms: Seventeen Fragments and an Archive 202
      Adam Zachary Newton

Part V. Elective Affinities 227

   9. The Balkan Notebooks 229
      Ann Cvetkovich

  10. A Polish Childhood 248
      Irene Kacandes

Afterword/Afterward: Eastern Europe, Unmapped and Reborn 269
    Vitaly Chernetsky

Index 282

List of Maps and Figures

MAPS

4.1. Graduated symbol map of *Kultura* authors by city (1947–89). 114

4.2. Graduated symbol map of *Kultura* authors by city—Europe (1947–89). 115

4.3. Graduated symbol map of *Kultura* authors by city—Europe (1954–63). 115

4.4. Graduated symbol map of *Kultura* authors by city—Europe (1974–81). 116

4.5. Graduated Symbol Map of *Kultura* authors by city—Europe (1982–89). 116

4.6. Cartogram of *Kultura* authors by country (1947–49). 117

4.7. Cartogram of *Kultura* authors by country (1960–64). 117

4.8. Graduated symbol map of *Kultura* letter writers by city (1950–89). 118

4.9. Graduated symbol map of *Kultura* letter writers by city—Europe (1954–63). 119

4.10. Graduated symbol map of *Kultura* letter writers by city—Europe (1974–81). 119

4.11. Graduated symbol map of *Kultura* funders by city (1947–89). 120

4.12. Graduated symbol map of *Kultura* funders by city (1955–63). 121

4.13. Graduated symbol map of *Kultura* funders by city (1974–81). 121

4.14. Graduated symbol map of *Kultura* funders by city (1982–89). 122

4.15. Cartogram showing the proportional amount of funding by country (1955–63). 123

4.16. Cartogram showing the proportional amount of funding by country (1974–81). 124

FIGURES

7.1. New Synagogue, Poznań, 1904–7. 179

7.2. Bet Tahara, Olsztyn, 1911–13, contemporary interior view. 181

7.3. Mossehaus, Berlin, 1923. 182

7.4. New Synagogue, Poznań, 2015. 185

7.5. Bet Tahara, Olsztyn, view of the dome after restoration, 2013. 188

11.1. Mykola Blazhkov, monument to Ludwik Zamenhof in Odessa, 1959. 270

Introduction
A Discontiguous Eastern Europe

Yuliya Komska

It is a rare journalistic account of World War II that leaves the episode with Stalin's blue pencil unmentioned. After the signing of the German-Soviet Treaty of Friendship, Cooperation and Demarcation (better known as the second Molotov-Ribbentrop Pact) in Moscow on 28 September 1939, a map accompanied refreshments. The treaty, as is well known, held the key to the foreseeable future of the populations in Poland, Lithuania, Ukraine, and Belarus. The map, for its part, was meant to be Hitler and Stalin's last word on the territories concerned. In particular, it outlined the border between the German and Soviet spheres of influence. Reviewing the course of this border, Stalin made an adjustment with a blue pencil. He extended the Soviet line further north of Rava-Ruska, a mixed-population Polish town just captured by Hitler's Wehrmacht. The flourish of Stalin's signature underneath proceeded to seal the fate of Poland, partitioned and stripped of sovereignty for the duration of the war, for decades to come.[1]

Retellings of the anecdote attest not only to Stalin and Hitler's geopolitical machinations or to the imperial whim (or "territorial writ") that has long held sway over the area historically known as Eastern Europe.[2] Most broadly, the story's recurrence reflects the degree to which this part of the world has been defined by its location on the map. The *cartographic mandate,* as we term this circumstance, refers not only to the practice of mapping itself, tied to the push-and-pull dynamic between "power and protest" and steeped in the hodgepodge of the cartographers' dissonant traditions, languages, and political affiliations that project order, authenticity, and accuracy but rarely live up to this façade.[3] Nor is it limited to popular revivals of geopolitical determinism, which wield maps to get at the causation of crises and conflicts and argue that such documents anticipate violence in "the dusty steppe" of Kosovo and Macedonia but not in "the cultured conviviality" of Prague or Budapest.[4] Outside journalistic writing and beyond cartography and the disciplines that it has traditionally served (statistics, economics, sociology, geopolitics), the idiom of geography, political or physical, is also deep-seated. The efficient "geographic shorthand"—admittedly less confusing than "an open-ended mélange of overlapping and incommensurable ... patterns"—functions as the all-too-rarely questioned bedrock for a wide gamut of references to the region.[5]

Undeniably, "metageography"—the breakdown of the world into East, West, North, and South—resonates already in the region's name.[6] The very designation "Eastern Europe"—along with such alternatives as Central, East Central, or Eastern and Central Europe (preferred by current scholars as well as the area's residents)—contains more than a hint at the physical coordinates.[7] The tendency to "geo-code," to borrow John Pickles's term, abides as one of the Enlightenment's holdovers. It occurs at the expense of highlighting the area's connections to other spaces, real and symbolic.[8] Such thinkers as Johann Gottfried Herder, once seminal for national revivals across the Continent's eastern half, generously endowed the region's inhabitants with a set of ties to natural geography but remained parsimonious with granting them connections to the less tangible realms. "The Slavic peoples," their foremost Enlightenment-era advocate ruefully noted, "occupy on Earth a greater space than [they do] in history."[9] Herder's sympathetic account of these Slavs proceeded to exacerbate the cliché by painting the subjects as "servile" and "obedient" peasants—in short, as antitheses of history-makers, sedentary and inseparable from their land.

In the Enlightenment's wake, the homegrown proponents of nineteenth-century Eastern European nationalisms echoed Herder by espousing the view that precisely land, and not "the narrative space of national history," held the greatest potential for cohesion.[10] Subsequently, land as the crucible of familial and social structures fueled imaginations of such Eastern European natives as the Ukrainian modernist writer Olha Kobylianska (*Land*, 1902) and filmmaker Alexander Dovzhenko (*Earth*, 1930). The conflation of territory and soil only boosted the impression of Eastern Europe's landlocked condition, in that most literal sense of being tied to the land.[11]

Likewise, scholarly methods and frameworks have not been exempt from geo-coding. As this introduction will flesh out in more detail, two terms underpin the cartographic mandate: *betweenness* and *contiguity*. From the viewpoint of imperial history, both feed into "typologies of empire," as Maria Todorova puts it. This is to say, they perpetuate contiguous (i.e., land) empire as a category that is not only pertinent to Eastern Europe but, as Timothy Snyder argues, also particularly pernicious.[12]

From the vantage point of area studies, betweenness and contiguity justify the prominence of *borderlands* and *neighbors* as the two currently dominant accents in thinking and writing about Eastern Europe across mediums, genres, and disciplines. These two frameworks have fed off the long-term transdisciplinary groundswell of efforts to tell stories about and from the vantage point of peripheries. They have drawn especially though not exclusively on the tenets of post-structuralism and postcolonial theory while acknowledging the limits of such imported insights' applicability to Eastern Europe. In this region, borders, as Eagle Glassheim points out, have often gone unnamed as such. Borderlands, for their part, have been a far cry from "the lively 'contact zones,' 'crossroads,' and 'fluid transitional spaces' associated with scholarship on North American border regions, which dominates the vigorous subfield of borderland studies."[13] Without a doubt, there have been good reasons for the prolonged scrutiny of borderlands and neighbors—as well as for the current dominance of the so-called borderlands paradigm in historical research and beyond.[14]

Borderlands contain the alluring promise of diversity and hybrid post-national coexistence. Yet the promise often falls flat when the "proximity and familiarity" of their populations unravel into "the kind of ruthless brutality that will transform friends and colleagues into faceless outsiders" or, worse, victims of violence and ethnic cleansing.[15] The promise further shatters against the seemingly unending "memory wars"—among them, the conflicts over the ownership of the material legacy of the past, the less tangible victimhood contests, and historical amnesia.[16] Ordinarily, these eclipse the much less overdetermined models of remembrance: the so-called knots of memory, for instance, which trade "geocultural hierarchies" for affective or ethical affinities between places, cast doubt on "the self-sameness of any site," and connect, to cite Michael Rothberg's example, a place like Warsaw not only with other European capitals but also with global metropolises like Atlanta, Gaza City, or Istanbul.[17] In short, the promise of borderlands stumbles over the many reminders of neighbors' un-neighborly behaviors—ethnic, racial, or religious hatred, suspicion, forgetting, and betrayal—of the kind highlighted in Jan T. Gross's writings about Polish antisemitism and, more recently, xenophobia.[18] The relatively recent backlash against Gross himself, accused of lacking patriotism by Poland's Law and Justice government, proves that the relevance of studying borderlands and neighbors knows no expiration date.[19]

At the same time, the "borderlands paradigm," refer as it may to the effects of mixing between ethnicities and traditions, implies and reinforces territorially limited engagements. Even as it eschews geopolitics by zooming in on peripheries rather than centers, it continues to owe a debt to the "geocultural hierarchies" that tie Eastern European locales to each other or to the counterparts in adjacent Western Europe and Russia. Studies of borderlands tend to focus on the "side-by-side" of proximate and sedentary populations.[20] To paraphrase Nick Baron and Peter Gatrell's formulation, many privilege *being* over *movement*—or else, they delimit movement.[21] When they do zoom in on mobility, as is the case with Baron and Gatrell's volume, the focus is typically on the internally displaced.[22] The result is, inevitably, only a partial ethnoscape, one with few "tourists, immigrants, refugees, exiles, [and] guestworkers" that are constitutive of Arjun Appadurai's original definition.[23] In turn, Appadurai's own formulations of various -scapes barely accommodate Eastern Europeans. His mentions of "Soviet Armenia and the Baltic Republics," Ukrainians, and Albanians remain brief, fleeting, and muddled.[24]

Therefore, we take this volume as an occasion to argue more concertedly than has been done before that geography circumscribes neither Eastern Europe's destiny nor its history or culture. The "geographic features," to draw on Paul Magocsi, hardly isolate the region from the rest of the world.[25] Nor can its "global moments," in Yaroslav Hrytsak's formulation, "be reduced to relations between core, periphery, and colony."[26] And so, if Vesna Goldsworthy's coinage "the imperialism of the imagination" exposed the tendency to substitute "real territories" with literary phantasms, we take issue with the tendency to overstate territoriality as such. For, just like Goldsworthy's notion of imperialist imagination, the trend impacts "how people view places, countries, and societies."[27] Its consequences resonate far and wide.

The area's natives, we point out, have consistently forged links to discontiguous lands and populations, whether willingly or by force.[28] In the same month as Stalin let his blue pencil loose on the map of Poland, for example, the renegade Polish writer Witold Gombrowicz got stranded in Argentina. It was a lonely sojourn in the "land lost in the oceans," he complained, lasting years instead of the anticipated two weeks.[29] Loneliness, however, was not for lack of compatriots—diplomats and exiles. Many nautical miles away from Europe, the author could hardly escape them and their parochialism, which he immortalized with scathing irony in the novel *Trans-Atlantyk* (1953).[30] Of course, an unforeseen "quirk of fate," as Gombrowicz put it, accounted for his refusal to board the ship that would have carried him back to Europe: his South American disembarkation coincided with Hitler's invasion of Poland.[31] But in countless other cases before and after his, people's choices were less accidental.[32]

Examples, some felicitous and others unfortunate, are too varied to sketch out here in anything but broad strokes. Many of them follow the ebbs and flows of various political and economic integrations and disintegrations that not only link Eastern European and global histories, as Snyder proposes, but also entwine the fates of concrete Eastern Europeans with those of the world.[33] Military servicemen, volunteers, and mercenaries received their baptism by fire in faraway lands, as did the eighteenth-century independence fighter and engineer Tadeusz Kościuszko when he joined in the American Revolutionary War in 1776. Emigrants moved from one continent to another in search of prosperity, freedom, and inclusion.[34] Refugees fled racial, religious, political, and ethnic persecution in the hopes of reaching more tolerant destinations. Their descendants now reunite in virtual city communities, where the "chronologically, spatially, and linguistically interconnected digital pathways" take on the function of physical streets.[35]

Besides, for many decades, merchants, industrial capitalists, and, subsequently, socialized enterprises traded with partners far removed from local, regional, national, or cross-border markets. In defiance of maps, landlocked countries such as Czechoslovakia staked out a place in maritime commerce.[36] The exports—in this case, metalwork, textiles, glass, musical instruments, costume jewelry, or furniture—served not peace alone. For better or worse, raw materials, military technologies, and scientific savvy also moved across the vast swathes of water.[37]

Neither were ideologies strangers to two-way transoceanic transfers. In Manhattan's Lower East Side of the early twentieth century, Yiddish-speaking immigrants, following the anarchist mastermind Mikhail Bakunin, repudiated "the rights and frontiers called historic" and trafficked in cosmopolitan diasporism instead.[38] Several decades later, disillusioned Marxists of Arthur Koestler's and Leszek Kołakowski's stature included anticommunism into this circuit of political ideas and influences. And after the end of the Cold War, democratization know-how became Eastern Europe's next export-import commodity, the legacy and permanence of which remain uncertain to this day: Eastern Europe inspires with the tenacity of its recurrent pro-democracy protests as much as it appalls with the force of deep-seated xenophobia.[39]

Against these backdrops, writers and filmmakers plotted their own extraterritorial lives and fantasies. A country like Poland provides plenty of examples that ring a bell to publics across borders. In the 1870s, the whale of English-language literature Joseph Conrad (born Józef Teodor Konrad Korzeniowski) took and wrote about a voyage on the Congo River in *The Heart of Darkness* (1899). To explain his fellow Eastern Europeans' retreat into privacy from his Cold War–era American exile, the dissident poet and writer Czesław Miłosz reached for the Persian term *ketman,* which he borrowed from the works of the French racialist, diplomat, and author Arthur de Gobineau. Back in Poland, the internationally renowned science-fiction genius Stanisław Lem, writing "with very little reference to concrete social and political changes," tested the limits of this trajectory by dispatching his protagonists to extraterrestrial worlds where their innermost thoughts, passions, as well as fears got unhinged—and borderlands or homelands mattered comparatively little.[40]

What were the reasons for these and other leaps of faith, ventures, and entanglements, we ask as we sample a cross-section (representative although by no means comprehensive) of topics from architecture to autobiography, from literature to religion? What new affiliations did these engagements engender? What benefits and pitfalls did they entail? What limits did they run up against? What *discontinuities*—ruptures in chronologies, traditions, historiographies, memory cultures, religious affiliations—do they involve? And did territorial *discontiguity*—the term that this book advances as both a counterweight and counterpart to "borderlands" and "neighbors"—provide the distance necessary for shaping a fresh critical outlook on the past, present, and future? Or did it, on the contrary, facilitate escapes from the unresolved dilemmas of proximate histories and memories?

To tie these central questions together, here we propose to *unmap* Eastern Europe. This term, we realize, requires a careful explanation. In this volume, unmapping does not deny geography's salience; such a stance would be both politically naïve and historically shortsighted. To clarify, unmapping here does not negate physical space. It does not fashion Eastern Europe into a utopia relegated to mental or fictional cartographies for which writers and thinkers toil as latter-day draftsmen.[41] Instead, the term takes issue with the cartographic mandate by bracketing the space defined by Eastern Europe's internal or external borders and by its relational proximity to Russia and Western Europe (including Germany and even Austria). All in all, unmapping extracts that to which "Eastern Europe" refers from the falsely exclusive contiguities ascribed to it: first and foremost spatial, but also temporal, ethnic, religious, intellectual, or cultural. It renders Eastern Europe as an entity that is neither merely a "connecting bridge" between its neighbors, nor an "intermediate region."[42] Eastern Europe, in brief, here amounts to more than its "situation," to use the onetime Czech dissident Milan Kundera's description of the area's Cold War–era political predicament.[43] Our aim, then, is to "decolonize" our way of thinking about this area, to invoke Madina Tlostanova's revision of the still-prevalent dichotomous paradigms—even if we, unlike Tlostanova, detach the process of revision from so-called border subjectivity.[44]

For this reason, this book does not open with a token map. If anything, we could begin with a map of the world, dotted with interconnected points. The problem with most conventional maps, however, is that they leave no room for depth perception and thus exclude any complicated territorial and temporal coincidences and overlaps. They fail to capture how in the passage and writing of history, to draw on Serguei Oushakine, "important locations are recaptured, renamed, or even repurposed." These rites of "stylistic gutting and retrofitting," Oushakine and others point out, never completely hide, let alone erase, earlier eras' traces.[45] Alan Dingsdale echoes this observation when he speaks of the region's "competing spatialities": local and national, continental, and global.[46] What map would make room for these layers? Certainly not the conventional kind.

Within the limited scope of this book, to name a few examples, unmapping amounts to asking why cultural figures who banded together under the name "the locals" remained outsiders in the country where they ostensibly belonged (as Tatsiana Astrouskaya investigates in her contribution); how a seemingly nation-centric publication enjoyed wide extraterritorial diffusion (to sum up Jessie Labov's argument); what accounts for the "dynamic state" of such a seemingly immobile work as a mural (in Adam Zachary Newton's interpretation); or what forces compelled Balkan Muslims—especially women—to choose pan-Islamism over Broz Tito's pan-Yugoslavism (a central question in Piro Rexhepi's essay). The variety of topics acts as a reminder of the region's lack of "overarching political cohesion, cultural integrity, or even a geographical identity" and suggests that precisely these shortages render it open to discontiguous engagements.[47]

It goes without saying that unmapping presupposes the possibility of remapping or re-spatialization. It is not a destruction but a "reconstruction of a spatial code," to invoke Henri Lefebvre's term for recovering unconventional (in his case, non-verbal or non-discursive) spatial practices on new terms. If anything, unmapping is an episode in "a series of separate and distinct assays of the world's space"—the assays that recapture, prominently, "the unity of dissociated elements."[48]

If the notes to the preceding pages are any indication, numerous individual studies have openly or implicitly contributed to this kind of re-envisioned spatial conception of Eastern Europe. Relationships between Eastern Europeans and their non-contiguous others—and with "the globalization momentum" at large—have played a role in research on military history, intellectual exchanges, modernities and modernisms, protest movements, travel, exile and (forced) migration, the "global circulation of blackness" in musical styles such as hip-hop, *samizdat/tamizdat* publishing, and Cold War broadcasting, to name just a few rubrics.[49] This book's greatest concern—as well as its *raison d'être*—is that so far, these individual efforts have failed to shape an assertive enough counterpoint to geography-as-destiny.[50] No journalist has yet written a bestseller about Eastern Europe gone global, but bestsellers about the doom of its maps continue to multiply.[51] Here, we are interested in asserting such a counterpoint and asking about the causes of its limited and delayed recognition thus far.

While the afterword addresses the stakes involved in this task—be it a choice (along the lines plotted in Irene Kacandes's essay), a postcolonial emancipatory gesture (along the lines suggest by Snyder and others), a commitment to bringing to light the typically overlooked histories and stories, or a combination of these factors—and envisions the task's future trajectory, the remainder of this introduction explains why now is the right moment to do so. The excursion starts with the specter of Eastern Europe's betweenness, then moves on to recap the quest for the alternatives to the interstitial position, and concludes with a note on the volume's timeliness and a brief overview of its structure.

THE SPECTER OF BETWEEN

More than a decade has passed since the accession of the first eight post-Soviet countries—the Czech Republic, Poland, Slovakia, Slovenia, Hungary, Estonia, Latvia, and Lithuania—to the European Union (EU). And yet, they are rarely described as being solidly within this alliance, both by outsiders and by their own political and cultural elites. Instead, they are perceived, in the words of the German weekly *Der Spiegel*, as "stuck in between"—in this case, between the East and the West.[52] The by now familiar specter of betweenness haunts also their neighbors to the immediate east and southeast:[53] the EU's most recent newcomers, such as Bulgaria, Romania, and Croatia; its official and potential candidates, among them Albania and Serbia; and its associates, including Moldova and, most obviously, war-torn Ukraine. Historian Larry Wolff's prophecy that "in the 1990s Eastern Europe will continue to occupy an ambiguous place between inclusion and exclusion" has extended well into the twenty-first century.[54]

And so, let us review the most significant recent preconditions for betweenness and then move on to the constraints that it entails. In the wake of 1989, when Wolff mused on the staying power of the Enlightenment's "mental map" of Eastern Europe, construed as alien to the West yet inalienable from the West's civilizational self-fashioning, the area's transition from socialism to the next milestone seemed to justify the turn to "between." Indeed, the shift engulfed—and, in many ways, continues to engulf—entire societies, not just their economies. At times, its impact was so overwhelming that it appeared to leave some states suspended between categories indefinitely, with political scientists wondering whether transition could still count as a liminal rite of passage or should be viewed, instead, as a permanent status quo, as its own kind of culture.[55]

More recent invocations of being "stuck in between," however, have been geopolitically motivated. As the media headlines in the last few years have made obvious, Eastern Europe's outlines depend not on mental mapping alone. Russia's annexation of Crimea in March 2014, along with its subsequent military intervention in mainland Ukraine, placed Eastern Europeans in the dual role of intrepid mediators between Western Europe and Russia and Russia's fearful victims-to-be. This turn of events marked yet another instrumentalization of history, since "between" looms large not only in the narratives of Eastern Europe's present. With even greater vigor, it molds views of its past.

Politicians, scholars, and media pundits in Eastern Europe and abroad have routinely described this part of the Continent as being or having been trapped betwixt the East and the West, Hitler and Stalin, Catholicism and Orthodoxy, Occidentalism and Orientalism.[56] In addition, "between" has provided the backdrop for discussions of global "eastness," predicated much more on drawing lines between adjacent entities than on difficult-to-extricate "nesting Orientalisms."[57] "Between," it bears reminding, only makes sense on a flat, surveyable surface: on a map that, to paraphrase Pickles, precedes the represented territory.[58]

Hypothetically, the interstitial position could have been a blessing: a much-needed third-way alternative to "dualistic East-West thinking," an overdue opposition to Russia's neither-West-nor-East ideology of Eurasia, or a synonym for the area's rich layering of cultures.[59] Yet in practice, it has borne closer resemblance to a curse. Elsewhere, spatial frames of reference—Germany's once-proverbial *Mittellage* (central position) comes to mind—eventually become consigned to history as it runs its course. With regard to Eastern Europe, however, the logic of "between" stubbornly endures, cementing the area's geographical position as all-important and indisputable.

Eastern Europe's "historical continuity," to cite an iteration of this cliché, derives "from its ill-fated location between the more organized and powerful neighbors."[60] In short, the rhetoric of "between" has been an instrument in the much larger project of casting geography as the area's inescapable, and unfortunate, destiny. In contrast to Russia, where since the nineteenth century space-as-destiny has stood (and was consciously chosen) in welcome opposition to Western Europe's self-definition through time and history, for Eastern Europe this "destiny" has had much more ambiguous implications.[61]

The list of the latter, spelled out below, proves that tropes "can be potentially reckless," as our contributor Adam Zachary Newton observes elsewhere.[62] The "trope of 'betweenness'" is no exception.[63] It brings about several interrelated, if partially unintended, side effects that shape the direction of our book. These go far beyond what Alexander Maxwell terms "geographic egoism," best paraphrased as a Kantian extension of one's subjective physical position to one's similarly subjective intellectual posture.[64] Betweenness has implications not for geopolitics alone.

Epistemologically, to borrow from Leslie Adelson, "between" "often functions literally like a reservation designed to contain, restrain, and impede new knowledge."[65] It hampers, in particular, the wider recognition and reappraisal of the area's connections to ideas, locales, or movements around the globe—the now proverbial ethnoscapes, mediascapes, technoscapes, finanscapes, and ideoscapes and their precursors.[66] Such links can be positive, based on interest or solidarity, as much as negative, that is, rooted in rejection, as this introduction suggests in closing.

Conceptually, to speak with Maxim Waldstein, "between" leaves Eastern Europe "in the blind spot on the map of contemporary social and cultural theory" as a consumer but not producer of methodological innovations.[67] Politically, it entrenches suspicions of Eastern Europe's territorial volatility (i.e., its "expanding and contracting areas with very fluid boundaries"),[68] its wanting sovereignty, its violent tangling and untangling of populations, and its colonial- or postcolonial-like subalterity, encapsulated in the moniker "the buffer zone."[69]

Culturally, "between" acts as the great homogenizer. For a lay observer, it feigns a semblance of unity among the area's constituents and is as easily mistaken for the area's most obvious defining feature as it is misconstrued as the glue that holds the widely disparate places together. Besides, "between" renders any attempted distinctions among the region's many aforesaid designations—Eastern, Central, or East Central Europe—null and void.[70] The inherent vagueness of these labels' "geographical domains" gives way, instead, to their mappability.[71] Consequently, "between" validates that prevalent Cold War–era label "Eastern Europe" as the proper umbrella term for the countries erroneously perceived as "geographically contiguous" and "structurally homogenous."[72]

THE LONG SEARCH FOR ALTERNATIVES

Just as "Europe" has been "more than a geographical expression," so have the designations describing Eastern Europe borne their fair share of myths and aspirations.[73] In the scheme of this volume—premised on the broadest possible definition of history that includes histories of religion, literature, and the arts—it means a great deal that the rebuttals to the cartographic mandate have been advanced by the literati. The eminent Cold War–era critic of Marxist thought Leszek Kołakowski, known for his Swiftian sensibilities, was among the first in his cohort to expose the overwhelming inutility of surface mapping.[74]

A satire of his, originally published in 1972, takes his readers on a search for the utopian Kingdom of Lailonia, populated with characters with such decidedly non–Eastern European names as Ajio, Kru, or Mek-Mek.[75] Unlike Robert Musil's better-known Kakania from *The Man without Qualities* (1930–43), Lailonia maintains no identifiable presence right in Europe's center. On the contrary, its location is as elusive as could be, much to the dismay of Kołakowski's narrator. Pinning it down takes so many maps, atlases, and globes that this character and his brother must sell most of their possessions and take special potions to shrink themselves in order to fit into their crammed apartment. And when they finally find the requisite map, it quickly gets lost in the clutter. Eventually, a package arrives confirming Lailonia's existence, but no postmaster can trace it back to the point of origin. Instead of more maps, the package contains a collection of the satirical tales that form the core of the book, warning the reader against conflating territory with content or substance.

Yet efforts such as Kołakowski's have more than once crashed against the pronounced inclination to overstate—or else simply leave unquestioned—Eastern Europe's link to the delimited physical space that it occupies.[76] To adopt a postmodern turn of phrase, Eastern Europe has been re-territorialized (i.e., linked back to its original physical space) much more frequently than it has been de-territorialized.[77] In this cycle, "between" has served as a vehicle for the region's geo-coding both by outsiders attempting to wrest control over it and, as Steven Seegel points out, by its resisting natives.[78]

Undoing Eastern Europe's territorial anchoring has been difficult even for those intent on making the leap. In his seminal essay "The Tragedy of Central Europe" (1984), often quoted in this volume, Kundera teetered on the verge on failing. On the one hand, he insisted that Central Europe is not a "coincidence of geography," typically dictated by the "always inauthentic" political borders. It is "not a state," but "a culture or a fate," he famously proclaimed, anticipating Timothy Garton Ash's nostalgic paean to just such a "kingdom of the spirit."[79] On the other hand, for all his attachment to symbolic geographies—the cornerstone of the ensuing years-long debate about the scope and meaning of Central Europe—not even Kundera could entirely shake off the spell of betweenness.[80] "What is Central Europe," he asked on the same page, but an "uncertain zone of small nations between Russia and Germany," one "vanished from the map of the West"? A fellow dissident

Miłosz, by then a Nobel Prize laureate, fell prey to a similar contradiction a few years on.[81]

The present obviousness of such inconsistencies signals our distance not only from the 1980s, when Kundera and Miłosz laid out their thoughts, but also from the more than two decades that followed 1989. That period, in Magdalena Marszałek's observation, was tantamount to a "spatial revolution," spurred by the "new [relative] freedom of movement" and "the drawing of new borders" within Europe.[82] The accompanying changes inaugurated a wave of Eastern Europe's political and literary mapping and re-mapping, informed by the broader interdisciplinary "spatial turn," whether as an indispensable counterpart of time in Eduardo Mendieta's "chronotopologies," as Appadurai's alternative global topography of various -scapes, or as Hillis Miller's literary topographies.[83]

Just as "phantasmagorical geography"[84] and so-called geopoetics—a "cultural self-determination of territories," originally formulated by Kenneth White—appealed to writers,[85] symbolic or imagined geography (focused on the perception of places and spaces, interlinked and mutable) and critical geopolitics (characterized by querying the geopolitical knowledge-making) became de rigueur among political scientists engaged with the region.[86] Given these decades-old counterweights to geopolitics, why is it that the cartographic mandate has lost none of its allure?

The pressing political crises and their geopolitically tinged media coverage surely account for some of the causes. At present, multiple factors have been conducive to upholding the master narrative of betweenness and contiguity: the East/West disparities with regard to taxation, migration, or asylum and minority rights within the EU; the well-publicized electoral gains of right-wing parties in countries such as Hungary and Poland; and Russia's threats, real and perceived, to the neighbors just west of it. Other circumstances have been cultural: the voices attuned to various discontiguities have tended to stress, perhaps too emphatically, the intangible worlds of fiction or the arts. What makes this volume so timely is the turning point that we observe with regard to these two vectors, political and creative. Therefore, in closing this introduction outlines the current constellation of forces that could enable a more robust narrative of Eastern Europe's discontiguous past and present. In this constellation, the intensities of fact and fiction align.

WHY NOW?

On the political front, discontiguities appear more pronounced than ever before. This is not only because Eastern Europe, as mentioned earlier, has become an eminent global exporter of democratic know-how, whether deservedly or not. Activism of such transition-era politicians as Lech Wałęsa has reached such remote places as Cuba, Iran, Tibet, Tunisia, and Burma. The agents in these transnational (and, at times, transcontinental) exchanges have functioned, in Tsveta Petrova's description, as "diffusion entrepreneurs" rather than recipients of democracy support, often to the chagrin of their Western European colleagues and in contradiction to their own not always democratic current opinions.[87]

Still more intriguing is the lead that the smallest Eastern European countries are taking in "virtualization of the state."[88] Until recently, physical territory used to be the linchpin for such demographic pillars as residency, frequently described by most states and supranational actors in bounded terms. This is how it appears in Article 13 of the Universal Declaration of Human Rights, which entitles individuals to "the right to freedom of movement and residence within the borders of each state."[89] However, in December 2014, the established territorial foundation of this and similar definitions felt a tremor when Estonia became the world's first country to introduce e-residency. The "transnational digital identity available to anyone in the world interested in administering a location-independent business online," as Estonia's exceedingly digital government describes the innovation, is still limited to fiscal matters.[90] But its blatant disregard for physical territory, commentators predict, will not remain thus circumscribed for long.[91] In Estonia, Appadurai's technoscapes and finanscapes overlap to cast doubt on Eastern Europe's geographically circumscribed destiny.

In a parallel to politics, discontiguity has picked up momentum in literature as well. Taking geopoetics beyond the bounded and self-referential Eastern European topographies are several widely translated and internationally well-received authors, some scrutinized in this volume. Georgi Gospodinov's novel *The Physics of Sorrow* (first published in Bulgarian in 2011), for example, experiments with radical ruptures of temporal continuity and familial lineage. In the prologue, the "I" introduces a vexing number of his multiple personalities, born, the reader learns, "at the end of August 1913," "on January 1, 1968," "on September 6, 1944," "always," or not yet: "We am," he agrammatically concludes. From this potpourri of years, any unambiguous indicators of place are conspicuously absent. For that, layers of history are all the more contemporaneous in the narrator's memory, which boasts equal access to "the beginning of the Ice Age and the end of the Cold War."[92] Capable of "get[ting] inside other people's memories," this narrator proceeds to recount "a story in which eras catch up with one another and intertwine. Some events happen now, others in the distant and immemorial past."[93] The distortion of chronologies, in turn, sweeps up the novel's spaces:

"The places are also confused, palaces and basements, Cretan kings and local shepherds build the labyrinth of this story about the Minotaur-boy, until you get lost in it. It winds like a maze and unfortunately I will never be able to retrace its steps."[94] The maze ends up being not only the text's mythological reference point but also its exaggerated pun on the "tangling" and "mixing" that usually pervade historical and fictional accounts of Eastern Europe. Mixed and tangled, that is, unmappable, here are not only populations but, primarily, memory, time, and space.

A comparably extraterritorial crescendo rises in the recent work of the Ukrainian writer and public figure Yurii Andrukhovych, one of the earliest and most consistent Eastern European champions of geopoetics. His *Lexicon of Intimate Cities* (2011) announces that "everything starts with maps," but to take this statement at face value would be rash.[95] For already its subtitle—*An Arbitrary Aid in Geopoetics and Cosmopolitics*—suggests cartography's limitations, underscored by the title's pun on the Ukrainian місто (city, town) and місце (place, and, in this context, also body part). Indeed, Andrukhovych begins the book with an "instructions-like prologue," which opens to the Cyrillic alphabet instead of a more traditional map. However, any reader who counts on the author to be his or her cicerone on this circumscribed linguistic terrain will walk away sorely disappointed. The *Lexicon,* in the author's admission, is a guide to disorientation instead. With its list of alphabetically arranged cities, meaningful within the author's private life, the book, Andrukhovych warns, is the worst possible reference work.

Admittedly, the actual maps' curious color-coding of countries may have once served him as an inspiration, but this gazetteer is no work of a cartographer. Towns and cities follow each other in a wild mash-up: "Aarau neighbors on Alupka, Balaklava on Barcelona, Haysyn has squeezed in between Heidelberg and Hamburg, Detroit has united with Dnepropetrovsk, Riga with Rome, Ternopil with Toronto, and Chicago with Chernivtsi." Furthermore, Andrukhovych's Cyrillic order does not mirror its Latin counterpart. Aware of the mismatch, the author rewrites his list of toponyms in Latin characters and comments on the resulting territorial incongruities: "It's clear: the original Quedlinburg [Кведлінбурґ, in Ukrainian] is not at all where it used to be. Salzburg is also in completely new environs, having swapped Zaporizhia for San Francisco." Seemingly baffled, in conclusion to his "instructions" Andrukhovych speculates on alternative ways of ordering, one more outlandish than the other: by years of visits; by adjoining rivers (in Ukrainian, another pun on *рік,* "year" and *річка,* "river"); or by the countries' latitudes. Wary of falling prey to cartography, he jokes about organizing cities by earthquakes, seasons, or types of landscape. But ultimately, he advises, such organization does not matter at all: the sequence, in the end, is in the eyes of the beholder.

All this said, it would be cynical to celebrate the narrative of discontiguity as a roster of achievements when failures to engage with non-neighbors loom as large in Eastern Europe's recent history as they do now. In 2015 and 2016, the political dreams of open borders and the literary dreams of phantasmagorical geographies ran up not only against the security fences erected by such countries as Hungary and Macedonia in response to the incoming waves of refugees. The dreams dissipated, first and foremost, in the chasm of racial, cultural, and religious intolerance—not to mention nationalism—that the crisis had put under the magnifying glass. When the leaders of such countries as Hungary or the Czech Republic balked at accepting refugee quotas and their constituencies demonstrated under the slogan "Have a nice, white day," it was "Eastern Europe" and "Central Europe"—not merely "Europe"—that were accused of heartlessness vis-à-vis the newcomers and of amnesia to the past migration ordeals of their own sons and daughters.[96]

To strike a balance, this volume does not shy away from conversations about Eastern Europe's relationships to space and the accompanying symbioses, positive or negative. On the contrary, it continues the search for new spaces, new relationships, and new methods and forms with which to process them—in the hope that its readers, in the spirit of Andrukhovych's gesture, will pick up the baton. The idea is not to replicate a map by giving a share of the book to every country or methodological concern, but to offer an array of new perspectives on some of the most striking discontiguities that cut across disciplines.

To this end, the following contributions are arranged into five parts, each corresponding to a specific category of analysis. To disencumber this introduction and offer more focused commentary, a brief editorial preface contextualizes each category within the broader scope of the volume's tasks, summarizing the contributions' central concerns and identifying the connections between them. It shall therefore suffice to indicate the units' thrusts here. Part 1, "Re-placed Religion," contributes to the writing of the area's religious history from its Jewish and Muslim margins. Part 2, "Dislodged Dissent," focuses on dissidence as the most recognizably unmapped rubric of the book. Part 3, "Fictional Cartographies and Temporalities," examines the global circulation of Eastern Europe on the printed page. Part 4, "Appropriated Afterlives," turns to architectural landmarks—entities usually anchored in place and its practices—that have been relocated physically and/or have been reassigned historically. Part 5, "Elective Affinities," underscores that learning, thinking, and writing about Eastern Europe is a choice that need not be determined by one's professional affiliations or genealogical roots. Finally, the volume concludes with an outlook onto the future directions of the intellectual trajectory plotted in the book.

Yuliya Komska is Associate Professor of German Studies at Dartmouth College, and is a cultural historian of the Cold War across the blocs. She is the author of *The Icon Curtain: The Cold War's Quiet Border* (University of Chicago Press, 2015) and a co-author of *Linguistic Disobedience: Restoring Power to Civic Language* (Palgrave, 2018). Recently, she has written about the transatlantic impact and memory of the broadcaster Radio Free Europe in both East and West.

NOTES

1. See, among others, Chris Bellamy, *Absolute War: Soviet Russia in the Second World War* (New York: Alfred A. Knopf, 2007), 84; and M. Allen Paul, *Katyn: Stalin's Massacre and the Triumph of Truth* (DeKalb: Northern Illinois University Press, 2010), 65. Accounts of the Potsdam Conference in July 1945 regularly feature another pencil on the map (along the Oder-Neisse line), this time Winston Churchill's.
2. On the "territorial writ," see Omer Bartov and Eric D. Weitz, "Introduction: Coexistence and Violence in the German, Habsburg, Russian, and Ottoman Borderlands," in *Shatterzone of Empires: Coexistence and Violence in the German, Habsburg, Russian, and Ottoman Borderlands,* ed. Omer Bartov and Eric D. Weitz (Bloomington: Indiana University Press, 2013), 1–2, 12.
3. Steven Seegel, *Mapping Europe's Borderlands: Russian Cartography in the Age of Empire* (Chicago: University of Chicago Press, 2012), 4–8; and Jason D. Hansen, *Mapping the Germans: Statistical Science, Cartography, and the Visualization of the German Nation, 1848–1914* (New York: Oxford University Press, 2015), 3–5.
4. Robert D. Kaplan, *The Revenge of Geography: What the Map Tells Us about Coming Conflicts and the Battle against Fate* (New York: Random House, 2012), especially 7–11. Scholars, in contrast, have long argued that "features of the natural world seldom conform to political terrains." Martin W. Lewis and Kären Wigen, *A Myth of Continents: A Critique of Metageography* (Berkeley: University of California Press, 1997), 8.
5. Lewis and Wigen, *A Myth of Continents,* 13.
6. Lewis and Wigen, *A Myth of Continents,* 7.
7. For a recent discussion of "Eastern Europe" as a pejorative term and an undesirable Cold War–era relic, see Anna Bischof and Robert Luft, "Radio Free Europe: Research and Perspectives: An Introduction," in *Voices of Freedom–Western Interference? 60 Years of Radio Free Europe,* ed. Anna Bischof and Zuzana Jürgens (Göttingen: Vandenhoeck & Ruprecht, 2015), 8.
8. John Pickles, *A History of Spaces: Cartographic Reason, Mapping, and the Geo-Coded World* (London: Routledge, 2004), 5.

9. Johann Gottfried Herder, *Ideen zur Philosophie der Geschichte der Menschheit* (Frankfurt am Main: Deutscher Klassiker Verlag, 1989), 696.
10. Derek Sayer, *The Coasts of Bohemia: A Czech History* (Princeton, NJ: Princeton University Press, 1998), 57.
11. Vratislav Pechota, "Czechoslovakia and the Third World," in *Eastern Europe and the Third World: East vs. South*, ed. Michael Radu (New York: Praeger, 1981), 77–105.
12. Maria Todorova, "On Public Intellectuals and Their Conceptual Frameworks," *Slavic Review* 74, no. 4 (2015): 710. A recent analysis of imperial contiguity in the context of Eastern Europe is Timothy Snyder, "Integration and Disintegration: Europe, Ukraine, and the World," *Slavic Review* 74, no. 4 (2015): 698, 701.
13. Eagle Glassheim, *Cleansing the Czechoslovak Borderlands: Migration, Environment, and Health in the Former Sudetenland* (Pittsburgh: University of Pittsburgh Press, 2016), 6–7.
14. Elke Hartmann, "The Central State in the Borderlands: Ottoman Eastern Anatolia in the Late Nineteenth Century," in Bartov and Weitz, *Shatterzone of Empires*, 172. Examples of works on borders/borderlands include but are not limited to Peter Judson, *Guardians of the Nation: Activists on the Language Frontiers of Imperial Austria* (Cambridge, MA: Harvard University Press, 2006); James Bjork, *Neither German nor Pole: Catholicism and National Indifference in a Central European Borderland* (Ann Arbor: University of Michigan Press, 2008); Holly Case, *Between States: The Transylvanian Question and the European Idea during World War II* (Stanford, CA: Stanford University Press, 2009); Peter Gatrell and Nick Baron, eds., *Warlands: Population Resettlement and State Reconstruction in the Soviet-East European Borderlands, 1945–1950* (London: Palgrave Macmillan, 2009). For a global perspective see Chad Bryant, Paul Readman, and Cynthia Radding, eds., *Borderlands in World History, 1700–1914* (London: Palgrave Macmillan, 2014).
15. Bartov and Weitz, "Introduction: Coexistence and Violence in the German, Habsburg, Russian, and Ottoman Borderlands," 12 and passim.
16. Uilleam Blacker and Alexander Etkind, introduction to *Memory and Theory in Eastern Europe*, ed. Uilleam Blacker, Alexander Etkind, and Julie Fedor (New York: Palgrave Macmillan, 2013), 3–5; and Omer Bartov, *Erased: Vanishing Traces of Jewish Galicia in Present-Day Ukraine* (Princeton, NJ: Princeton University Press, 2007).
17. Michael Rothberg, "Between Paris and Warsaw: Multidirectional Memory, Ethics, and Historical Responsibility," in Blacker, Etkind, and Fedor, *Memory and Theory in Eastern Europe*, 82.
18. Jan T. Gross, *Neighbors: The Destruction of the Jewish Community in Jedwabne, Poland* (Princeton, NJ: Princeton University Press, 2001). On the twenty-first-century refugee crisis, see his "Eastern Europe's Crisis of Shame," https://www.project-syndicate.org/commentary/eastern-europe-refugee-crisis-xenophobia-by-jan-gross-2015-09?barrier=true, accessed 13 September 2015.
19. Alex Duval Smith, "Polish Move to Strip Holocaust Expert of Award Sparks

Protest," *The Guardian,* 13 February 2016, http://www.theguardian.com/world/2016/feb/14/academics-defend-historian-over-polish-jew-killings-claims, accessed 13 February 2016.
20. Bartov and Weitz, "Introduction: Coexistence and Violence in the German, Habsburg, Russian, and Ottoman Borderlands," 1–2, 12.
21. Nick Baron and Peter Gatrell, introduction to *Homelands: War, Population and Statehood in Eastern Europe and Russia, 1918–1924,* ed. Nick Baron and Peter Gatrell (London: Anthem Press, 2004), 1.
22. See also Lewis H. Siegelbaum and Leslie Page Moch, *Broad Is My Native Land: Repertoires and Regimes of Migration in Russia's Twentieth Century* (Ithaca, NY: Cornell University Press, 2014).
23. Arjun Appadurai, "Disjuncture and Difference in the Global Cultural Economy," *Theory, Culture & Society* 7 (1990): 297.
24. Appadurai, "Disjuncture and Difference," 295, 301, 307.
25. Paul Robert Magocsi, "Geography and Borders," in *History of the Literary Cultures of East-Central Europe: Junctures and Disjunctures in the 19th and 20th Centuries,* vol. 2, ed. Marcel Cornis-Pope and John Neubauer (Amsterdam: John Benjamins Publishing Company, 2004), 19.
26. Yaroslav Hrytsak, "The Postcolonial Is Not Enough," *Slavic Review* 74, no. 4 (Winter 2015): 736.
27. Vesna Goldsworthy, *Inventing Ruritania: The Imperialism of the Imagination* (New York: Columbia University Press, 2013), ix.
28. On the history and politics of "human dumping" with respect to Eastern European minority populations, see Tara Zahra, *The Great Departure: Mass Migration from Eastern Europe and the Making of the Free World* (New York: W. W. Norton, 2016), 9–11 and passim.
29. Witold Gombrowicz, *Diary,* vol. 3, trans. Lillian Vallee (Evanston, IL: Northwestern University Press, 1993), 108.
30. Witold Gombrowicz, *Trans-Atlantyk,* trans. Carolyn French and Nina Karsov (New Haven, CT: Yale University Press, 1994).
31. Gombrowicz, *Diary,* vol. 3, 108.
32. For detailed case studies of the forced migrations and population swaps within Europe, see Philipp Ther and Anna Siljak, eds., *Redrawing Nations: Ethnic Cleansing in East-Central Europe, 1944–1948* (Lanham, MD: Rowman & Littlefield, 2001) and Gatrell and Baron, *Warlands.*
33. Snyder, "Integration and Disintegration," 707.
34. For the most recent account of the exodus from Eastern Europe and its effects at home, see Zahra, *The Great Departure.*
35. The flight and expulsion of minorities from Eastern Europe, displacement of Jews and stateless people, as well as the trajectories of Cold War–era political refugees are briefly outlined in Peter Gatrell, *The Making of the Modern Refugee* (Oxford: Oxford University Press, 2013), especially 62–69, 91–93, 109–15. On the virtual networks, see Marianne Hirsch and Leo Spitzer, "The Web and the Reunion: http://czernowitz.ehpes.com/," in *Rites of Return: Diaspora Practices and*

the *Politics of Memory*, ed. Marianne Hirsch and Nancy K. Miller (New York: Columbia University Press, 2011), 59–71, here 62.

36. The relevant company's Cold War–era establishment and its relationships with China and Cuba are described in Lenka Krátká, *A History of the Czechoslovak Ocean Shipping Company, 1948–1989: How a Small, Landlocked Country Ran Maritime Business during the Cold War* (Stuttgart: Ibidem Verlag, 2015). The legacy of similar transatlantic transactions persists, and press reports of Cuba's late-2016 offer to pay its $276-million debt to former Czechoslovakia are but an example. Ishaan Tharoor, "Cuba Wants to Pay Off Some of Its Cold War Debt in Rum," *Washington Post*, 15 December 2016, https://www.washingtonpost.com/news/worldviews/wp/2016/12/15/cuba-wants-to-pay-off-some-of-its-cold-war-debt-in-rum/?utm_term=.76f309009b07, accessed 15 December 2016.

37. The ties between Cold War–era Warsaw pact countries and the Third World are particularly well studied. The most comprehensive early survey is Michael Radu, ed., *Eastern Europe and the Third World: East vs. South* (New York: Praeger, 1981). Czechoslovakia's machinery, arms, and dry goods deals with African countries, from Egypt to Morocco, Somalia, and Ghana, are outlined in Philip Muehlenbeck, *Czechoslovakia in Africa, 1945–1968* (London: Palgrave Macmillan, 2016). An overview of Czechoslovak and Czech/Slovak exports appears in Alice Teichova, "Czechoslovakia and the Czech and Slovak Republics," in *The Oxford Encyclopedia of Economic History*, ed. Joel Mokyr (New York: Oxford University Press, 2003), 58–60.

38. Kenyon Zimmer, *Immigrants against the State: Yiddish and Italian Anarchists in America* (Urbana: University of Illinois Press, 2015), 7, 13–16.

39. See, for example, Zdenek Červenka, *African National Congress Meets Eastern Europe: A Dialogue on Common Experiences* (Uppsala: Nordiska Afrikainstitutet, 1992). Eastern European legacies of anti-authoritarian protest—and their fragility—became a subject of rekindled discussions following Donald Trump's election to the US presidency. See, among others, Timothy Snyder, *On Tyranny: Twenty Lessons from the Twentieth Century* (New York: Tim Duggan Books, 2017).

40. Istvan Csicsery-Ronay, "Lem, Central Europe, and the Genre of Technological Empire," in *The Art and Science of Stanisław Lem*, ed. Peter Swirski (Montreal: McGill-Queen's University Press, 2006), 146. It is worth noting that adaptations of Lem's works, Andrei Tarkovsky's *Solaris* in particular, revert to territoriality and highlight the pull of homes/homelands.

41. See Gilles Deleuze's dictum "To write is to draw a map," in *Foucault*, trans. Paul Bove (Minneapolis: University of Minnesota Press, 1988), 44.

42. Csaba G. Kiss, "Central European Writers about Central Europe: Introduction to a Non-Existent Book of Readings," in *In Search of Eastern Europe*, ed. George Schöpflin and Nancy Wood (Oxford: Polity Press, 1989), 127. See also Philip Ther, "Caught in Between: Border Regions in Modern Europe," in Bartov and Weitz, *Shatterzone of Empires*, 487.

43. Milan Kundera, "The Tragedy of Central Europe," *New York Review of Books*, 26 April 1984, 33.

44. Madina Tlostanova, *Gender Epistemologies and Eurasian Borderlands* (London: Palgrave Macmillan, 2010), 4.
45. Serguei Alex. Oushakine, "Postcolonial Estrangements: Claiming a Space between Stalin and Hitler," in *Rites of Place: Public Commemoration in Russia and Eastern Europe*, ed. Julie Buckler and Emily D. Johnson (Evanston, IL: Northwestern University Press, 2013), 286; and Tarik Cyril Amar, "Different but the Same or the Same but Different? Public Memory of the Second World War in Post-Soviet Lviv," *Journal of Modern European History* 9, no. 3 (2011): 373–96.
46. Ian Dingsdale, *Mapping Modernities: Geographies of Central and Eastern Europe, 1920–2000* (London: Routledge, 2002), 5.
47. Blacker and Etkind, introduction to *Memory and Theory in Eastern Europe*, 1.
48. Henri Lefebvre, *The Production of Space*, trans. Donald Nicholson-Smith (Oxford: Blackwell, 2012), 64–65.
49. Vitaly Chernetsky, *Mapping Postcommunist Cultures: Russia and Ukraine in the Context of Globalization* (Montreal: McGill-Queen's University Press, 2007), xiv. Other examples include Nikola Petković, *Srednja Europa: zbilja, mit, utopija: postmodernizam, postkolonijalizam, postkomunizam i odsutnost autentičnosti* (Rijeka: Adamić, 2003); Dingsdale, *Mapping Modernities*; Friederike Kind-Kovács and Jessie Labov, eds., *Samizdat, Tamizdat, and Beyond: Transnational Media during and after Socialism* (New York: Berghahn Books, 2013); and Adriana N. Helbig, *Hip Hop Ukraine: Music, Race, and African Migration* (Bloomington: Indiana University Press, 2014). Currently, the British Arts and Humanities Research Council is funding the research project *Socialism Goes Global: Cold War Connections between the "Second" and "Third World" 1945–1991*, with publications pending.
50. On alternating conjunctures and disjunctures, see Marcel Cornis-Pope and John Neubauer, general introduction to *History of the Literary Cultures of East-Central Europe: Junctures and Disjunctures in the 19th and 20th Centuries*, ed. Marcel Cornis-Pope and John Neubauer, vol. 1 (Amsterdam: John Benjamins, 2004), 8.
51. Most recently, Kaplan's argument has been rearticulated in Tim Marshall, *Prisoners of Geography: The Maps That Explain Everything about the World* (New York: Scribner, 2015).
52. Jurek Skrobala, "Gespenster vor den Scheiben," *Der Spiegel*, 1 December 2014, http://www.spiegel.de/spiegel/print/d-130630612.html, accessed 4 December 2014.
53. Various interstitial tropes are surveyed in Alexander Maxwell, "Introduction: Bridges and Bulwarks; A Historiographic Overview of East-West Discourses," in *The East-West Discourse: Geography and Its Consequences*, ed. Alexander Maxwell (Frankfurt am Main: Peter Lang, 2011), 1–32.
54. Larry Wolff, *Inventing Eastern Europe: The Map of Civilization on the Mind of the Enlightenment* (Stanford, CA: Stanford University Press, 1994), 9.
55. Michael D. Kennedy, *Cultural Formations of Postcommunism: Emancipation, Transition, Nation and War* (Minneapolis: University of Minnesota Press, 2002).
56. A wide range of historical examples is listed in Maxwell, "Introduction: Bridges and Bulwarks," 1–32.

57. On "eastness," see Tomasz Zarycki, *Ideologies of Eastness in Central and Eastern Europe* (London: Routledge, 2014); and Wolfgang Stephan Kissel, ed., *Der Osten des Ostens: Orientalismen in slawischen Kulturen und Literaturen* (Frankfurt am Main: Peter Lang, 2012). On "nesting Orientalisms," see Milica Bakić-Hayden, "Nesting Orientalisms: The Case of Former Yugoslavia," *Slavic Review* (1995): 917–31.
58. Pickles, *A History of Spaces*, 5.
59. Magdalena Marszałek, "On Slavs and Germans: Andrzej Stasiuk's Geopoetics of Central European Memory," in *Re-mapping Polish-German Historical Memory: Physical, Political, and Literary Spaces since World War II*, ed. Justyna Beinek and Piotr H. Kosicki (Bloomington: Slavica, 2012), 189; Marlène Laruelle, "Space as Destiny: Legitimizing the Russian Empire through Geography and Cosmos," in *Empire De/Centered: New Spatial Histories of Russia and the Soviet Union*, ed. Sanna Turoma and Maxim Waldstein (London: Ashgate, 2013), 85–104; and Ther, "Caught in Between," 485.
60. Alexander V. Prusin, *The Lands Between: Conflict and the East European Borderlands, 1870–1992* (New York: Oxford University Press, 2010), 1.
61. Laruelle, "Space as Destiny," 89.
62. Adam Zachary Newton, *The Elsewhere: On Belonging at a Near Distance; Reading Literary Memoir from Europe to the Levant* (Madison: University of Wisconsin Press, 2005), 7.
63. Leslie A. Adelson, "Against Between: A Manifesto," in *Unpacking Europe: Towards a Critical Reading*, ed. Salah Hassan and Iftikar Dadi (Rotterdam: NAI Publishers, 2001), 245.
64. Maxwell, "Introduction: Bridges and Bulwarks," 27. Immanuel Kant, "What Does It Mean to Orient Oneself in Thinking?" in *Kant's "Critique of Practical Reason" and Other Writings on Moral Philosophy*, ed. and trans. L. W. Beck, vol. 8 (Chicago: University of Chicago Press, 1949), 133–45.
65. Adelson, "Against Between: A Manifesto," 245, 246.
66. Appadurai, "Disjuncture and Difference in the Global Cultural Economy," 296.
67. Maxim Waldstein, "Theorizing the Second World: Challenges and Prospects," *Ab Imperio* 1 (2010): 98–99, 101. For a related argument on how the West's "coloniality of knowledge" impacts perceptions of Eastern Europeans' agency, see Madina Tlostanova, "Can the Post-Soviets Think? On Coloniality of Knowledge: External Imperial and Double Colonial Difference," *Intersections: East European Journal of Society and Politics* 1, no. 2 (2015): 38–58.
68. Adrian Webb, *The Routledge Companion to Central and Eastern Europe since 1919* (London and New York: Routledge, 2008), 2.
69. Maxwell, "Introduction: Bridges and Bulwarks," 1–32.
70. On the distinction between the designations, see Cornis-Pope and Neubauer, general introduction to *History of the Literary Cultures of East-Central Europe*, vol. 1, 2–6. Central and Eastern Europe in particular are defined in Larry Wolff, "The Traveler's View of Central Europe: Gradual Transitions and Degrees of Difference in European Borderlands," in Bartov and Weitz, *Shatterzone of Empires*, 23–41.

71. Wolff, "The Traveler's View of Central Europe," 32.
72. László Kontler, "Introduction: Reflections on Symbolic Geography," *European Review of History–Revue européenne d'Histoire* 6, no. 1 (1999): 11.
73. Zara Steiner, *The Triumph of the Dark: European International History* (New York: Oxford University Press, 2011), 2.
74. Louise Sweeney, "Jefferson Lecturer Speaks Candidly about Global Politics," *Christian Science Monitor* (8 May 1986), http://www.csmonitor.com/1986/0508/dkol-f.html, accessed 13 April 2015.
75. Leszek Kołakowski, *Tales from the Kingdom of Lailonia and the Key to Heaven,* trans. Agnieszka Kołakowska (Chicago: University of Chicago Press, 1989).
76. See, for example, Gyula Horvath, *Spaces and Places in Central and Eastern Europe: Historical Trends and Perspectives of Regional Development* (London: Routledge, 2015).
77. On the summary of the terms' original figurative uses in the work of Deleuze and Guattari, see Eugene W. Holland, "Deterritorializing 'Deterritorialization': From the 'Anti-Oedipus' to 'A Thousand Plateaus,'" *SubStance* 20, no. 3 (1991): 55–65. On the adoption (and, in some cases, rejection) of the term by geographers and anthropologists—in its more literal meaning—see Stuart Elden, "Missing the Point: Globalization, Deterritorialization, and the Space of the World," *Transactions of the Institute of British Geographers* 30, no. 1 (2005): 8–19.
78. Seegel, *Mapping Europe's Borderlands,* 89–109, 175–85, and passim.
79. Kundera, "The Tragedy of Central Europe," 34–35; and Timothy Garton Ash, *Uses of Adversity: Essays on the Fate of Central Europe* (New York: Random House, 1989), 189.
80. Useful summaries include Tony Judt, "The Rediscovery of Central Europe," *Daedalus* 119, no. 1 (1990): 23–54; and Timothy Garton Ash, "Mitteleuropa?," *Daedalus* 119, no. 1 (1990): 23–54, 1–21.
81. Czesław Miłosz, "O naszej Europie," *Kultura* (1986), 3, no. 12, quoted in Marszałek, "On Slavs and Germans," 193. Marszałek notes the contradiction without discussing it further.
82. Marszałek, "On Slavs and Germans," 202, 185. See also Marszałek and Sylvia Sasse, "Geopoetiken," in *Geopoetiken: Geographische Entwürfe in den mittel- und osteuropäischen Ländern* (Berlin: Kulturverlag Kadmos, 2010), 7–11.
83. Eduardo Mendieta, "Chronotopology: Critique of Spatiotemporal Regimes," in *New Critical Theory: Essays on Liberation,* ed. William S. Wilkerson and Jeffrey Paris (Oxford: Rowman & Littlefield, 2001), 175–97; Appadurai, "Disjuncture and Difference"; J. Hillis Miller, *Topographies* (Stanford, CA: Stanford University Press, 1995). Much of this interdisciplinary interest in mapping is described in Michael Dear, "Creative Places: Geocreativity," in *Geohumanities: Art, History, Text at the Edge of Place,* ed. Michael Dear et al. (New York: Routledge, 2011), 7.
84. Marszałek, "On Slavs and Germans," 194.
85. Igor Sid, "Osnovnoy voipros geopoetiki," presented at the conference "Ot geopolitiki–k geopoetike," Moscow, 24 April 1996, http://liter.net/geopoetics/, accessed 22 April 2015. See also Marszałek, "On Slavs and Germans," 188.

86. A summary and additional sources appear in Joshua Hagen, "Redrawing the Imagined Map of Europe: The Rise and Fall of the Center," *Political Geography* 22 (2003): 490–91.
87. Tsveta Petrova, *From Solidarity to Geopolitics: Support for Democracy among Postcommunist States* (New York: Cambridge University Press, 2014), 1–5, 17, 20, and passim. Wałęsa's post-1989 politics and, more recently, his collaboration with Poland's secret police have come under scrutiny.
88. Eric B. Schnurer, "E-stonia and the Future of the Cyberstate," *Foreign Affairs*, 28 January 2015, https://www.foreignaffairs.com/articles/eastern-europe-caucasus/2015-01-28/e-stonia-and-future-cyberstate, accessed 20 January 2015.
89. The Universal Declaration of Human Rights, http://www.un.org/en/documents/udhr/, accessed 1 July 2015.
90. "What is e-Residency?," https://e-estonia.com/e-residents/about/, accessed 25 June 2015.
91. Schnurer, "E-stonia and the Future of the Cyberstate."
92. Georgi Gospodinov, *The Physics of Sorrow*, trans. Angela Rodel (Rochester: Open Letter, 2015), 7.
93. Gospodinov, *The Physics of Sorrow*, 18, 15.
94. Gospodinov, *The Physics of Sorrow*, 15.
95. Yurii Andrukhovych, *Lexykon intymnykh mist: Dovilnyi posibnyk z geopoetyky ta kosmopolityky* (Chernivtsi: Meridian, 2011). The following quotes stem from pages 9–13. Translations are my own.
96. See, among others, Paul Hockenos, "The Stunning Hypocrisy of Mitteleuropa," *Foreign Policy*, 10 September 2015, http://foreignpolicy.com/2015/09/10/the-stunning-hypocrisy-of-mitteleuropa-refugees-poland-hungary-czech-republic/, accessed 12 September 2015; and Bartosz Marcinkowski, "Cold War Split in Europe over Refugee Crisis," *New Eastern Europe*, 22 September 2015, http://neweasterneurope.eu/articles-and-commentary/1719-cold-war-split-in-europe-over-refugee-crisis, accessed 23 September 2015.

WORKS CITED

Adelson, Leslie A. "Against Between: A Manifesto," in *Unpacking Europe: Towards a Critical Reading*, edited by Salah Hassan and Iftikar Dadi, 244–55. Rotterdam: NAI Publishers, 2001.
Amar, Tarik Cyril. "Different but the Same or the Same but Different? Public Memory of the Second World War in Post-Soviet Lviv." *Journal of Modern European History* 9, no. 3 (2011): 373–96.
Andrukhovych, Yurii. *Lexykon intymnykh mist: Dovilnyi posibnyk z geopoetyky ta kosmopolityky*. Chernivtsi: Meridian, 2011.
Appadurai, Arjun. "Disjuncture and Difference in the Global Cultural Economy." *Theory, Culture & Society* 7 (1990): 295–310.
Ash, Timothy Garton. "Mitteleuropa?" *Daedalus* 119, no. 1 (1990): 1–21.

———. *Uses of Adversity: Essays on the Fate of Central Europe*. New York: Random House, 1989.
Bakić-Hayden, Milica. "Nesting Orientalisms: The Case of Former Yugoslavia." *Slavic Review* (1995): 917–31.
Baron, Nick, and Peter Gatrell. Introduction to *Homelands: War, Population and Statehood in Eastern Europe and Russia, 1918–1924*, edited by Nick Baron and Peter Gatrell, 1–9. London: Anthem Press, 2004.
Bartov, Omer. *Erased: Vanishing Traces of Jewish Galicia in Present-Day Ukraine*. Princeton, NJ: Princeton University Press, 2007.
Bartov, Omer, and Eric D. Weitz. "Introduction: Coexistence and Violence in the German, Habsburg, Russian, and Ottoman Borderlands." In *Shatterzone of Empires: Coexistence and Violence in the German, Habsburg, Russian, and Ottoman Borderlands*, edited by Omer Bartov and Eric D. Weitz, 1–20. Bloomington: Indiana University Press, 2013.
Bellamy, Chris. *Absolute War: Soviet Russia in the Second World War*. New York: Alfred A. Knopf, 2007.
Bischof, Anna, and Robert Luft. "Radio Free Europe: Research and Perspectives: An Introduction." In *Voices of Freedom–Western Interference? 60 Years of Radio Free Europe*, edited by Anna Bischof and Zuzana Jürgens, 1–14. Göttingen: Vandenhoeck & Ruprecht, 2015.
Bjork, James. *Neither German nor Pole: Catholicism and National Indifference in a Central European Borderland*. Ann Arbor: University of Michigan Press, 2008.
Blacker, Uilleam, and Alexander Etkind. Introduction to *Memory and Theory in Eastern Europe*, edited by Uilleam Blacker, Alexander Etkind, and Julie Fedor, 1–22. New York: Palgrave Macmillan, 2013.
Bryant, Chad, Paul Readman, and Cynthia Radding, eds. *Borderlands in World History, 1700–1914*. London: Palgrave Macmillan, 2014.
Case, Holly. *Between States: The Transylvanian Question and the European Idea during World War II*. Stanford, CA: Stanford University Press, 2009.
Červenka, Zdenek. *African National Congress Meets Eastern Europe: A Dialogue on Common Experiences*. Uppsala: Nordiska Afrikainstitutet, 1992.
Chernetsky, Vitaly. *Mapping Postcommunist Cultures: Russia and Ukraine in the Context of Globalization*. Montreal: McGill-Queen's University Press, 2007.
Cornis-Pope, Marcel, and John Neubauer. General introduction to *History of the Literary Cultures of East-Central Europe: Junctures and Disjunctures in the 19th and 20th Centuries*, edited by Marcel Cornis-Pope and John Neubauer, vol. 1, 1–18. Amsterdam: John Benjamins, 2004.
Csicsery-Ronay, Istvan. "Lem, Central Europe, and the Genre of Technological Empire." In *The Art and Science of Stanisław Lem*, edited by Peter Swirski, 130–51. Montreal: McGill-Queen's University Press, 2006.
Dear, Michael. "Creative Places: Geocreativity." In *Geohumanities: Art, History, Text at the Edge of Place*, edited by Michael Dear, Jim Ketchum, Sarah Luria, and Doug Richardson, 5–8. New York: Routledge, 2011.

Deleuze, Gilles. *Foucault.* Translated by Paul Bove. Minneapolis: University of Minnesota Press, 1988.
Dingsdale, Alan. *Mapping Modernities: Geographies of Central and Eastern Europe, 1920–2000.* London: Routledge, 2002.
Elden, Stuart. "Missing the Point: Globalization, Deterritorialization, and the Space of the World." *Transactions of the Institute of British Geographers* 30, no. 1 (2005): 8–19.
Gatrell, Peter. *The Making of the Modern Refugee.* Oxford: Oxford University Press, 2013.
Gatrell, Peter, and Nick Baron, eds. *Warlands: Population Resettlement and State Reconstruction in the Soviet–East European Borderlands, 1945–1950.* London: Palgrave Macmillan, 2009.
Gombrowicz, Witold. *Diary.* Vol. 3. Translated by Lillian Vallee. Evanston, IL: Northwestern University Press, 1993.
———. *Trans-Atlantyk.* Translated by Carolyn French and Nina Karsov. New Haven, CT: Yale University Press, 1994.
Gospodinov, Georgi. *The Physics of Sorrow.* Translated by Angela Rodel. Rochester: Open Letter, 2015.
Gross, Jan T. *Neighbors: The Destruction of the Jewish Community in Jedwabne, Poland.* Princeton, NJ: Princeton University Press, 2001.
Hagen, Joshua. "Redrawing the Imagined Map of Europe: The Rise and Fall of the Center." *Political Geography* 22 (2003): 489–517.
Hansen, Jason D. *Mapping the Germans: Statistical Science, Cartography, and the Visualization of the German Nation, 1848–1914.* New York: Oxford University Press, 2015.
Hartmann, Elke. "The Central State in the Borderlands: Ottoman Eastern Anatolia in the Late Nineteenth Century." In *Shatterzone of Empires: Coexistence and Violence in the German, Habsburg, Russian, and Ottoman Borderlands,* edited by Omer Bartov and Eric D. Weitz, 172–90. Bloomington: Indiana University Press, 2013.
Helbig, Adriana N. *Hip Hop Ukraine: Music, Race, and African Migration.* Bloomington: Indiana University Press, 2014.
Herder, Johann Gottfried. *Ideen zur Philosophie der Geschichte der Menschheit.* Frankfurt am Main: Deutscher Klassiker Verlag, 1989.
Hirsch, Marianne, and Leo Spitzer. "The Web and the Reunion: http://czernowitz.ehpes.com/." In *Rites of Return: Diaspora Practices and the Politics of Memory,* edited by Marianne Hirsch and Nancy K. Miller, 59–71. New York: Columbia University Press, 2011.
Hockenos, Paul. "The Stunning Hypocrisy of Mitteleuropa." *Foreign Policy,* 10 September 2015. Accessed 12 September 2015. http://foreignpolicy.com/2015/09/10/the-stunning-hypocrisy-of-mitteleuropa-refugees-poland-hungary-czech-republic/.
Holland, Eugene W. "Deterritorializing 'Deterritorialization': From the 'Anti-Oedipus' to 'A Thousand Plateaus.'" *SubStance* 20, no. 3 (1991): 55–65.
Horvath, Gyula. *Spaces and Places in Central and Eastern Europe: Historical Trends and Perspectives of Regional Development.* London: Routledge, 2015.

Hrytsak, Yaroslav. "The Postcolonial Is Not Enough." *Slavic Review* 74, no. 4 (2015): 732–37.

Judson, Peter. *Guardians of the Nation: Activists on the Language Frontiers of Imperial Austria.* Cambridge, MA: Harvard University Press, 2006.

Judt, Tony. "The Rediscovery of Central Europe." *Daedalus* 119, no. 1 (1990): 23–54.

Kant, Immanuel. "What Does It Mean to Orient Oneself in Thinking?" In *Kant's "Critique of Practical Reason" and Other Writings on Moral Philosophy,* edited and translated by L. W. Beck, vol. 8, 133–45. Chicago: University of Chicago Press, 1949.

Kaplan, Robert D. *The Revenge of Geography: What the Map Tells Us about Coming Conflicts and the Battle against Fate.* New York: Random House, 2012.

Kennedy, Michael D. *Cultural Formations of Postcommunism: Emancipation, Transition, Nation and War.* Minneapolis: University of Minnesota Press, 2002.

Kind-Kovács, Friederike, and Jessie Labov, eds. *Samizdat, Tamizdat, and Beyond: Transnational Media during and after Socialism.* New York: Berghahn Books, 2013.

Kiss, Csaba G. "Central European Writers about Central Europe: Introduction to a Non-Existent Book of Readings." In *In Search of Eastern Europe,* edited by George Schöpflin and Nancy Wood, 125–36. Oxford: Polity Press, 1989.

Kissel, Wolfgang Stephan, ed. *Der Osten des Ostens: Orientalismen in slawischen Kulturen und Literaturen.* Frankfurt am Main: Peter Lang, 2012.

Kołakowski, Leszek. *Tales from the Kingdom of Lailonia and the Key to Heaven.* Translated by Agnieszka Kołakowska. Chicago: University of Chicago Press, 1989.

Kontler, László. "Introduction: Reflections on Symbolic Geography." *European Review of History–Revue européenne d'Histoire* 6, no. 1 (1999): 9–14.

Krátká, Lenka. *A History of the Czechoslovak Ocean Shipping Company, 1948–1989: How a Small, Landlocked Country Ran Maritime Business during the Cold War.* Stuttgart: Ibidem Verlag, 2015.

Kundera, Milan. "The Tragedy of Central Europe." *New York Review of Books,* 26 April 1984, 33–38.

Laruelle, Marlène. "Space as Destiny: Legitimizing the Russian Empire through Geography and Cosmos." In *Empire De/Centered: New Spatial Histories of Russia and the Soviet Union,* edited by Sanna Turoma and Maxim Waldstein, 85–104. London: Ashgate, 2013.

Lefebvre, Henri. *The Production of Space.* Translated by Donald Nicholson-Smith. Oxford: Blackwell, 2012.

Lewis, Martin W., and Kären Wigen. *A Myth of Continents: A Critique of Metageography.* Berkeley: University of California Press, 1997.

Magocsi, Paul Robert. "Geography and Borders." In *History of the Literary Cultures of East-Central Europe: Junctures and Disjunctures in the 19th and 20th Centuries,* edited by Marcel Cornis-Pope and John Neubauer, vol. 2, 19–30. Amsterdam: John Benjamins, 2004.

Marcinkowski, Bartosz. "Cold War Split in Europe over Refugee Crisis." *New Eastern Europe,* 22 September 2015. Accessed 23 September 2015. http://neweasterneurope.eu/articles-and-commentary/1719-cold-war-split-in-europe-over-refugee-crisis.

Marshall, Tim. *Prisoners of Geography: The Maps That Explain Everything about the World.* New York: Scribner, 2015.
Marszałek, Magdalena. "On Slavs and Germans: Andrzej Stasiuk's Geopoetics of Central European Memory." In *Re-mapping Polish-German Historical Memory: Physical, Political, and Literary Spaces since World War II,* edited by Justyna Beinek and Piotr H. Kosicki, 185–204. Bloomington: Slavica, 2012.
Marszałek, Magdalena, and Sylvia Sasse, "Geopoetiken." In *Geopoetiken: Geographische Entwürfe in den mittel- und osteuropäischen Ländern,* edited by Magdalena Marszałek and Sylvia Sasse, 7–11. Berlin: Kulturverlag Kadmos, 2010.
Maxwell, Alexander. "Introduction: Bridges and Bulwarks; A Historiographic Overview of East-West Discourses." In *The East-West Discourse: Geography and Its Consequences,* edited by Alexander Maxwell, 1–32. Frankfurt am Main: Peter Lang, 2011.
Mendieta, Eduardo. "Chronotopology: Critique of Spatiotemporal Regimes." In *New Critical Theory: Essays on Liberation,* edited by William S. Wilkerson and Jeffrey Paris, 175–97. Oxford: Rowman & Littlefield, 2001.
Muehlenbeck, Philip. *Czechoslovakia in Africa, 1945–1968.* London: Palgrave Macmillan, 2016.
Newton, Adam Zachary. *The Elsewhere: On Belonging at a Near Distance; Reading Literary Memoir from Europe to the Levant.* Madison: University of Wisconsin Press, 2005.
Oushakine, Serguei Alex. "Postcolonial Estrangements: Claiming a Space Between Stalin and Hitler." In *Rites of Place: Public Commemoration in Russia and Eastern Europe,* edited by Julie Buckler and Emily D. Johnson, 285–314. Evanston, IL: Northwestern University Press, 2013.
Paul, M. Allen. *Katyn: Stalin's Massacre and the Triumph of Truth.* DeKalb: Northern Illinois University Press, 2010.
Pechota, Vratislav. "Czechoslovakia and the Third World." In *Eastern Europe and the Third World: East vs. South,* edited by Michael Radu, 77–105. New York: Praeger, 1981.
Petković, Nikola. *Srednja Europa: zbilja, mit, utopija: postmodernizam, postkolonijalizam, postkomunizam i odsutnost autentičnosti.* Rijeka: Adamić, 2003.
Petrova, Tsveta. *From Solidarity to Geopolitics: Support for Democracy among Postcommunist States.* New York: Cambridge University Press, 2014.
Pickles, John. *A History of Spaces: Cartographic Reason, Mapping, and the Geo-Coded World.* London: Routledge, 2004.
Prusin, Alexander V. *The Lands Between: Conflict and the East European Borderlands, 1870–1992.* New York: Oxford University Press, 2010.
Radu, Michael, ed. *Eastern Europe and the Third World: East vs. South.* New York: Praeger, 1981.
Rothberg, Michael. "Between Paris and Warsaw: Multidirectional Memory, Ethics, and Historical Responsibility." In *Memory and Theory in Eastern Europe,* edited by Uilleam Blacker, Alexander Etkind, and Julie Fedor, 81–101. New York: Palgrave Macmillan, 2013.
Sayer, Derek. *The Coasts of Bohemia: A Czech History.* Princeton, NJ: Princeton University Press, 1998.

Schnurer, Eric B. "E-stonia and the Future of the Cyberstate." *Foreign Affairs*, 28 January 2015. Accessed 20 January 2015. https://www.foreignaffairs.com/articles/eastern-europe-caucasus/2015-01-28/e-stonia-and-future-cyberstate.

Seegel, Steven. *Mapping Europe's Borderlands: Russian Cartography in the Age of Empire*. Chicago: University of Chicago Press, 2012.

Siegelbaum, Lewis H., and Leslie Page Moch. *Broad Is My Native Land: Repertoires and Regimes of Migration in Russia's Twentieth Century*. Ithaca, NY: Cornell University Press, 2014.

Snyder, Timothy. "Integration and Disintegration: Europe, Ukraine, and the World." *Slavic Review* 74, no. 4 (2015): 695–707.

———. *On Tyranny: Twenty Lessons from the Twentieth Century*. New York: Tim Duggan Books, 2017.

Steiner, Zara. *The Triumph of the Dark: European International History*. New York: Oxford University Press, 2011.

Teichova, Alice. "Czechoslovakia and the Czech and Slovak Republics." In *The Oxford Encyclopedia of Economic History*, edited by Joel Mokyr, 58–60. New York: Oxford University Press, 2003.

Ther, Philipp. "Caught in Between: Border Regions in Modern Europe." In *Shatterzone of Empires: Coexistence and Violence in the German, Habsburg, Russian, and Ottoman Borderlands*, edited by Omer Bartov and Eric D. Weitz, 485–502. Bloomington: Indiana University Press, 2013.

Ther, Philipp, and Anna Siljak, eds. *Redrawing Nations: Ethnic Cleansing in East-Central Europe, 1944–1948*. Lanham, MD: Rowman & Littlefield, 2001.

Tlostanova, Madina. "Can the Post-Soviets Think? On Coloniality of Knowledge: External Imperial and Double Colonial Difference." *Intersections: East European Journal of Society and Politics* 1, no. 2 (2015): 38–58.

Todorova, Maria. "On Public Intellectuals and Their Conceptual Frameworks." *Slavic Review* 74, no. 4 (2015): 708–14.

Waldstein, Maxim. "Theorizing the Second World: Challenges and Prospects." *Ab Imperio* 1 (2010): 98–117.

Webb, Adrian. *The Routledge Companion to Central and Eastern Europe since 1919*. London and New York: Routledge, 2008.

Wolff, Larry. *Inventing Eastern Europe: The Map of Civilization on the Mind of the Enlightenment*. Stanford, CA: Stanford University Press, 1994.

———. "The Traveler's View of Central Europe: Gradual Transitions and Degrees of Difference in European Borderlands." In *Shatterzone of Empires: Coexistence and Violence in the German, Habsburg, Russian, and Ottoman Borderlands*, edited by Omer Bartov and Eric D. Weitz, 23–41. Bloomington: Indiana University Press, 2013.

Zahra, Tara. *The Great Departure: Mass Migration from Eastern Europe and the Making of the Free World*. New York: W. W. Norton, 2016.

Zarycki, Tomasz. *Ideologies of Eastness in Central and Eastern Europe*. London: Routledge, 2014.

Zimmer, Kenyon. *Immigrants against the State: Yiddish and Italian Anarchists in America*. Urbana: University of Illinois Press, 2015.

Part I

Re-placed Religion

To avoid the pitfall of situating Eastern Europe's confessional landscape in the familiar coordinates between Orthodoxy and Catholicism, this section contributes to writing the area's religious history from what is typically described as "the margins." The focus here is on the two groups that have been essential to the region's habitus but hardly in control of it: Jews and Muslims. Deliberations about the agency of these "insider-outsiders" (Udel) and its limits link the contributions by Miriam Udel and Piro Rexhepi.

Udel turns to the resurgence of an age-old papal fantasy in two Jewish literary texts from the 1940s—one a work of juvenile fiction and the other a story by the perhaps best-known author of Yiddish literature, Isaac Bashevis Singer. In both tales, a Jewish character has a chance to attain—and possibly even surpass—the status of a Catholic pope, only to rediscover Jewishness by choice and on his own terms, that is, on those not prescribed by his co-territorial Gentile neighbors. Against the contextual backdrop of their rabbinic precursors and real-life antecedents, these writings thematize what Udel justly terms "the plasticity" of religious and ethnic affiliations. Accompanied by significant but never irrevocable crossings of interreligious or interethnic lines in both directions, the stories' use of the papal fantasy questions the presumed unidirectionality of passing.

Forms of resistance against the compulsion to pass—as European historical subjects, this time around—crystallize in Piro Rexhepi's essay on Muslims in the Balkans. Historiography of so-called Balkan Islam, he argues, has erroneously upheld the colonial-era narrative of this brand's difference—in effect, its discontiguity—from Islam elsewhere. The goal has been to assimilate the religion into the civilizational fabric of forward-looking Europe, suppress the voices insistent on alternative temporalities or spatialities, and fracture any cross-border solidarities among Muslim coreligionists. To expose the shortsightedness of this kind of isolation from the vantage points of history and current politics alike, Rexhepi dwells on a string of twentieth- and twenty-first-century case studies that highlight the close, diverse, far-reaching, and at times alarming continuum of ties between the Muslims in what is now Kosovo, Albania, and Bosnia and the transnational pan-Islamic movements from Mecca to Lahore and Cairo. Islam in the Balkans, Rexhepi provocatively insinuates, does not exist if it is construed as intrinsic to Europe but extrinsic to the rest of this global religion.

Given the scope of these two essays, the section's title, "Re-placed Religion," stands deliberately ambiguous or, rather, polysemous. On the one hand, at stake is "replacing" in the most literal sense: the possibility of swapping one religion for another and the unexpected ease with which the attendant contiguities can crumble or become reshuffled in the process. On the other hand, re-placing is also a symbolic search for alternative matrices of ideological and even ontological self-anchoring in time and space. This vantage point emphasizes that the margins are usually constituted in the eye of the beholder: one community's margins could be another's centers, as Rexhepi's piece suggests. Contiguity and discontiguity, likewise, are not absolute paradigms waiting to be debunked or installed, but historically conditioned regimes in need of close scrutiny.

Chapter One

The "Jewish Pope" in the 1940s
On Jewish Cultural and Ethnic Plasticity

Miriam Udel

Yiddish letters furnish a found experiment, however imperfect and uncontrolled, in the audacity of unmapping. Just how far might a text—or a person—be removed from the cartographic bounds (and bonds) of Eastern Europe and remain Eastern European? How about a story composed in New York, set in the seat of Western European religious culture, and addressed to young Americans? Or one set in Poland and canonized in the West through translation? Do these kinds of discontiguities mark the Jewish experience in relation to Eastern Europe as a peculiar one, or do they instead help us to establish and refine the very paradigm of unmapping?

In 1947, Yudl Mark (1897–1975)—renowned Yiddish educator, grammarian, philologist, translator, and author of textbooks and historical children's books—published a different sort of work altogether. *Der yidisher poyps* (*The Jewish Pope*) might be classed today as a novella for young adults and marketed as a lightly fictionalized historical account of the succession of Pope Anaclet II to the throne of Saint Peter in 1130. In fact, it appeared as part of the Kinder-Ring Library's series "Historical Figures."[1] However, a more complex truth is proclaimed on the title page, where the book is characterized as "a web of legend, history and fantasy." The final term of this triumvirate underscores this novella's contribution to a venerable and polymorphous motif in the Jewish cultural imaginary: namely, the recurrent fantasia of a Jew who ascends to the papacy itself or otherwise to a status "more Catholic than the pope." Dating back at least to the Talmudic period, and rooted in the biblical Joseph cycle, the most persistent version of this fantasy is the narrative of the Catholic pope of Jewish origin.

One of the notable aspects of this malleable and evergreen fantasy is the way it combined and recombined with the other terms of the title page: legend and history. It surfaces in a variety of eras and places and always has the potential to illuminate, through the special European Jewish role as consummate insider-outsider, historical tensions (papal schism, imperial expansion) that implicated but did not fundamentally originate with or depend upon the Jews. This essay concentrates on the notable resurgence of the Jewish pope motif during the 1940s in Yiddish letters specifically, where its popularity highlights a cluster of spatial and linguistic discontiguities particular to Eastern European Jewish identity. The Jewish boy's ascension to the papacy suggested to a transnational Yiddish readership not only that geography was not destiny, but that neither was ethnicity or confessional affiliation. Poignantly countervailing this message of plasticity, though, were the inescapable realities to which the Yiddish medium was itself subject. "Jewish Eastern Europe" might find safe harbor in New York, but the constitutive language of Jewish Eastern European identity would encounter a more complicated fate.

The texts on which I focus are Mark's novella and a short story by Isaac Bashevis Singer, "Zeydlus der ershter" ("Zeidlus the First"; 1943). Targeting, respectively, juvenile and adult audiences and featuring radically divergent plot lines, these two stories that appeared just four years apart at once demonstrate the unity and multifariousness of the papal motif as a tool for grappling with the limits of Jewish identity and agency. Given the way it overleaps religious, temporal, and spatial boundaries, this motif might be considered as a peculiarly Jewish instance of geopoetics.[2]

PLOT OF *DER YIDISHER POYPS*

Until recently, there was no secondary literature on Mark's novella.[3] Because the text is both intricate and substantial,[4] a summary of key plot points follows. The story opens with a sympathetic view of Theresa, an impoverished Catholic woman taking confession for the sin of working as a *shabes goy* (a non-Jew who lights the oven fires and does other tasks prohibited to Jews on the Sabbath) in local Jewish homes, labor that is formally interdicted by church law. Her confessor, Father Thomas, insists that the only measure that will compensate for her blemished soul is to deliver him a new soul—that is, a Jewish child who can be converted. Overcoming her qualms, Theresa dutifully abducts Elchanan, the sickly six-year-old son of Mainz's distinguished rabbinic leader, Rabbi Simeon the Great. During a daring midnight attempt at escape, the boy falls ill. He awakens recaptured but now entrusted to the care of Father Felix, whose compassion and delicacy begin to wear away at Elchanan's dogged resistance to proselytizing. On the way to Rome, the priest instructs the boy in Latin and catechism.

In Rome, Elchanan is adopted by the wealthy and powerful Pierleoni family, themselves Jewish converts. Rechristened Petrus/Peter, Elchanan witnesses the schismatic violence between the Pierleonis and the rival Frangipanis, as well as Urban II's initiation of the First Crusade, with its unintended (as the text presents them) consequences for German Jewry. As a twelve-year-old boy, Elchanan/Petrus learns of the decimation of the Jews of Mainz and other German communities, including, presumably, his birth parents. The ostensibly orphaned Petrus journeys to France to study (with Peter Abelard, no less) and enters the church, rising to the rank of cardinal while still a young man. Traveling to Germany on a papal diplomatic mission, his carriage is stopped by a poor Jew who begs his assistance in rescuing his daughter, Rebecca, from the rapacious Knight of the Red Plains. The first half of the novella closes with Petrus's election as the "legitimate" Pope Anaclet II in Rome, while his peers clandestinely elevate one of their number as the "illegitimate" Pope Innocent II.

The novella's second half focuses increasingly on the pull that the Jewish pope feels toward the faith of his forebears. Father Felix, now blind and impoverished, makes a pilgrimage and begs forgiveness for his involvement in the abduction, revealing that Elchanan's father is still alive. Drawn to his coreligionists, the Jewish pope attends the Kol Nidre service incognito and resolves to summon the leaders of Mainz in the hopes that his father will be among them. Devising a ruse that will compel his aged father's attendance, Elchanan-Petrus-Anaclet promulgates an extravagantly harsh decree against the Jews of Mainz that no bishop can overturn but that may be rescinded only by the pope himself. The punitive dispensation has its intended effect, and Rabbi Simeon arrives in person to plead for his community. The obligatory anagnorisis follows, with Anaclet, Joseph- or Odysseus-like, disclosing his identity to his father. Ultimately, the Jewish pope devises a strategy to escape his station unnoticed and to return to the home and faith of his parents in Mainz—with the resolute and beautiful Rebecca as his bride.

THE EVENTS IN HISTORY AND LEGEND

As a literary product of the 1940s, *Der yidisher poyps* is marked by a high degree of narratorial omniscience and access to several (though not all) of the characters' feelings, thoughts, and motivations. The historical plot is interwoven with a suitably medieval romantic one, and the whole is subordinated to the overarching drama of Jewish identity compromised, forfeited, and then joyfully reclaimed. The folk and historical sources on which Mark drew were more circumspect albeit thoroughly recognizable in his embroidered text. The "legend" to which the title page alludes is first elaborated in Yiddish in the *Mayse bukh,* a collection of rabbinic and folk material published in Basel in 1602. Totaling eight pages (in Moses Gaster's English translation[5]), the *Mayse bukh* presentation of "The Jewish Child Who Was Stolen by a Servant and Later Became Pope" is considerably more bare-bones than Mark's novella, but quite prolix relative to the rest of the collection. It establishes wide-ranging narratorial access but uses this omniscience to offer a very cursory, exterior view of the early events of Elchanan's life and character formation, eschewing any account of the various characters' inner motivations except to justify the Jewish pope's decision to remain among the Christians, "as one may well imagine, considering that it went well with him and that he was held in high esteem" (412). The early modern text gives only glancing treatment to Elchanan's boyhood, either in Mainz or in Rome. Most of its emphasis (six of the eight pages) is placed on the father-son reunion, which recapitulates several aspects of the biblical Joseph's reunion with his brothers and then with his father, Jacob.[6] Chief among these is the lopsided nature of an encounter in which a long-lost son, not only acculturated but having succeeded to fabulous power within his adoptive surroundings, lures his father to a meeting through a manufactured crisis; son knows father's identity, but the reverse is not true. Recognition is established gradually by signs and tokens, such as the pope's uncannily deep facility with Talmudic argumentation and his knowledge of an idiosyncratic and masterful chess move transmitted early on in life by Rabbi Simeon to Elchanan. Not only does the pope rescind his harsh decree at the encounter, but in its aftermath, he authors a polemic against Catholicism, which he orders every subsequent candidate for the papacy to read; then he escapes Rome in order to return to Mainz and become "a good Jew again" (417). His father, in turn, authors a liturgical poem (*piyyut*) commemorating the story, an assertion the *Mayse bukh* proffers as an attestation of the events' facticity: "Therefore do not think that this is mere fiction" (417). The legend thus accounts for the provenance of a composition that is still recited on Rosh Hashanah.[7]

Perhaps the most poignant moment of the reunion comes just after Elchanan's disclosure of identity, when the son asks his father, "Can you advise me how I can atone for my sin?"—that is, the sin of retaining his Christian identity and practice into adulthood while knowing of his Jewish parentage.[8] His father's reply invokes the pertinent rabbinic legal designation, consonant with the kidnapped boy's lack of volition: "You need not worry, it was against your will, for you were only a child when you were taken away from me" (416). The concept of the "captive child" originates in Talmudic argumentation[9] and grows into a capacious legal category for unwitting sin that still figures prominently in Jewish legal discussions of the status of nonobservant Jews. The leniency that the rabbis carved out entailed an implicit recognition of the overwhelming power of co-territorial—that is, non-Jewish—societies and religions in general, and then in medieval Europe, of the Catholic Church specifically. The resonance of the papal motif comes through its promise of Jewish power, consolidated under adversity but then benignly exercised: "For its part," writes Joseph Sherman, "impotent Jewry invented a fantasy that there might one day be crowned a truly Jewish pope—not an apostate, but a crypto-Christian—who, by remaining true to the faith of his people, would help to reverse that people's powerlessness" (18–19). In fact, the most realistic hopes for Jewish attainment of power in the real world lay precisely in unidirectional and unrepentant apostasy.

The historical record of the turn of the twelfth century attests to this, reflecting a schismatic moment in which a family of recent Jewish extraction played a pivotal role. Banker to Pope Leo IX (1049–54) and other high church officials, the Jewish Baruch/Benedictus was converted (along with his son Leo) under the direct sponsorship of the supreme pontiff. Leo's son, Peter Leo / Pietro di Leone, lent the family its surname and continued to offer financial support to various popes and church elites. He and his brothers were supporters of Urban II (1088–99), who died in one of the family's homes, near the Trastevere, Rome's Jewish quarter. A son—not adoptive—of Pietro Pierleoni who shared his father's name entered the church, rose to cardinal in 1120 and pope in 1130, reigning in Rome as Pope Anaclet II until his death in 1138. Meanwhile, a rival faction of cardinals regarded Anaclet as an antipope and instead designated Innocent II (1130–43),[10] who fled to a far more hospitable France after the contested election. Although, as Sherman notes (18), his family history raised no objections during his tenure as cardinal and papal legate, polemics against Pope Anaclet II dwelled heavily on his Jewish heritage, imputing to him a racist panoply of "Jewish" sins and impurities, including avarice, usury, gluttony, and even incest with his sister Tropea.[11]

A RECENT PRECEDENT: THE MORTARA AFFAIR

With a documented history encompassing such rhetorical excesses, we can hardly be surprised at Yudl Mark's elision of legend, history, and fantasy. Hovering over his fictionalized, retrograde story is a set of real-life events that take on an even more mythopoeic cast for their temporal proximity to his own lifetime and its defining traumas. In the year 1858, a six-year-old boy named Edgardo Mortara[12] was taken by the military police of the Papal States from the care of his Jewish parents in their Bologna apartment and remanded to the custody of the church under the direct authority of the inquisitor, Father Pier Gaetano Feletti. Edgardo was abducted in this legally sanctioned fashion because word had reached the inquisitor that during an illness in his infancy, the boy had been hastily baptized by the family's then-fourteen-year-old Catholic domestic servant. Under canon law, a baptized child was considered Catholic, and a Catholic child could not be left in the care of Jewish parents. That the baptism itself was haphazard, hasty, remote, and unwitnessed was all irrelevant once word of the event reached the inquisitor.

Thus, the boy was placed in the House of the Catechumens, an institution founded in Rome in the sixteenth century as a kind of instructional halfway house for those converting to Catholicism from other religions. Pope Pius IX took the child on as his own son, keeping close track of his religious education and ensuring that his parents could see him only occasionally and under church supervision. They mounted endless appeals involving the communal leadership of Roman Jewry and extending to international Jewish notables and philanthropists (such James and Lionel Rothschild and Moses Montefiore) and even world leaders, including Napoleon III and the British foreign secretary. Political pressure and legal appeals were in vain; the boy came to embrace his new identity and eventually entered the church as a monk, a vocation in which he remained during a long lifetime of missionary preaching, contemplation, study, and prayer in a Belgian abbey. He died at age eighty-eight in March 1940, just a month before the Nazis entered Belgium "to begin rounding up all those tainted with Jewish blood."[13]

The phenomenon of papal abductions neither began nor ended with Edgardo's, although his became the most internationally notorious case. Much as Anaclet's election took place against the backdrop of papal schism and internecine conflict in Rome and throughout Catholic Europe, so were the Mortaras unwittingly caught in the cross-fire of the Risorgimento and the death throes of papal temporal rule. The papal abductions of children implicitly affirmed the plasticity of affiliation and therefore of identity, averring that religion was a matter of mutable faith rather than of immutable blood. By the 1940s, the Jews of Europe had been trapped by a European imperial conflict on the grandest scale yet. The Nazis were renovating the racialized doctrine of *limpieza de sangre* that had taken hold in fifteenth-century Spain: once again, any Jewish blood constituted an ineradicable taint. In this context, the very idea of fungible lines between Jew and Christian that had been anathema to Jews in nineteenth-century Italy (how dare the church claim their children as Catholics!) yielded to a fantasy of lifesaving escape.

LEV NUSSIMBAUM: A SELF-MADE LEGEND

For an indication of how pervasive the Jewish preoccupation with "escape" was in Europe in the first decades of the twentieth century, as well as for a real-life study in ethno-religious plasticity, it is worth digressing briefly to consider the life of Lev Nussimbaum. Born to a prosperous Jewish oil family in pre-revolutionary Baku, Nussimbaum fled the Russian Revolution as a high schooler, together with his father, and undertook an itinerant course through Turkey and eventually various locales in Western Europe. He became a prolific and commercially successful writer, reinventing himself along the way as the Arab potentate Essad Bey and eventually perhaps as Khurban Said, author of the Azerbaijani national novel *Ali and Nino*. As a teenager, he was intrigued with the Muslim Orient, and as a university student in England, he undertook serious study of Arabic and the Near East. He converted to Islam, dressed in mufti in the interwar cafés, and was generally known as a Muslim. Ill and alone in middle age, Nussimbaum died at a pension in wartime Italy. Tom Reiss's captivating account of his life[14] makes the case for Nussimbaum's being one and the same as Khurban Said, although this identification has been questioned by others.

Many of the discontiguities that surface in the legend of the Jewish pope also converge in Nussimbaum's life. His consciousness straddled historical periods and places so that as a young man, "he was becoming a believer in a kind of monarchy of his own imagining that was a blend of the Ottoman and czarist legacies with those of the ancient Jewish kingdom of the Khazars and the Crusader clans of Khevsuria. It would be a monarchy that existed in an unreal space between Europe and Asia."[15] His peripeteia was set in motion by the realization that it was utterly and increasingly hopeless to map that unreal space onto the actual map of twentieth-century Eastern Europe. Like Yudl Mark, Nussimbaum had to make great spatiotemporal leaps—to unmap himself, as it were—in order to imagine a *modus vivendi*; the difference is that he tried actually to live out these leaps alongside his fictional creations, outfitted in mufti, for example, while holding forth in Berlin cafés. Reiss contextualizes Nussimbaum within a real-life group of Jewish Weimar Republic intellectuals who indulged a benignly intended Orientalism:

> Like Lev, these Weimar figures—many from a wing of the Zionist movement that sought a pan-Asiatic merger with Muslims—found in the Orient a kind

of escape hatch from the encroaching threats of brutal modernity.... They reinvented the historical Muslim Orient as a place free from clear ethnic and sectarian lines, and most especially free from antisemitism—no matter that the reality was more complex than that. (229)

Set alongside Mark's novella, it is striking how these various Jewish inhabitants of that "unreal space between Europe and Asia" imaginatively constructed a time and a place where ethno-religious passing was relatively frictionless, and even bidirectional in the case of the Jewish pope. But as Weimar Republic–era freedoms gave way to National Socialist–Nuremberg restrictions, Nussimbaum found little protection in his assumed—or more accurately, transformed—identity. As Reiss indicates, the walls of Europe were closing in:

> European Jews had been the greatest beneficiaries of liberalism, which had allowed them to live and prosper as individuals; the new tribalism was re-creating the ghetto walls. They were imperiled by the sudden collapse of the old imperial and monarchical regimes, even though this was what many of them had worked toward and wanted. The old empires and autocracies, even at their most oppressive, had provided space in which people could get on with their business. The totalizing, ideological systems of Lev's lifetime would not allow such space. The new map of Europe would be fraught with ubiquitous peril for liberals, for free thinkers, for misfits, and, above all, for Jews. The quest for a way out took on an undercurrent of desperation. (228)

A German literary rival of Nussimbaum's, also exiled in Italy in 1941, derided the spectacle of his competitor's life as "the horrifying fairy tale of a young, unhappy, apostate Jew!"—"one [trying to] make a fairy tale out of his life in order to escape sad reality."[16]

All of the passages cited above include the word "escape"; it is startling to realize that this word recurs no fewer than twenty-seven times in Reiss's book. Ending in dashed hopes, Nussimbaum's life of elected apostasy and unelected flight ultimately illustrates Europe's limitations on ethno-religious plasticity. In this respect, it sets the stage for the compressed but masterful wartime instantiation of the Jewish pope motif by Isaac Bashevis Singer.

A REPUDIATION OF THE LEGEND

In his 1943 short story "Zeydlus der ershter" ("Zeidlus the First"),[17] Isaac Bashevis Singer subverts virtually every aspect of the Jewish pope legend. As if immediately to signal a radically new perspective, the first-person narrator of Bashevis Singer's tale is an ambitious demon seeking to improve his standing in the underworld by delivering Jewish souls to his satanic overlord.[18] His eye quickly alights on the misanthropic Talmud scholar Zeydl Cohen of Janov. At once wealthy, ascetic by nature, and impervious to sensual pleasures, Zeydl is proof against all the usual means of demonic seduction. But the narrator eventually notes in Zeydl "much more than that sliver of vanity which the Law permits the scholar" (172): at last he has found his mark's exploitable yearning. To Zeydl, the demon makes a strong, if perverse, argument for apostasy, a cardinal sin:

> You know the Jews have never honored their leaders: they grumbled about Moses; rebelled against Samuel; threw Jeremiah into a ditch; and murdered Zacharias. The Chosen People hate greatness. In a great man, they sense a rival to Jehovah, so they love only the petty and mediocre. Their thirty-six saints are all shoemakers and water-carriers. The Jewish laws are concerned mainly with a drop of milk falling into a pot of meat or with an egg laid on a holiday. They have deliberately corrupted Hebrew, degraded the ancient texts. Their Talmud makes King David into a provincial rabbi advising women about menstruation. The way they reason, the smaller the greater, the uglier the prettier. Their rule is: The closer one is to dust, the nearer one is to God. So you can see, Reb Zeidel, why they find you a thumb in the eye—you with your erudition, wealth, fine breeding, brilliant perceptions, and extraordinary memory. (172–73)

While Zeydl's erudition is underappreciated among the Jews, the demon argues, it would be treasured among the Christians. "Having totally accepted the Christian definition of themselves as inferior beings,"[19] European Jews have actually become, the demon argues, blinkered, petty, and self-loathing—a community cut off from the grandeur of its own history, textual traditions, and aspirations. As if this were not bad enough, the Jews fail to define themselves affirmatively and instead measure themselves in every way as being what the Christians are not. Thus, Christian culture and religion are entrenched as the arbiter of value, and their Jewish neighbors are reduced to playing hopeless catch-up at best or a destructive game of self-negation at worst.

Accepting the demon's logic, Zeydl converts to Christianity and labors over a brilliant polemical attack on Judaism. The driven scholar, with his formidable mastery of Bible and rabbinics, quickly takes in Polish, Latin, and New Testament Greek. "After a while he was so thoroughly versed in Christian theology that the priests and monks were afraid to talk to him for with his erudition he found mistakes everywhere" (175). The renamed and reborn Zeidlus has become more Catholic than the pope. But while confessional affiliation might be malleable, changed circumstances are no match for ingrained temperament: Zeidlus languishes unappreciated among the Gentiles, finally losing his newly acquired wealth, his eyesight, and with it all of his learning except for the pages of Talmud memorized in his youth. Despite his intellectual acuity, he cannot see that he is valued by his new associates not as a scholar or an individual of any kind, but rather only as an apostate—that is, a "living witness to the superiority of the Christian faith."[20]

THE RHETORIC OF ANTITHESIS: *LEHAVDL-LOSHN*

The devil is the consummate double-voiced speaker,[21] and he often speaks out of both sides of his mouth. His flattery takes the form of insults, and he speaks in ironic paradoxes. As the narrator makes the case to Zeydl, "The Gentiles are the antithesis of the Jews. Since their God is a man, a man can be a God to them. Gentiles admire greatness of any kind and love the men who possess it: men of great pity or great cruelty, great builders or great destroyers, great virgins or great harlots, great sages or great fools, great rulers or great rebels, great believers or great infidels" (173). This verbally acrobatic passage offers the clearest formulation of one of the signature rhetorical strategies of Bashevis Singer's demons: the clever use of antithesis. A key feature of the Bashevian underworld is that the moral order is intact but precisely inverted. The demon has only to argue that *his* moral order is the true one, and the whole structure of moral reasoning is automatically reconfigured to accord Satan the uppermost. Antithesis recurs as both a verbal tactic and a theme in Bashevis-Singer's demon tales, and in all its variations it points to the blurring or overturning of the moral order, as when another demonic narrator confides to the object of his seduction, "I lie only with married women, for good actions are my sins; my prayers are blasphemies; spite is my bread; arrogance, my wine; pride, the marrow of my bones."[22] These inversions often convey irony that, while apparent to the reader, is lost on the victim. Even as Zeydl's tempter lauds the Gentiles' robust admiration for greatness, he criticizes their lack of discrimination between pity and cruelty, builders and destroyers, virgins and harlots, sages and fools.

At the philological level, this antithesis is borne out by the liberal use of pejorative, culturally distinctive *lehavdl-loshn*[23]: antithetical or oppositional language. David Roskies identifies this linguistic phenomenon at work in Bashevis Singer's stories, describing it thus:

> Within Yiddish itself there had come into being what Max Weinreich termed *lehavdl-loshn*, a built in, double vocabulary to distinguish or differentiate the Jewish from the Christian realm. Since, from the Jewish point of view, what is

"ours" is automatically better than what is "theirs," the words that signify their world are loaded with pejorative meaning. More than a motley of ethnic slurs ... this is a linguistic structure that serves to insulate the Jews even as they live and work among Christians. (286)

Lehavdl-loshn takes its name from a verbal tic generally associated with piety, the insertion of the word *lehavdl* (meaning "to make a distinction") before any reference to things base, profane, or simply foreign. The term expands to include a whole dual lexicon where the term applied to what is "Jewish" carries a neutral or positive connotation and the corresponding term for what is Christian or "other" carries a negative one.

In "Zeidlus," the devil's speech is rife with such fraught language. As Roskies and Sherman point out, the devil does not avail himself of the neutral Yiddish words for "pray in a church," but rather expresses the same idea with a phrase that translates literally as "to blather in a pagan house of worship." Even as the devil argues that there is no immanent, personal God, that "the earth and its inhabitants are no more than a swarm of gnats" in His eyes, and that there are no substantive differences between Jew and Christian, he does so using *lehavdl-loshn*:

> You'll continue to study, to wear a long coat and skullcap. The only difference will be that instead of being stuck away in a remote village among Jews who hate you and your accomplishments, praying in a sunken hole of a study house where beggars scratch themselves behind the stove, you will live in a large city, preach in a luxurious church where an organ will play, and where your congregation will consist of men of stature whose wives will kiss your hand. If you excel and throw together some hodgepodge about Jesus and his mother the Virgin, they will make you a bishop, and later a cardinal—and God willing, if everything goes well, they'll make you a Pope one day. (174)

The sentence about Jesus and the Virgin has been translated with ecumenical tact for Western eyes. A more tonally faithful rendering might read, "And if you really do it up and throw together some kind of bullshit [*treyf-posl*] about Jeezus and his mother, the so-called virgin...." Roskies notes the ironic divide between what the devil preaches (apostasy) and the specific language in which he does so—a vocabulary pervaded by Ashkenazic anti-Christian polemicism and dripping with scorn.[24] By employing traditionally pious rhetoric, the devil at once ironizes that rhetoric and mocks Zeydl, who is willing to transgress and ignore the protective adaptive benefits of Jewish antipathy toward Christianity. The devil, always for Bashevis Singer rooted firmly in Jewish language, culture, history and even religion, knows his proper place. *He* will not be taken in by the promises to which Zeydl succumbs; even as he bobs and weaves and obfuscates matters to the detriment of his mark, he revels in the clarity of a stark separation between Jew and Christian.

The ultimate wages of all Zeydl's elaborate discussions with the devil is deep confusion—moral, practical, philosophical, and verbal. The man begins as an intellectual if not a moral seeker who presses to know, if indeed there is no reward or punishment in the next world:

> "Then what is there?" Zeidel asked me, fearful and confused.
> "There is something that exists, but it has no existence," I answered in the manner of the philosophers. (173)

Following his conversion, Zeydl only grows more disillusioned and uncertain: "After years of effort, he was so fatigued that he could no longer distinguish between right and wrong, sense and nonsense, between what would please and what displease the Church. Nor did he believe any more in what is called truth and falsehood" (176). This confusion is not the result of any logical failure on the devil's part. On the contrary, Bashevis Singer artfully conveys his critique of Enlightenment rationalism by constructing a devil whose arguments are perfectly logical, if topsy-turvy. The chief target of his demons' speech is the logocentric, intellectual platitudes of modern Jewry—seeking refuge in "the manner of philosophers." That manner is a sophisticated but ultimately hollow discourse of one kind or another to justify what Bashevis Singer deems to be the self-destructive programs of assimilation and social progress for which apostasy is a premodern analogue.

In refashioning the triumphant myth of the Jewish pope into a wry parable of failed apostasy, he drags a storyline in which Jews have figured tangentially in other peoples' conflicts and schisms into the very center of the Jewish street. He restages the clash as the indigenously (if not exclusively) Jewish one between traditional piety and its various substitutes, including Enlightenment ("reformed" religion), secular humanism, and Christianity. Though these departures from tradition might be placed along a continuum, Bashevis Singer views all of them as fairly interchangeable iterations of the same execrable thing. In almost all of his fiction, Bashevis Singer systematically forecloses to his characters potential avenues of escape or redemption: traditional Judaism, modernized Judaism, other religions, secularism. His flight-obsessed protagonists can go nowhere and end up immobilized and even immured, whether literally (*Magician of Lublin*) or figuratively (*Shadows on the Hudson*). But what Yudl Mark accomplishes with the honey of elective affinity, Bashevis Singer manages with the vinegar of consignment to one's fate: whether through celebration or condemnation, both authors reinforce the inevitability of Jewishness for the Jews.

Surprisingly, some of Isaac Bashevis Singer's most darkly ironic tales end on a curious note of affirmation, albeit what we would have to call negative affirmation. The passage to the next world holds out the promise of an end to the confusion that Zeydl has experienced in this one. Humbled, blind, and destitute in his final days, the reclusive priest finds that "one yearning still plagued him: to know the truth" about the cosmos and its Creator. Thus when the devil appears to escort him to hell, Zeydl greets him with serenity bordering on joy:

> "Where are you taking me?" he asked.
> "Straight to Gehenna."
> "If there is a Gehenna, there is also a God," Zeidel said, his lips trembling.
> "This proves nothing," I retorted.
> "Yes it does," he said. "If Hell exists, everything exists. If you are real, He is real. Now take me to where I belong. I am ready." (178)

It is significant that over a lifetime of conversing with the devil, this is the first time that Zeydl—now blind—ever sees him. Adding the visual dimension to that of pure conversation breaks the rhetorical spell of demonic seduction. Once again, the broken man regains some of the old forensic acumen of his days as a Talmud scholar. He turns one of Satan's favorite rhetorical maneuvers against his tempter by naming the greatest antithesis of the cosmos: if there is a devil, there must be a God. If so much power is brought to bear by the forces of evil, they must be joined in battle against a genuine, if sensually imperceptible, force for good. Zeydl's life has been ruined by the illusion of a dichotomous world in which suffering among the Jews must imply glory among the Gentiles. Now, he throws the dichotomy back at his tormentor, embracing what one interpreter calls a "backdoor policy for approaching God."[25] Too late to enter heaven but still in time to satisfy his earthly curiosity, the man who would never be pope learns the cosmic truth.

PASSING UP PASSING: AN ASSERTION OF AGENCY

By the time Yudl Mark's novella was published, Eastern European Jewish culture found itself in redoubled exile: the age-old Jewish exile from the Holy Land was now trebled by the further displacement of the vast majority of remaining Yiddish speakers to the Americas or Palestine. Yet Mark demonstrated that if Jews could pass as Gentiles, and even rise to the top of Gentile power structures, then they could pass right back into Jewishness.

The re-articulation of the papal legend took on tremendous power in the shadow of the Holocaust. The Nazis had damned the Jews to insuperable alterity by their very blood, but what if it were possible to assimilate into (Christian) normalcy by some combination of coercion and suasion? The Jewish pope motif located that very possibility within Christian theology itself and so de-racialized religious identity. Moreover, the myth hazarded a corresponding claim for a kind of Jewish agency: anyone who *could* choose to live as a Christian but did not was affirmatively electing Jewish identity rather than merely defaulting to the lachrymose fate dictated by the "wrong" ancestry. Perhaps the Jews could pass up passing altogether. The preadolescent and teenage audience for Mark's novella—being reared to read or at least to comprehend a fairly ornate narrative in the Yiddish language, and that immediately after the decimation of Europe's Yiddish speakers—found themselves in a threshold position similar to Elchanan's at the moment of his abdication and return to Mainz. If there is no *limpieza de sangre,* and apostasy and assimilation are viable choices, then so is Jewishness. As a grammarian and linguist, Mark made a career-spanning investment in preserving the Yiddish language. Surely, he hoped that what was true of Jewish identity (*yidishkeyt*) might also be true of Yiddish: that the juvenile readers of his tale might affirmatively choose to embrace all elements of the religio-cultural-linguistic complex to which they were heir. Passing up passing might mean not only staking a robust claim on Jewishness but passing up the seemingly inevitable process of linguistic assimilation.

With respect to these works' publication, the *where* is as significant as, and finally quite inseparable from, the *when.* Isaac Bashevis Singer made his way, with his brother's help, to New York in 1935; Yudl Mark came the following year. Both writers arrived as part of an outrageously fortunate trickle of would-be refugees rather than with the torrent of two million European Jews who had immigrated to the United States in the four decades preceding the Immigration Act of 1924 and established an infrastructure of Yiddish cultural and educational institutions. Whereas earlier arrivals enjoyed the luxury of imagining their move to the New World as provisional and perhaps reversible, there could be no doubt by the mid-thirties that this relocation was irrevocable. Yiddish fictions representing life in Europe would increasingly be read, if they were read at all, by people living elsewhere. Those who chose to pursue life in Yiddish—whether artistic or political—had to grapple with the radical discontiguity between the roots of their language and their new surroundings.[26] They chose to dwell, however tenuously or temporarily, in a Yiddishland whose very essence was its unmappability, its sometimes dogged, sometimes spritely resistance to the cartographic mandate. This interwar and postwar Yiddishland was unbound from the ordinary geographical contiguities, recognizing any potential borderland as precarious and contingent.

For a time, Yiddish cultural activists made sure that Jewish "Eastern Europe" lived on stateside as a linguistic community, a strategy that after all represents more of a continuation than a rupture with the perpetual self-understanding of exilic and diasporic Jewish nationhood. As Jeffrey Shandler points out in his seminal article on Yiddish in America:

> Yiddish has never stood alone. Its speakers have always been in contact with non-Jews and have always been multilingual, and this has shaped the content and structure of the language. Moreover, the choice of speaking in Yiddish (or not) has always been charged with meaning, and especially so in the modern era, as traditional patterns of Ashkenazic multiglossia gave way to a much more open and contentious configuration of language use among East European Jews.[27]

The fact that this community is constituted by its commitment to a *hybrid* tongue necessarily poses questions of betweenness that are analogous to the potential betweenness of Eastern Europe itself. Does Yiddish exist "between" its constituent elements of German, Russian, Polish, Hebrew, and Romance? Is it a cast-off *zhargón* or a chosen language, tethered to a civilization and thought system, but hovering over or, web-like, linking its constituent languages and cultures? For the multiglossic speakers and readers of newly American Ashkenaz, was Yiddish to be a repository of precious cultural distinctiveness or a gloomy linguistic catacomb? The respective fates of these two papal stories are just as instructive as their plots. Through translation,[28] the Jewish-Polish "Bashevis" found his way out of the linguistic ghetto and into an American identity as "Singer."[29] The story of Zeidlus is widely read in English and many other languages besides. Yudl Mark's work, on the other hand, languished for decades untranslated and therefore unknown beyond a small coterie of aging Yiddish after-school students.[30] Translation itself is a radical deed of unmapping, of negating or overcoming spatial and linguistic discontiguities; it may be enacted more subtly or brutally, according to the approach of the translator and the consciousness of the audience. In these cases, translation from the Yiddish is no neutral passage from one language to another of equal status. It is rather the granting of safe transit to a small set of texts as outrageously fortunate as their authors. The original Yiddish stories are refugees, not tourists in America. To translate them is to unmake their places of origin in favor of another, ostensibly safer destination.

Collaborating with his translators, viewing their work as the production of "a second original,"[31] Bashevis Singer seems to have won by wagering heavily on translation as a preservative for his literary legacy. No scholar has overlooked his crusty Zeidlus. It is curious that despite Joseph Sherman's exceedingly thorough treatment of the papal motif, he bypasses Mark's novella altogether, even though it is far longer than any of the sources that are analyzed.[32] Perhaps this reflects a straightforward bias against children's literature, or perhaps the work simply escaped his notice. But it is an omission worth redressing, for the particular circumstances of a juvenile audience—and *this* postwar juvenile audience—lend resonance to an already rich master narrative. The child's core reality is one of narrowly constrained agency in the present and immediate future, offset by the imagined prospect of limitless agency in the hazy and remote time to come known as adulthood. The actual process of maturation is a gradual reckoning with the limitations of that eventual agency. Thus does Mark emphasize Elchanan's powerlessness, desperation, and fear during the early phases of his abduction, contrasting them with his eventual power as pope; the ultimate manifestation of that power, of course, is abandoning the papacy for a life of his own choosing. Bashevis Singer writes not only for adults chastened by the normal processes of growing up and seeing the far horizon of limitless possibility draw nearer, but also for those traumatized by the violent and horrific revocation of their agency. While Zeidlus's overeager pedantry and arrogance condemn him to fail in carrying out the "terms" of the papal legend, his final negative affirmation of ineluctable Jewishness nonetheless reinforces the deep truth that the legend presents.

We might concur with David Levine Lerner that in its medieval manifestations, the papal legend was "an expression of Jewish defiance in the face of political subordination to the Church."[33] However, by the end of the 1940s the motif has come to represent a very complex interweaving of resistance and resignation to cultural, linguistic, religious, and cartographic mandates. In insisting on a remainder of agency, however compromised, and in privileging a Yiddishland of the mind over terrains that are contiguous on the map, the would-be Jewish pope claims geopoetics as a last redoubt against the sober dictates of geopolitics.

Miriam Udel is associate professor of German studies and Jewish studies at Emory University, where her research and teaching focus on Yiddish modernism in the context of the modern Jewish literary complex. She is currently at work on a project about twentieth-century Yiddish children's literature that encompasses a translated, annotated anthology as well as a scholarly study of the corpus. Udel's book *Never Better! The Modern Jewish Picaresque* has recently appeared in the University of Michigan Press series "Studies in Comparative Jewish Cultures" and won a National Jewish Book Award.

NOTES

For AZ

1. In a similar vein, Yudl Mark published lives of the explorer David Hareuveni and the messianic reverse-converso Solomon Molkho, two medieval Jewish figures whose exploits are wreathed in myth and mystery. By contrast, the same author wrote biographies for young readers of unimpeachably real figures in Jewish intellectual history including Maimonides, Rashi, and Rabbenu Gershom. See his *Der rambam* (New York: Arbeter ring, 1947) and *Rabenu Gershom, Rashi, Yehuda Khosid* (New York: Kinder ring, 1941).
2. See the distinction between geopoetics and geopolitics in Komska's introduction to this volume.
3. For a brief but trenchant discussion of the novella, see Naomi Prawer Kadar's sweeping study of Yiddish children's periodicals *Raising Secular Jews: Yiddish Schools and Their Periodicals for American Children, 1917–1950* (Waltham, MA: Brandeis University Press, 2016).
4. A digital version of the Yiddish original may be accessed through the Spielberg Library on the website of the National Yiddish Book Center: https://archive.org/details/nybc208511, accessed 25 January 2017. For a translation of the text, see Ruth Fisher Goodman, *The Jewish Pope: A Yiddish Tale* (McKinleyville, CA: Daniel and Daniel, 2006).
5. Moses Gaster, ed. and trans., *Ma'aseh Book: Book of Jewish Tales and Legends* (Philadelphia: Jewish Publication Society, 1934), vol. 1, tale 188, 410–18. A facsimile of the original Yiddish was annotated and translated into French and published as a lavish bilingual edition by Astrid Starck, *Un beau livre d'histoires* (Basel: Schwabe, 2004), 518–26. In Starck's numbering, it is tale 187. For a thorough textual reconstruction and thematological analysis, see Joseph Bamberger, *Ha'afifior hayehudi. Letoldoteha shel 'aggadà mime' habenaym be'ashkenaz* [*The Jewish Pope. History of a Medieval Ashkenazic Legend*] (Ramat-Gan: Bar-Ilan University Press, 2009). See also the discussion of the Jewish pope legend in Eli Yassif, *Sippur ha-'am ha-'ivri: toldotav, sugav, umashma'uto* (Jerusalem: Mosad Bialik, 1992), 334ff.
6. See Joseph Sherman's *The Jewish Pope: Myth, Diaspora and Yiddish Literature* (Oxford: Oxford Legenda, 2003) for an exhaustive treatment of the textual parallels, both in direct relation to the *Mayse bukh* account (71) and, more broadly, in relation to the motif of the Jewish pope (26–66). For a compact, yet wide-ranging schema of the medieval attestations of this motif (including Sephardic sources) as well as two twentieth-century revisitations, see David Levine Lerner, "The Enduring Legend of the Jewish Pope," *Judaism* 40, no. 2 (Spring 1991): 148–70.

7. The poem plays on the name Elchanan, breaking it into its constituent words "*El hanan nahalato beno'am lehashper*" (God bestowed grace upon His Portion [Israel], adorning them with his favor). I am grateful to Bernard Septimus, who aided in the translation of this difficult line and helped me to locate the annotated *piyyut* in *Rosh ha-Shanah Mahzor*, edited by Daniel Goldschmidt (Jerusalem: Koren, 2009), 47–50. See Avraham Grossman's, *Hakhme ashkenaz harishonim* (Jerusalem: Magnes, 1989), 86ff. On Elhanan, see 89ff. Grossman mentions the custom of early Ashkenazic liturgical poets to allude to their children in their compositions.
8. Several Hebrew and Sephardic sources require Elchanan's martyrdom for the full expiation of his sin. However, the Yiddish version recorded in the *Mayse bukh* does not. See a discussion of a possible reason for this divergence in Sherman, *The Jewish Pope*, 14.
9. See Babylonian Talmud, Shabbat 68b and Shavuot 5a.
10. For accounts of the historical events, see Mary Stroll, *The Jewish Pope: Ideology and Politics in the Papal Schism of 1130* (Leiden: Brill, 1987); George L. Williams, *Papal Genealogy: The Families and Descendants of the Popes* (Jefferson, NC: McFarland, 1998), 24; and Joachim Prinz, *Popes from the Ghetto* (New York: Schocken Books, 1968).
11. For an analysis of the racial dimension of Anaclet's election and this papal schism, see Irven M. Resnick "Race, Anti-Jewish Polemic, Arnulf of Seéz, and the Contested Papal Election of Anaclet II (A.D. 1130)," in *Jews in Medieval Christendom: Slay Them Not*, ed. Kristine T. Utterback and Merrall L. Price (Leiden: Brill, 2013), 45–70. See also Resnick's *Marks of Distinctions: Christian Perceptions of Jews in the High Middle Ages* (Washington, DC: Catholic University of America Press, 2012), 270–85.
12. For a thorough and gripping account of the Mortara episode in its historical and cultural context, see David I. Kertzer, *The Kidnapping of Edgardo Mortara* (New York: Knopf, 1997). Also useful is Kertzer's follow-up work, an account of top-down Catholic antisemitism and anti-Judaism, *The Popes against the Jews: The Vatican's Role in the Rise of Modern Anti-Semitism* (New York: Vintage, 2001).
13. Kertzer, *Mortara*, 298.
14. See Tom Reiss, *The Orientalist: In Search of a Man Caught Between East and West* (London: Vintage, 2006).
15. Reiss, *The Orientalist*, 126.
16. This "frenemy" was Armin Wegner. Reiss cites from his daybook, *The Orientalist*, 336.
17. The original Yiddish version of the story was published in the New York journal *Svive* and later reprinted together with his novel *Der Sotn in Goray. A mayse fun fartsaytns un andere dertseylungen* (New York: Matones, 1943; reprint, Jerusalem: Akademon, 1972; Tel Aviv: Peretz, 1992). Joel Blocker and Elizabeth Pollet translated the tale into English, under the title "Zeidlus the Pope," where it appears in the collection *Short Friday and Other Stories* (New York: Farrar, Straus and Giroux, 1964) and also in *The Collected Stories of Isaac Bashevis Singer* (New

York: Farrar, Straus and Giroux, 1983). All English citations are from the latter edition.
18. Bashevis Singer gave free rein to clever demonic seducers in a series of stories published in the early 1940s. In introducing the first of these, "Zeydlus der ershter" (translated as "Zeidlus the Pope"), he anticipates publishing a collection to be known as the *Yeytser-hore mayses* (Memoirs of the Evil One)—mostly monologic tales told by demons about their verbal exploits among human beings. Three more of these tales appeared in 1943 with "Zeidlus." Together, they forge a distinctive vocabulary for discussing the besetting crises of Jewish modernity, including secularization, urbanization, and assimilation.
19. Sherman, *The Jewish Pope*, 124.
20. Sherman, *The Jewish Pope*, 124.
21. David Roskies, "Di shprakh fun derekh-haSaM: Vi der sotn redt af yidish," in *Hahut shel hen: shai leHava Turnianski [A Touch of Grace: Studies in Ashkenazi Culture, Women's History, and the Languages of the Jews Presented to Chava Turniansky]*, ed. Israel Bartal, Galit Hasan-Rokem, et al. (Jerusalem: Zalman Shazar Center for Jewish History and the Center for Research on Polish Jewry, the Hebrew University, 2015), 69–85, here 69.
22. The demonic narrator in *Der shpigl: A monolog fun a shed* ["The Mirror"]. The citation is from Norbert Guterman's English translation of the tale in *The Collected Stories of Isaac Bashevis Singer*. New York: Library of America, 2004, 62.
23. Sherman offers a granular discussion of the story's use of *lehavdl-loshn* in *The Jewish Pope*, 126–30. Max Weinreich, *History of the Yiddish Language*, trans. Shlomo Noble with Joshua A. Fishman (Chicago: University of Chicago Press, 1980), 193ff. See also the discussion in David G. Roskies's *A Bridge of Longing: The Lost Art of Yiddish Storytelling* (Cambridge, MA: Harvard University Press, 1996), 286–88.
24. Roskies, *Bridge of Longing*, 287.
25. See Mark Spilka's "Empathy with the Devil: Isaac Bashevis Singer and the Deadly Pleasures of Misogyny," *Novel* 31, no. 3 (Summer 1998): 430–44. Explicating the short story "The Witch," Spilka writes that "Singer himself discovered his backdoor policy for approaching God: like his parents before him, he uses devils, imps, and demons to prove that the world makes religious sense after all, that miraculous irrational forces exist which must have been put there by a God in whom it is otherwise rationally impossible to believe. There is a positive stake, then, in Singer's world, in presenting such perversely negative experiences from the devil's point of view." Roskies, in noting the same language of inversion, takes a slightly different approach: "Should life on earth continue, there would have to be a metaphysical counterweight to evil.... Over Kant and Nietzsche, Zeidel reaches back to reclaim the negative theology of Lurianic Kabbalah" (*Bridge*, 289). See also Sanford L. Drob, *Kabbalah and Postmodernism: A Dialogue* (New York: Peter Lang, 2009), especially 129–33 on the concept of *coincidentia oppositorum* in kabbalistic thought.

26. In a well-known essay, Bashevis Singer proposed as a solution to this conundrum that Yiddish writers continue to depict only Jewish life in Europe, so as not to have to sully the language with terms to describe the technological and other accoutrements of modern American life. See I. B. Singer, "Problemen fun der yidisher proze in amerike," ["Problems of Yiddish Prose in America,"] *Svive* 2 (1943): 2–13; reprinted in English in *Prooftexts* 9 (1989): 5–12.
27. Shandler, Jeffrey. "Beyond the Mother Tongue: Learning the Meaning of Yiddish in America," *Jewish Social Studies* 6, no. 3 (2000): 97–123, here 100.
28. See the entire volume *The Hidden Isaac Bashevis Singer,* ed. Seth L. Wolitz (Austin: University of Texas Press, 2001) and particularly Joseph Sherman's essay "Bashevis/Singer and the Jewish Pope," 13–27. See also Asaf Galay's 2014 film, *The Muses of Isaac Bashevis Singer.*
29. As is well known among his Yiddish readers, the author wished to distinguish himself from his already prominent elder brother Israel Joshua and so followed the Yiddish nomenclatural convention of adopting a matronymic, after his mother Batsheva. Yiddish pronunciation elides the "t" sound in this biblical name, producing the possessive "Bashevis." When not writing under one of several pseudonyms, he signed himself in Yiddish "Yitskhok Bashevis."
30. Goodman's translation, cited above, has not yet had a wide impact.
31. See Anita Norich, "Isaac Bashevis Singer in America: The Translation Problem," *Judaism* 44, no. 2 (Spring 1995): 208–18.
32. Similarly, Lerner's otherwise very comprehensively sourced article "The Enduring Legend" bypasses Mark's novella.
33. Lerner, "The Enduring Legend," 164.

WORKS CITED

Bamberger, Joseph. *Ha'afifior hayehudi. Letoldoteha shel 'aggadà mime' habenaym be'ashkenaz* [*The Jewish Pope: History of a Medieval Ashkenazic Legend*]. Ramat-Gan: Bar-Ilan University Press, 2009.

Bashevis Singer, Isaac. "The Mirror." Translated by Norbert Guterman. In *The Collected Stories of Isaac Bashevis Singer.* New York: Library of America, 2004.

———. "Problemen fun der yidisher proze in amerike," *Svive* 2 (1943): 2–13; reprinted in English as "Problems of Yiddish Prose in America" in *Prooftexts* 9 (1989): 5–12.

———. "Zeidlus the Pope." Translated by Joel Blocker and Elizabeth Pollet. In *Short Friday and Other Stories.* New York: Farrar, Straus and Giroux, 1964. Reprinted in *The Collected Stories of Isaac Bashevis Singer.* New York: Farrar Straus Giroux, 1983.

———. "Zeydlus der ershter." *Svive* 1, no. 2 (January–February 1943). Reprinted in *Der Sotn in Goray. A mayse fun fartsaytns un andere dertseylungen.* New York: Matones, 1943; reprint, Jerusalem: Akademon, 1972; Tel Aviv: Peretz, 1992.

Drob, Sanford L. *Kabbalah and Postmodernism: A Dialogue.* New York: Peter Lang, 2009.

Gaster, Moses, ed. and trans. *Ma'aseh Book: Book of Jewish Tales and Legends*. Philadelphia: Jewish Publication Society, 1934.
Goldschmidt, Daniel, ed. *Rosh ha-Shanah Mahzor*. Jerusalem: Koren, 2009.
Grossman, Avraham. *Hakhme ashkenaz harishonim*. Jerusalem: Magnes, 1989.
Kadar, Naomi Prawer. *Raising Secular Jews: Yiddish Schools and Their Periodicals for American Children, 1917–1950*. Waltham, MA: Brandeis University Press, 2016.
Kertzer, David I. *The Kidnapping of Edgardo Mortara*. New York: Knopf, 1997.
——. *The Popes against the Jews: The Vatican's Role in the Rise of Modern Anti-Semitism*. New York: Vintage, 2001.
Lerner, David Levine. "The Enduring Legend of the Jewish Pope." *Judaism* 40, no. 2 (Spring 1991): 148–70.
Mark, Yudl. *Der rambam*. Nyu York: Arbeter ring, 1947.
——. *Der yidisher poyps*. New York: Arbeter ring, 1947.
——. *The Jewish Pope: A Yiddish Tale*. Translated by Ruth Fisher Goodman. McKinleyville, CA: Daniel and Daniel, 2006.
——. *Rabenu Gershom, Rashi, Yehuda Khosid*. New York: Kinder ring, 1941.
The Muses of Isaac Bashevis Singer. Directed by Shaul Betser and Asaf Galay. Tel Aviv: Antenna Productions, 2014.
Norich, Anita. "Isaac Bashevis Singer in America: The Translation Problem." *Judaism* 44, no. 2 (Spring 1995): 208–18.
Prinz, Joachim. *Popes from the Ghetto*. New York: Schocken Books, 1968.
Reiss, Tom. *The Orientalist: In Search of a Man Caught between East and West*. London: Vintage, 2006.
Resnick, Irven M. *Marks of Distinctions: Christian Perceptions of Jews in the High Middle Ages*. Washington, DC: Catholic University of America Press, 2012.
——. "Race, Anti-Jewish Polemic, Arnulf of Seéz, and the Contested Papal Election of Anaclet II (A.D. 1130)." In *Jews in Medieval Christendom: Slay Them Not*, edited by Kristine T. Utterback and Merrall L. Price, 45–70. Leiden: Brill, 2013.
Roskies, David G. *A Bridge of Longing: The Lost Art of Yiddish Storytelling*. Cambridge, MA: Harvard University Press, 1996.
——. "Di shprakh fun derekh-haSaM: Vi der sotn redt af yidish." In *Hahut shel hen: shai leHava Turnianski [A Touch of Grace: Studies in Ashkenazi Culture, Women's History, and the Languages of the Jews Presented to Chava Turniansky]*, edited by Israel Bartal, Galit Hasan-Rokem, et al., 69–85. Jerusalem: Zalman Shazar Center for Jewish History and the Center for Research on Polish Jewry, the Hebrew University, 2015.
Shandler, Jeffrey. "Beyond the Mother Tongue: Learning the Meaning of Yiddish in America." *Jewish Social Studies* 6, no. 3 (2000): 97–123.
Sherman, Joseph. *The Jewish Pope: Myth, Diaspora and Yiddish Literature*. Oxford: Oxford Legenda, 2003.
Spilka, Mark. "Empathy with the Devil: Isaac Bashevis Singer and the Deadly Pleasures of Misogyny." *Novel* 31, no. 3 (Summer 1998): 430–44.
Starck, Astrid. "Conte 187." In *Un beau livre d'histoires*, 518–26. Basel: Schwabe, 2004.

Stroll, Mary. *The Jewish Pope: Ideology and Politics in the Papal Schism of 1130*. Leiden: Brill, 1987.
Talmud Bavli. Shabbat 68b and Shavuot 5a.
Weinreich, Max. *History of the Yiddish Language*. Translated by Shlomo Noble with Joshua A. Fishman. Chicago: University of Chicago Press, 1980.
Williams, George L. *Papal Genealogy: The Families and Descendants of the Popes*. Jefferson, NC: McFarland, 1998.
Wolitz, Seth L., ed. *The Hidden Isaac Bashevis Singer*. Austin: University of Texas Press, 2001.
Yassif, Eli. *Sippur ha-'am ha-'ivri: toldotav, sugav,umashma'uto*. Jerusalem: Mosad Bialik, 1992.

Chapter Two

Unmapping Islam in Eastern Europe
Periodization and Muslim Subjectivities in the Balkans

Piro Rexhepi

> At present, driven back into its Asiatic and African quarters, and tolerated only in one corner of Europe through the jealousy of Christian powers, Islam has forever vanished from the state of history at large, and has retreated into Oriental ease and repose.
> —Bart Labuschagne and Timo Slootweg, eds.,
> *Hegel's Philosophy of the Historical Religions*[1]

The idea of Islam's retreat from Europe is almost as old and persistent as the idea of Europe itself. Lecturing at the University of Berlin in the 1820s, Hegel expressed confidence that Islam was being driven back into its Oriental and African quarters, a sentiment that coincided well with the emerging idea of unified "Europe" at the time. A decade after the Congress of Vienna and during the Greek War of Independence, touted throughout Europe as the last effort to rid the continent from Islam, Hegel's suggestions that Islam had already vanished from history not only locates history as a solely European mandate, it also outlines a persistent predicament in Europe's subsequent articulation of its spatial and temporal coordinates, which situated Islam outside the continent's cartographic imagination.

Ironically, Hegel's conceptualization of Islam as an encroachment on *natural* Europe unfolded at the height of European colonial expansion, a project that would contribute to the disintegration of the Ottoman Empire. The Great Eastern Crisis and the subsequent Congress of Berlin solidified the "notional shape of Europe"[2] through the production of the idea of the Ottoman Empire as sick and mired in the past and of Europe as a unified whole en route to the future. The post-Ottoman Christian states in the Balkans, established with Western Europe's support in the second half of the nineteenth century, designated the Continent's new frontiers. These states would be charged with overseeing their Muslim populations, now segregated in just one corner of Europe. Considered a colonial project, Muslims in the Balkans, particularly the non-Slavic Muslims, became a "problem" that had to be addressed through cleansing, expulsion, elimination, or assimilation. In the words of a Serbian official writing in 1935, "No victims are too many for this problem to be solved."[3]

The task of cleansing Europe from the Islamic minorities after the disintegration of the Ottoman Empire requires a *longue durée* investigation of the colonial projects enacted in the Balkans, both by European empires and by their local vassal states at the expense of the "left-behind" Muslims. The "left behind" label negates the Muslim communities' belonging to Europe, while at the same time drawing a separation line between them and the *ummah* (the entire community of Muslims bound together by the foundational principles of Islam). In the context of this volume's concerns, the idea of "left behind" marks a discontiguous time and place—not so much the in-betweenness of Europe and Islam as the Muslim communities' asymmetrical lag in the corridors of time, their purported unwillingness to wait to become European or to respond to Europe. In this chapter, asking the question about discontiguity helps us register the imposed violent fragmentation of Muslims and their subsequent othering, both of which bound them to new non-Muslim centers while subverting solidarities among peripheries. Discontiguity may also be understood as *fitnah,* the tension of trials among the known assurances and the unfamiliar divisions and possibilities.

This chapter challenges the fixed spatial and temporal discontiguities of the borders between East and West and Europe and Islam that contribute to the physical and discursive separation of Balkan Muslims from the larger Muslim world. It draws on the works of twentieth-century Islamic scholars and activists, particularly women and underprivileged minorities, such as Melika Salihbegović, Hidajeta Mirojević, Safija Šiljak, Sheikh Haxhi Qamili, Muhammad Nasir-ud-Din al-Albani, Vehbi Sulejman Gavoçi, and Abdul-Kader Aranauti, whose intellectual labor has traversed the East/West, Ottoman/post-Ottoman, and Communist/post-Communist thresholds. Examining Muslim histories in Eastern Europe beyond the confines of these spatiotemporalities opens up multiple perspectives on past and present political struggles of Muslims in Eastern Europe, allowing us to explore histories and subjectivities of those who saw their lived experiences not in relation to

Europe, but as constitutive parts of the Muslim world. Their perspectives and insistence on an Islamic way of life provide an alternative reading of the history of Muslims in the Balkans, not isolated by their immediate surroundings, but as members of a transnational struggle against colonialism and coloniality throughout the twentieth century.

Any serious consideration of their work and self-perceptions within collective formations of resistance to nationalism and colonialism implies a dissatisfaction with the current state of research on Islam in Eastern Europe. The main flaw of existing studies, reliant on the linear, forward-looking post-Ottoman and post-socialist temporalities, is to suggest that following the collapse of the Ottoman Empire and during the socialist period, Muslims in Eastern Europe were successfully and completely isolated from the rest of the *ummah* and concomitantly attached to European geo-temporalities. Taking the idea of discontiguous affiliations seriously and choosing to learn about the self-perceptions of individuals on the fringes of their own communities lead me to deconstruct anticolonial and post-socialist nationalist narratives that have been proposed and defended primarily by privileged men.

The idea of the separation of Muslims in the Balkans from the rest of the Muslim world is not recent. It dates back to at least the late nineteenth and early twentieth centuries, that is, to colonial and nationalist narratives, where synchronizing Muslims in the Balkans with the historical timeline and space of Europe was a political goal. The post-Ottoman reconfiguration of time and space, enacted by European and Balkan historiographies, sought to establish continuity with the European histories. Contemporary European integration projects aim similarly at a merger with Europe as the preordained goal. Leaving Islamic pasts behind, this arrangement of time puts Muslims in the Balkans into the future-oriented teleology, ignoring or obscuring those who interrupt this destined path, go against time, or intentionally or unintentionally subvert the forward-moving European time. Along with this temporal cleavage, the geographical conception of viewing the Balkans and "Balkan Islam" as discontiguous from neighbors further east and south also reinforces a notion of these lands and communities as separate and distinct from other former Ottoman lands, such as the Levant or Egypt.

The fragmentation of Islam along national typologies has been a key feature of the late nineteenth- and early twentieth-century European colonial projects, denying commonalities to Muslims from Kashgar to Marrakech. Colonialism has historically worked to prevent the emergence of common narratives of oppression and resistance among peripheries, particularly of those with shared historical pasts. Its spatial and temporal configurations are organized to this end, dividing peripheries into mandates that take their own political meanings, with alternatives rendered impossible. In *The Ethnographic State: France and the Invention of Moroccan Islam*, for instance, Edmund Burke III points out how the legitimization of French colonial power in Morocco was facilitated by the production of a "Moroccan Islam."[4] Burke delineates the production of "Moroccan Islam" as a discursive space that forges a brand of Islam acceptable to the French colonial administration while preventing the emergence of common anticolonial narratives among Muslims in North Africa. Recent attempts by Pankaj Mishra, Sohail Daulatzai, and Gary Wilder[5] to deconstruct postcolonial narratives that privilege nationalism as a response to colonial separation and violence have contributed to the reconsideration of the bonds between the peripheries. They have shed light on alternative decolonizing projects of belonging and becoming that are not coherent with imperial geo-temporalities or nationalist imaginaries.

My project operates in parallel with these ideas, seeking to bring attention to Muslim revolutionaries, thinkers, and activists who resisted the European colonial advancement in the Balkans—not in isolated national liberation projects, but as members of a transnational resistance against colonialism and against the discontiguities produced by the Eurocentric narratives of history. What possibilities were precluded by the violence of the nation-state building project? Who was given voice and who was silenced in privileging the European? How can we rethink and retell the story of Muslims in the Balkans outside the secular submission to Europe and as part of a trans-temporal "Muslim International"?

AN *UMMAH* AFTER THE *UMMAH*: PARTITIONS, RESISTANCE, AND REFORMATION

In June 1914, Sheikh Haxhi Qamili led a Muslim uprising challenging the legitimacy of the newly established Albanian state and its partition from the Ottoman Empire. The insurgents demanded the removal of the German prince, Wilhelm of Wied, installed by European powers through the International Control Commission.[6] As the European powers behind the commission rejected proposals for the appointment of a Muslim prince, the uprising gathered momentum. The insurgents demanded that Albania be returned to the sovereignty of the *khalīfah* (the Ottoman sultan) as an autonomous province governed by a Muslim prince and that the Arabic alphabet be restored.[7] Qamili, a sheikh of the Melâmî Sufi *tarqia* (school) practicing intentional poverty,[8] also demanded the abrogation of land privileges that the Albanian aristocracy had acquired though the so-called Organic Statute. The land, according to Qamili, was to be subsequently redistributed among peasants.[9] The statute, which served as a provisional constitution for the new Albanian state, transformed all *Arazi Mirie* (crown lands)—the Ottoman-owned public property bestowed for use to loyal subjects—to *Arazi Memluke* (private lands).[10] Beneficiaries of these reforms were the small group of landed Albanian aristocracy who supported the prince.

In less than two months, the insurgents seized most of the territory of the Albanian state. Durres, the capital, remained the only territory controlled by Prince Wied, his provisional Albanian government, and the International Control Commission. It should be noted that the prince's recruits, who served as a provisional army, when sent to extinguish the insurgency, refused to fight their "Muslim brothers."[11] In a letter to the Foreign Ministry in Vienna, written in response to the prince's ouster, the Austro-Hungarian ambassador to Rome, Kajetan Mérey von Kapos-Mére, stressed that unless the European powers collectively intervened to suppress the uprising, the "credibility of European prestige"[12] would be on the line. In addition to the requirement that such an intervention should explicitly call for the protection of the prince and his family, it was supposed to "teach Albanian rebels a lesson on European unity."[13] By 5 September 1914, the rebels had taken over Durres, entered the royal palace, and replaced the Albanian flag with the Ottoman one. They proceeded to govern Albania for the following eight months. By May 1915, the Serbian state, facing an Austro-Hungarian invasion and seeking access to the Adriatic, had successfully organized the "Albanian expedition" led by Esad Pasha Toptani, invading Albania and ending its short-lived return to the *khalīfah*. Haxhi Qamili was hanged on 16 August of that year.[14] The Serbian expedition is notable not only for its role in ending the first organized Muslim resistance to a European incursion into the Ottoman lands. It was equally emblematic of how the newly established Christian states in the Balkans adopted Western European colonial practices—along with the rhetoric of "liberating" Europe from the last remaining Muslims—to recolonize Muslim populated areas.

Despite its failure, this short-lived resistance to European intervention in the Ottoman Empire resonated deeply with Muslims elsewhere. For instance, in an article titled "A Pan-Islamic Movement in Albania," the *Tribune* in Lahore judged the rebels' demands for using the Arabic alphabet unreasonable and worried that it could harm an otherwise "justifiable movement."[15] The All-India Muslim League protested the maltreatment of the Muslims in the conflict and warned against the perils of such an international intervention. Two thousand international volunteers responded to an appeal to fight alongside the rebels in Albania. In Singapore, the newspaper

Majalah al-Islam condemned the intervention of Western powers into what it considered the internal affairs of the Ottoman Empire.[16] In addition, in a piece titled "In Praise of the Rebels," the *Times of India* wrote that "Moslems are apprehensive that they will be persecuted by the Christian government of Albania as they are in Montenegro and Serbia, where hundreds of families are being forced into exile because they are Albanian Mohammedans."[17]

When various efforts to resist the encroachment of European and Balkan powers failed during the interwar period, waves of migration and displacement from the Balkans to the Ottoman "rump state" followed.[18] Muslims in the emerging unified Yugoslavia faced additional setbacks when the Kingdom of Serbs, Croats, and Slovenes (renamed Kingdom of Yugoslavia in 1929) sought to assimilate the ethnically Slavic Muslims and expel all others from the Albanian populated areas through settler colonial practices.[19] One of the foremost ideological proponents of this idea, Vasa Čubrilović, a Yugoslav academic and politician, published a manifesto in 1937. Under the title *Expulsion of the Albanians*, it contained detailed policy recommendations on how to deal with the Muslim question:

> Let it suffice to mention that with the elimination of the Albanians, the last link between our Moslems in Bosnia and Novi Pazar and the rest of the Moslem world will have been cut. They are becoming a religious minority, the only Moslem minority in the Balkans, and this fact will accelerate their assimilation.[20]

We should note specifically that the spirit expressed in Čubrilović's manifesto is also meant to erode any sense of affiliation between the Muslim populations in other Balkan regions and their coreligionists in non-contiguous parts of the Muslim world.

Later, in socialist Yugoslavia, Čubrilović would become a noted public intellectual and a key commentator on Balkan politics, establishing the Institute for Balkan Studies at the Serbian Academy of Sciences and Arts in 1969. As his recognition foretells, he was far from the only Yugoslav public figure to advocate for the expulsion of Muslims. Ivo Andrić, who in 1961 would receive the Nobel Prize in Literature, also promoted the expulsion of Muslims and the annexation of Albania by Yugoslavia in 1939:

> After the partition of Albania, Kosovo would lose its attraction as a center for the Albanian minority, which, under the new situation, could be more easily assimilated. We would eventually gain 200,000 to 300,000 Albanians, but these are mostly Catholics whose relations with the Moslem Albanians have never been good. The deportation of Moslem Albanians to Turkey could then be carried out since, under the new circumstances, there would be no major impediment to such a move.[21]

Confronting the threat of expulsion, the Muslims in interwar Yugoslavia formed several state-sanctioned organizations: the Jugoslavska Muslimanska Organizacija in Bosnia and Sandzak (Yugoslav Muslim Organization) and the Islam Muhafazai Hukuk Cemiyet (Islamic Association for the Defense of Justice) in Kosovo. Mladi Muslimani (Young Muslims) would be established in 1939 as a response to further co-optation. The politics of elimination, separation, and assimilation of Muslims, at the basis of the interwar politics of Balkan nation-states, resulted in a wave of policies enacted by the Yugoslav Kingdom to colonize the Muslim-populated areas in Bosnia, Macedonia, and Kosovo.[22] Specifically, the expropriation of agricultural land and the concomitant impoverishment of the Muslim population resulted in further migrations of Muslims from Bosnia, Kosovo, and Macedonia to Turkey, Syria, and Egypt. When Muslims refused to emigrate, their names were entered in government registers so that they could be "refused government jobs or services."[23] In Albania, the increased control of the Muslim community by state-structured religious institutions would also see a wave of Muslim *muhacirs* (migrants) to the Middle East.[24] The expulsion and displacement continued in the immediate aftermath of World War II. Turkey reported receiving an estimated 170,000 migrants from Socialist Yugoslavia between 1953 and the 1960s.[25] The reasons for these population shifts are too many and too complex to be addressed here, yet it should be noted that the new constraints on religious practice in postwar socialist Yugoslavia and the suspension of sharia courts may have played a role. Significantly, unlike the *muhacirs* from the Balkan Wars, whose ties with the Balkans were, to a large extent, discontinued, the *muhacirs* from the 1930s, '40s, and '50s would maintain the connections to their families and home communities in the following decades. The journeys of Muhammad Nasir-ud-Din al-Albani, Vehbi Sulejman Gavoçi, Abdul-Kader Arnauti, and Mahmud Arnauti can help us understand not only how Balkan *muhacirs* fostered the links between the Muslim world and Muslims in the Balkans, but also how their experiences as *muhacirs* informed their intervention into the debates on the challenges of the Muslim world during and after the Cold War.

THE HAJJ, SOLIDARITY, AND THE MUSLIM INTERNATIONAL

> When descending the valley you may feel that you are going to collapse. But then, the Kaaba appears! The Kaaba, toward which Muslims face when praying, is the center of existence, faith, love and life. It is the direction in which the beds of patients in agony are placed. It is also the direction in which the dead are buried.
> —Ali Shariati, *Hajj: A Reflection on Its Rituals*

In 1981, two Muslimas from Bosnia, Hidajeta Mirojević and Safija Šiljak, drove their Yugoslav Zastava 750 to the hajj. Writing about their meetings with the Balkan *muhacirs* as they drove through Turkey and Syria, Mirojević noted that "everyone was happy that Yugoslavs were coming to the hajj." While in the presence of Muslims from around the world at the Umayyad Mosque in Damascus, Mirojević saw herself as belonging to a "lasting and beautiful brotherhood and unity."[26] During the Cold War, the hajj gained a new meaning for Muslims in the nonaligned world, as it allowed them to develop a sense of belonging beyond the binaries of socialism and democracy. It offered a point of unity as the center of "existence, faith, love, and life" that evoked solidarity and a safe haven. The hajj became a "Muslim International" that for Sheriati, hadži Hidajeta Mirojević, hadži Safija Šiljak, hadži Halide Mehmeti, and (on the other side of the Atlantic) el-Hajj Malik el-Shabazz (Malcolm X) allowed an escape from the sense of otherness, violence, and discrimination they experienced in their respective home societies. During the hajj, the Cold War–era divisions between the so-called First, Second, and Third Worlds seemed to dissolve. While Malcolm X experienced a "spirit of unity and brotherhood" that he had never before believed "could exist between the white and non-white"; Mirojević "had a feeling that the entire world remained behind, here in Kaaba ... finally understanding the meaning of the hajj."[27] Returning to Skopje from the hajj in 1983, Halide Mehmeti wrote that the journey had "strengthened my *istikam* [fortification or faith] ... like all Muslims in Yugoslavia I considered myself orphaned; walking the *tawaf* [the ritual of circling the Kaaba during hajj] around the Kaaba, I finally met all of my family."

Contemporary scholarship of Islam in the Balkans has mostly employed post-socialist, post-conflict transition-focused frameworks, where the "re-emergence of Islam" or the "rediscovery of the *ummah*" falls under the more general rubric of the "return of God in post-communism."[28] Other studies, focusing on the rise of extremist Islam in the Balkans, have stressed the role of foreign influences in what is otherwise European "Balkan Islam."[29] An Islam distinct from its other kinds, the Balkan Islam, according to such scholars, stands as secular, white, and European, against its darker and more fanatical counterpart located farther east and further back in time. The concept of a locally "reemerging Islam" suggests, again, that under socialism Balkan Muslims were isolated from the rest of the Muslim world, whereas the testimonies quoted above demonstrate that this was more complicated. Earlier global ties, according to the logic of "reemerging Islam," weakened or discontinued after the collapse of the Ottoman Empire and during the socialist period, rendering the practitioners as observers but not co-creators of Islam's broad changes.

The nonaligned movement of the socialist period did allow Muslims from Yugoslavia to communicate extensively with Muslims throughout nonaligned countries. Syrian, Iraqi, and Palestinian students studied in Yugoslav universities, while Bosnians, Macedonians, and Albanians read the Qur'an in Damascus, Cairo, and Baghdad. Over four hundred new mosques went up in socialist Yugoslavia between 1945 and 1985, many of them with support from Muslim countries and communities in the nonaligned movement to which Yugoslavia belonged. Muslims from Bosnia beseeched Iran to use its oil trade with Yugoslavia to improve their conditions and to exert more influence with the authorities. As Yugoslavia grew in prominence in the nonaligned movement, its Muslims saw their country's international self-positioning as hypocritical given the discriminatory conditions against them. Active practitioners of Islam were kept away from decision-making positions. Conversely, secular Muslims were frequently rewarded for implementing various "emancipatory" projects in their communities. Džemal Bijedić, for instance, who in 1950 introduced legislation to ban the veil and "end the century old symbol of inferiority and cultural backwardness of Muslim women," would go on to become the Yugoslav prime minister and the country's key liaison to the nonaligned movement.[30] As Muslims found themselves employed in the service of Yugoslavia's nonaligned ambitions, a new Muslim commons emerged, resisting what its members saw as an instrumentalization of their faith.

Addressing the subject of an emerging Muslim International, one that did not belong to the state-sanctioned, nonaligned conferences but that was nonetheless enabled by them, Alija Izetbegovic argued that "self-styled reformers in the present-day Muslim countries may be recognized by the pride in what they should rather be ashamed of and their shame in what they should be proud of."[31] Izetbegovic was inspired by the revival of pan-Islamism that had started to succeed pan-Arabism, which until the 1960s had overshadowed Islamism as the vanguard of decolonization. He would advocate a "folk pan-Islamism," one that would be guided and influenced not by the project of liberal or socialist modernity but instead by an Islamic sense of belonging. "How is it then," he asks,

> that this "folk pan-Islamism" ... does not have much effect on the everyday life and practical policy of the Muslim countries? Why does it remain just a feeling, never rising to a real awareness of common destiny? How to explain the fact that although news of suffering of Muslims in Palestine or the Crimea, in Sinkiang, Kashmir or Ethiopia arouse feelings of dejection and unanimous condemnation everywhere, at the same time, action is either lacking or is not at all in proportion to the feeling which exists?[32]

Izetbegovic's universalization of the challenges that Muslims faced in Yugoslavia was inspired by the Islamic decolonization thinkers vocal in Iran of the 1960s, particularly Jalal Al-E Ahamad and Ali Shariati. These masterminds of the Islamic Revolution saw the struggle for liberation not along national but along international anti-imperialist lines. The Sarajevo Process of 1983—resulting in the arrest and sentencing of Izetbegovic and twelve other Bosnian Muslim men and women of the Mladi Muslimani for challenging the constitutional order with pan-Islamist and fundamentalist projects, and for considering Iran's Islamic Revolution to be their own—highlighted not only a continuity of relations between Muslims in Yugoslavia and the rest of the Muslim world. It also illustrated the state's aggressive intervention into the mainstream Muslim International discourse calling for solidarity and cooperation beyond the prescribed parameters.[33]

In 1988, under a general Yugoslav amnesty for political prisoners, the members of the Sarajevo Trial were set free. By this time, however, the anti-Muslim rhetoric had become rampant in the public discourse. As Yugoslavia was plagued by economic crises, the demands of Kosovo Albanians for autonomy within the federation played into the hands of Serbian nationalists. Slobodan Milošević would frequently capitalize on pre-existing European Islamophobia to justify his attacks on Muslim populations.[34] The disintegration of Yugoslavia is still filed under "inter-ethnic violence," the blurred notion that obscures the role of Islamophobia, the historical facts of public trials and imprisonment of Muslim activists, and, crucial to my larger argument, an identification on the part of such individuals with non-neighbors, that is, with communities and cultures discontiguous to Yugoslavia. A decade later, this discourse would prove disastrous in the hands of Serbian nationalists in Bosnia and Kosovo.

On a research visit to Yugoslavia in 1989, political scientist and author Sabrina Ramet recorded her interviewees' Islamophobic remarks, which pivoted on blaming Muslims for the disintegration of Yugoslavia:

> Albanian Muslims and Bosnian Muslims are in this together.... They have big families in order to swamp Serbia and Yugoslavia with Muslims, and turn Yugoslavia into a Muslim republic. They want to see a Khomeini in charge here. But Belgrade is not their final goal. They will continue to advance until they have taken Vienna, Berlin, Paris, London—all the great cities of Europe. Unless they are stopped.[35]

These and other such apprehensions generated during the socialist years bear a striking resemblance to the (post-)socialist and post-9/11 anxieties, both rooted in the suggestion that borders must be reinforced to prevent the Balkan Muslims from being "together." As Melika Salihbegović, who was imprisoned during the Sarajevo Process and spent five years in jail, would note after the Yugoslav Wars, the "democratic majors differ from former Communist invaders of the justice and freedom only by the absence of dirt under their fingernails."[36] The anxiety over solidarity between the Muslims in the Balkans and Europe with those in the rest of the world continues to reproduce these borders as a necessity against a perceived "Islamic threat." Pan-Islamic solidarity between Muslims in socialist Yugoslavia and Islam writ large may only be remembered as a surmounted danger and a site of violence that continues to justify organized Islamophobia in the name of security.

The Muslim International within the socialist and nonaligned world, however, was not limited to Yugoslavia. The atheist regime of Enver Hoxha in Albania sustained close relations with the Muslim world in the context of the Sino-Soviet split and the nonaligned world.[37] Addressing Iran's anti-colonial struggle, Hoxha noted that the "anti-feudal and anti-imperialist revolution of the Iranian people is considerably rooted in the spirit of the Shiite clerics"[38] and that although "Islamism in general plays an active role in the liberation and anti-imperialism of the Muslim people,"[39] it would take time for the revolution to progress to a full Marxist liberation. Celebratory telegrams were sent from Albania to Khomeini announcing the success of the revolution. In return, an Iranian delegation visited Albania in 1982.[40] Obviously, the anti-imperialisms of Hoxha and Khomeini differed greatly. While Khomeini was set on awakening Islam, Hoxha was concerned with creating the new Communist man with Stalinist methods. The early stages of solidarity were largely cursory exchanges of camaraderie without much articulation of differences beyond a shared sense of past belonging and anti-imperial goals. Both Albania's Hoxha and Yugoslavia's Broz Tito tried to utilize Islamic solidarity for economic and political ends, mostly for inexpensive oil and development projects, a strategy deployed since the end of World War II.[41] Islamic scholars and activists in Yugoslavia, conversely, adopted this opportunity to join and develop a transnational network debating the future of Islam beyond the socialist and liberal frameworks.

Whatever the objectives of the Yugoslav and Albanian party leaders may have been, they unwittingly allowed the fermentation of solidarity that often escaped official channels. Muslims in the Balkans grew aware of various Third World movements that merged Islamic thought with Marxism and Islam, such as Nasakom in Indonesia. The Algerian War of Independence and the Israeli-Palestinian conflict resonated deeply with them, too. A year after the massacre of Tal al-Zaatar in 1977,[42] a Kosovo Muslim poet would write, "You are the first and the last sura of a new Qur'an."[43] To invoke the solidarity of common Islamic legacies, the poet replaces the Qur'an with the pain and suffering of Palestinians—the new reference point of the global discourse on disenfranchised minorities. Similarly, the Albanian poet Adelina Mamaqi, in solidarity with the Algerian revolutionaries, contributed the following: "We have been murdered in the past and we are still being murdered, under these dark clouds! You can't murder an entire nation with bullets! We Algerians have fire in our blood, such offspring has Africa, it has Lumumbas."[44]

The intersection between the Second and Third World Marxist and Islamic resistance did not confine the imagination of the Balkan Muslims to Muslim struggles alone. Above all, it allowed them to see themselves as members of a larger Third World liberation movement—whatever its specific profile. More than any event, however, the Iranian Revolution compelled Muslims, particularly those in Yugoslavia, to think more critically of their position in their country of residence and their othering in the process of socialist modernization. Thus, transnational solidarity of the Balkan Muslims with the *ummah* in the nonaligned world can be approached relationally across time. Such an exercise would by necessity include the earlier cases of post-Ottoman resistance against the European effort to colonize and reform Balkan Muslims while cutting them off from the rest of the Muslim world.

MEETING EUROPEAN EXPECTATIONS: BALKAN ISLAM—SUSPECTS, VICTIMS, AND VILLAINS

> The struggle for Sarajevo and the fate of the area's diverse population is rapidly transforming into a proxy battlefield for the future and fortunes of the growing Muslim community of Western Europe. This fact directly affects the extent and nature of the assistance provided by several outside powers led by Iran to the local Muslim authorities.... Thus, Tehran and its allies are using the violence in Bosnia-Hercegovina as a springboard for the launching of a jihad in Europe.
> —Yossef Bodansky and Vaughn S. Forrest, "Iran's European Springboard?"

The disintegration of Yugoslavia has served as a frequent reference point for the proponents of the clash-of-civilizations debate that accompanied the end of the Cold War. As the war broke out in Bosnia, the links between the Muslims in the Balkans and the *ummah* were considered a new post–Cold War phenomenon and thus became the target of various Islamophobic attacks that described this relationship as a threat to Western Europe. The US House Republican Research Committee's Task Force on Terrorism and

Unconventional Warfare argued that Bosnia had become a "springboard for jihad in Europe." Along similar lines, in the article "A Threat to Europe? Middle East Ties with the Balkans," Magnus Ranstorp and Gus Xhudo suggested:

> The possibility for recruitment from this area of Europe had long been examined by Middle East organizations due simply to the fact that the Balkans contain over eight million people of Islamic persuasion. While the majority of these are secular, or non-practicing Muslims, the small minority which profess total adherence to Islam may have offered militant groups the nucleus they were seeking for possible recruitment and expansion into Europe.[45]

The image of the Balkan Muslims not only as suspect communities, but also as potential victims of militant groups, calls for their supervision. It is not surprising that Serbian nationalists frequently deployed similar rhetoric in defense of their wartime atrocities against Muslim populations. Moreover, the early view that conceived of the Balkan Muslims as mostly secular or non-practicing—the kind that the West need not fear—produced practicing Muslims as a threat a priori. Their faith alone, according to this narrative, heralded the possibility of a new Middle Eastern front in Europe. This pervasive positioning of Muslims has joined the long lineage of efforts to sever the Balkan Muslims from the Middle East. The view has consequently allowed for the policing, surveillance, and detention of those Muslims who operate outside the designated representational mandate of this group. Since 9/11, such a premise was operative in the EU assemblages of securitization policies and enacted in the European "integration" processes that have sought to create and secure the geopolitical borders in the Balkans. Notable is the shift in the vocabulary of European integration, from the early flourishes of Central and Eastern Europe's "return to Europe" to the tense characterizations of Balkan integration—particularly with regard to Muslim-majority countries—as a security measure.[46] Hence, the desired EU borders not only demarcate the physical frontiers but also operate as an enactment of the clash-of-civilization ideology that produces representational mandates for secular and loyal good Muslims and suspect Muslim others.

Addressing the post-9/11 securitization and counterterrorist logic, Puar and Rai's brilliant observation of how this viewpoint "organizes representations (discourses of civilizations, sexuality, races, nations, democracy, good, evil), temporalities (present modernity and archaic other), [and] spaces"[47] is pivotal for grasping the contemporary efforts to enact discursive and material borders between the Muslims in the "Balkans" and those in the "Middle East." The panic over the migrant Balkan route is no less significant in considering the importance of these bordering projects for the EU. Thus, it is not merely the coercive EU bordering and securitization policies that restrict the movement of Balkan Muslims across internal borders of the so-called Fortress Europe. Identifying them as spatially and temporally alienated from the rest of the *ummah* is a significant contributing factor. By claiming to be "Islam-blind" in its enlargement process, the EU not only silences the Balkan Muslims by treating them as secular nation-state subjects. It also glosses over the systemic practices of surveillance and detention to which Muslims across the Balkans have been subjected in the last decade, all in the name of European security and integration.[48]

In the summer of 2013, in Tirana, Prishtina, and Sarajevo, citizens gathered to protest the coup of the Egyptian military that removed President Mohamed Morsi from office.[49] Similarly, citizens demonstrated in support of Palestine during the Israeli shelling of Gaza in 2014.[50] The role and visibility of Islamist movements in organizing these events is noteworthy not only because the demonstrators came from a range of organizations that cut across religion, ethnicity, and class, but also because of the backdrop to these events: the entrenched rhetoric of a reverential attitude of the Balkan Muslims toward the United States and the EU.

The emergence of YouTube videos of a handful of Muslims from the Balkans fighting for DAESH (popularly known as the Islamic State or ISIS) raised the alarm about a resurgent Islamic extremism in the region. The tendency has been to present participants in these movements as victims of yet another wave of contaminating Islamist extremism imported from the Middle East. In April 2015, a report sponsored by the US embassy in Kosovo sought to explain the reasons for the regional emergence of extremist Islam. Anchoring the Balkan Muslims in the "Western Hemisphere," the report locates extremist Islamic ideologies outside the geographical imaginaries of this half of the world. Instead, the authors place them in the prisons of Egypt, subsequently spread through "imams who have visited and studied in the Middle East."[51]

The inclination to explain extremism in the Balkans as always "imported" provides a vivid example of drawing a clear distinction between the Balkan Muslims and the rest of the *ummah* at the same time that it establishes a hierarchy of suspect populations. Salafist interpretations and practices of Islam in the Balkans are routinely categorized as a strictly foreign intrusion from the Arab world—one that manifestly clashes with the local secular, or at least more centrist and moderate, Balkan Islam. This gesture equates the fundamentalist interpretations of Islam with the Arab world, while ignoring the fact that a foremost ideological founder of the Salafist movement was the Albanian Islamic scholar Nasir-ud-Din al-Albani.[52]

Al-Albani was born in Shkodër, Albania, in 1914. His story is significant not only in that he was a prolific self-taught hadith scholar who challenged the currents of hadith studies in Islamic scholarship of the 1960s and 1970s. What matters is also the manner in which his scholarship was influenced by his personal experience as a *muhacir* from the Balkans.[53] Breaking the ranks of the close-knit Najd religious establishment, al-Albani asserted himself as the one of the most significant Islamic thinkers of the twentieth century. He became an itinerant proponent of close examination of the hadiths. Although he is frequently associated with Wahhabis, who rely on a literalist interpretation of the Qur'an and *al-salaf al-salih* (the pious ancestors), al-Albani was primarily concerned with the science of the hadiths.[54] While he did receive an invitation to teach at the University of Medina between 1961 and 1962, his lax position on female face-covering did not resonate with the Saudi religious establishment, which therefore requested his departure.

In 1993, al-Albani proceeded to issue a controversial fatwa asking all Muslims to leave Palestine and migrate to a territory where they could practice their religion freely. The conditions in the occupied territories, he believed, made it impossible for them to do so.[55] While this drew wide condemnation in Islamic intellectual circles as being an unjustifiable demand on the Palestinian people,[56] al-Albani's motivations may have stemmed from his own experience. He considered his emigration with his father from Albania to Syria as one of the most significant transpositions of his life, because it was this move, he believed, that allowed him to contribute to the "correction of the creed and the abandonment of bigotry towards the schools of thought, warning them against weak and fabricated hadith, encouraging them to revive the authentic Sunnah which the elite among them had killed off."[57] Subsequently, he espoused leaving Palestine as the only way for Muslims to find salvation from "colonization, humiliation and ignominy that has afflicted them."[58]

Although al-Albani was against the politicization of Islam, his work would prove problematic for various religious and political establishments, forcing him to circulate for the rest of his life between Syria and Jordan and Lebanon. For the Balkan Muslims moving to or visiting the Middle East, on the other hand, he was a magnet. As a result, a community of scholars traversing any boundaries set between the Balkans and the Muslim world organized around him. Another member of this community was Suleiman Gavoçi, who visited Yugoslavia in 1974 and became a favorite with the Balkan diaspora in Europe.[59] During the Cold War, Gavoçi would write frequently in the Arab press to raise awareness about the conditions of Muslims in Albania and Yugoslavia.[60] His student Abdul-Kader Arnauti, placed under house arrest by the Assad regime in Syria in the late 1970s, in the

1990s would take to recording messages in cassettes and VHS tapes alerting Muslims around the world to come to the aid of Muslims in the Balkans.[61] Arnauti advised his compatriots and coreligionists to "resist divisions and become aware of the conditions of Muslims around the world."[62] Today, a mosque in Skopje bears his name, while his son Mahmud Arnauti, exiled by the Assad regime, moved to Kosovo in 2012 and has become an authority on the contribution of Islamic scholars from the Balkans in Islamic thought.

The converging histories of these scholars who traversed spatial and temporal divides, to become centerpieces of transnational Islam, undermine the myth of an isolated "Balkan Islam" and continue to challenge the physical and discursive partition of Muslims in the Balkans from the larger Muslim world. Challenging the spatial and temporal fragmentation of the relations between these two entities is essential, lest it foster fear of and violence against those Balkan Muslims who object to their separation from the *ummah*. Equally, limiting the separation of the Muslims in the Balkans from the *ummah* to socialist and post-socialist temporalities conceals the historical mapping of Muslims in Europe as separate from their coreligionists in the Middle East and North Africa during the post-Ottoman and particularly interwar eras.

While this chapter has addressed some conflicts and the people behind them, considerable work remains to be done to better understand Muslim struggles in the Balkans and their connections to larger geographies of liberation. The role of Muslim decolonizing efforts in the nonaligned movement, especially the relations between the so-called Second and Third Worlds, remains to be explored more fully, since research on Islam in the Balkans to date has mainly approached Islam as a post-socialist phenomenon and has not addressed its historical continuity and change. The post-socialist framework provides insufficient means for challenging the spatial and temporal divisions of the Balkan Muslims from the *ummah*. Besides, such challenges must go beyond their usual Euro-American temporalities. They require wider historical frameworks and the study of the *longue durée*. We need to seek out more information about those Muslims who resisted and continue to resist dominant discourses, including those of historiography itself; they understood their work and their lives through decidedly decolonizing perspectives. That being said, it would be a mistake to replace Eurocentric periodization with an equally essentialist Islamic timeline. My aim, rather, has been to open up and invite additional multiple perspectives of the past and present roles of Islam in the Balkans.

Piro Rexhepi is a research fellow at the Max Planck Institute for the Study of Religious and Ethnic Diversity in Göttingen, Germany. He holds a PhD in politics from the University of Strathclyde, UK, and has held research fellowships at the Centre for Southeast European Studies at the University of Graz and the Center for Advanced Studies of Southeastern Europe at the University of Rijeka and teaching positions at the State University of New York, City University of New York, and New York University.

NOTES

1. Bart Labuschagne and Timo Slootweg, eds., *Hegel's Philosophy of the Historical Religions,* vol. 6 (Leiden: Brill, 2012), 225.
2. For a detailed account of how the notional shape of Europe was constructed through the decline of the Ottoman Empire, see Matthew Smith Anderson, *The Eastern Question, 1774–1923: A Study in International Relations,* vol. 146 (London: Macmillan, 1966).
3. "Zapisnik interministerijalne konferencije, održane u Ministarstvu inostranih poslova 20. septembra 1935. god. po pitanju iseljenja neslovenskog stanovništva iz Južne Srbije," Archives of Yugoslavia, Fond: "Poslanstvo Kraljevine Jugoslavije u Turskoj-Carigrad, Ankara (370)," Folder 9, Archival Unit 42, pages 637–43.
4. Edmund Burke III, *The Ethnographic State: France and the Invention of Moroccan Islam* (Berkeley: University of California Press, 2014).
5. Pankaj Mishra, *From the Ruins of Empire: The Intellectuals Who Remade Asia* (London: Palgrave Macmillan, 2012); Sohail Daulatzai, *Black Star, Crescent Moon: The Muslim International and Black Freedom beyond America* (Minneapolis: University of Minnesota Press, 2012); and Gary Wilder, *Freedom Time: Negritude, Decolonization, and the Future of the World* (Durham, NC: Duke University Press, 2014).
6. For more on the International Commission of Control, see Erwin A. Schmidl, "The International Operation in Albania, 1913–14." *International Peacekeeping* 6, no. 3 (1999): 1–10.
7. D. Heaton Armstrong, *Prince Vidi: Gjashtë muaj mbretëri* (Tirana, 1995), 74.
8. The Malami order spread in the Balkans during the late nineteenth century through the teachings of the Egyptian sheikh Muhammad Nur al-Arabi, who had settled in Skopje. For more on this, see Harry Thirlwall Norris, *Islam in the Balkans: Religion and Society between Europe and the Arab World* (Columbia: University of South Carolina Press, 1993); and Robert Elsie, *A Dictionary of Albanian Religion, Mythology, and Folk Culture* (New York: New York University Press, 2001), 177.
9. For a broader analysis of the demands of the uprising, see Arben Puto, *Çështja shqiptare në aktet ndërkombëtare të periudhës së imperializmit,* vol. 2 (Tirana: 8 Nëntori, 1987), 597.
10. For more on the transformation, see Arben Puto, Çështja *shqiptare në aktet ndërkombëtare të periudhës së imperializmit,* vol. 2 (Tirana: 8 Nëntori, 1987), 597.

11. Arben Puto, *Pavarësia shqiptare dhe diplomacia e fuqive të mëdha* (Tirana: 8 Nëntori, 1978).
12. Kajetan Mérey von Kapos-Mére, cited in Marenglen Verli, *Shqiptarët në optikën e diplomacisë Austro-Hungareze (1877–1918): studime, analiza, dokumente* (Tirana, Albania: Klean, 2014).
13. "Protecting Prince William," *Times*, 5 June 1914, 7.
14. Owen Pearson, "Albania and King Zog," *Independence, Republic and Monarchy* (New York: New York University Press, 2004).
15. "A Pan-Islamic Movement in Albania," *Tribune* (Lahore), 14 June 1914, 1.
16. "Kuasa sunia: Satu bantahan bagi siasah," *Majalah al-Islam* 6, no. 6 (1914): 188–96.
17. "The Albanian Revolt," *Times of India*, 23 June 1914.
18. See, for instance, Justin McCarthy, *Death and Exile: The Ethnic Cleansing of Ottoman Muslims, 1821–1922* (Princeton, NJ: Darwin, 1995); Kemal H. Karpat, *Ottoman Population, 1830–1914: Demographic and Social Characteristics* (Madison: University of Wisconsin Press, 1985): 208–10; and Kemal H. Karpat, "The Migration of the Bosnian Muslims to the Ottoman State, 1878–1914: An Account Based on Turkish Sources," in Markus Koller and Kemal H. Karpat, eds., *Ottoman Bosnia: A History in Peril* (Madison: University of Wisconsin Press, 2004).
19. For a detailed account on the nature of the colonization, including settler colonial practices, see Đorđo Krstić, *Kolonizacija u južnoj Srbiji* (Sarajevo: Đ. Krstić, 1928).
20. *Iseljavanje arnauta*, Belgrade, 7 March 1937. Manuscript in the Institute of Military History of the Yugoslav People's Army (Vojno Istorijski Institut JNA). Retranslated from the Serbo-Croatian by Robert Elsie on the basis of an existing English version and first published in Elsie, ed., *Gathering Clouds: The Roots of Ethnic Cleansing in Kosovo and Macedonia; Early Twentieth-Century Documents* (Pejë: Dukagjini, 2002), 97–130.
21. Ivo Andrić, quoted in Bogdan Krizman, "Elaborat dra Ive Andrica o Albaniji iz 1939, godine," *Casopis za suvremenu povijest* 9, no. 2 (1977): 77–89. Retranslated from the Serbo-Croatian by Robert Elsie on the basis of an existing English version and first published in Elsie, *Gathering Clouds*, 131–48.
22. The documents include "Preliminary Provisions for Agrarian Reform" (25 February 1919); "The Decree on the Colonization of the Southern Regions" (24 September 1920); "The Law on the Colonization of Southern Regions" (11 June 1931); "The Law on Regulation of Agrarian Relations in the Former Regions of Southern Serbia and Montenegro" (December 1931) and "The Law on Settlement Southern Regions" (15 December 1921).
23. "Zapisnik interministerijalne konferencije, održane u Ministarstvu inostranih poslova 20. septembra 1935. god. po pitanju iseljenja neslovenskog stanovništva iz Južne Srbije," Archives of Yugoslavia, Fond: "Poslanstvo Kraljevine Jugoslavije u Turskoj-Carigrad, Ankara (370)," Folder 9, Archival Unit 42, pages 637–43.
24. For more on the institutional organization of religion in interwar Albania, see Roberto Morozzo Della Rocca, *Nazione e religione in Albania* (Lecce: Besa, 2002).

25. Halim Çavuşoğlu, "Yugoslavya-Makedonya topraklarından Türkiye'ye göçler ve nedenleri," *Bilig. Bahar* 41 (2007): 123–54.
26. Hidajeta Mirojević, quoted in "Vozila sam auto kroz Arabiju do Meke," *Denevni Avaz*, http://www.avaz.ba/clanak/136368/vozila-sam-auto-kroz-arabiju-do-meke #sthash.YKpDbAfo.dpuf, accessed 18 September 2014.
27. Hidajeta Mirojević, "25 September 1985," *Putopis* (self-published).
28. Boris Buden, *Zone des Übergangs: Vom Ende des Postkommunismus* (Frankfurt: Suhrkamp, 2009); Kristen Ghodsee, *Muslim Lives in Eastern Europe: Gender, Ethnicity, and the Transformation of Islam in Postsocialist Bulgaria* (Princeton, NJ: Princeton University Press, 2009); Ina Merdjanova, *Rediscovering the Umma: Muslims in the Balkans between Nationalism and Transnationalism* (New York: Oxford University Press, 2013); Eldar Sarajlić, "The Return of the Consuls: Islamic Networks and Foreign Policy Perspectives in Bosnia and Herzegovina," *Southeast European and Black Sea Studies* 11, no. 2 (2011): 173–90; and Gëzim Krasniqi, "'The Forbidden Fruit': Islam and Politics of Identity among Albanians in Kosovo and Macedonia," unpublished paper, presented at the "After the Wahabi Mirage: Islam, Politics and International Networks in the Balkans" conference, European Studies Centre, University of Oxford, June 2010.
29. Danuta Gibas-Krzak, "Contemporary Terrorism in the Balkans: A Real Threat to Security in Europe," *Journal of Slavic Military Studies* 26, no. 2 (2013): 203–18; Şenol Korkut, "The Diyanet of Turkey and Its Activities in Eurasia after the Cold War," *Acta Slavica Iaponica* 28 (2010): 117–39; and Ann Ross Solberg, "The Role of Turkish Islamic Networks in the Western Balkans," *Südosteuropa* 55, no. 4 (2007): 429–62
30. Robert J. Donia, *Sarajevo: A Biography* (Ann Arbor: University of Michigan Press, 2006).
31. Alija Izetbegović, *The Islamic Declaration: A Programme for the Islamization of Muslims and the Muslim Peoples*, Sarajevo, 1990, http://profkaminskisreadings.yola site.com/resources/Alija%20Izetbegovic-%20The%20Islamic-Declaration%20%28 1990%29.pdf, accessed 20 August 2015.
32. Izetbegović, *The Islamic Declaration*, 62.
33. Izetbegovic, in his defense statement, explained how he had learned about the Muslim Brotherhood in Egypt through a Sudanese student studying architecture in Sarajevo and his other peers from Lebanon, Saudi Arabia, Kuwait, and Egypt studying in Yugoslavia. Sarajevo District Court, Court Decision No. K212/83, 1983, Archives of the Federation of Bosnia and Herzegovina, File 61.
34. For more on this, see Louis Sell, *Slobodan Milosevic and the Destruction of Yugoslavia* (Durham, NC: Duke University Press, 2003).
35. Sabrina Ramet, "Islam in Yugoslavia Today," *Religion, State and Society* 18, no. 3 (1990): 226–35.
36. Melika Salihbegović Bosnawi, "Hijab Is a Guarantor of Freedom of Conscience: An Imaginary Interview," Melika Salihbeg Bosnawi, http://www.bosnawi.ba/ en/essay/194-hijab-is-a-guarantor-of-freedom-of-conscience#sthash.py75mmap .dpuf, accessed 15 June 2015.

37. Enver Hoxha, *Reflections on the Middle East: 1958–1983*, Marxists Internet Archive, https://www.marxists.org/reference/archive/hoxha/works/ebooks/reflections_on_the_middle_east.pdf, accessed 15 June 2015.
38. Enver Hoxha, *Shënime mbi Lindjen e Mesme* (Tirana: 8 Nëntori, 1984), 213.
39. Hoxha, *Shënime mbi Lindjen e Mesme*, 369.
40. For more on this subject, see Odile Daniel, "The Historical Role of the Muslim Community in Albania," *Central Asian Survey* 9, no. 3 (1990): 1–28.
41. See, for instance, the Tirana edition of *Gazeta Bashkimi*, 25 December 1949.
42. Tal al-Zaatar was a massacre at a Palestinian refugee camp during the Lebanese Civil War. For a detailed account, see Saleem Al-Bahloly, "The Persistence of the Image: Dhākira Hurra in Dia Azzawi's Drawings on the Massacre of Tel al-Zaatar," *Art Margins* 2, no. 2 (2013): 71–97.
43. Muhamed Mufaku (Arnauti), "Lidhjet Letrare Shqiptare—Arabe," *Qendra Shqiptare për Studime Orientale*, 2009, 178.
44. Mufaku, "Lidhjet Letrare Shqiptare," 174.
45. Magnus Ranstorp and Gus Xhudo, "A Threat to Europe? Middle East Ties with the Balkans and Their Impact upon Terrorist Activity throughout the Region," *Terrorism and Political Violence* 6, no. 2 (1994): 196–223.
46. Piro Rexhepi, "Mainstreaming Islamophobia: The Politics of European Enlargement and the Balkan Crime-Terror Nexus," *East European Quarterly* 43, nos. 2–3 (2015): 189–214.
47. Jasbir K. Puar and Amit Rai, "The Remaking of a Model Minority: Perverse Projectiles under the Specter of (Counter)Terrorism," *Social Text* 22, no. 3 (2004): 75–104.
48. See "Jihad Made in Kosovo," http://www.dw.de/jihad-made-in-kosovo/a-17874069, accessed 24 August 2014; Vesna Peric Zimonjic, "BALKANS: Arrest of Wahhabis Highlight Extremist Threats," *Interpress News Service*, 11 February 2010, http://www.ipsnews.net/2010/02/balkans-arrest-of-wahhabis-highlights-extremist-threat/; "Operacioni 'Balcania,' 14 të arrestuar në shqipëri dhe itali," *Mapo*, 4 June 2015, http://www.mapo.al/2015/06/operacioni-balcania-14-te-arrestuar-ne-shqiperi-dhe-itali, accessed 20 August 2015.
49. See "Shkup, protestë solidarizimi me egjiptianët," *Shekulli*, 23 August 2013, http://www.shekulli.com.al/p.php?id=29214, accessed 20 August 2015; "Sarajevo: Peaceful Protests to Support Morsi," *R4BIA Platform*, http://www.r4biaplatform.com/content/news-story/sarajevo-peaceful-protests-support-morsi, accessed 20 August 2015; "Dhuna në Egipt, protestë edhe në Tiranë," *Gazeta Tema*, http://www.gazetatema.net/web/2013/08/23/dhuna-ne-egjipt-proteste-edhe-ne-tirane-foto/, accessed 20 August 2015.
50. Elvira M. Jukic, "Sarajevans Protest over Bombing of Gaza," *Balkan Insight*, 18 July 2014, http://www.balkaninsight.com/en/article/sarajevo-protest-against-killings-in-gaza, accessed 20 August 2015; "Skopje: Solidarity Protests in Support of Gaza Strip, Islamic Religious Community Opposes," *Independent*, 25 July 2014, http://www.independent.mk/articles/7631/Skopje+Solidarity+Protests+in+Support+of+Gaza+Strip,+Islamic+Religious+Community+Opposes, accessed 20

August 2015; "LISBA Protests in Support of Gaza," *Kosova Press*, http://www.kosovapress.com/en/nacional/lisba-protests-in-support-of-gaza-22466/?deviceView=desktop, accessed 20 August 2015.

51. Shpend Kursani, *Report Inquiring into the Causes and Consequences of Kosovo Citizens' Involvement as Foreign Fighters in Syria and Iraq* (Kosovo: Kosovar Center for Security Studies, 2015), 51.
52. Kamaruddin Amin, "Nasiruddin Al-Albani on Muslim's Sahih: A Critical Study of His Method," *Islamic Law and Society* 11, no. 2 (2004): 149–76.
53. Abu Nasir Ibrahim Abdul Rauf; Abu Maryam Muslim Ameen, *The Biography of Sheikh Muhammad Nasiruddin Al-Albani* (Houston, TX: Dar-Us-Salam Publications 2007).
54. Stephane Lacroix, "Al-Albani's Revolutionary Approach to Hadith," *ISIM Review* 21 (2008): 6, https://openaccess.leidenuniv.nl/handle/1887/17210.
55. *Al-Liwa'* (Beirut), 7 August 1993.
56. See, for instance, Muhammad Sa'id Ramadan al-Buti, *Al-Jihad fil Islam: Kayfa mafhamuhu wa kayfa numarisuhu?* (Damascus: Dar Al-Fikr, 1997).
57. Esaam Moosa Haadi, *The Life of Shaikh al-Albaani: May Allaah, the Most High, Have Mercy upon Him: In His Own Words*, trans. and ed. Ahmed Abu Turaab (Amman, 2011), https://shaikhalbaani.files.wordpress.com/2011/03/bio-latest.pdf, accessed 24 August 2016.
58. Haadi, *The Life of Shaikh al-Albaani*, 35.
59. "Njëqind personalitetet shqiptare te kultures Islame," *Komuniteti mysliman shqiptar*, 2014, 263–64
60. Suleiman Gavoçi, *Letra të një emigranti* (Shkodër: Myftinia Shkodër 1995).
61. The role of the circulation of cassette and VHS taped sermons in the Balkans during this period is another subject that deserves more attention in the contemporary history of Islam in the Balkans. For a more comprehensive account of the role of cassettes in the wider Muslim world, see Charles Hirschkind, *The Ethical Soundscape: Cassette Sermons and Islamic Counterpublics* (New York: Columbia University Press, 2006).
62. Abdul Kader Arnauti, "Këshillë për Kosovën nga imam abdul kader arnauti," *IslamShqip*, 22 March 2012, http://www.islamshqip.com/keshille-per-kosoven-nga-imam-abdul-kader-arnauti/, accessed 20 August 2015.

WORKS CITED

Al-Bahloly, Saleem. *The Persistence of the Image: Dhākira Hurra in Dia Azzawi's Drawings on the Massacre of Tel al-Zaatar*. Cambridge, MA: MIT Press, 2013.
"The Albanian Revolt." *Times of India*, 23 June 1914.
Al-Buti, Muhammad Sa'id Ramadan. *Al-Jihad fil Islam: Kayfa mafhamuhu wa kayfa numarisuhu?* [Strife in Islam]. Damascus: Dar Al-Fikr, 1997.
Al-Liwa' (Beirut). 7 August 1993.

Amin, Kamaruddin. "Nasiruddin Al-Albani on Muslim's Sahih: A Critical Study of His Method," *Islamic Law and Society* 11, no. 2 (2004): 149–76.
Anderson, Matthew Smith. *The Eastern Question, 1774–1923: A Study in International Relations*. London: Macmillan, 1966.
Armstrong, D. Heaton. *Prince Vidi: Gjashtë muaj mbretëri*. Tirana, 1995.
Arnauti, Abdul Kader. "Këshillë për Kosovën nga imam abdul kader arnauti." *Islam-Shqip*, 22 March 2012. Accessed 20 August 2015. http://www.islamshqip.com/keshille-per-kosoven-nga-imam-abdul-kader-arnauti/.
Bodansky, Yossef, and Vaughn S. Forrest. "Iran's European Springboard?" *Srpska Mreza–Serbian Network*. Accessed 20 August 2015. http://www.srpska-mreza.com/library/facts/bodansky1.html.
Bosnawi, Melika Salihbeg. "Biography/Identity Card." Accessed 15 June 2015. http://www.bosnawi.ba/en/biography-identity-card.
———. "Hijab Is a Guarantor of Freedom of Conscience: An Imaginary Interview." Accessed 15 June 2015. http://www.bosnawi.ba/en/essay/194-hijab-is-a-guarantor-of-freedom-of-conscience#sthash.py75mmap.dpuf.
Buden, Boris. *Zone des Übergangs: Vom Ende des Postkommunismus*. Frankfurt: Suhrkamp, 2009.
Burke, Edmond, III. *The Ethnographic State: France and the Invention of Moroccan Islam*. Berkeley: University of California Press, 2014.
Çavuşoğlu, Halim. "Yugoslavya—Makedonya Topraklarından Türkiye'ye Göç ve Nedenleri." *Bilig* 41 (Spring 2007).
Daniel, Odile. "The Historical Role of the Muslim Community in Albania." *Central Asian Survey* 9, no. 3 (1990): 1–28.
Daulatzai, Sohail. *Black Star, Crescent Moon: The Muslim International and Black Freedom beyond America*. Minneapolis: University of Minnesota Press, 2012.
Dello Rocca, Roberto Morozzo. *Nazione e religione in Albania*. Lecce: Besa, 2002.
"Dhuna në Egipt, protestë edhe në Tiranë." *Gazeta Tema*, 23 August 2013. Accessed 20 August 2015. http://www.gazetatema.net/web/2013/08/23/dhuna-ne-egjipt-proteste-edhe-ne-tirane-foto/.
Donia, Robert J. *Sarajevo: A Biography*. Ann Arbor: University of Michigan Press, 2006.
Elsie, Robert. *A Dictionary of Albanian Religion, Mythology, and Folk Culture*. New York: New York University Press, 2001.
———. *Gathering Clouds: The Roots of Ethnic Cleansing in Kosovo and Macedonia*. Peja, Kosovo: Dukagjini Balkan Books, 2002.
Gavoçi, Suleiman. *Letra të një emigranti*. Shkodër: Myftinia Shkodër, 1995.
Ghodsee, Kristen. *Muslim Lives in Eastern Europe: Gender, Ethnicity, and the Transformation of Islam in Postsocialist Bulgaria*. Princeton, NJ: Princeton University Press, 2009.
Gibas-Krzak, Danuta. "Contemporary Terrorism in the Balkans: A Real Threat to Security in Europe." *Journal of Slavic Military Studies* 26, no. 2 (2013): 203–18.
Haadi, Esaam Moosa. *The Life of Shaikh al-Albaani: May Allaah, the Most High, Have Mercy upon Him: In His Own Words*. Translated and edited by Ahmed Abu Turaab.

Amman, 2011. Accessed 28 August 2016: https://shaikhalbaani.files.wordpress.com/2011/03/bio-latest.pdf.
Hirschkind, Charles. *The Ethical Soundscape: Cassette Sermons and Islamic Counterpublics.* New York: Columbia University Press, 2006.
Hoxha, Enver. *Reflections on the Middle East: 1958–1983.* Marxists Internet Archive. Accessed 15 June 2015. https://www.marxists.org/reference/archive/hoxha/works/ebooks/reflections_on_the_middle_east.pdf.
———. *Shënime mbi Lindjen e Mesme.* Tirana: 8 Nëntori, 1984.
Izetbegovic, Alija. *The Islamic Declaration: A Programme for the Islamization of Muslims and the Muslim Peoples.* Sarajevo, 1990. Accessed 20 August 2015. http://profkaminskisreadings.yolasite.com/resources/Alija%20Izetbegovic-%20The%20Islamic-Declaration%20%281990%29.pdf.
"Jihad Made in Kosovo." *Deutsche Welle.* Accessed 24 August 2014. http://www.dw.de/jihad-made-in-kosovo/a-17874069.
Jukic, Elvira M. "Sarajevans Protest over Bombing of Gaza." *Balkan Insight,* 18 July 2014. Accessed 20 August 2015. http://www.balkaninsight.com/en/article/sarajevo-protest-against-killings-in-gaza.
Karpat, Kemal. "The Migration of the Bosnian Muslims to the Ottoman State, 1878–1914: An Account Based on Turkish Sources." In *Ottoman Bosnia: A History in Peril,* edited by Markus Koller and Kemal H. Karpat. Madison: University of Wisconsin Press, 2004.
———. *Ottoman Population, 1830–1914: Demographic and Social Characteristics.* Madison: University of Wisconsin Press, 1985.
Korkut, Şenol. "The Diyanet of Turkey and Its Activities in Eurasia after the Cold War." *Acta Slavnocia Iaponica* 28 (2009): 117–39.
Krasniqi, Gëzim. "'The Forbidden Fruit': Islam and Politics of Identity among Albanians in Kosovo and Macedonia." Unpublished paper, presented at the "After the Wahabi Mirage: Islam, Politics and International Networks in the Balkans" conference, European Studies Centre, University of Oxford, June 2010.
Krstić, Đorđo. *Kolonizacija u južnoj Srbiji.* Sarajevo: Đ. Krstić, 1928.
"Kuasa sunia: Satu bantahan bagi siasah." *Majalah al-Islam* 6, no. 6 (1914): 188–96.
Kursani, Shpend. *Report Inquiring into the Causes and Consequences of Kosovo Citizens' Involvement as Foreign Fighters in Syria and Iraq.* Kosovo: Kosovar Center for Security Studies, 2015.
Labuschagne, Bart, and Timo Slootweg, eds. *Hegel's Philosophy of the Historical Religions.* Vol. 6. Leiden: Brill, 2012.
Lacroix, Stephane. "Al-Albani's Revolutionary Approach to Hadith." *ISIM Review* 21 (2008): 6. Accessed 26 January 2017. https://openaccess.leidenuniv.nl/handle/1887/17210.
"LISBA Protests in Support of Gaza." *Kosova Press.* Accessed 20 August 2015. http://www.kosovapress.com/en/nacional/lisba-protests-in-support-of-gaza-22466/?deviceView=desktop.
McCarthy, Justin. *Death and Exile: The Ethnic Cleansing of Ottoman Muslims, 1821–1922.* Princeton, NJ: Darwin, 1995.

Merdjanova, Ina. *Rediscovering the Umma: Muslims in the Balkans between Nationalism and Transnationalism.* Oxford: Oxford University Press, 2013.
Mirojević, Hidajeta. "25 September 1985." *Putopis* (self-published).
Mishra, Pankaj. *From the Ruins of Empire: The Intellectuals Who Remade Asia.* London: Palgrave Macmillan, 2012.
Mufaku (Arnauti), Muhamed. "Lidhjet Letrare Shqiptare–Arabe." *Qendra Shqiptare për Studime Orientale,* 2009.
"Njëqind personalitetet shqiptare te kultures Islame." *Komuniteti mysliman shqiptar* (2014): 263–64.
Norris, Harry Thirlwall. *Islam in the Balkans: Religion and Society between Europe and the Arab World.* Columbia: University of South Carolina Press, 1993.
"A Pan-Islamic Movement in Albania." *Tribune* (Lahore), 14 June 1914.
Pearson, Owen. *Albania and King Zog: Independence, Republic and Monarchy 1908–1939.* New York: New York University Press, 2004.
"Protecting Prince William." *Times,* 5 June 1914.
Puar, Jasbir K., and Amit Rai. "The Remaking of a Model Minority: Perverse Projectiles under the Specter of (Counter) Terrorism." *Social Text* 22, no. 3 (2004): 75–104.
Puto, Arben. *Çështja shqiptare në aktet ndërkombëtare të periudhës së imperializmit.* Vol. 2. Tirana: Shtëpia Botuese "8 Nëntori," 1987.
———. *Pavarësia shqiptare dhe diplomacia e fuqive të mëdha.* Tirana: 8 Nëntori, 1978.
Ramet, Sabrina P. "Islam in Yugoslavia Today." *Religion in Communist Lands* 18, no. 3 (Summer 1990): 226–35.
Ranstorp, Magnus, and Gus Xhudo. "A Threat to Europe? Middle East Ties with the Balkans and Their Impact upon Terrorist Activity throughout the Region." *Terrorism and Political Violence* 6, no. 2 (1994): 208.
Rexhepi, Piro. "Mainstreaming Islamophobia: The Politics of European Enlargement and the Balkan Crime-Terror Nexus." *East European Quarterly* 43, nos. 2–3 (2015): 189–214.
Sarajevo District Court. Court Decision No. K212/83, 1983. Archives of the Federation of Bosnia and Herzegovina, File 61.
"Sarajevo: Peaceful Protests to Support Morsi." *R4BIA Platform.* Accessed 20 August 2015. http://www.r4biaplatform.com/content/news-story/sarajevo-peaceful-protests-support-morsi.
Sarajlić, Eldar. "The Return of the Consuls: Islamic Networks and Foreign Policy Perspectives in Bosnia and Herzegovina." *Southeast European and Black Sea Studies* 11, no. 2 (June 2011): 173–90.
Schmidl, Erwin A. "The International Operation in Albania, 1913–14." *International Peacekeeping* 6, no. 3 (1999): 1–10.
Sell, Louis. *Slobodan Milosevic and the Destruction of Yugoslavia.* Durham, NC: Duke University Press, 2003.
Shariati, Ali. *Hajj: A Reflection on Its Rituals.* Mustbe Interactive, 2014.
"Shkup, protestë solidarizimi me egjiptianët," *Shekulli,* 23 August 2013. Accessed 20 August 2015. http://www.shekulli.com.al/p.php?id=29214.

"Skopje: Solidarity Protests in Support of Gaza Strip, Islamic Religious Community Opposes." *Independent*, 25 July 2014. Accessed 20 August 2015. http://www.independent.mk/articles/7631/Skopje+Solidarity+Protests+in+Support+of+Gaza+Strip,+Islamic+Religious+Community+Opposes.

Solberg, Anne Ross. "The Role of Turkish Islamic Networks in the Western Balkans." *Southeast Europe Journal of Politics and Society* 4 (2007): 429–62.

Verli, Marenglen. *Shqiptarët në optikën e diplomacisë Austro-Hungareze (1877–1918): studime, analiza, dokumente*. Tirana: Klean, 2014.

"Vozila sam auto kroz Arabiju do Meke." *Denevni Avaz*, 18 September 2014. Accessed 18 September 2014. http://www.avaz.ba/clanak/136368/vozila-sam-auto-kroz-arabiju-do-meke#sthash.YKpDbAfo.dpuf.

Wilder, Gary. *Freedom Time: Negritude, Decolonization, and the Future of the World*. Durham, NC: Duke University Press, 2014.

"Zapisnik interministerijalne konferencije, održane u Ministarstvu inostranih poslova 20. septembra 1935. god. po pitanju iseljenja neslovenskog stanovništva iz Južne Srbije." Archives of Yugoslavia, Fond: "Poslanstvo Kraljevine Jugoslavije u Turskoj-Carigrad, Ankara (370)." Folder 9, Archival Unit 42, pages 637–43.

Zimonjic, Vesna Peric. "BALKANS: Arrest of Wahhabis Highlight Extremist Threats." *Interpress News Service*, 11 February 2010. Accessed 20 August 2015. http://www.ipsnews.net/2010/02/balkans-arrest-of-wahhabis-highlights-extremist-threat/.

———. "Operacioni 'Balcania,' 14 të arrestuar në shqipëri dhe itali," *Mapo*, 4 June 2015. Accessed 20 August 2015. http://www.mapo.al/2015/06/operacioni-balcania-14-te-arrestuar-ne-shqiperi-dhe-itali.

Part II

Dislodged Dissent

Among this book's rubrics, dissent, with its time-tested link to exile, is one that is most recognizably unmapped in geographical terms. And yet, rather than capitalizing on the association with exile, this section dislodges oppositional Eastern Europe in other complementary ways. Dissent, so goes the overarching theme, need not be predicated on geographical distance and its paradoxical accessory—the tenacious link to a stable homeland, real or imagined. Instead, the two chapters introduce alternative kinds of distances: those between cultural canons and ways of interpreting them.

A group of cultural and political dissidents in Soviet Belarus, called, significantly, the Tuteishyia ("locals"), is the centerpiece of Tatsiana Astrouskaya's essay. Here, the author traces several important discontiguities in the relatively little-known history of Belarusian protest movements. Not only did the emergence of the group itself mark a rupture in the former republic's tradition of nonconformity: the Tuteishyia's willingness to take a political stance contrasted with their precursors' single-minded dedication to (national) culture. Discontinuities were also temporal (forging links to earlier periods by omitting the Soviet era) and thematic. With regard to themes, the group spearheaded several literary and linguistic shifts: from rural to urban, from folkloric to avant-garde, and last but not least, from national to local. With the help of these, at the close of the last Soviet decade the Tuteishyia envisioned a more open third space, one that was neither Soviet nor unerringly nation-bound. There, the "spiritual ancestry" of global cultural authorities had precedence, however briefly, over national heroes.

"Distancing" takes on its perhaps broadest meaning in Jessie Labov's piece about new approaches to re-evaluating *Kultura,* one of the most important Polish émigré cultural journals. In contrast to the existing studies of the periodical, focused on close readings of individual texts or on specific authors, Labov's computational mapping aims to get at the global circulation of this outlet not only among its producers but also among its donors and, above all, its audiences across the globe—in the diaspora and also in Poland. Her adoption of "distant reading" (an aggregate analysis of vast and diverse data) enables a new look at the otherwise difficult-to-investigate dissemination and reception of what she calls "extraterritorial literature." For, akin to the Tuteishyia, *Kultura* participated in the making of a delimited public sphere (the surrogate national kind, in this case) as much as it imploded the limits of this creation.

Chapter Three

Located on the Archipelago
Toward a New Definition of Belarusian Intellectuals

Tatsiana Astrouskaya

> For we came when the rest had given up, and had not expected anyone. We came as salvation, but also as revenge.
> —Ігар Бабкоў, *Хвілінка,* Ihar Babkoŭ, *Khvilinka*[1]

> We have appeared to be, where we did not intend to arrive, we have found ourselves where we did not want to be.
> —Валянцін Акудовіч, *Вялікая Здрада,*
> Valiantsin Akudovich, "Vialikaia zdrada"[2]

The notion of Eastern Europe as the "space between," trapped in its transition from the Communist rule to Western-type democracies, has been applied to Belarus (until 1990: the Belarusian Soviet Socialist Republic, the BSSR) arguably more than to the other parts of this geographical and mental imaginary.[3] Soviet Belarus, with its reputation as the repository of socialism during the postwar period, became notorious as perestroika-era Vendée at the end of the Soviet era.[4] In the last some twenty years, ruled by President Aliaksandr Lukashenka, the present-day Republic of Belarus is believed to march on the tricky path of conserving the Soviet order.[5] The political quarantine that was first framed by the Iron Curtain and then by Lukashenka's authoritarian isolationism has lasted almost an entire century, excluding short periods of remission.[6] However stuck in its "stability" and however politically fenced in the world Belarusian reality may look, it obviously cannot escape the whirlpool of globalization and rapid political and economic transformations. The stubborn intention of political elites to preserve the status quo is unfeasible and produces a peculiar understanding of space as well as time. In the foreword to his influential study *Historiker und Herrschaft*, German historian Rainer Lindner noted that some European countries represent old and new periods simultaneously, Belarus being among them.[7] In addition, despite its geographical location and historical ties to Europe, Belarus's political development has resembled that of Latin American autocracies; it followed the path of Eurasian economic integration more than that of the EU.[8] This valuation is very much in line with Belarus's aforesaid "betweenness" and Eastern Europe's perceived interstitial condition, summarized in Yuliya Komska's introduction to this book.[9] In other words, what was once an aberration for the national revival activists and for Soviet Belarusian dissidents, who continually underscored their countrymen's Europeanness and their dissimilarity vis-à-vis Russians, has become today's everyday reality.[10] Belarus has often been mentioned as Europe's (and recently even as Ukraine's)[11] "silent other, in the mirror of whom, one can enjoy the glance of its own democratic institutions."[12]

My intention here, however, is not to retell the story of Belarusian post-Soviet political development, but rather to shed light on some of the intellectual projects of the last thirty years (starting with perestroika) that negotiated the established cartography of Belarusian culture and offered in one way or another the notion of contested cultural spatiality.[13] The pathways of culture penetrate political as well as physical borders and expose the construction of space and time in more complex and perplexing relations than might seem possible at first glance.

I address here the generation of the Tuteishyia, named after a group of young authors who gathered together briefly in the wake of perestroika.[14] The contemporaries of the Tuteishyia from other parts of the former USSR had often been referred to as the generation of the 1980s, by analogy with the *shestidesiatniki,* or the generation of the 1960s. The word *tuteishyia* literally means "locals" or "natives."[15] It was borrowed from a play written in 1922 by the national poet Yanka Kupala and banned by the Soviet censors at the time of its original publication, with the ban lasting through the years of the group's emergence. I will return to the play and to the meaning of the term *tuteishyia* below.

This generation of the 1980s, despite its initially productive creative impulse and its continuous domination in the (underground) Belarusian cultural landscape of the 1990s–2000s, was described as "lost" by native commentators.[16] Due to its use of the Belarusian language and its intellectualism, the active representatives of this generation have never gained wide popular support. Moreover, unlike intellectuals in other Eastern and Central European countries, who after the fall of Communism "attained almost unprecedented heights in terms of social esteem and of moral and political legitimacy," the members of the group also never entered politics.[17] Still, Belarusian intellectuals have never been completely isolated from the state and the populace that they have observed and studied. Grounded in the locality, they simultaneously search for distinctive global connections. Edward Said's oft-cited definition of the intellectual as an exile and outsider suits well Belarusian intellectual elites over the course of the whole twentieth century.[18] With regard to Belarus, internal exile also becomes relevant. I would like to propose that the position of exile within the society, on the archipelago, as philosopher Valiantsin Akudovich once called it, allows intellectuals, who are simultaneously this society's insiders and outsiders, to challenge the established political and cultural categories.[19] Parallel to Soviet-era self-publishing (samizdat) and its extra-territorial networks, the creative works of intellectuals in contemporary Belarus penetrate and recast borders.[20] The designation "lost," in this regard, can be understood in the light of a procreant marginality that endows intellectual projects with the advantage of being set free from society's normative prescriptions and limitations and, arguably, from the burden of the political, cultural, and geographical betweenness.

LOCALS AND THE ARCHIPELAGO OF THE BELARUSIAN INTELLIGENTSIA

Akudovich employs Said's notion of the marginal to explain the emergence and development of the local intelligentsia during the second half of the nineteenth century. At that time, the Northwestern Krai of the Russian Empire, once part of the Great Duchy of Lithuania and, later, of the Polish-Lithuanian Commonwealth, had become the epicenter of several different national intelligentsias: Polish, Lithuanian, Russian, Belarusian, Ukrainian, and Jewish.[21] At this stage, fluidity between distinct national projects was widespread. The emerging Belarusian intelligentsia, deprived of national schools and universities, obtained intellectual training, social status, and identity as the foster children in non-Belarusian contexts.[22] In particular, its university degrees came from Petersburg, Tartu (then Dorpat/Dörpt, later Jur'ev), Cracow, and Vienna. Therefore, learning to write in Belarusian, after first writing in other languages, had to be a deliberate decision and not a mere default.

Here are a few examples of how such marginality worked. Raised and educated in Russia, Maksim Bahdanovich (1883–1917) initially published poetry, short prose works, and critical articles in Russian—despite being celebrated as the most talented Belarusian modernist poet.[23] His only collection of verse came out in Vilna (now Vilnius, Lithuania), at that time the center of Belarusian culture, and his burial site was Yalta (now in occupied Crimea). Belarusian-Jewish poet and writer Samuil Plaŭnik (pen name: Zmitrok Biadulia, 1886–1941) first wrote in Hebrew, then in Russian, becoming famous for his Belarusian-language stories.[24] Many more such examples could be cited, making the pattern typical rather than exceptional.

The life and works of Yanka Kupala (pen name of Ivan Lutsevich, 1882–1942), described as the national Belarusian poet, can also be perceived in the light of such heterogeneous identity formations. Born into a family of landed gentry and initially writing in Polish, he became the bard of Belarusian peasantry. His poetry forestalled the national revival of the early twentieth century. Yet, during Soviet rule, it was assigned to the classics of Belarusian Soviet literature and simultaneously nourished the national sentiments of its opponents, the Belarusian émigré diaspora.[25] Kupala died in Moscow under murky circumstances, but accounts of his person, as well as his poetry, have not for a moment disappeared from Belarusian literary textbooks.

Still, one of Kupala's greatest works, the tragicomic play *Tuteishyia,* written in 1922, did not share the success of his poetry.[26] Published only once during the Soviet era, *Tuteishyia* was subsequently banned by Soviet censorship, both for publication and for staging.[27] The play reappeared only in September 1988, more than three years after the start of perestroika.[28] Staging it was again prohibited in 2007, despite its invariable success with audiences in the brief instances when it could be performed.

Tuteishyia, the play, is set in Minsk between the years 1918 and 1922. Various political forces arrive and try to establish themselves in town, first the Germans, then the Soviets, after that the Poles, and again the Soviets. The play recounts how the locals cope with and survive the misleading parade of armies and authorities, as well as the shifting borders. Identities change and overlap with one another, provoking confusing, comical, but also tragic situations. A cross-section of locals is represented and examined in Kupala's piece: clergy, peasantry, intelligentsia, gentry, bureaucrats, and prostitutes. These diverse groups speak Russian, Polish, Belarusian, and also a mixture of all three languages. The play depicts these locals (*tuteishyia*) trying to survive under the pressure of foreign cultures and ideologies by choosing protean identities, aligning themselves with East or West, not conforming fully to either and thus remaining true to themselves against all odds.

The main character, Mikita Znosak, embodies this strategy most consistently. The peculiarity of this identity is its ability to connect and metamorphose: the local could easily become someone else. Philosopher Ihar Babkoŭ expresses this as "coloniality as it is, with its mimicry, imitation of the dominating identity, and, simultaneously, with the internal distancing from whatever identity."[29] In *Native Realm,* Czesław Miłosz depicted with subtlety this process of a deliberate, often pragmatic choice of identity that he saw to be a trait of this part of Europe.[30] As we have learned from Homi Bhabha and other postcolonial theorists, ambivalent identification characterizes the relations between local and colonial forces all over the globe.[31] Another context in which we can understand the play is as Kupala's attempt to examine and expose the identity of local people and specifically their indifference to the intelligentsia's calls for an "awakening."

"Nothing has changed since then," states Babkoŭ elsewhere.[32] Kupala's protagonists, the *tuteishyia,* who were attached to the place of their birth and residence, have survived attempts of conversion into nationalism (at the beginning and at the end of the twentieth century) and have proved to be vigorous in sticking to their own identity.[33] By the beginning of the twenty-first century, the idea of local identity, supported by this time by state patriotism, has once again become influential. Free from nationalism, in its classical meaning, speaking Russian or the mixed Belarusian-Russian language called *trasianka,* and also (silently) critical of the authoritarianism of Lukashenka—who in turn, as Andrej Kazakevich has noticed, also emphasizes the connections to the land and to the territory—Belarusian citizens express strong feelings of belonging to the land and, one can assume, through that concrete connection to the contiguous, of bearing the same (local) identity.[34] Ironically, such an identity combines the fear of capitalism and the longing for consumption, the wish for stability within state borders and the feeling of brotherhood with other Eastern Slavs.

THE TUTEISHYIA GROUP

As I have mentioned, citizens of Soviet Belarus were often considered the "most Soviet" in the USSR, having lacked both dissent and national sentiments. This image is not entirely groundless, considering the results of the 1991 Soviet Union referendum, which, as David Marples put it, "indicated strong support for the continuation of a revised USSR, in the BSSR as elsewhere," as well as the later establishment of authoritarian rule.[35] Yet the flourishing of political and cultural life in the late 1980s and early 1990s should not be considered solely the result of the democratization and glasnost "from above."[36] Contrary to conventional wisdom, it was also inspired by dissent and samizdat that were both present in the BSSR.[37] As was the case across the entire USSR, in the BSSR various expressions of disagreement with the Communist ideology got a new lease on life after Josef Stalin's death in 1953. Admittedly, the so-called nonconformism unfolded in spaces discontiguous to those occupied by ordinary BSSR citizens and was concentrated in the small circles of the intelligentsia.[38] Starting in 1979, just as the first secretary of the Belarusian Communist Party, Piotar Masheraŭ, paid tribute "above all [to] the great Russian people," ideological, cultural, and political opposition was spreading and consolidating.[39]

In 1988, the Department of Agitation and Propaganda of the Minsk Party Committee secretly reported the existence of 566 non-formal youth associations in the city at that moment. The Tuteishyia group was identified as one of the most problematic, because of its political and social engagement.[40]

The group, an underground association of young poets, writers, artists, and scholars, first gathered on 12 February 1987, with the aim of discovering and promoting a new definition of Belarusian culture. The sixty to seventy members of the association were very diverse in their creative activity. One could describe the group as a laboratory of transition, where multifaceted projects of identity were conceived and varied roles for the intellectual elites were first tried out.[41]

All over the collapsing Soviet Union, these new intellectuals, while emerging as a social force distinct from the old Soviet intelligentsia, to borrow from Dubravka Ugrešić, had to simultaneously appeal to their local communities, to Europe, and to the increasingly globalizing world, and to be, as Leonidas Donskis aptly noticed, "faster than history."[42] For the Belarusian national elites, this task was most evident in the need to balance the preservation of the native language and culture while connecting Belarus and themselves to the world. In addition, the legacy of Russian and Soviet imperialism had to be weighed against the increasing influence of the West's continued "invention" of Eastern Europe, including Belarus, as one of its alter egos.[43]

By 1987, the members of the group had acquired both the experience of samizdat (which continued even after the abolition of the Law on Censorship on 12 June 1990) and the profound knowledge of history and literature, which had been banned by the Soviets. At the same moment when Russification was at its peak and the view of Belarusians as oppressed and sedentary peasants emancipated by Soviet rule still prevailed, the alternative Belarus that the Tuteishyia were able to discover (from older colleagues, from propaganda literature that nonetheless contained a bit of historical knowledge, from occasional forays into closed library departments) changed their worldview suddenly and radically, giving birth to another "here" in Soviet Belarus.[44] Many well-educated young people then abruptly changed their language and Weltanschauung by abandoning the Soviet identity and subscribing to that other "here," as locals, or Tuteishyia. Given that national tendencies had previously been marginal and thus never been adopted concertedly by the population, young intellectuals made a leap over contiguities and continuities and chose a protean locality as their point of departure.

"Belarus does not exist yet," claimed the Tuteishyia, "therefore Belarusians do not exist either, there are only locals [*tuteishyia*], and we belong to them."[45]

So, as regards the end of the twentieth century, we could say that not only locals and the intelligentsia were discontiguous to each other. The intelligentsia itself was claiming and occupying discontiguous time and spatial coordinates. There existed not only the "old" Soviet, and the "new," national intelligentsia, but the dividing line between them was much more subtle. Thus, many ardent party functionaries remained not less ardent supporters of the Belarusian language and culture throughout the late Soviet period. Similarly, the arising post-Soviet intellectuals should not necessarily be seen as those who picked up the torch of the national awakening at the common outburst of the national sentiments of the late 1980s to early 1990s.

One can trace at least two such trajectories within the Tuteishyia from its beginnings by examining the paths of the group's two prominent leaders: Anatol Sys (1959–2005) and Adam Hlobus (pen name of Uladzimir Adamchyk, born in 1958).[46] Sys, a charismatic cult figure, absorbed and reinterpreted the pathos of national renaissance and saw his mission as the awakening of the people. Arnold McMillin characterizes Sys as follows:

> A truly patriotic poet, whose poems are deeply embedded in the cultural and spiritual past of his country, he expressed most vividly his hopes and, particularly, despair in view of what seemed to him a catastrophic decline in his beloved native culture.[47]

In some ways Sys's opponent Hlobus became best known for new urban prose, moving the focus from rural areas, favored by the preceding traditions of romantic nationalism and Soviet Belarusian literature, to the city. He combined his roles as a successful writer and an artist, as many members of the Tuteishyia did. His urban stories appeared in the second half of the 1980s, and by the early 1990s, he also opened up the field of erotic novels, previously an absolute taboo in Soviet Belarusian literature.[48]

As a leader of the Tuteishyia, Hlobus was able to unite a group of associates (Maksim Klimkovich, Miraslaŭ Shajbak, Ŭladzimir Stsiapan) to cooperate on new venues for the Belarusian language. They experimented with haiku, published numerous detective stories, and explored the genre of children's literature, editing such outlets as the youth magazine *Biarozka*

(Little Birch). Not less challenging were their attempts to deconstruct the newly surfacing national mythologies. For example, in the play *Vita Brevis or The Trousers of St. George,* where the first (Belarusian) printer Francishak Skaryna meets Martin Luther in Wittenberg, Skaryna, a Belarusian cult national figure, is depicted as a wag, dodger, and a philanderer.[49] Written in 1990, at the height of national sentiments among the intelligentsia of the Soviet republics, the play by Shajbak and Klimkovich insisted on transcending them. The transition from Communism was accompanied, as is well known, by a drastic economic crisis, with its impoverishment of vast segments of post-Soviet societies, including the intelligentsia. Hlobus and his counterparts found their way out of the economic straits by writing and publishing popular Russian-language literature, which they successfully sold all over the former Soviet Union, thus supporting the publishing of an intellectual Belarusian literature.[50]

In 1988, under the official name "the Association of Young Literati," the Tuteishyia became affiliated with the official Writers Union of the BSSR. The affiliation did not satisfy all members, but it did enable the publication of otherwise unauthorized texts and result in the ability to function within the established writers' institutions. Ironically perhaps, Ales Arkush, one of the fellows, considered this attainment of recognition to be the main reason for the fading of the group's activity and its subsequent dissolution around 1990.[51]

Thus, the only official collective anthology of the Tuteishyia was published in 1989.[52] It included the poetry and prose of nearly forty authors, among them short translations of the Chinese poet Li Bai (Li Po) and of the classical writers Anacreon and Horace, who were evidently awarded honorary membership and considered to be the group's spiritual ancestors. The inclusion of these names can be considered another kind of discontiguity, demonstrating the Tuteishyia's ambition to circulate in a wider cultural context, to question the East-West opposition, as well as to distance themselves from immediate past history and contiguous neighbors.

Critic Jan Maksimiuk wittily noted, with a reference to Nikita Khrushchev's dictum from 1961, that this generation had had to live under Communism and must have completely forgotten Belarusian.[53] Moreover, the gamut of their activities cannot be reduced to the fluctuation between the adepts of nationalism and the "ambassadors of the West" (as Mark Andryczyk called it) that one could expect from the wave of national revival of the late 1980s to early 1990s.[54] Some authors of the generation of the Tuteishyia continued to function past the point that one would imagine possible. Below I take up two more individual biographies to show how the spirit of the Tuteishyia informed those individuals' activities even after the group had dissolved. Both

Sjarhej Dubavets and Ihar Babkoŭ attempted to situate and imagine Belarus in mental and geographical coordinates non-contiguous to the Soviet.

DUBAVETS AND *NASHA NIVA*

Sjarhej Dubavets (born in 1959), a journalist, publicist, and one of the leaders of the Tuteishyia, was an active member of the underground youth movement already from the very beginning of the 1980s. In 1979–80, Dubavets participated in the publication of the illegal periodical *Liustra Dzion* (Daily Mirror),[55] which still expressed a hope for reformation of the socialist system. Dubavets and his counterparts juxtaposed *tut* (here), understood as the then declining socialist system in Soviet republics, absolutely dependent on Moscow's will, and the *tam* (there), evoking the so-called "socialism with a human face" and national foundations—for example, the Polish People's Republic, Yugoslavia, or (in their idiosyncratic interpretation) Soviet Lithuania. The publishers of the uncensored *Liustra Dzion* seem to have truly believed that national rebirth could bring democratization and prosperity. Later, in his writings of the later 1980s and early 1990s, Dubavets generalized "here" as the countries captive by Communist rule and compared it to "there," which now appeared to be the West. Dubavets, like many Eastern European intellectuals who witnessed the fall of the Iron Curtain, was enchanted by the West and its culture:

> If you would have been born there you would pay money and wouldn't be troubled with your cultural life. You wouldn't be informed that you could get Dumas [in exchange] for waste paper, that Solzhenitsyn was in *spetskhrans* and Poe was sold out.... But you were born *here*.[56]

In the 1986 samizdat (self-published) periodical *Burachok* (Beetroot), issued at the onset of perestroika, Dubavets and his counterparts already advanced claims for Belarusian independence and cultural and national revival.[57] These were accompanied by an agitation campaign aimed at the masses, reaching back to draw on the spirit of national revival from the beginning of the twentieth century. Dubavets himself contributed to this campaign by publishing polemical articles in the official press.[58] Such attempts to return to the road of national development, considered as "interrupted, on stage B," to use Miroslav Hroch's classification, by the establishment of the Soviet rule, did not succeed, at least not with the initial purpose of national consolidation. Yet these efforts can still be said, in my estimation, to have consolidated the national elites and have relaunched a long-dormant intellectual culture. One interesting effect, to be sure, was the changing meaning of the opposition between "here" and "there."

How was such a reaching back or, better yet, jumping back in time effected or at least attempted? In 1991 in Vilnius, where he moved together with his family, Dubavets re-founded *Nasha Niva* (Our Field). Between 1906 and 1915, an eponymous newspaper had become the main periodical of the early twentieth-century Belarusian revival.[59] Through that newspaper, as Lindner observes, for the first time the Belarusian people acquired a historiography as well as a working literary language.[60] Despite the attempts to explain the new *Nasha Niva* project as the simple rehearsal of the rhetoric and pathos of that earlier revivalist wave, during the period of Dubavets's editorship (1991–96), it neither became the flagship of the new nationalism, nor did it fulfill the image of the "people's newspaper."[61] It intended of course to inform and to appeal to the (whole) nation, yet the actual results incurred reproaches for "intellectualism," directed at the *Nasha Niva* editorial board and its contributors. While the leitmotif of the old *Nasha Niva,* as Nelly Bekus put it, was "hard life on the native land, injustice, and social inequality," for Dubavets and his companions the field (*niva*) appeared to be a contemporary Belarusian culture that they purposed to create and contextualize.[62] A work in progress, this culture showed interest in both contiguities and discontiguities. The periodical contained, for example, translations of J. D. Salinger and Jorge Luis Borges, Czesław Miłosz, Tomas Venclova, and other authors previously unavailable in Belarusian translation, historical studies, critical reviews (especially of publications on Poland and Lithuania), philosophical essays, and metaphysical poetry.

Thus *Nasha Niva* can be treated also as a project of cultural cartography, which intended to imagine Belarus as an inseparable part of Europe and the Western world. For this reason, perhaps, the editorial board decided to locate itself in Vilnius (Vilnia in Belarusian), the first center of Belarusian urban culture in the first half of the twentieth century that, with its rich heritage, has been often perceived as the nearest frontier to the West.[63]

BABKOŬ AND *FRAHMENTY*

Ihar Babkoŭ, was born in Homel in 1964; precisely in the second half of the 1980s he trained as a philosopher in Minsk, where he became a fellow of the Tuteishyia. He is a talented poet, novelist, philosopher, translator, and one-time editor of two intellectual magazines: a Belarusian-language *Frahmenty* (Fragments, together with Valer Bulhakaŭ and issued in 1996–2006) and

Perekrestki (Crossroads, 2001–14; Babkoŭ was the editor-in-chief 2001–7).⁶⁴ Since space does not permit me to present all the exciting projects initiated or created by Babkoŭ, I will focus on *Frahmenty* to demonstrate how Babkoŭ and his team created an alternative cultural spatiality in the late 1990s.

Frahmenty appeared in 1996 as the first intellectual journal founded in post-Soviet Belarus, following Lukashenka's election to the presidency of Belarus and the notorious referendums of 1995 and of 1996, which altered the constitution and established a new authoritarianism.⁶⁵ These years can also be considered formative for a new relationship within the triangle of the populace, intellectuals, and the state. Michel Foucault's conclusion about the wake of the May 1968 events in Paris—that is, that "the intellectual discovered that the masses no longer need him to gain knowledge: they know perfectly well, without illusion; they know far better than he and they are certainly capable of expressing themselves"—applies also to the relationship between post-Soviet intellectuals and the populace.⁶⁶

In Belarus, after a short period of large-scale social support, growing runs of books and periodicals, and ardent public discussions, the populace has made its choice—choosing Lukashenka—and it was not in the intellectuals' favor.⁶⁷ After 1996, an enlarging gulf between the "here" imagined by the intellectuals and the "here" desired by the populace became clear. The intellectuals and the populace spoke different languages and located post-Soviet Belarusia within different political and geographical coordinates. Beyond the most obvious opposition of pro-Western and pro-Russian, pro-democratic and pro-authoritarian choices, this also included the search for extraterritorial connections and the closing on the locality. The appearance of *Frahmenty* and intellectual magazines after the onset of authoritarianism can be viewed as the results of the intellectuals' disappointment that "Belarus will never be *solely* Belarusian" (emphasis in original).⁶⁸ Though this is the phrase of philosopher and essayist Valiantsin Akudovich, it reflects the general state of mind of many intellectuals at the close of the 1990s. Not surprisingly, in the second issue of the magazine, Babkoŭ declared the death of the people (*narod*).⁶⁹ In a déjà vu, the drastic chasm between intellectuals and public became obvious.

As the editor of *Frahmenty,* Babkoŭ did probably more than others among the Tuteishyia to destroy Belarus's "cartographic mandate."⁷⁰ *Frahmenty* unceasingly questioned contiguity with Eastern European and/or post-Soviet lands. Babkoŭ sought to present perspectives that could, rather, explain Belarus and Eastern Europe in any other but the usual categories. Symptomatic is the journal's systematic introduction of postcolonial studies to the Belarusian audience: the translations and discussions of works by Said,

Homi Bhabha, Gayatri Spivak, and other theorists of postcolonialism. Although the text's limited applicability has later been noticed, a postcolonial perspective on Eastern European countries served to overcome, to borrow Timothy Snyder's recent expression, the "traditional difference between European and global history" that places "Europeans (and sometimes Americans and occasionally the Japanese) on one side of a divide and the rest of the world and its inhabitants in the other."[71]

The need for such an overcoming was realized by the editorial board already at the end of the 1990s.[72] To provide an example, I will refer to the fifth issue of the journal that appeared in 1998, entitled "*Kultura*: The Belarusian issue." It would have been immediately clear to readers from the title that the issue was devoted to the famous Polish émigré magazine *Kultura*, discussed at length in this volume by Jessie Labov. It should be noted that Jerzy Giedroyc, *Kultura*'s editor, was born in Belarus's present-day capital Minsk and had ardently supported Belarusian (as well as Ukrainian and Russian) independence and free cultural development.[73] Giedroyc and his *Kultura* became the source of inspiration, an example of openness, political engagement, high-quality intellectual production, and, not least, intellectual networks that could extend beyond the national or regional.

The issue starts with Babkoŭ's editorial. Impressed by his recent meeting and conversation with Giedroyc, Babkoŭ writes:

> We were sitting in his study, and I was talking about the events that took place in Minsk recently, he was listening with interest, but also with some distance, with the distance, we all dream of. And suddenly, he took a typewritten text from the beginning of the [twentieth] century out of his table's drawer and started to talk about the Belarusian roots of Mickiewicz's "Dziady" and talked from there, from the beginning of the nineteenth century, [then] switched to the latest Brzezinski's book, about Europe's future and talked already from somewhere in the future, he was moving across time and space easily and without an effort, I was just following him.[74]

In this anecdote we can locate again the kernel of my argument about the particularities of "local" identities and their mutual discontiguity. Obviously, Giedroyc, as well as Tadeusz Kościuszko, Adam Mickiewicz, Mark Chagall, and many others who were born in the territory of present Belarus, cannot be treated as Belarusian.[75] And yet, they can be and indeed are treated by some as locals, *tuteishyia*. They partly belong to this place with its blurred identity, grounded in the land and bounded by some sense of common identity. These acts of identifying become the precondition for overcoming established political, geographical, and cultural categories of contiguity.

CONCLUSION

In 1996, Dubavets resigned from his position on the editorial board of *Nasha Niva* and moved to Minsk, and under the editorship of Andrej Dynko and Andrej Skurko, the paper was gradually transformed into a tabloid of sorts. Although its intellectual stature diminished, by the end of the first decade of the twenty-first century *Nasha Niva* did become what it aimed for at its founding: a people's newspaper.[76] The restrictions on non-state media and the development of the Internet happened in Belarus almost simultaneously. This produced the unexpected side effect of interest in independent (often Belarusian-language) media: decent quality and critical points of view were able to attract a wider (although not necessarily Belarusian-speaking) audience. The intellectual archipelago that once emerged as an endeavor to connect to and preserve the local has recently been drifting all over the globe. Cited in the epigraph of the novel *Khvilinka*, published by Babkoŭ in 2013, the main character Bahdan, a prototype of Eastern or Central European intellectual, secludes himself on an isolated island with a Chinese book and a bottle of whiskey and finally cannot find his way off it. No matter. The island resembles the topography of the Belarusian Polesie.[77]

Tatsiana Astrouskaya is a PhD candidate in East European history at the University of Greifswald, Germany, who has just finished writing her doctoral dissertation on the intelligentsia, nonconformism, and samizdat in late Soviet Belarus. She has published articles on memory and identity in contemporary Belarus and is a recipient of OSF, DFG, and Kryżowa Foundation fellowships.

NOTES

The author would like to thank warmly the editors of this volume, Irene Kacandes and Yuliya Komska, for all their kind assistance during the preparation of this essay.
1. "Бо мы прыйшлі тады, калі яны ўжо здаліся і нікога больш не чакалі. Прыйшлі як выратаванне, але і як помста." Ihar Babkoŭ, *Khvilinka. Try historyi* (Minsk: Lohvinaŭ, 2013), 191. All translations are mine, unless otherwise noted.
2. "Мы патрапілі зусім не туды, куды імкнуліся, мы наўсьцяж апынуліся ня там, дзе хацелі быць." Valiantsin Akudovich, "Vialikaia zdrada," *Dzeyasloŭ* 10 (2004): 211.
3. Throughout the volume and the essay, the designation "Belarus" and its derivatives, such as the adjective "Belarusian," are used to reflect the spelling and

use in the Belarusian language before, during, and after the Soviet era. BSSR (Belarusian Soviet Socialist Republic) is occasionally used in reference to the Soviet years. The names in the citations remain unchanged.
4. A well-known definition of Soviet Belarus as Vendée of perestroika was introduced by writer and publicist Ales' Adamovich (1927–94) in the late 1980s, in response to the Belarusian Communist party elites' reaction to perestroika and their denial of the real scale of the Chernobyl disaster. See Ales' Adamovich, "Nash vek dakazaŭ biassille ŭsiakaj sily. Hutarka z zhurnalistam Aliaksandram Lukashukom 8 Snezhnia 1994 hoda ŭ Maskoŭskim Instytutse Prablem Kinamastactva," in *Vybranyia tvory* (Minsk: Knihazbor, 2012), 468.
5. This point of view appears both in Western and Belarusian (nongovernmental) media and in scholarship. The latter considers Lukashenka's authoritarianism, his intention to maintain close relations with Russia, and the cultivated praising of the Soviet past as leading to the construction of a new Soviet identity in Belarus.
6. The BSSR as a western border of the USSR was exposed to intensive ideological and border control. Enormous military forces, composing 30 percent of the entire Soviet military complex, were concentrated on its territory.
7. Rainer Lindner, "Pradmova da belaruskaha vydannia," in *Historyki i ŭlada. Natsiatvorchy praces i histarychnaia palityka ŭ Belarusi XIX-XX st.* (St. Petersburg: Neŭski prasciach, 2005), 7. Originally published as Rainer Lindner, *Historiker und Herrschaft. Nationsbildung und Geschichtspolitik in Weißrussland im 19. und 20. Jahrhundert* (Munich: R. Oldenbourg Verlag, 1999).
8. Here I mean, above all, the Eurasian Economic Union (EAEU), to the foundation and the development of which Belarus was amenable already in 1995. I also refer to the attempts of the Belarusian government to establish and maintain relationships with such countries as China and Iran.
9. See Yuliya Komska's introduction to this volume.
10. The attempts to claim the radical difference of the foundations of Belarusian and Russian identity formations were of particular concern for activists of the Belarusian revival of the beginning of the twentieth century. Under Soviet rule, similar claims appeared to be the core theme of samizdat (Belarusian: *samvydat*)—self-published and illegally distributed texts. To name a few publications: Ihnat Abdziralovich, *Advechnym shliacham: dasledziny belaruskaha svetahliadu* (Vilnia: Belaruskae Vydaveckae Tavarystva, 1921); Genrikh Rakutovich, *Polozhenie v Belorusi, 1974 god* (Mogilev, 1974); *Letter to a Russian Friend. A "Samizdat" Publication from Soviet Byelorussia* (London: Association of Byelorussians in Great Britain, Ukrainian Publishers Limited, 1979).
11. For juxtaposing Belarus and Ukraine, see, for instance, George Grabowicz's article on the Ukrainian culture, where he several times refers to Belarus as a "perpetual caution" for Ukraine. George G. Grabrowicz, "Ukraine after Independence: A Balance Sheet for Culture," in *Society in Transition: Social Change in Ukraine in Western Perspectives,* ed. Wsevolod Isajiv (Toronto: Canadian Scholars Press, 2003), 325. In her recent blog entry on *Deutsche Welle,* a Ukrainian writer,

Oksana Zabuzhko, has also claimed that Ukraine by no means can be compared to Belarus. Oksana Zabuzhko, "'Ukraina ni Bilorus', abo Pisliaslovo do kyivskoho vizitu Svitlani Aleksievych," *Deutsche Welle*, 17 April 2016, accessed 24 April 2016, http://dw.com/p/1IXBB.

12. Hleb Hobzem, "Listy z Niamechchyny," *Frahmenty* 11 (2006): 244. Compare to Maria Todorova's apt critique of the prevailing Western view of the Balkans: "The Balkans have served as a repository of negative characteristics against which a positive and self-congratulatory image of the 'European' and the 'West' has been constructed"; *Imagining the Balkans* (Oxford and New York: Oxford University Press, 2009), 188.
13. One or another aspect of this has been studied by David Marples in *Our Glorious Past": Lukashenka's Belarus and the Great Patriotic War* (Stuttgart: ibidem-Verlag, 2014); Andrew Wilson, *Belarus: The Last European Dictatorship* (New Haven and London: Yale University Press, 2011); Brian Bennett, *The Last Dictatorship in Europe. Belarus under Lukashenko* (London: Hurst & Company, 2011); Nelly Bekus, *The Struggle over Identity: The Official and the Alternative Belarusiannes* (Budapest and New York: CEU Press, 2010); David Marples, *The Lukashenka Phenomenon: Elections, Propaganda, and the Foundations of Political Authority in Belarus* (Trondheim: Program on East European Cultures and Societies, 2007).
14. In the following, the capitalized plural form "Tuteishyia" refers to the name of the nonconformist group and to the eponymous play of Yanka Kupala, while the lower-case *tuteishyia* designates the general term for locals or native people in Belarus. *Tuteishy*, which appears in Vitaly Chernetsky's epilogue, is the singular form.
15. For Ukraine, see Mark Andryczyk, "New Images of the Intellectual in Post-Soviet Ukrainian Literature," in *Ukraine on Its Meandering Path Between East and West*, ed. Andrej N. Lushnycky and Mykola Riabchuk (Bern: Peter Lang, 2009), 183.
16. Hanna Kislitsyna, "Novaia litaraturnaia situatsyia," *Belaruski Kalehiium*, accessed 12 February 2014, http://bk.baj.by/lekcyji/litaratura/kislicyna03.htm.
17. András Bozóki, ed., *Intellectuals and Politics in Central Europe* (Budapest: CEU Press, 1999), 6.
18. Edward W. Said, *Representations of the Intellectual*, 1993 Reith Lectures (New York: Vintage Books, 1994), xvi.
19. The metaphor of the archipelago is well-known because of Alexander Solzhenitsyn's monumental work *The Gulag Archipelago*. Valiantsin Akudovich applied it to Belarusian society. The whole society he describes as an immense sea of Russianness, with the small islands of those who speak and write in Belarusian bobbing on it. He is mainly referring to Belarusian-speaking intellectuals. See Valiantsin Akudovich, "Archipelah Belarus: zamest pradmovy," in *Miane niama: rozdumy na ruinach chalaveka* (Minsk: EŭroForum, 1998), 3.
20. Frederike Kind-Kovács and Jessie Labov, "Samizdat and Tamizdat: Entangled Phenomena?," in *Samizdat, Tamizdat, and Beyond: Transnational Media during and after Socialism*, ed. Frederike Kind-Kovács and Jessie Labov (New York and Oxford: Berghahn Books, 2013), 1.

21. Timothy Snyder gives a convincing and multifaceted picture of the emerging of nations in the territory of former Polish-Lithuanian Commonwealth in *The Reconstruction of Nations: Poland, Ukraine, Lithuania, Belarus 1569–1999* (New Haven and London: Yale University Press, 2003), 15–104.
22. Valiantsin Akudovich, *Kod adsutnastsi. Asnovy belaruskaj mentalnastsi* (Minsk: Lohvinaŭ, 2007), 41.
23. Bahdanovich had also written and published numerous critical articles on Belarusian culture and the Belarusian intelligentsia. Interestingly, his Belarusian-language articles appeared in *Nasha Niva,* and some Russian and Ukrainian-language publications appeared in Russian and Ukrainian newspapers and magazines essentially all at the same time. He attempted to introduce the Belarusian national movement to a larger context, writing about the process of self-determination of other Slavic nations. See Uladzimir Konan, "Publitsystyka Maksima Bahdanovicha," in *Poŭny zbor tvoraŭ* u 3 t., vol. 3, *Publitsystyka*, by Maksim Bahdanovich (Minsk: Navuka i tekhnika, 1995), 264–65.
24. Uladzimir Kazberuk, "Budz' sam saboiu belarus," in *Vybranyia tvory*, by Zmitrok Biadulia (Minsk: Knihazbor, 2006), 5.
25. See, for instance, the admiring recollections of émigré writers about Kupala in Barys Sachanka, ed., *Na sud historyi* (Minsk: Mastatskaia litaratura, 1994), accessed 25 April 2016, http://kamunikat.org/usie_knihi.html?pubid=6916. The Belarusian minority in Poland also valued Kupala's poetry. One of the first Belarusian-language samizdat publications was a collection of Kupala's poems called "To the Youth." See Yanka Kupala, *Moladzi* (Belastok: Berah, 1988). For a detailed bibliography of Yanka Kupala's publications in the West, see Vitaŭt Kipel and Zora Kipel, *Yanka Kupala i Yakub Kolas na Zakhadze: Bibliiahrafiia* (New York: Ross, 2004).
26. It is important for the argument of this chapter to underscore the canonicity of Kupala's works. Yet it should be noted that *Tuteishyia* is not his only work to have been prohibited and closed in *spetskhrans*. Despite the official recognition and the title of "the people's poet" that was bestowed on Kupala in 1925, he also went through the periods of significant harassment and persecution. The first wave of terror swept Kupala as early as 1921 (the same year in which Russian Akmeist poet Nikolai Gumilev was executed). Better known are the persecutions against "national democratism" in 1930–31 in the BSSR, but also in other Soviet republics. When the case of the "Union of Liberation of Belarus" had been initiated by the GPU, Kupala was meant to be its leader. For more on this topic, see Per Anders Rudling, *The Rise and Fall of Belarusian Nationalism* (Pittsburgh: University of Pittsburgh Press, 2015), 290–98, 318.
27. *Polymia* 2–3 (1924).
28. Yanka Kupala, "Tuteishyia," *Polymia* 9 (1988): 13–62.
29. Ihar Babkoŭ, "Henealiohiia belaruskaj idei," *Arche* 3 (2005): 157.
30. Czesław Miłosz, *Native Realm: A Search for Self-Definition* (London: Sidgwick & Jackson, 1981).

31. Homi Bhabha, *The Location of Culture* (London and New York: Routledge, 1994), 62.
32. Ihar Babkoŭ, "Krytychnyia intelektualy," in *Vytlumachenne ruinaŭ* (Minsk: Lohvinaŭ, 2005), 70.
33. Per Anders Rudling observes that at the end of the 1980s, 69 percent of Belarusians (more than in any other Soviet republic) considered themselves to be the "Soviet people" (Per Anders Rudling, "Belarus in the Lukashenka Era: National Identity and Relations with Russia," in *Europe's Last Frontier?: Belarus, Moldova, and Ukraine Between Russia and the European Union,* ed. Oliver Schmidtke and Serhy Yekelchyk [New York and Houndmills, UK: Palgrave Macmillan, 2008], 61). Present-day surveys, however, indicate the will of the majority to keep a distance from both Russia and the European Union. The warm relationship with Russia and positive attitude toward integration grew colder after Putin's 2002 "proposal" to annex Belarus (as a federal *okrug*). The majority has also been cautious about European integration, though this majority does not include many young people, cultural elites, and Lukashenka's opponents. See the most recent results of a sociological review conducted by the Independent Institute of Socio-Economic and Political Studies (IISEPS): "Trends in Change in Belarusian Public Opinion," *IISEPS,* accessed 2 May 2016, http://www.iiseps.org/?p=114&lang=en.
34. Andrej Kazakevich, "Kulturny fon belaruskaj palityki," in *Najnoŭshaia historyia belaruskaha parlamentaryzmu,* ed. Valer Bulhakaŭ, 132–46 (Minsk: Analitychny Hrudok, 2005), accessed 6 May 2016, http://kamunikat.org/download.php?item=3390-7.html&pubref=3390.
35. David R. Marples, *Belarus: A Denationalized Nation* (Amsterdam: Harwood Academic, 1999), 59.
36. Compare to the approach of Costica Bradatan and Serguei Oushakine, who point out that the perception of perestroika as a radical break is exaggerated. To be sure, there existed a certain continuity of intellectual elites: "Some of the intellectual actors who came to shape the public discourse in Eastern Europe and Russia in the 1990s had in fact been involved in the production of the mainstream knowledge under the Communist regime in their respective countries." Bradatan and Oushakine, introduction to *In Marx's Shadow: Knowledge, Power and Intellectuals in Eastern Europe and Russia,* ed. Costica Bradatan and Serguei Alex. Oushakine (New York: Lexington Books, 2010), 3. Other authors, like Robert Horvath, argue for a succession in dissident thought that shaped perestroika (e.g., in *The Legacy of Soviet Dissent: Dissidents, Democratization and Radical Nationalism in Russia* [London and New York: Routledge Curzon, 2005], 50–80).
37. There has been no systematic research on dissent and samizdat in Soviet Belarus, or at least, none has been published thus far in Belarus or beyond. Two Belarusian reference books provide only a brief treatment. See Juras' Laŭryk and Larysa Androsik, eds., *Pazatsenzurny peryiadychny druk Belarusi 1971–1990* (Minsk: BHAKC, 1998); and Aleh Dziarnovich, ed., *Nonkanfarmizm ŭ Belarusi:*

1953–1985 (Minsk: Athenaeum, 2004). Some of the samizdat publications have been digitized and are available at www.vytoki.net, accessed 28 April 2016.

38. To name a few lesser-known examples: Akademichny asiarodak (Academic Circle, 1960s–early 1970s) and the illegal artistic association Na paddašku (Under the Leads, 1965–85); both aimed at the re-creation of the non-Soviet version of Belarusian history and identity. In 1964–65, a self-taught historian, Mikola Ermalovich, produced some fifty issues of a samizdat periodical, *Hutarki* (Conversations), filled with a pointed and subtle critique of Soviet social and national policies. *Hutarki* has been published as "Ab usim, shto balits Hutarki' Mikoly Ermalovicja," in *Jaho chakala Belarus chatyry stahoddzi. Zbornik dakumentaŭ i materyialaŭ da 85-hoddzia z dnia naradzhennia Mikoly Ermalovicha,* ed. Anatol Bely and Anatol Valakhnovich (Minsk: Kamunikat, 2007), 171–41. In 1974, an art historian (and an influential politician of the 1990s), Zianon Pazniak, published the Russian-language brochure *Polozhenie v Belorusi* (Situation in Belorus), with a program of emancipation for Soviet nations. See Rakutovich, *Polozhenie v Belorusi.*
39. Cited in David Roger Marples, *Belarus from Soviet Rule to Nuclear Catastrophe* (Edmonton: University of Alberta Press, 1996), 6.
40. "Nekotorye aktualnye voprosy ideologicheskoi raboty v sovremennykh usloviiakh (v poriadke orientirovaniia dlia sekretarej partijnykh komitetov)" (n.p., 1988), 2, 4, accessed 11 April 2016, http://vytoki.net/?docs=00017343.
41. Zygmunt Bauman characterizes this very region as "a laboratory in which the labors and struggles still awaiting most of the planet are currently rehearsed through a succession of trials and errors, forward leaps and reveals of fortune." See his preface to Leonidas Donskis, *Loyalty, Dissent, and Betrayal: Modern Lithuania and East-Central European Moral Imagination* (Amsterdam and New York: Rodopi, 2005), xii.
42. Dubravka Ugrešić, "The New Eastern European Intellectual: 'A Culture of Lies,'" *Context* 18 (2005), accessed 2 March 2016, www.dalkeyarchive.com/the-new-eastern-european-intellectual-a-culture-of-lies/; Donskis, *Loyalty, Dissent, and Betrayal,* 3.
43. Larry Wolff, *Inventing Eastern Europe: The Map of Civilization on the Mind of the Enlightenment* (Stanford, CA: Stanford University Press, 1994).
44. Marples, *Belarus: A Denationalized Nation,* 50. Soviet historian Lavrentij Abecedarskij, the author of canonical history textbooks in the BSSR, was among the promoters of this view. See Lavrentij Semenovich Abecedarskij et al., *Istoriia BSSR: Uchebnoe posobie dlia uchashchikhsia srednikh shkol* (Minsk: Narodnaia asveta, 1968); several further editions of the textbook followed between 1972 and 1987.
45. Ales Arkush, "Viartanne ŭ 'Tuteishyia," in *Asklepki vialikaha maliunku* (Minsk: Lohvinaŭ, 2007), 52.
46. Sys's bibliography includes *Ahmen* (1988), *Pan Les* (1989), and *Sys* (2000). The name of Ales Bialiatski (born 1962), which does not appear in the main text, should also be mentioned. Bialiatski was among the group's leaders, who, above all, promoted its political activity. He was one among several organizers of the "Dziady" meeting of 31 October 1988—the first mass demonstration in the

BSSR. He is well known for his political and rights-defending activity. In 1996, at the height of the protests against violation of the constitution by the president, Lukashenka, Bialiatski founded the Viasna (Spring) Human Rights Center. In 2011–14 he was imprisoned by the regime.

47. Arnold McMillin, *Writing in a Cold Climate: Belarussian Literature from the 1970s to the Present Day* (London: Maney Publishing, 2010), 541.
48. Some books published by Hlobus in the 1980s–90s include *Park* (1988), *Adzinota na Stadyione* (1988), *Damavikameron* (1994), and *Tolki ne havary maioj mame* (1995).
49. Maksim Klimkovich and Miraslaŭ Shajbak, "Vita Brevis albo Nahavicy Sviatoha Heorhiia," in *Litaratura* 2 (n.p., 1990), 2–24.
50. "U nas dzve dushy'. Razmova z Adamam Hlobusam," in *Zrabavany narod: razmovy z belaruskimi intelektualami*, by Malhazhata Nocyn and Andzhej Bzhezetski (Harodnia-Wroclaw: Haradzenskaia Bibliateka, 2009), 110, 116.
51. Arkush, *Asklepki vialikaha maliunku*, 46.
52. Siarhej Dubavets, ed., *"Tuteishyia." Tvorchasts siabroŭ tavarystva* (Minsk: Mastatskaia litaratura, 1989).
53. Jan Maksymiuk, "Imiona umartwionej mowy. Esej o sredniomłodej literaturze białoruskiej (niektóre imiona)," *Kartki* 1 (1997): 6, cited in Siarhej Kavalioŭ, "Preparavanne mifa: tavarystva 'Tuteishyia' ŭ Liusterku krytyki," *Dzejasloŭ* 2 (2013): 308.
54. Andryczyk, *New Images of the Intellectual*, 188.
55. *Liustra Dzion*, n.p., n.d. [c. 1980], accessed 31 January 2016, http://vytoki.net/?docs=00005721.
56. Siarhej Dubavets, "Tut," in *Praktykavanni* (Minsk: Mastatskaia litaratura, 1992), 99 (emphasis mine). *Spetskhrans* were special storage departments in the USSR, the reserves of the books banned in the Soviet Union. Access to them was strictly limited.
57. *Burachok* 1 (n.p., n.d. [c. 1986]); *Burachok* 2 (n.p., n.d. [c. 1987]).
58. See, for instance, Siarhej Dubavets "Prablemy sapraŭdnyia i uiaŭnyia," *LiM* 26 (1986): 5; Siarhej Dubavets, "Vivat Palemika," *LiM* 41 (1996): 5.
59. To illustrate the importance of the old *Nasha Niva*: during 1906–15 there were issued 320 Belarusian-language publications with a total run of 615,000 copies. See Ihar Babkoŭ, "Henealiohiia belaruskaj idei," 151. By comparison, during the previous two centuries the number of published books in Belarusian did not exceed a few dozen.
60. Lindner, *Historiker und Herrschaft*, 38. A few issues of the newspaper appeared also in 1920–21. More on the old *Nasha Niva* in Rudling, *The Rise and Fall of Belarusian Nationalism*, 52–65; and in Andrej Unuchak, *"Nasha Niva" i belaruski nacyianalny rukh* (Minsk: Belaruskaja navuka, 2008).
61. Thus, Andrew Wilson argues that "a new anti-Soviet opposition tried to revive the Nashanivtsy [sic] tradition in the late 1980s and early 1990s, but failed to become hegemonic" (Wilson, *Belarus*, 139).
62. Nelly Bekus, "Nationalism and Socialism: Phase D in the Belarusian Nation-Building," in *Nationalities Papers* 38, no. 6 (November 2010): 833.

63. For more about Vilnia/Vilnius as a contested Belarusian-Lithuanian city, see Snyder, *The Reconstruction of Nations,* 40–42. For the meaning of Vilnia for the Belarusian national movement, consult Lindner, *Historiker und Herrschaft,* 57–69.
64. Babkoŭ's major publications, in addition to those already mentioned, include *Zasynats, prachynatstsa, sluchats halasy ryb* (Minsk: Lohvinaŭ, 2009); *Adam Klakotski i iahonyia tseni* (Minsk: Lohvinaŭ, 2001); and *Heroj vajny za prazrystasts* (Minsk: Ėŭraforum, 1998). A yearly digest of *Perekrestki/Crossroads* appeared in English and is available at http://www.ehu.lt/ru/research/izdateljstvo-egu/zhurnal. Last accessed 11 May 2015.
65. For more on the referendums of 1995 and 1996, see Marples, *Belarus: A Denationalized Nation,* 72–77 and 96–99, respectively.
66. Michel Foucault, "Intellectuals and Power," in *Language, Counter-Memory, Practice: Selected Essays and Interviews by Michel Foucault,* ed. Donald W. Bouchard (New York: Cornell University Press, 1977), 207.
67. The period of rapid democratic transformation of the late 1980s to early 1990s all over Eastern and Central Europe was characterized by intensive intellectual engagement. Later, however, followed a "period of lost illusions" for intellectuals, as András Bozóki called it. These crises, it should be noted, were mostly caused not by the establishment of authoritarianism, but rather by the introduction of market economies. See Bozóki, *Intellectuals and Politics in Central Europe,* 7.
68. Akudovich, *Kod adsutnastsi,* 131.
69. Ad redaktara, *Frahmenty,* nos. 1–2 (1997). Cited in Ihar Babkoŭ, "Pra narod," in *Vytlumachenne ruinaŭ,* 69.
70. For more on the concept of the "cartographic mandate," see Komska's introduction to this volume.
71. Timothy Snyder, "Integration and Disintegration: Europe, Ukraine, and the World," *Slavic Review* 74, no. 4 (Winter 2015): 696.
72. It seems that the editorial board was itself composed with an eye to overcoming the geographical borders of Eastern Europe. In other words, the scholars on the board were themselves located in other cities, like Minsk, New York, Kyiv, Paris, Prague, and Sofia.
73. For more on *Kultura* in a global framework, see chapter 4 in this volume, "Rereading *Kultura* from a Distance," by Jessie Labov.
74. *Frahmenty* 5 (1998): 6.
75. There is also a whole issue of *Frahmenty* devoted to Mickiewicz. See *Frahmenty: Mickiewicz i Dekanstrukcyia,* nos. 1–2 (2001). This, however, should not be interpreted as an attempt to appropriate Mickiewicz or endow him with the identity of a Belarusian poet. The internationally renowned poet was born in Navahradak (territory of present-day Belarus), died in Paris, wrote in Polish, and considered himself to be a patriot of the Polish state (Polish-Lithuanian Commonwealth). Still, he founded his poetry on Lithuanian mythology and Belarusian traditions. Publishing him was one of the attempts of *Frahmenty*'s editorial board to overcome national, but also region-locked perspectives. The meaning

of the figure of Tadeusz Kościuszko is discussed by Kacandes in chapter 10 in this volume.
76. *Nasha Niva* exists now as a popular, well-curated, and well-visited website, www .nn.by, and a (less-popular) weekly publication that, as was recently announced, will be transformed into a monthly. It is one among very few non-state periodicals founded in the early 1990s that has been able to survive all the public-sphere limitations imposed in Belarus since 1995.
77. Babkoŭ, *Khvilinka,* 169–74.

WORKS CITED

Adamovich, Ales. *Vybranyia tvory.* Minsk: Knihazbor, 2012.
Akudovich, Valiantsin. *Kod adsutnastsi. Asnovy belaruskaj mentalnastsi.* Minsk: Lohvinaŭ, 2007.
———. *Miane niama: rozdumy na ruinach chalaveka.* Mensk: EŭroForum, 1998.
———. "Vialikaia zdrada." *Dzeyasloŭ* 10 (2004): 211–28.
Arkush, Ales. *Asklepki vialikaha maliunku.* Mensk: Lohvinaŭ, 2007.
Babkoŭ, Ihar. "Henealiohiia belaruskaj idei." *Arche* 3 (2005): 136–64.
———. *Khvilinka. Try Historyi.* Minsk: Lohvinaŭ, 2013.
———. *Vytlumachenne Ruinaŭ.* Minsk: Lohvinaŭ, 2005.
Bahdanovich, Maksim. *Poŭny zbor tvoraŭ* u 3 t. Vol. 3, *Publitsystyka.* Minsk: Navuka i technika, 1995.
Bekus, Nelly. "Nationalism and Socialism: Phase D in the Belarusian Nation-Building." In *Nationalities Papers* 38, no. 6 (November 2010): 829–46.
———. *The Struggle over Identity: The Official and the Alternative Belarusiannes.* Budapest and New York: CEU Press, 2010.
Bhabha, Homi. *The Location of Culture.* London and New York: Routledge, 1994.
Biadulia, Zmitrok. *Vybranyia Tvory.* Minsk: Knihazbor, 2006.
Bozóki, András, ed. *Intellectuals and Politics in Central Europe.* Budapest: CEU Press, 1999.
Bradatan, Costica, and Serguei Alex. Oushakine, eds. *In Marx's Shadow: Knowledge, Power, and Intellectuals in Eastern Europe and Russia.* New York: Lexington Books, 2010.
Burachok 1. N.p., [c. 1986].
Burachok 2. N.p., [c. 1987].
Donskis, Leonidas. *Loyalty, Dissent, and Betrayal: Modern Lithuania and East-Central European Moral Imagination.* Amsterdam and New York: Rodopi, 2005.
Dubavets, Siarhej, ed. *Tuteishyia. Tvorchasts siabroŭ tavarystva.* Minsk: Mastatskaia litaratura, 1989.
Hobzem, Hleb. "Listy z Niamechchyny." *Frahmenty* 11 (2006): 241–47.
Horvath, Robert, *The Legacy of Soviet Dissent: Dissidents, Democratization and Radical Nationalism in Russia.* London and New York: Routledge Curzon, 2005.

Kavalioŭ, Siarhej. "Preparavanne mifa: tavarystva 'Tuteishyia' ŭ liusterku krytyki." *Dzejasloŭ* 2 (2013): 307–20.
Kazakevich, Andrej. "Kulturny fon belaruskaj palityki." In *Najnoŭshaia historyia belaruskaha parlamentaryzmu*, edited by Valer Bulhakaŭ, 132–46. Minsk: Analitychny hrudok, 2005. Accessed 6, May 2016. http://kamunikat.org/download.php?item=3390-7.html&pubref=3390.
Kind-Kovács, Frederike, and Jessie Labov, eds. *Samizdat, Tamizdat, and Beyond: Transnational Media during and after Socialism*. New York and Oxford: Berghahn Books, 2013.
Kipel, Vitaŭt, and Zora Kipel. *Yanka Kupala i Yakub Kolas na Zachaddze: Bibliiahrafiia*. New York: Ross, 2004.
Kislitsyna, Hanna. "Novaia litaraturnaia situacyia." *Belaruski Kalehiium*. Accessed 12 February 2014. http://old.belcollegium.org/lekcyji/litaratura/kislicyna04.html.
Klimkovich, Maksim, and Miraslaŭ Shajbak. "Vita Brevis albo nahavitsy sviatoha Heorhiia." In *Litaratura* 2, 2–24. N.d. [1990].
Kupala, Yanka. *Moladzi*. Belastok: Berah, 1988.
———. "Tuteishyia." *Polymia* 9 (1988): 13–62.
Lindner, Rainer. *Historiker und Herrschaft. Nationsbildung und Geschichtspolitik in Weißrussland im 19. und 20. Jahrhundert*. Munich: R. Oldenbourg Verlag, 1999.
Liustra Dzion. N.p., n.d. [c. 1980]. Accessed 31 January 2016. http://vytoki.net/?docs=00005721.
Lushnycky, Andrej N., and Mykola Riabchuk, eds. *Ukraine on Its Meandering Path between East and West*. Bern: Peter Lang, 2009.
Marples, David Roger. *Belarus: A Denationalized Nation*. Amsterdam: Harwood Academic, 1999.
———. *Belarus from Soviet Rule to Nuclear Catastrophe*. Edmonton: University of Alberta Press, 1996.
———. *The Lukashenka Phenomenon: Elections, Propaganda, and the Foundations of Political Authority in Belarus*. Trondheim: Program on East European Cultures and Societies, 2007.
McMillin, Arnold. *Writing in a Cold Climate: Belarussian Literature from the 1970s to the Present Day*. London: Maney, 2010.
Miłosz, Czesław. *Native Realm: A Search for Self-Definition*. London: Sidgwick & Jackson, 1981.
"Nekotorye aktualnye voprosy ideologicheskoj raboty v sovremennykh usloviiakh (v poriadke orientirovaniia dlia sekretarej partijnykh komitetov)." N.p., 1988. Accessed 11 April 2016. http://vytoki.net/?docs=00017343.
Notsun, Malhazhata, and Andzhej Bzhezetski. *Zrabavany narod: razmovy z belaruskimi intelektualami*. Harodnia-Wroclaw: Haradzenskaia bibliiatėka, 2009.
Rudling, Per Anders. *The Rise and Fall of Belarusian Nationalism*. Pittsburgh: University of Pittsburgh Press, 2015.
Sachanka, Barys, ed. *Na sud historyi*. Minsk: Mastatskaia litaratura, 1994.
Said, Edward W. *Representations of the Intellectual*. 1993 Reith Lectures. New York: Vintage Books, 1994.

Snyder, Timothy. "Integration and Disintegration: Europe, Ukraine, and the World." *Slavic Review* 74, no. 4 (Winter 2015): 695–707. Accessed 16 May 2016. doi: 10.5612/slavicreview.74.4.695.

———. *The Reconstruction of Nations: Poland, Ukraine, Lithuania, Belarus 1569–1999.* New Haven and London: Yale University Press, 2003.

Todorova, Maria. *Imagining the Balkans.* Oxford and New York: Oxford University Press, 2009.

Ugrešić, Dubravka. "The New Eastern European Intellectual: 'A Culture of Lies.'" *Context* 18 (2005). Accessed 2 March 2016. www.dalkeyarchive.com/the-new-eastern-european-intellectual-a-culture-of-lies/.

Wilson, Andrew. *Belarus: The Last European Dictatorship.* New Haven and London: Yale University Press, 2011.

Wolff, Larry. *Inventing Eastern Europe: The Map of Civilization on the Mind of the Enlightenment.* Stanford, CA: Stanford University Press, 1994.

Chapter Four

Re-reading *Kultura* from a Distance

Jessie Labov

Most literary scholars are specialists in the small, the textual, the local, and the specific. The challenge of reading texts across borders and beyond contiguities is a dramatic shift in scale. In the following study of the Polish émigré journal *Kultura,* I would like to reflect carefully on what it means to work on different geographical and temporal scales: on the level of an individual writer, an individual editor, a series of publications over years or decades, individual readers who sometimes respond, and much larger numbers of readers who usually remain silent. The first impulse when scaling up might be to reach for theories of the global, and in particular those transnational flows of capital and information that seem to produce recognizable parameters in many different settings. However, what is most productive and unexpected about reading *Kultura* is that it is *not* simply global, that it is rather suspended between the regional ("Eastern Europe") and the global (Polish-language diaspora)[1] at a scale that we do not yet know exactly how to name. This is perhaps another way of expressing what Yuliya Komska labels "betweenness" in her introduction to this volume, but instead of being tied to a particular territorial zone like the borderlands, the émigré nature of *Kultura* allows us to focus on the consequences of mobility and diaspora. Instead of simply demonstrating discontiguity in space, these centrifugal movements over time show how little contiguity has to do with identity. The farther Poles travel temporally and spatially from "Eastern Europe," the more determined they are to perform their Polishness via *Kultura,* subverting the equivalence of blood and soil.

In her essay on "The Scale of World Literature," Nirvana Tanoukhi challenges us to make "cracks in the geography of 'world literature'" by focusing on scale and to "conceptualize the dialectic of lived time and lived space in and around literature—in order to understand the entanglement of literature in the history of the production of space."[2] While her objects of analysis are postcolonial literature and the literary landscape she calls "Africa-of-the-Novel," which is produced by those texts, her arguments apply just as cogently to the case of *Kultura*. Terms like "postcolonial" or "post-socialist" produce metaphoric spaces, but they mask the relational, embedded character of geographical spheres of experience. *Kultura* was not just an émigré journal that published essays and poems by isolated members of a diaspora. Over the course of its monthly publication from 1947 to 2000 it became a site of condensed experience—both a channel of communication between those in the homeland and those abroad and a conduit to an earlier era in Polish culture that no longer existed.

Chronology itself is subject to conditions when we adjust for scale. Historian Dina Mishkova works through different articulations of historical time (using Ferdinand Braudel) before she reaches her own position in her 2010 article on Balkan history and the concept of scale and historiography.[3] Most useful for our thought experiment on Eastern European contiguities is Mishkova's further development of Mark von Hagen's basic gesture, Eurasia as anti-paradigm.[4] In the case of Balkan historiography and Southeastern European studies more broadly, Mishkova argues, "Different objects (i.e., spaces) of enquiry are coextensive with different temporal layers each of which demand[s] a different methodological approach."[5] Following Jacques Revel, she notices that different features of Southeastern Europe emerge depending on the scale of analysis and that the various formulations of national and regional/"meso-regional" scale were often motivated by embedded prejudices of each Balkanist charting his or her own "horizon of expectation."[6] Scaled up to the East European dimension, we see how moving beyond this unit of measure forces us to shift to other scales of analysis, keyed to particular historical moments. It brings into relief features that cannot be seen closer up (such as rivers that flow through formerly hostile territories). Simultaneously, it effaces boundaries and crystalizes, at a smaller scale, categories to which we have become attached (such as the formerly Soviet or the post-socialist). This brings us back to the question, how do we read at such a large scale? What are the techniques and methodologies that can help to disrupt those old forms of knowledge?

In this essay, I will use the case of *Kultura* to illustrate the formation of a new Polish cultural identity in emigration on two scales: first on the familiar, microscale of literary history, as I trace the evolution of *Kultura* via its most famous contributor, Witold Gombrowicz, and its chief editor, Jerzy Giedroyc; then on the quantitative, macroscale of GIS analysis, as I map the concentric circles of the journal's reception among readers and writers of Polish. The goal is to try to reread *Kultura*'s material traces of meaning via a wider geographical sphere of experience and a broader temporal window rather than the more traditional context of the Cold War. Furthermore, as a byproduct of this cartographic exercise, I will simultaneously "unmap" the East Europeanness of the journal and its reception and work against the logic of geo-coding that ties place to space. The readers of *Kultura* construct their own sphere of belonging, which extends before (and after) the People's Republic of Poland and far beyond its borders.

KULTURA ON THE SCALE OF GOMBROWICZ

It is hard to overstate the importance of *Kultura* in postwar Polish culture: every major writer, essayist, journalist, and poet who lived in emigration during this period aspired to publish in its pages. After the mid-1950s, it became known to readers in Poland as well and included many writers from socialist-era Poland who published anonymously or pseudonymously at first, then more openly as censorship eased. During the martial law crisis of the early 1980s, *Kultura* took on an even greater importance, as it was the chief *tamizdat* (émigré publishing) venue for free expression for Polish-language writers. A scholar of Polish or Central European literature on the North American continent is most likely to first encounter *Kultura* through reading Witold Gombrowicz and Czesław Miłosz (e.g., Gombrowicz's *Diary* was originally published in *Kultura,* in installments beginning in 1957). But *Kultura* was not just the vehicle of transmission for Gombrowicz's work; it was also in part its subject. Scanning the first year of his *Diary*, one sees that more than a third of the entries begin with references to *Kultura, Wiadomości, Orzeł Biały,* and other émigré journals: "Thursday. Lechoń's article entitled 'Polish Literature and Literature in Poland' in *Wiadomości*"; "Saturday. From B. T.'s article in *W*"; "Tuesday. Another review, this time in *Orzeł Biały*."[7] This conversation across pages is emblematic of the émigré journal's privileged genres of essay, feuilleton, and *publicystyka*: they are meant to serve as a starting point for discussion. Every so often, Gombrowicz records a self-consciously mundane detail of life ("Monday. I ate a tasty fish")[8] in the midst of his more arcane polemics about literature or philosophy. The references to articles in émigré journals can be seen in a similar light, in that they ground the reader in the writer's unmistakable (and inescapable) physicality. Gombrowicz has to eat, he has to drink; he buys shoes, he holds a piece of paper in his hand that links him to an ever-widening diaspora. In the context of *Diary*, these pieces of paper link Gombrowicz's daily life in Argentina with his diaspora polemics, his physical reality with his mental chain of associations—and this is not such a straightforward process for the creator of metaphysical puzzles such as Philifor and Philimor.

Back in Poland between the two world wars, Gombrowicz frequented cultural institutions such as the Café Ziemiańska or Café Zodiak, similar to other cafés across turn-of-the-century Europe that fostered circles of artists and writers in a more public and fluid instance of patron-based salon culture. The writer's daily encounters with peers and rivals in the same physical space led him to publish in the proliferation of literary journals, each with its own agenda and politics, as was characteristic in the interwar era.[9] Yet in the postwar emigration, there were no longer cafés that could serve as a central gathering place. Journals—dailies, weeklies, monthlies, quarterlies, even yearbooks—took the place of the communal *kawiarnia* in émigré communities. The physical trail left in émigré journals, printings and reprintings of letters, ripostes, lectures, and responses—that is how we, too, experience the transcontinental discussion that took place just after World War II, separated now by time as well as distance. If we were to read the texts of émigré writers without embedding them in this context, they might appear to have been written in isolation, an impression enhanced at times by émigré writers' own fascination with the condition they call "exile." I will argue here against exile and isolation as the fundamental paradigm by which diaspora writing should be understood.[10] Without dismissing the psychological trauma induced by leaving one's homeland and language, it should still be possible to foreground the intricate virtual network of writers and readers that extended Polish culture far beyond its borders throughout the Cold War.

THE *LONGUE DURÉE* OF *KULTURA*: THE PUBLISHING ODYSSEY OF JERZY GIEDROYC

The postwar émigré publishing world was dominated by two men who began their careers in the interwar years in Warsaw: Jerzy Giedroyc (1906–2000) and Mieczysław Grydzewski (1894–1970). This story begins, therefore, between the wars, because the shape of Polish culture in emigration was determined as much by the cultural milieu that these men came from as by conditions abroad. By the end of the brief interwar period of Polish independence in 1939, Giedroyc and Grydzewski had become anchors of their respective milieus: Grydzewski as editor of the literary monthly *Skamander* and the weekly *Wiadomości Literackie* (Literary News), Giedroyc as editor of the political journals *Bunt Młodych* (Youth Rebellion) and *Polityka*. In what follows, I interpret the editor as part participant, part observer, and part invisible dictator and claim an influence often overlooked in literary or political histories. In Miłosz's 1969 *History of Polish Literature,* neither Grydzewski nor Giedroyc are mentioned in reference to interwar literature, even though Miłosz knew both and was published in their journals. The presence of these editors is perhaps more detectable in the titles of such studies as *Kultura i jej krąg* (Culture and Its Circle); *Wiadomości i ich krąg* (Wiadomości and Its Circle); *Wiadomości i okolice* (Wiadomości and Its Environs); *Styl politycznego myślenia wokół "Buntu Młodych" i "Polityki"* (The Style of Political Thinking around *Bunt Młodych* and *Polityka*). There is a sphere of influence that emanates from these publications, a circle of writers, friends, and intellectuals. And it is the editor who draws people into this circle and who sometimes keeps others out.

Giedroyc's prewar career was more political than literary. He was born into a family of landed gentry from the *kresy* (or eastern borderlands, now part of Ukraine) and his coming-of-age coincided with Poland's new independence. In a resulting surge of patriotism, he enlisted at the age of fourteen as a communications clerk in the Russo-Polish War of 1920.[11] This experience made a strong impression on him; soon after he found his political and editorial voice as a law student at the University of Warsaw and joined the executive committee of a small neoconservative party, the Myśl Mocarstwowa (Thought and World Power).[12] In the early 1930s, he divided his time between the journal *Bunt Młodych–niezależny organ młodej inteligencji* (Youth Rebellion–Independent Organ of the Young Intelligentsia) and his job as a civil servant. He moved around within the government bureaucracy, beginning in the Ministry of Agriculture, then, after falling out of favor with the director, moving to the Ministry of Industry and Trade.

The worlds of politics and *publicystyka* were closely related for Giedroyc. An issue that concerned him, such as Polish relations with Ukrainian nationalists in eastern Galicia, would appear first on his agenda as an administrator and then as a feuilleton in the pages of his journal. Out of this interest in things Eastern, he frequented a circle of Russian émigrés living in Warsaw, where he met Dmitri Filosov and Josef Czapski.[13] In 1937, Giedroyc's biweekly *Bunt Młodych* became *Polityka*,[14] and its polemic with the Socialist and National Democratic Parties increased in volume. In 1938, the group around *Polityka* published a collective work, *Polska idea imperialna* (The Polish Imperial Idea), which described the current state of false party demagoguery and misguided economic strategies, a program to overcome Polish-Ukrainian antagonisms, and a contentious solution to "the Jewish question" in the form of a mass emigration to Palestine. The driving force behind most of these arguments (however misguided some of them might be in hindsight) was the right to self-rule; because of this, Marcin Król argues, we should understand that the context for the term *mocarstwowość* (imperialness) was different from the way we would use it today:

> For now, let's just say that the postulate "mocarstwowość" meant only the following assumption: the creation of a strong state is the only way to protect the Polish right to existence between two great powers. "Imperialism," this was no stirring dream about colonies, nor any kind of imperialism as we understand it today, but the expression of a conviction and not a totally naive one, that in order to preserve its independence, Poland must be "an imperium"—that is, a large, strong state.[15]

From the first issue of *Bunt Młodych*, Giedroyc instituted an ongoing polemic with *Wiadomości Literackie*; as strange as it may seem, Giedroyc's political journal virtually defined itself in opposition to Grydzewski's literary one. In his recent biography of Giedroyc, Andrzej Kowalczyk suggests that this largely unilateral attack was due in some part to a generational difference and that the young writers of *Bunt Młodych* (most of whom ascribed to the Myśl Mocarstwowa as well) perceived the "liberalism, pacifism, eclecticism, and leftist sympathy" of Grydzewski's journal as symptomatic of the "weak spirit and disorientation of the older generation."[16]

At the start of World War II, Giedroyc found himself in Budapest as the personal secretary to the Polish ambassador, where he was able to receive several Polish journals that continued publication during the war, including Grydzewski's *Wiadomości Polskie*.[17] Over the next three to five years, Giedroyc traveled around the Near and Middle East, where he met several of his future colleagues at *Kultura*, including Zofia and Zygmunt Hertz and Juliusz Mieroszewski. He worked on the military newsletter *Orzeł Biały* with Józef Czapski and became the head press officer of General Anders's army. In his capacity as minister of intelligence of the Polish government-in-exile, Adam Pragier was responsible for bringing Giedroyc to London late in 1944, to direct the Department on Continental Affairs. While in London, Giedroyc was able to convince the government-in-exile of the value of establishing his Instytut Literacki but was unable to secure funding for it. This is where the idea of a privately funded, independent press took root. Giedroyc was sent back to Rome in late 1945 with a "mandate" to found an institute in the name of the Polish government and even received an official order from General Anders to carry out this task. Financial support then followed in the form of private donations from the soldiers and officers of Anders's Second Corps. The rest of the funding for the first year of the institute's existence came in the form of postwar *kombinacja* (a Polish term for circumventing official channels in order to gain access to resources).[18] At the close of the war,

Giedroyc ended up in Rome, where together with Czapski, the Hertzes, and Gustaw Herling-Grudziński he established the Instytut Literacki and eventually began to publish *Kultura*. A few years later the whole operation moved to a villa on the outskirts of Paris, in the township of Maisons-Laffitte.

The achievement of the first issue of *Kultura* was its unusual claim to independence, with almost entirely private funding and an initial statelessness. As a new publication, it began with a preface about the current crisis in European civilization (in this case, "European" is meant to encompass both Western Europe and Poland, although it is not clear how far this boundary extends to the east). Within the text of the essay, Poland is not even directly mentioned.[19] Instead, we find statements by Paul Valéry (in 1919), Benedetto Croce, and André Malraux (in 1946) about the state of Europe after two world wars. At the end of the two-page preface, the goals of *Kultura* are clearly set out, including its intentions toward its divided audience of Polish readers:

> *Kultura* wants to bring home to the Polish readers, who, having chosen political emigration, find themselves beyond the borders of their native country, that the cultural circle in which they live is not an extinct one.
>
> *Kultura* wants to reach the readers in Poland and strengthen their belief that the values that are dear to them have not yet collapsed under the outbreak of brute force.
>
> *Kultura* wants to seek in the civilized Western world this "will to live, without which the European will die out like the leaders of so many layers of ancient empires before us."[20]

Instead of taking on the task of self-consciously presenting Polish culture to the West, Giedroyc and his colleagues decided that *Kultura* would be a working part of European culture as a whole, that it could offer some answers not found in Italy, France, or England to the new challenges of the postwar period. Both this mission statement and the above list of goals show traces of prewar Giedroyc, except that the critical strength of the Polish "imperium" now applies to Western values pitted against those dominant in the East.

It is worth noting that Giedroyc entered the world stage from the cultural landscape of independent Poland, and his drive to publish as a means of self-determination and self-definition grew directly out of that world. What happens to that drive to publish in emigration? Because of the logistics of the war, neither Giedroyc nor the other residents of Maisons-Laffitte experienced a sudden separation from their native language, audience, direct circles of friends, or, even more importantly, institutions that could offer support to their publishing enterprises. In this way, their situation did set the pattern for the following generations of Central European émigrés.

What stands out from Giedroyc's experience is the belief in periodical publication as a cohering force for an audience dispersed across borders and oceans. This belief predates interwar Poland and can be traced to the spiritual inheritance handed down from the nineteenth century by the editors of *Tygodnik Literacki* (Literary Weekly, which ran from 1838 to 1845 in Paris).[21]

It was in the first ten years of *Kultura*'s existence that Giedroyc developed the journal's complex political profile, both as a reaction to the more conservative, London-based *Wiadomości* (published by Grydzewski, Giedroyc's longtime antipode) and as a negotiation of the realpolitik demanded by the new postwar era in Western Europe, in the very early stages of the Cold War.[22] The first major issue to ignite tension between the two journals and their followers was a resolution passed in June of 1947 by Związek Pisarzy Polskich na Obczyźnie (the Association of Polish Writers Abroad, based in London and linked to *Wiadomości*), signed by forty writers, not to publish either old or new works in the press and publishing houses of Poland.[23] Many of the writers associated with *Kultura* did not agree with this resolution, and Herling-Grudziński in particular objected that this action would lead to a cultural ghetto in emigration.

This was the background against which the "Miłosz affair" was staged, which then defined *Kultura*'s political profile for much of the rest of the Cold War era. When Miłosz decided to break with Communism in January 1951, he began life in the West in Maisons-Laffitte and soon after published an essay in *Kultura*. It was during this period that he drafted *The Captive Mind*, a seminal text on the forces that drive writers to turn to Communism, as well as their subsequent disillusionment.[24] His confessional self-criticism was received with mistrust and accusations in *Wiadomości*, including a personal attack by Grydzewski; because of Miłosz's former position as a diplomat, he was labeled a "collaborator."[25] In subsequent issues of both journals, the debate continued, and Miłosz was defended by Juliusz Mieroszewski, Giedroyc, and other *Kultura* writers. During the thaw of October 1956, many prominent émigrés decided to return to Poland, and hopes were raised for cooperation with Władysław Gomułka's new government. The staff of *Kultura* was initially among those supporting Gomułka. In October of that year, the Association of Polish Writers in London convened and issued a statement reasserting their proclamation of 1947, insisting on their embargo on Polish presses despite the changes in government. In response, *Kultura* conducted a survey of well-known writers and intellectuals living in emigration and published thirty-three answers of various lengths and opinions in the December 1956 issue. The majority opposed the proclamation. Not long after, *Kultura* reversed its position on the Gomułka government, but still refused to participate in London's boycott of Polish publishing.[26]

Those events represent only a sample of the constant stream of editorials, feuilletons, and general polemic that characterized émigré publishing, but it gives a sense of the political chess game that went on during these two decades. When looking at a piece in *Kultura,* such as the December 1956 survey, one can see Giedroyc's refashioned liberalism—not necessarily in a political sense, but in the sense of inclusivity, of allowing a range of opinions to coexist in the journal, trusting the readers to navigate on their own. Both Kowalczyk and Supruniuk note the leftist influence that Czapski and the Hertzes had on Giedroyc's politics and on the politics of *Kultura*. From this point of view, the resulting political stance of *Kultura* could be seen as more of a synthesis of their views than a single-handed shift on the part of Giedroyc. Giedroyc was a politician first, one whose views were formed around Ukrainian cultural politics and in a circle of Russian émigrés; because of this he seems ideally suited to navigate the complex interaction between culture and politics in postwar emigration. *Kultura* developed as *Bunt Młodych* and *Polityka* did during the interwar period, in the negative space left by more traditional or conservative émigré publications. I would trace this relationship back to its original setting, in interwar Poland, where the history of individual periodicals or literary circles does not seem to explain the intensity and quality of overall cultural production. We should look at the interaction of these different circles, where an editor ran two very different publications, where writers published in several places at once, and the ideological and/or aesthetic territory between these journals overlapped, was contested, created polemics, and caused some publications to fail and new ones to emerge.

GETTING SOME DISTANCE FROM *KULTURA*

Giedroyc and the Hertzes, the regular editors of the journal, sometimes refer directly to their audience or answer letters directly, but these are just sporadic glimpses of the readership as a whole. Who was reading *Kultura* and why? How did the different political events and shifts in editorial policies affect that readership? These were the initial questions that motivated the quantitative study I carried out on the geographical reach of *Kultura* across several dimensions of the Polish diaspora. As a methodological experiment in digital/quantitative approaches to literary studies, it is meant to illustrate a side of the political-cultural journal that cannot be seen from the microscale presented above. Working with a small research team, I extracted information about when and where people contributed to *Kultura*. This included the authors published in the journal, along with basic metadata on the volume, year, and issue number. We then estimated where the authors were located when they wrote the piece in question.[27] We also recorded the date and location of letter writers to *Kultura*; the date, location, and amount of donations sent in by supporters of the journal; and, when available, the date and location of those whose contributions *Kultura* rejected. We then generated maps with the help of GIS specialists to illustrate the larger reach and impact of this journal.[28]

While mapping *Kultura* might at first glance look like a straightforward application of communication or social network theory to literary history, it is rather an intervention in the sphere of literary criticism itself. The study of cultural expressions such as journals with heterogeneous materials has been bound by either ideological frameworks—politicized or biographical readings—or strictly material literary histories—content analysis or anecdotes of production. Meanwhile, literary criticism practiced during the fifty years when *Kultura* was published has been largely associated with close readings of individual texts. Even the more socially or materially grounded analyses of the "cultural turn"—postcolonial theory, gender and ethnic studies—still rely on close reading as a fundamental mode of inquiry. More recently literary scholars of broader phenomena, such as Franco Moretti and Pascale Casanova, have turned to metrics that they have sometimes labeled "distant reading," an attempt to illuminate new aspects of literary form and culture by looking through a macro lens, including large-scale changes over space and time.[29] These loosely grouped practices of distant reading can be carried out through quantitative analysis, such as Moretti's, or via qualitative models borrowed from the social sciences, but then reconfigured with literary or cultural variables, following Casanova. The fundamental idea is that if we change our scope, patterns begin to emerge that challenge assumptions behind our gaze. That is why we are *re*-reading *Kultura* again from a distance.

THE AUTHORS OF *KULTURA*

The first set of maps that accompany this chapter show where the authors of *Kultura* were located at the time their texts were published in the journal. There were regular reports from cities important to the diaspora: London, Brussels, and Berlin. There are pockets of émigrés in some places further afield, like Buenos Aires, New York, and Toronto. Map 4.1, "*Kultura* authors by city," shows authors writing in the journal from 1947 to 1989. Map 4.2 provides a closer view of the continent of Europe for these same figures. Immediately evident from this quick reduction in scale is the fact that the majority of authors contributing to the journal during the Cold War were

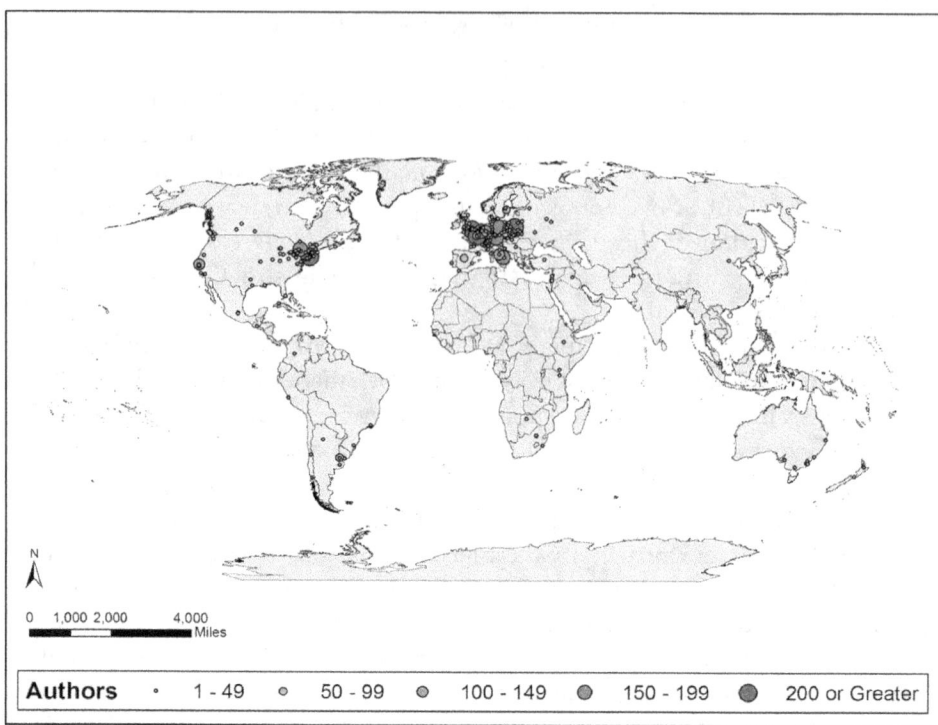

Map 4.1. Graduated symbol map of *Kultura* authors by city (1947–89). All maps in this chapter were produced by Jessie Labov and Taylor Beale for a project funded by Ohio State University, 2014.

living in either Europe or North America. After looking more closely at the map of Europe, we notice that the continent is not starkly divided between East and West: this is the first striking view of the movement of texts across the Iron Curtain.

In the following series of maps 4.3–5, these same authors contributing to *Kultura* are represented over different periods of time on the European continent. There are several compelling narratives to be drawn from these maps, some of which reflect the dialogue between *Kultura* and its homeland during different moments of tension and thaw during the Cold War. During the journal's first period, there are almost no contributors located in Poland, but after Giedroyc's new openness of the 1950s (when he began to reach out to authors publishing in Poland, even those whose texts appear officially), more begin to appear. As *samizdat/tamizdat* traffic picked up in the late 1960s and early 1970s, the number of contributors from Poland grows significantly, and the next map (1974–81) includes the period of Solidarity and open publishing from Poland. The last map (1982–89) is again counterintuitive: martial law (1981–83) did not stop the flow of texts from Poland to the West. In fact, the numbers of authors from Poland publishing in *Kultura* increases as samizdat and "second circulation" publishing reaches its peak in the mid-1980s.

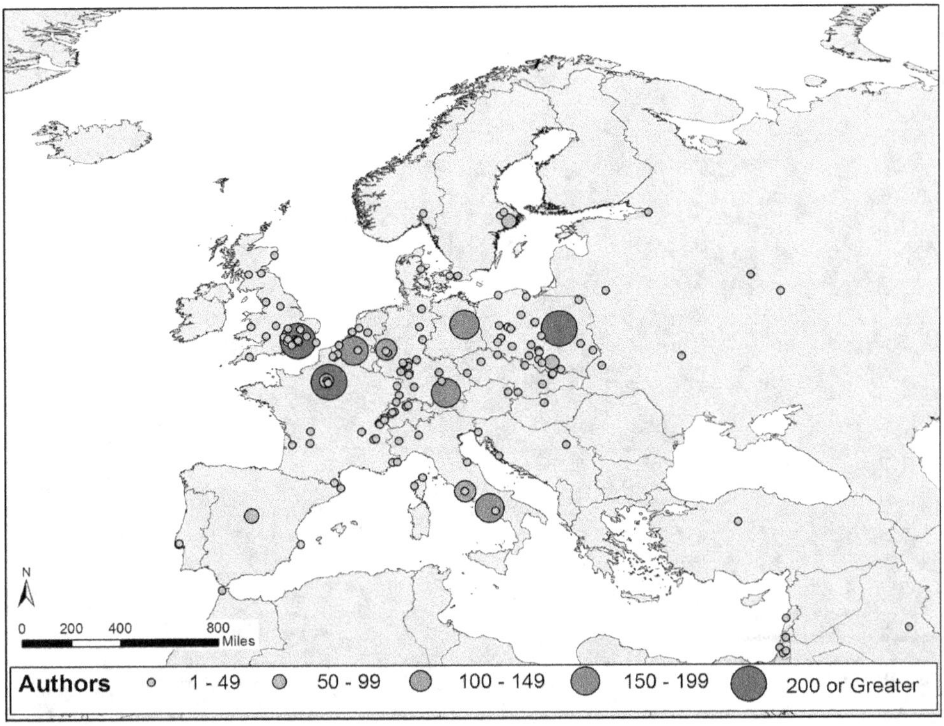

Map 4.2. Graduated symbol map of *Kultura* authors by city—Europe (1947–89).

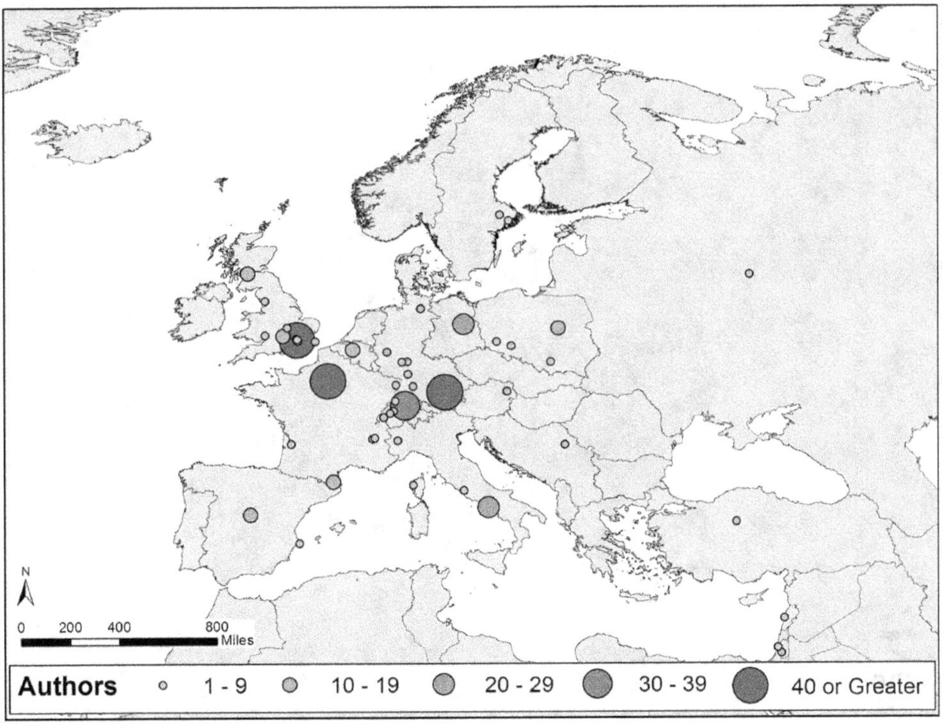

Map 4.3. Graduated symbol map of *Kultura* authors by city—Europe (1954–63).

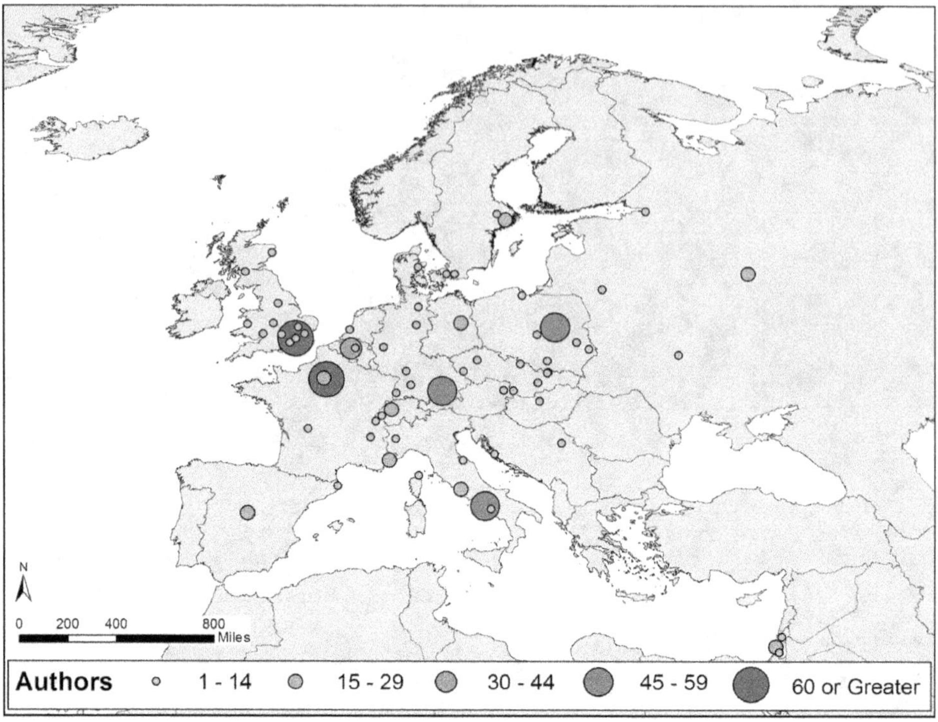

Map 4.4. Graduated symbol map of *Kultura* authors by city—Europe (1974–81).

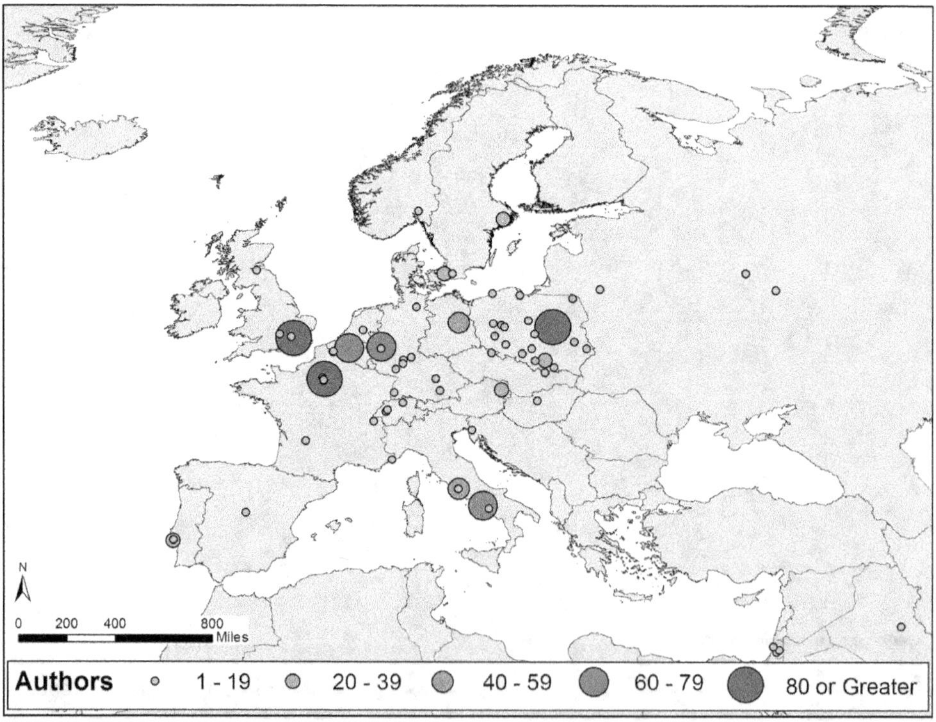

Map 4.5. Graduated symbol map of *Kultura* authors by city—Europe (1982–89).

Different stories can be read from these maps about the role of various European cities as points of transfer and resettlement for emigrants: apart from London and Paris, there is a great deal of variation in the number of contributing authors from cities like Stockholm, Naples, Munich, and Frankfurt. Here I will single out Munich as the seat of Radio Free Europe. Due to this circumstance, the city's role as home to *Kultura* authors is directly related to the wave of émigrés who left Poland in the wake of 1956. There is a threefold increase in the number of contributions from Munich between the first and second periods; the number steadily decreased over the remainder of the Cold War, as those who emigrated to Munich disseminated to points farther west. Maps 4.6 and 4.7 show the same authors in cartograms[30] by country, first in the period between 1947 and 1949 and then for

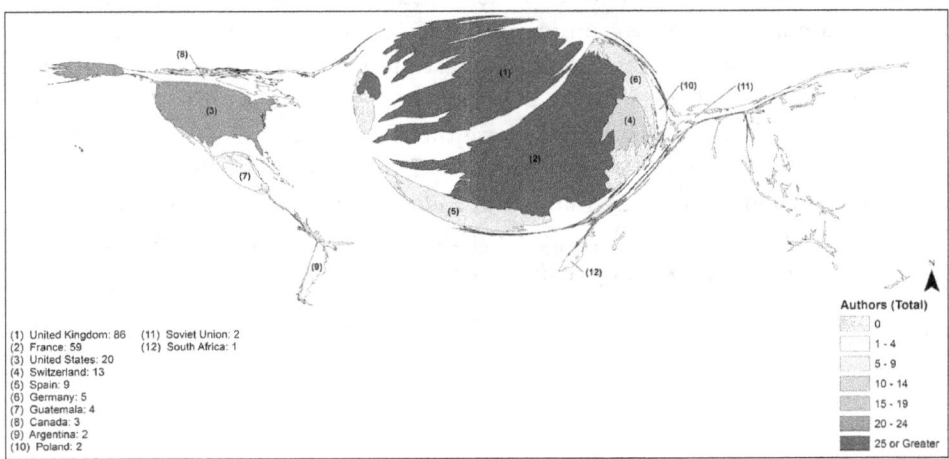

Map 4.6. Cartogram of *Kultura* authors by country (1947–49).

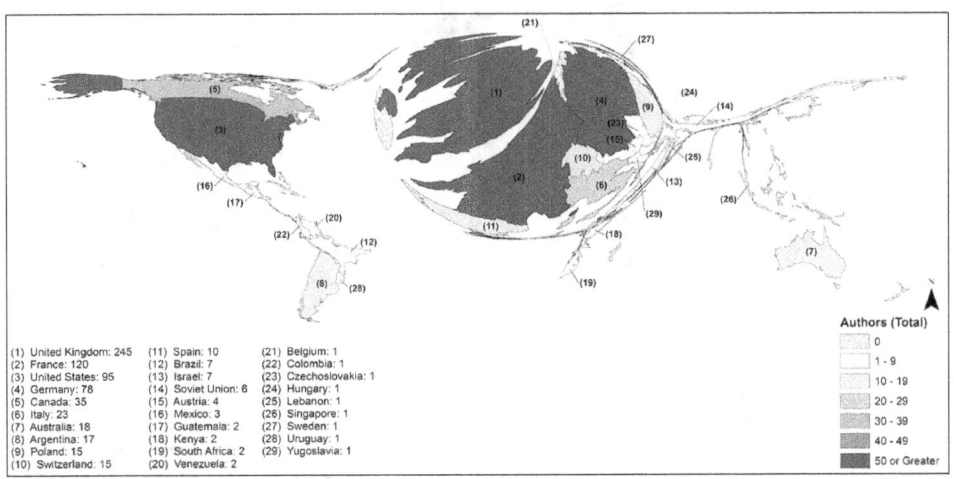

Map 4.7. Cartogram of *Kultura* authors by country (1960–64).

contrast that between 1960 and 1964. One of the most evident patterns to run through both sets of maps is the high number of authors coming from the United Kingdom and the increase in authors from the United States, Canada, and Poland (a trend which continues after 1968). This resonates with what we know about the dynamic between Giedroyc and Grydzewski, as well as the changing patterns of where different waves of Polish émigrés settled.[31]

THE LETTER WRITERS OF *KULTURA*

If the different constituencies of the journal can be represented as concentric circles of engagement, the next widest ring of engagement would include those who sent letters to the journal. Sometimes the letter writers were authors themselves, commenting on another piece or responding to a letter. Most typically, however, they illustrate which of the regular readers of *Kultura* felt that their voices belonged in the journal alongside those of the authors. Maps 4.8–10 show where the letter writers can be found, first in cities, then by country proportionally. The maps of letter writers by city reveal a broadening of the imprint of *Kultura*: whereas the authors become more concentrated in certain political and academic capital cities, the letter writers are moving in an opposite direction. As a result, we see more points

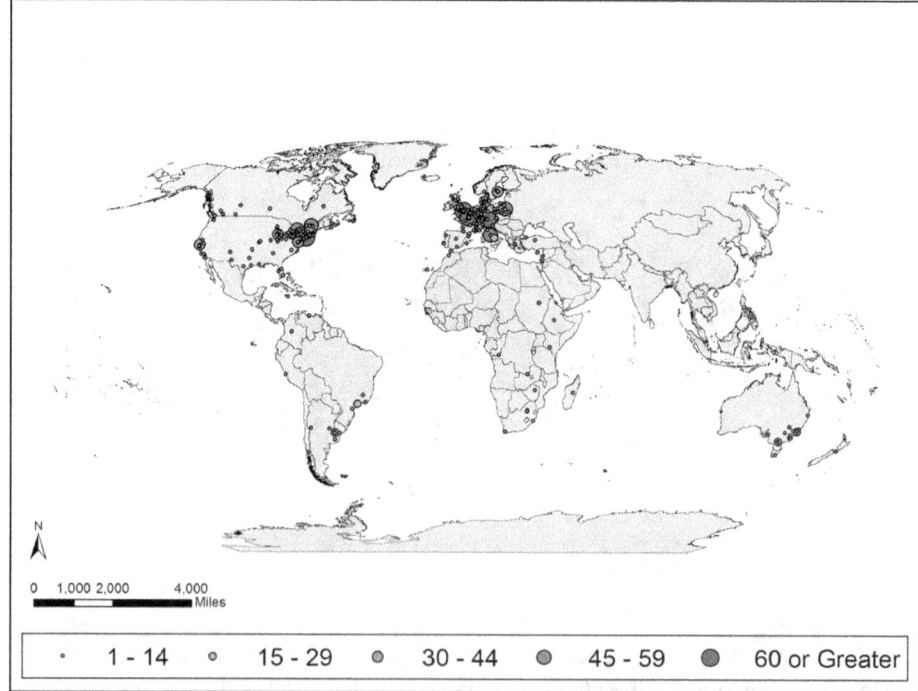

Map 4.8. Graduated symbol map of *Kultura* letter writers by city (1950–89).

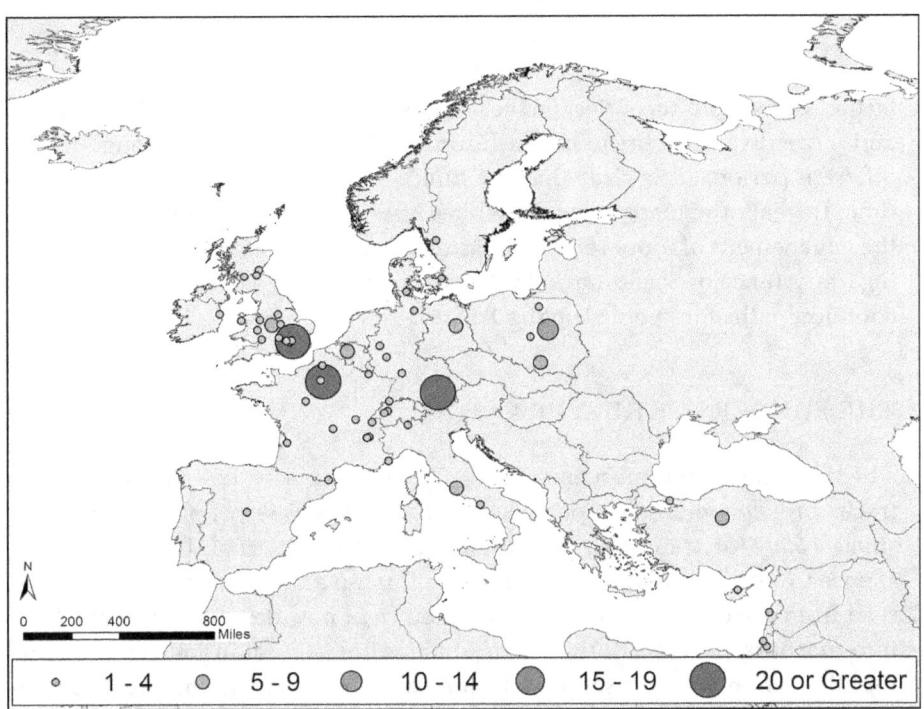

Map 4.9. Graduated symbol map of *Kultura* letter writers by city—Europe (1954–63).

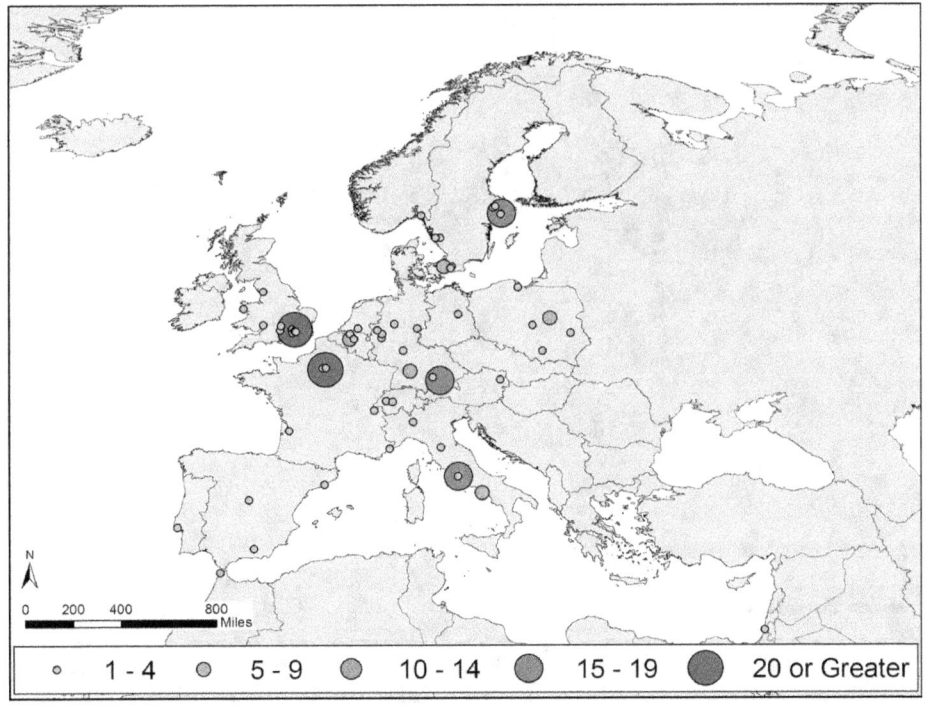

Map 4.10. Graduated symbol map of *Kultura* letter writers by city—Europe (1974–81).

farther away from the cities, farther across the United States and Australia, and more diversely spread out in Europe. With just a glance through these different periods, it is clear that the number of letters did not change over time. Instead, the maps show the circles of readership broadening to reflect the engagement of more remote émigrés. These maps also show the increasing importance of Scandinavia in the years after 1968, as that was one of the common paths for people leaving Poland.

THE FUNDERS OF KULTURA

The last, widest, and most compelling circle of diaspora Poles who left their tracks on *Kultura* are the journal's funders. These are people who sent in small *wpłaty* (or transfers), initially to support the journal, but later in response to world events. More so than authorship and letter writing, funding read from the distance gives us a new picture of how deeply *Kultura* reached into diaspora pockets. Rather than functioning as a salon journal only for the elite (a frequent accusation that came both from Communist Poland and from the more nationalist corners of the Polish and Russian diaspora), maps 4.11–14 show an active use of the journal as a medium of communication

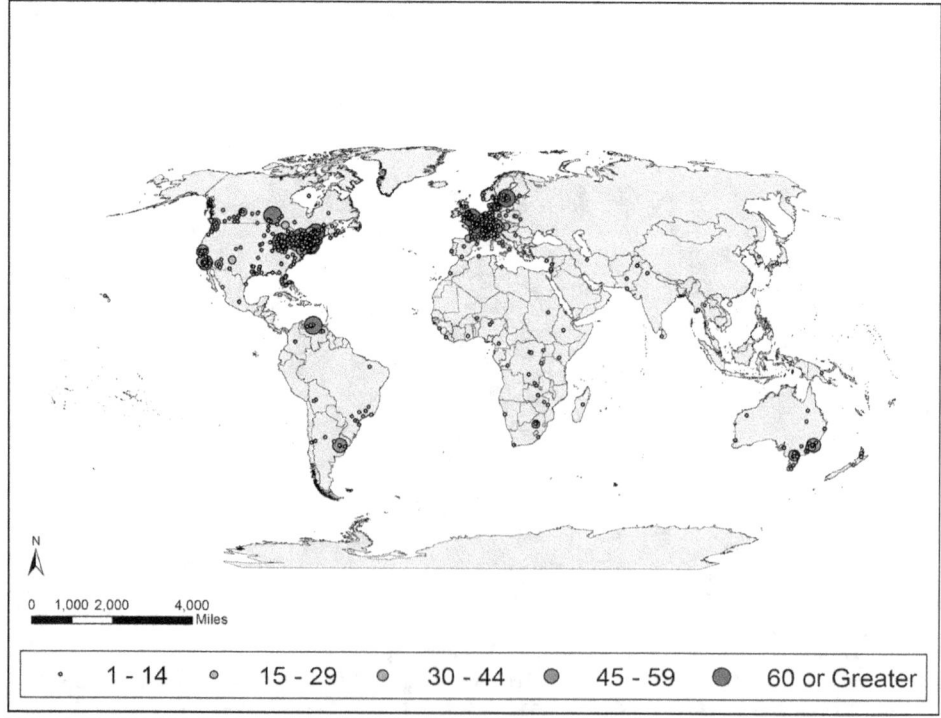

Map 4.11. Graduated symbol map of *Kultura* funders by city (1947–89).

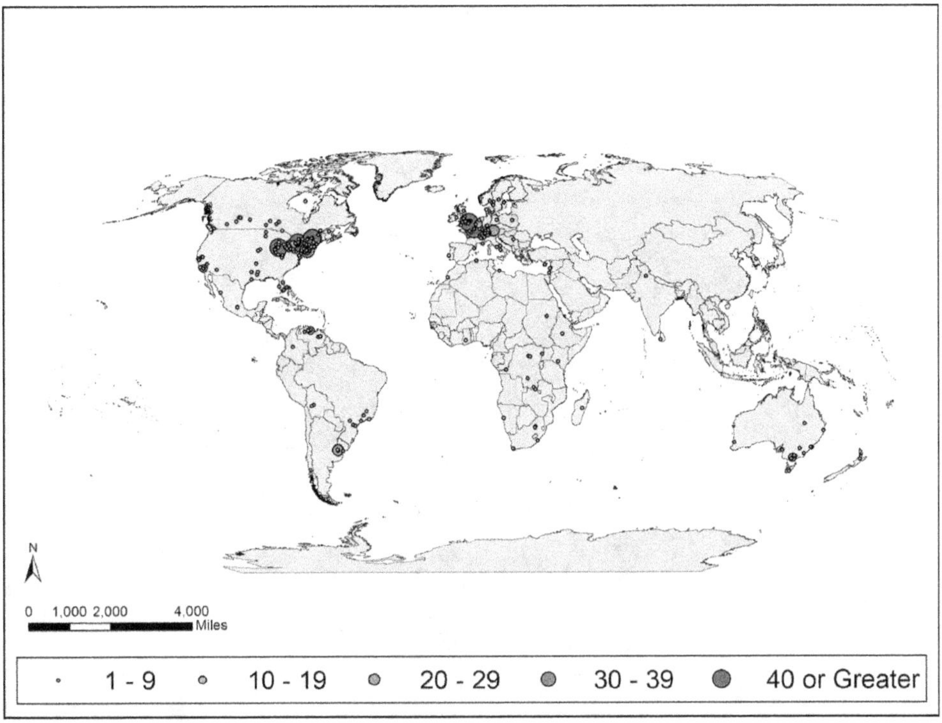

Map 4.12. Graduated symbol map of *Kultura* funders by city (1955–63).

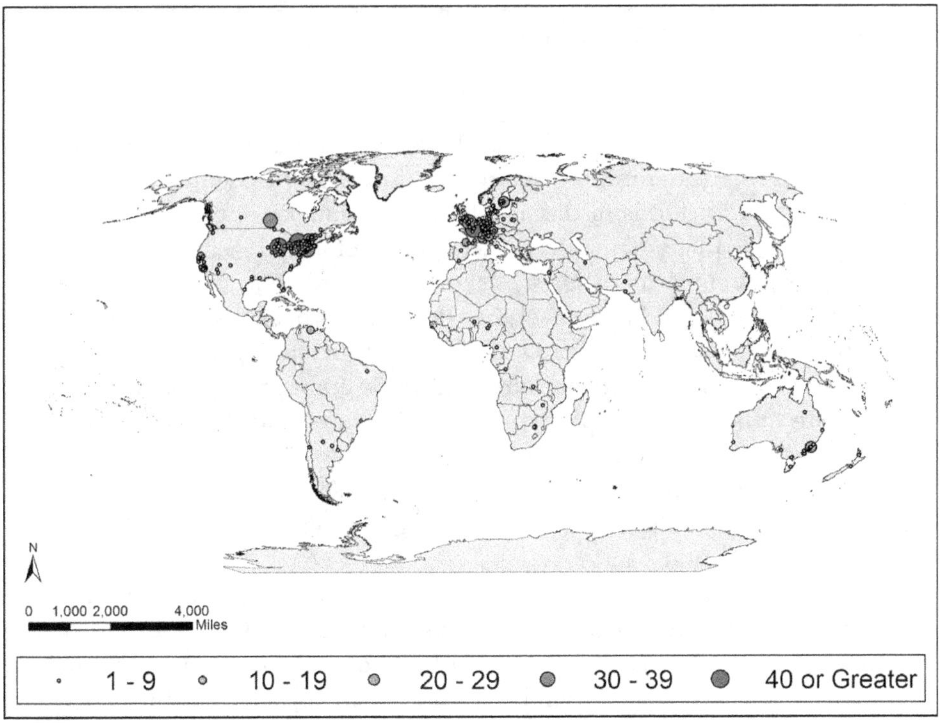

Map 4.13. Graduated symbol map of *Kultura* funders by city (1974–81).

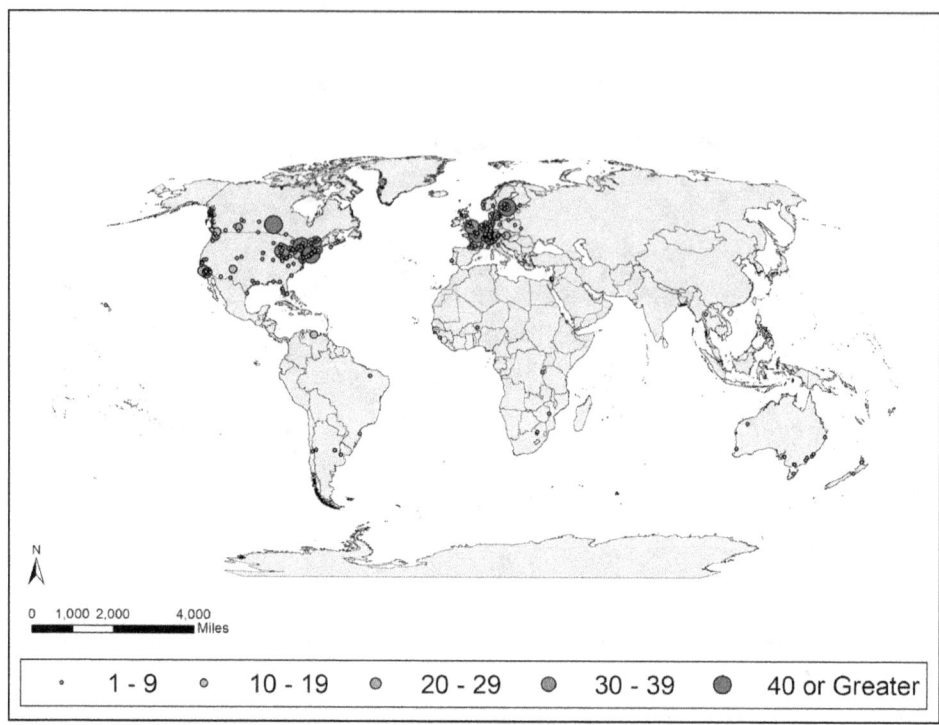

Map 4.14. Graduated symbol map of *Kultura* funders by city (1982–89).

and connection with the homeland.[32] If we look at the general trends starting in 1955 (there were no contributions sent in until Giedroyc made his famous appeal for funds in the mid-1950s), we can see noticeable patterns of response to different politically sensitive moments. Seeing the funders of the journal represented this way shows the third concentric ring of participation: those who did not feel that their voices belonged in the journal but still wanted to play a role in sustaining it. Of course, some authors and letter writers did send contributions in as well, but the maps make very clear that more individuals are participating as funders, and they are in different places. The funders are located deeper in the diaspora, in small ethnic pockets spread all the way across the North American continent, Western Europe, and Australia as well as in strategic locations in Latin America, Africa, and the Middle East.

From the cartograms (maps 4.15 and 4.16), it might look like more funders from the United States and Australia were able to donate larger sums of money. This is slightly misleading, for in fact the large amounts of money represented at certain points (for example, Australia in 1970) are

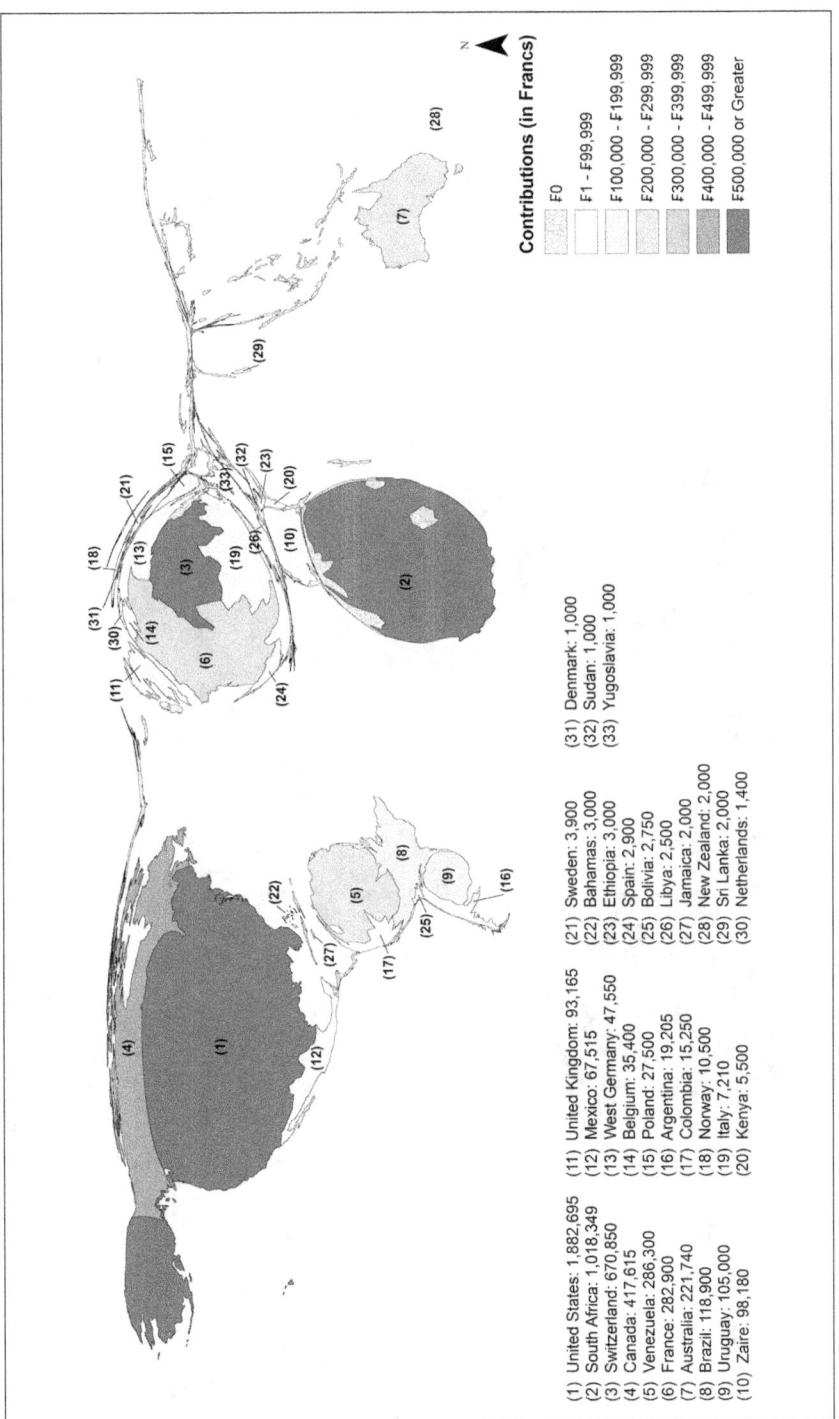

Map 4.15. Cartogram showing the proportional amount of funding by country (1955–63).

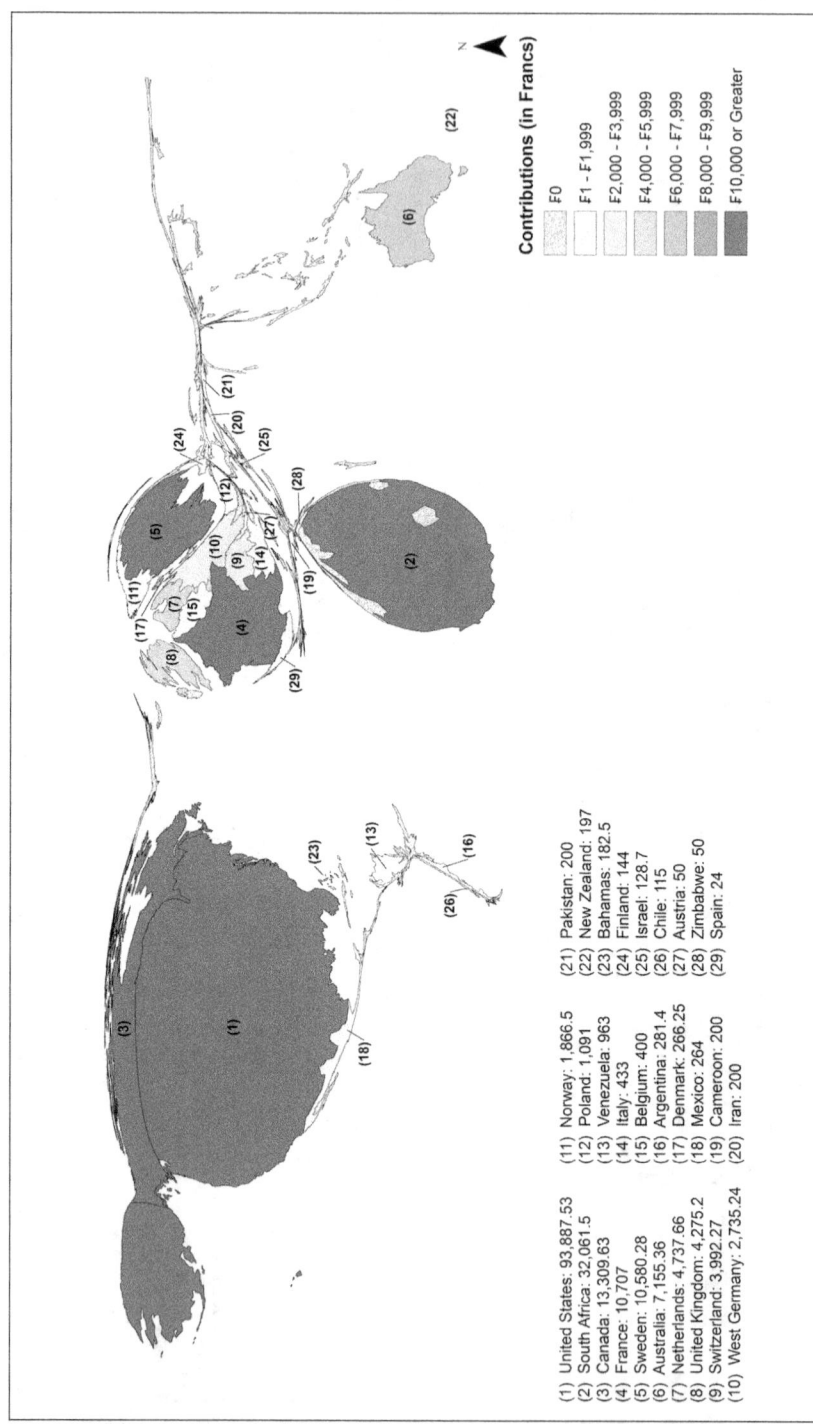

Map 4.16. Cartogram showing the proportional amount of funding by country (1974–81).

the result of one very wealthy donor sending extremely large sums on three consecutive occasions. So while the numbers of funders do steadily increase in response to particular political events, the vast majority of them are giving small amounts. I find this type of contribution more significant, in fact, than a wealthy donor giving a large amount of money. Some of the most touching "notes" specify exactly what the funds are to be used for. In the beginning, they were almost entirely for the *Kultura* foundation, that is, to sustain the journal. There are occasionally suggestions that the funders are sending donations to honor loved ones "*zamiast kwiatów*" (instead of flowers) or suggest personal greetings. But over the course of the 1970s, the notes start to acquire more political valence, culminating with funds earmarked for KOR (the Committee to Defend Workers, an early version of Solidarity), Solidarity, the independent press in Poland, "straight to the hands of Lech Wałęsa," and so forth.

The numbers of authors and letter writers from Poland grew over time, in synchronicity with Giedroyc's policies of keeping the door to the homeland open, while there were very few financial contributions from Poland itself. Yet for those in the furthest reaches of the diaspora, with the strongest connection to the home country, *Kultura* was entirely about that open door. They could get news of Poland and frozen memories of Polish culture from *Wiadomości*, but by sending a donation to *Kultura* they could actually come into virtual contact with Poland. The flowers and greetings that émigrés sent might be intended for fellow émigrés, but often other missives were for people back home. And over the course of the 1970s (1968 through martial law in 1982), donations soared in number, amount, and specificity, until there were hundreds listed in each issue.

TOWARD AN EXTRATERRITORIAL LITERATURE ON BOTH SCALES

In one sense, the outpost of the *Kultura* editorship could be read as an isolated minority group, free from the Polish postwar mandate to build and fortify a national literature. But was this really the case? Could Poles in emigration leave the nation-building literature to the so-called social realists in Warsaw? Because of the political constraints on aesthetic development in Poland, this function of the literary establishment was left to the emigration as well. As a result, readers looked to *Kultura* as a surrogate for all aspects of Polish culture, from the aesthetics of its poets to the ethics (or antipolitics) of its essayists. At times it reflected the religious conservatism of the diaspora alongside the revisionist Marxism of Gomułka's generation.

Reading *Kultura* from a distance demonstrates that the small crew at Maisons-Laffitte was not at all alone or isolated. The strongest corrective that this project offers to the wider understanding of the relationship between *Kultura* and its audience is that it defies the stereotype that *Kultura* was a journal only for intellectuals and political elites (seemingly evident when looking only at the authors who published it). The great majority of the diaspora is usually assumed to have more conservative, reactionary, and nationalist affinities, which is why small diaspora groups almost always publish a newsletter with that character. And although we could tell from the subscription records that small diaspora groups would order the journal, it was not at all clear until now what they did with those journals full of political ambiguity and compromises with individual writers from behind the Iron Curtain. After looking carefully at the intersecting rings of activity that emanate from this publication, we see that diaspora groups really did accept *Kultura* as a part of their émigré lifestyle and used it as a platform for the expression of their hopes and desires for the future—both in emigration and at home. In other words, while the territorial *discontiguity* of Polish diaspora life might have brought about a new imagining of the homeland, it remained anchored by *Kultura* in the Polish national present.

What have we gained by reading *Kultura* on a micro- and then a macro-scale? The very important layering of literary history and its variegated affective realities for the people who encounter literary artifacts. This is a quantitative view that is deeply grounded in the material, but which is also screened through the conceptual framework of biography. Giedroyc's shifts in editorial policy and his explicit communications to his readers allow us to anticipate when we might see changes on a large scale in the dataset. At the same time, there are clearly shifts in the use of *Kultura* as a medium for reaching the homeland—shifts that reflect new political realities beyond Maisons-Laffitte.

It is Warsaw as seen from New York via Paris. It is New York as seen from Stockholm via Paris.

It is Poland as seen from South Africa via France. It is Canada as seen from Poland via France.

It is North America as seen from Europe. It is Australia as seen from Europe.

It is not Eastern Europe, and it is not global; it is something in between.

Jessie Labov is resident fellow at the Center for Media, Data and Society at Central European University. Recent publishing projects include her co-edited volume *Samizdat, Tamizdat and Beyond* (Berghahn Books, 2013) and a forthcoming monograph entitled *Transatlantic Central Europe: Contesting Geography and Re-defining Culture Beyond the Nation* (Central European University Press, forthcoming 2018). In addition to writing on Polish film, Yugoslav popular culture, and Central European Jewish identity, she has also worked on a variety of digital humanities projects concerned with issues of canon formation.

NOTES

Parts of this chapter are based on chapter 3 in *Transatlantic Central Europe: Counting Geography and Redefining Culture Beyond the Nation,* to be published by Central European University Press.
1. This term denotes several generations of Polish-speaking migrants settled around the globe, both those in identifiable pockets of Polish émigré culture and those who have assimilated more thoroughly into the host culture. For a nuanced treatment of the Polish-language diaspora in the United States and UK, see Ewa Morawska, "'Diaspora' Diasporas' Representations of the Homelands: Exploring the Polymorphs," *Ethnic and Racial Studies* 34, no. 6 (June 2011): 1029–48. For a more general consideration of the relationship between migration and culture, see the introduction to Robin Cohen and Gunvor Jónsson, eds., *Migration and Culture* (Cheltenham, UK, and Northampton, MA: Edward Elgar, 2011).
2. Nirvana Tanoukhi, "The Scale of World Literature," *New Literary History* 39, no. 3 (2008): 600, 613.
3. Dina Mishkova, "What Is Balkan History? Spaces and Scales in the Tradition of Southeast-European Studies," *Southeastern Europe* 34 (2010): 55–86, 57–59.
4. In "Empires, Borderlands, Diaspora: Eurasia as Anti-Paradigm for Post-Soviet Era," von Hagen argues that the disciplines of comparative literature and anthropology have offered a much-needed critique of the European imperial project and that "Eurasia serves as a displacement—or a deflection—of the question of whether Russia belongs to Europe or Asia" (458). *The American Historical Review* 109, no. 2 (2004): 445–68.
5. Mishkova, "Balkan History," 60.
6. Mishkova, "Balkan History," 80–82.
7. Witold Gombrowicz, *Diary,* vol. 1, trans. Lillian Vallee (Evanston, IL: Northwestern University Press, 1988), 4, 9, 21.
8. Gombrowicz, *Diary,* 227.
9. Cafés were the spawning grounds for the very forms of the newspaper, the journal, and the periodical. See, for example, chapter 2 (on authorship) in Peter Stallybrass and Allon White, *The Poetics and Politics of Transgression* (Ithaca, NY: Cornell University Press, 1986). This is a more material and restrained claim

than similar arguments by Jürgen Habermas about the origins of the public sphere.

10. In this context, Robin Cohen's notion of a "deterritorialized diaspora," one that denotes "collective identities and homelands/homes as a fluid, vibrant and frequently changing set of cultural interactions" (124) might be useful. See chapter 7 of Robin Cohen, *Global Diasporas: An Introduction*, 2nd ed. (New York: Oxford University Press, 2008), 124–40.
11. Andrzej Kowalczyk, *Giedroyc i "Kultura"* (Wroclaw: Wydawnictwo Dolnośląskie, 1999), 8.
12. Marcin Król, *Styl politycznego myślenia wokol "Buntu Młodych" i "Polityka"* (Paris: Libella, 1979), 9–11.
13. For a detailed and well-illustrated portrait of Giedroyc at this age, see Kowalczyk, *Giedroyc*, chapter 1. Also see Timothy Snyder, *The Reconstruction of Nations: Poland, Lithuania, Ukraine, Belarus, 1599–1999* (New Haven, CT: Yale University Press, 2003), 218–20.
14. Król, *Styl politycznego myślenia*, 13.
15. "Teraz, powiedzmy tylko tyle, że postulat 'mocarstwowości' oznaczał jedynie założenie następujące: stworzenie silnego państwa jest jedynym sposobem ochrony racji istnienia Polski między dwiema wielkimi potęgami. 'Imperializm'–to nie było wzruszające marzenie o koloniach, ani jakikolwiek imperializm, tak jak go dzisiaj pojmujemy, ale wyraz przekonania–nie całkiem przecież naiwnego, że Polska, jeśli ma zachować niepodległość, musi być 'imperium,' czyli dużym, silnym państwem" (Król, *Styl politycznego myślenia*, 9–10). My translation.
16. Kowalczyk, *Giedroyc*, 44.
17. For a full description of Giedroyc's activities during the war, see Kowalczyk, *Giedroyc*, chapter 2, and Mirosław Adam Supruniuk, *"Kultura": Materiałow do dziejów Instytutu Literackiego w Paryżu* (Torun: Uniwersytet Mikolaja Kopernika, 1994), 1–15.
18. Kowalczyk, *Giedroyc*, 70–71.
19. It is interesting to note that while the linguistic idiom of *Kultura* is Polish, the journal is only indirectly linked to the formation of a Polish national identity, unlike the Belarusian writers of the Tuteishyia group described in chapter 3 of this volume.
20. *Kultura* 1, no. 1 (June 1947): ii. The last quote appears without a clear reference. When not otherwise noted, all translations from *Kultura* are mine.
21. The best source comparing the political and literary activities of the nineteenth-century Polish emigration to more recent ones is no doubt Andrzej Friszke, Paweł Machcewicz, and Rafał Habelski, *Druga wielka emigracja 1945–1990* (Warsaw: Więź, 1999).
22. For a more detailed and nuanced description of the political life of *Kultura*, see Konstanty Jeleński's introduction to Robert Kostrzewa, *Between East and West: Writings from* Kultura (New York: Hill and Wang, 1990). Among the interesting details that he relates are stories behind *Kultura*'s funding, its profound inter-

generational dialogue, its enthusiasm for Gomułka in 1956, and its "constant efforts to distinguish between Russia and the U.S.S.R" (18).
23. Tadeusz Radzik, *Z dziejów spółeczności polskiej w Wielkiej Brytanii po drugiej wojnie światowej (1945–1990)* (Lublin: Wydawnictwo Uniwersytetu Marii Curii-Skodowskiej, 1991), 68.
24. Czesław Miłosz, *Zniewolony umysł* (Paris: Instytut Literacki, 1953).
25. Kowalczyk, *Giedroyc,* 179–80.
26. T. Radzik, *Z dziejów spółeczności polskiej,* 68–69.
27. This was a research task carried out over several years and with input from many different research assistants and secondary sources. It was often difficult to determine exactly where a given author was in the postwar years, due to spontaneous travel and emigration, unreliable information provided by contemporary encyclopedias of emigration, and the common use of pseudonyms in the journal. The most intensive work was done by Rebecca Dulemba, Patricija Pawłowska, Ewa Zegler-Poleska, and myself; our database of *Kultura* metadata will be available online in an open-access format, and we will encourage modifications from the scholarly community in order to continue to improve the accuracy of the dataset.
28. In particular, Adam Pruss and Taylor Beale provided the knowledge and expertise to carry out this task.
29. See, for example, Franco Moretti, *Graphs, Maps, Trees* (London: Verso, 2007); Pascale Casanova, *The World Republic of Letters* (Cambridge, MA: Harvard University Press, 2004); N. Katherine Hayles, "Combining Close and Distant Reading: Jonathan Safran Foer's *Tree of Codes* and the Aesthetic of Bookishness," *PMLA* 128, no. 1 (2013): 226–31.
30. A cartogram illustrates the relative weight of each country's contribution by distorting the size of the country to represent its relative proportion of the total contributions.
31. See Kazimierz Dopierała, *Encyklopedia emigracji polskiej i Polonii* (Toruń: Oficya Wydawnicza Kuharski, 2003).
32. When viewing the two sets of maps above, there are a few very important variables to keep in mind: (a) the initial city-based maps are measuring number of contributions, while the second, country-based cartograms are measuring total contributions of each country in francs; (b) these amounts in francs are adjusted for inflation in France but do not take into account fluctuations in the exchange rate between countries. Therefore, some countries' contributions might seem higher than those of others because of weaker and stronger currencies.

WORKS CITED

Casanova, Pascale. *The World Republic of Letters.* Cambridge, MA: Harvard University Press, 2004.

Cohen, Robin. *Global Diasporas: An Introduction*. 2nd ed. New York: Oxford University Press, 2008.
Cohen, Robin, and Gunvor Jónsson, eds. *Migration and Culture*. Cheltenham, UK, and Northampton, MA: Edward Elgar, 2011.
Dopierała, Kazimierz. *Encyklopedia emigracji polskiej i Polonii*. Toruń: Oficya Wydawnicza Kuharski, 2003.
Friszke, Andrzej, Paweł Machcewicz, and Rafał Habelski, *Druga wielka emigracja 1945–1990*. Warsaw: Więź, 1999.
Gombrowicz, Witold. *Diary*. Vol. 1. Translated by Lillian Vallee. Evanston, IL: Northwestern University Press, 1988.
Hayles, N. Katherine. "Combining Close and Distant Reading: Jonathan Safran Foer's *Tree of Codes* and the Aesthetic of Bookishness." *PMLA* 128, no. 1 (2013): 226–31.
Kostrzewa, Robert. *Between East and West: Writings from Kultura*. New York: Hill and Wang, 1990.
Kowalczyk, Andrzej. *Giedroyc i "Kultura."* Wroclaw: Wydawnictwo Dolnośląskie, 1999.
Król, Marcin. *Styl politycznego myślenia wokoł "Buntu Młodych" i "Polityka."* Paris: Libella, 1979.
Miłosz, Czesław. *Zniewolony umysł*. Paris: Instytut Literacki, 1953.
Mishkova, Dina. "What Is Balkan History? Spaces and Scales in the Tradition of Southeast-European Studies." *Southeastern Europe* 34 (2010): 55–86.
Morawska, Ewa. "'Diaspora' Diasporas' Representations of the Homelands: Exploring the Polymorphs." *Ethnic and Racial Studies* 34, no. 6 (June 2011): 1029–48.
Moretti, Franco. *Graphs, Maps, Trees*. London: Verso, 2007.
Radzik, Tadeusz. *Z dziejów spółeczności polskiej w Wielkiej Brytanii po drugiej wojnie światowej (1945-1990)*. Lublin: Wydawnictwo Uniwersytetu Marii Curii-Skodowskiej, 1991.
Snyder, Timothy. *The Reconstruction of Nations: Poland, Lithuania, Ukraine, Belarus, 1599–1999*. New Haven, CT: Yale University Press, 2003.
Stallybrass, Peter, and Allon White. *The Poetics and Politics of Transgression*. Ithaca, NY: Cornell University Press, 1986.
Supruniuk, Mirosław Adam. *"Kultura": Materiałow do dziejów Instytutu Literackiego w Paryżu*. Torun: Uniwersytet Mikolaja Kopernika, 1994.
Tanoukhi, Nirvana. "The Scale of World Literature." *New Literary History* 39, no. 3 (2008): 599–617.

Part III

*Fictional Cartographies
and Temporalities*

While the region of the world to which this volume devotes itself has been repeatedly defined by those from "without," in this section, the authors take two very different lenses to explore the senses of place and of history by various "insiders." Despite the differences among them, the critiques offered by those insiders involve often dizzying manipulations of geography and chronology that explode some dearly held truisms, be they the lack of historical agency of the small nations in Central Europe or of the deep hatred and misunderstandings between peoples of the Balkans. No new re-vision reigns.

Daniel Pratt considers the framework for understanding time in Central Europe, as proposed by Josef Kroutvor in his 1986 article "Střední Evropa: Torzo omílené historií" (Central Europe: The Torso Eroded by History), published in the dissident journal *Svědectví* under the pseudonym Josef K. According to Kroutvor, Central Europe does not have a History with a capital *H,* or an overarching narrative of progress engendered by a combination of social and institutional will, due to the violent incursions of other nations on its development. Instead, the anecdote, the distinctly social, non-objective, nonlinear, nonprogressive form of storytelling must take its place. Pratt then tries reading two works of Bohumil Hrabal—*Ostře sledované vlaky* (*Closely Watched Trains,* 1965) and *Obsluhoval jsem anglického krále* (*I Served the King of England,* 1971)—as emblematic of Kroutvor's theory of anecdote and history, only to discover that Hrabal's protagonists cannot be exonerated by their geographical, social, and political situations, as Kroutvor's theories would imply.

Focusing on the imaginaries of Balkan capitals and towns in the work of Miroslav Penkov and Aleksandar Hemon, Ioana Luca examines the way post-Communist spaces are rendered to global audiences. In exploring new fictional images and histories, she foregrounds the significance of these post-socialist authors writing in the United States about the Balkans for American and world readers. The literary cartographies in these writers' work, Luca demonstrates, belie notions of betweenness and contiguity, offering, rather, geographical erasures and recalibrations, multiple imperial dominations, and political hegemonies. In Penkov's stories, for instance, anything west of Bulgaria is the West; and in Hemon's novels, Sarajevans envision their native city in constant dialogue with locations in present-day Ukraine, Romania, and the United States. Such moves go beyond nostalgia or Orientalizing topoi and lead to a transnational understanding of Eastern European spaces, so far poorly held together by older (Balkanist) or newer ("powder keg"–style) discourses.

Chapter Five

Troubles with History
The Anecdote, History, and the Petty Hero in Central Europe

Daniel Pratt

Set at the close of World War II, Bohumil Hrabal's *Closely Watched Trains* (*Ostře sledované vlaky*, 1965) begins with the young narrator, Miloš Hrma, approaching a recently downed plane. In a field near his small town, his neighbors have already begun dismantling the aircraft: "Within five minutes our townspeople had made a clean sweep of all the plates and sheet-metal from this wing, and the pieces reappeared the very next day as little roofs for rabbit-hutches and hen-houses."[1] As the narrator gets nearer to the scene, he finds that

> in every crystal of snow there seemed to be an infinitely tiny second hand ticking, the snow crackled so in the brilliant sunlight, shimmering in many colours. Then it seemed to me that I could hear these tiny hands ticking away not only in every crystal of snow, but somewhere else as well. There was the ticking of my watch, of course, I heard that quite distinctly, but I could hear another ticking, too, and this one came from the aeroplane, from this heap of wreckage in front of me. And there it was, the clock on the instrument panel, actually still going, and it even showed the exact time, I compared it with the hands of my watch.[2]

The gesture of matching time between Hrma's watch and the plane's chronometer reflects a momentary synchronization of the grand historical temporality of the war and the quotidian, circular temporality of village life, where metal parts become more useful as rabbit hutches than as cutting-edge technological material.

Although *Closely Watched Trains* is set during World War II, it is not about the war, with only a few scenes dealing explicitly with the (Nazi) Protectorate of Bohemia and Moravia. The bulk of the work describes ridiculous sexual escapades among Czech railroad workers, activities that make more sense in the context of gossip than in that of a moral panic, horrifying war atrocities, and human suffering on the grandest scale. Hrabal uses the war as a backdrop to the action of the novel, emphasizing the rift between the historical temporality of the war and the quotidian world of the village. The war seems to have little effect on the village world—other than the occasional gift of materials—despite the horrors occurring around it.

Closely Watched Trains ends with another moment of synchronization between the two temporalities of the quotidian and historical. Hrma overcomes his problems with premature ejaculation during a sexual encounter with a spy and then volunteers to bomb a Nazi train for her, ultimately being shot and killed in the process. Josef Škvorecký writes in the forward to the English translation that Hrma "commits an act of heroism that is more a consequence of sexual euphoria than premeditated patriotism."[3] Hrma is the product of the historical moment; he is angered at the Nazi invasion and subsequent killing of his grandfather at their hands. However, his choice to sabotage the Nazis at this very moment is not entirely the result of any grand feeling of patriotism, nor is it caused entirely by his "sexual euphoria," but rather by the momentary synchronization of the two realms of history, personal history and History with a capital *H*. If Hrma had not been given a bomb at just the right time, if the Nazis had not killed his grandfather, if he had not just had his first positive sexual encounter, then he would not have committed his act of petty heroism.

Hrma has become an example of the ubiquitous Czech trope of petty heroism, both through Hrabal's novel and through the more widely known Oscar-winning film adaptation by Jiří Menzel (1966). In Czech culture, an array of figures has performed small, even insignificant, acts of resistance against what are now considered illegitimate regimes. They have often done so as much for personal reasons as out of some grander ideological, philosophical, or religious conviction. Jaroslav Hašek's Švejk represents one of the most famous and earliest examples, as he resists deployment in the Great War not through any real act of resistance, but through an incongruous literary display of idiocy and brilliance. More recently, the film *Cozy Dens* (*Pelíšky*, 1999) contains a scene in which the ardent opponent of Communism Kraus shouts out of his window at the Communists, giggling to himself for his daring, despite no one paying any attention to his sudden outburst that emerges more from personal frustrations than ideological ones. The film is loosely based on a book by Petr Šabach, whose works contain further examples of the petty hero, such as the boys in *National Identity Card* (*Občanský průkaz,* 2006), who decide to rip out the thirteenth page of their identification booklet in protest of the thirteenth meeting of the Communist Party of Czechoslovakia, although only one dares to carry out the decision.[4] The boys' petty vandalism should be attributed more to teenage rebellion than to ideological antagonism. These acts of Czech petty heroes have little effect on any larger stage, but for the individuals in question, they engender feelings of grandeur.

According to Josef Kroutvor (1942–), the only theorist to scrutinize petty heroism in this context, the trope emerges from a disjunction between the temporalities of personal and historical events—in his terminology, between the anecdotal and the Historical—something he sees as a fundamental problem for the small nations of Central Europe. In an article first published in the dissident journal *Svědectví* in 1981 under the pseudonym Josef K and later collected with three other essays in *Troubles with History* (*Potíže s dějinami,* 1990), Kroutvor argues that Central Europeans do not actively participate in the march of History but rather limit themselves to everyday life: "history rolls across Central Europe, but it doesn't matter at all to a person from Prague or Budapest" who cares more about local concerns than the tide of History.[5] Like Hrma above, if a Central European has an effect upon the larger sweep of History, then he or she acts primarily out of personal concerns and not out of any sense of connection to History writ large. For Kroutvor, there is no connection to the larger process of Historical progress because the countries between Russia and Germany have lacked any real agency on the Historical stage, experiencing History more as victim than in a leading role.

In the introduction to this volume, Yuliya Komska cites Johann Gottfried Herder's claim that "the Slavic peoples occupy on Earth a greater space than [they do] in history."[6] The quote underlines a disjuncture between the geographical importance of Central and Eastern Europe and the role that its inhabitants have played in the larger historical narrative. Although the bulk of this volume focuses on discontiguities in space, this chapter examines discontiguities of time, that is, it concerns itself with Herder's contention about the marginal role of the Slavs and other Central and Eastern Europeans in history. Certainly since the age of Herder, Central and Eastern European nations, Russia in particular, have come to play a greater role. And yet, the Czechs in particular have seen themselves in only minor roles despite being "present" for much of the action. For instance, the Czechoslovak government did not participate in the 1938 Munich Accords, known in Czech as *Mnichovská zrada,* or the "Munich Betrayal." That their state could be dismembered without their involvement in the decision caused feelings of "powerlessness and humiliation."[7] Ten years later, the Communist government put an end to the multiparty parliament with the help of the Soviet Union, and then in 1968, the Warsaw Pact armies invaded Czechoslovakia, emphasizing that the Czechs' "destiny was not entirely in their own hands."[8] Due to this perceived (and, one could argue, objective) lack of agency over its course, History has become discontiguous, separated into discrete units not by the acts of Czechs themselves, but by outsiders who interrupt or inhibit a Czech role in History.

The Czechs are not alone in this perception of a lack of agency over the course of History. When the term "Central Europe" re-emerged in the 1980s, Milan Kundera, Czesław Miłosz, and György Konrád all focused on historical experience as the defining feature of Central Europe. Konrád saw History's intrusion into the lives of people as what connected them, all of whom "are sure to have, in an otherwise banal and normal life-history, some quite colorful personal anecdote in which they were heroes in spite of themselves, heroes in the Švejkian sense of Jaroslav Hašek's novel."[9] Kundera claims that History "judges us and arbitrates our fate" and that Central Europeans "represent the wrong side of this history; they are its victims and outsiders."[10] Miłosz claims that Central Europe is "hardly a geographical notion," but "the most striking feature in Central European literature is its awareness of history past and present."[11] History is what creates the space for Central Europe, demonstrating the overlap of the temporal and the spatial.

This concept of History, or rather this perceived lack of agency over History, can be understood in terms of Appadurai's ideoscape. Central Europe is an imagined geography created by the concept of a disjointed History, implying that there could be, and even *should be,* a continual and progressive development over time. This notion of History as progress aligns with the "elements of the Enlightenment world-view" that Appadurai cites.[12] Petty heroism then becomes a kind of Central European local answer to the pervasive idea that there should be a progressive history. To put it yet otherwise, it is a reaction to the ideoscape of the Enlightenment figuration of the path of Historical progress.

To return to the case I know best, the trope of petty heroism can thus be viewed as a method of re-inscribing Czech agency, of creating a narrative of Czechs acting instead of being acted upon. To be clear, this is a historical trope, not "real" history in the sense of what historians do; as in the quotes from historians above, the emphasis is on a reaction to historical events, a widespread commentary on historical events, a *feeling* of "powerlessness," not any absolute interpretation of history. To be sure, such feelings, justified or not, find their expressions in petty heroism, in narratives of victimization and of loss of agency. They are fundamental to a constructed national narrative, especially as it is conveyed in the arts, such as the books, essays, and films discussed in this chapter. Along with Benedict Anderson, I would argue that despite no claim to objectivity, these tropes and their expression in cultural production contribute in critical ways to Czechs' sense of their national community.[13]

Although the complaint of the lack of agency is common across the region, the strong development of the petty hero is not. In an interview, Péter Esterházy wrote about Hrabal's novels, claiming, "It is interesting how Hrabalian anecdotes differ from Hungarian, in which the hero always wins. Hrabal's stories are stories of failure. The Hungarians rather only cry, that they lose, but when they speak about themselves, they always win. So to see something like this, as in Czech culture, literature, it's always a big help."[14] Esterházy critiqued his own culture for its insistence on traditional heroes and found an alternative within the Czech context, something that he would use in his own novel *The Book of Hrabal*. Jan Błoński similarly critiqued Polish literature for being too "obsessed with history, because history has interfered with its process too much."[15] For Błoński, Polish culture focuses too much on the large Historical moments, filled with grand heroics. The Czech novel, however, can show "the life of the man of the street, the day-to-day life," a regular person.[16] Błoński is pointing to the type of petty heroics that have become such a hallmark of Czech culture, but one that is deeply appreciated by leading authors and critics in Central Europe.

At best, the petty hero undermines the Romantic hero trope, opposing the "great man" of History, showing how an insignificant figure can have an effect on the larger stage. The trope is attractive, especially in the context of the twentieth century, with so many troubling rulers and "great men." This decidedly humanist construction of the individual emphasizes human agency, especially on a small scale, as well as implies that the broader society had little to do with the construction of the world in which events took place. The scale of History may be beyond the agency of a single person, but there is nonetheless heroism in utilizing the limited amount of agency any individual actually has.

At its worst, the petty hero can reinforce the moral superiority of those who occasionally act in opposition to various regimes but never in any sustained or productive way. In opposing Romantic heroism, or idealistic acts meant to apply to the grand scale, the petty hero keeps his or her focus on the immediate, local concerns, implying that those who act on the grand Historical scale are ignoring what is actually most important for human life. The trope can imply that anyone attempting to act on the scale of History rejects the human dimension and thus is morally reprehensible. Extending the trope to the entire nation, as the various cited examples have often done, petty heroism relieves the small countries of responsibility for the greater events on the historical scale. If the small person or small country has reduced agency but nonetheless attempts even a minuscule act of resistance, then he or she has demonstrated opposition to the regime and reaffirmed the restricted amount of agency meted out to oppressed people, while also maintaining a narrative of victimization. The trope becomes not only a literary construction, but also the source of comfort for those who lived through an oppressive regime, especially if they may have committed a minor act of petty resistance or have even felt momentarily the urge to oppose, as Esterházy suggests above, and yet have not engaged in any broader or sustained resistance to the regime. As we know, tropes are dynamic. Despite creating one of the most famous examples of the petty hero, Bohumil Hrabal's later work *I Served the King of England*, written in 1971, six years after his *Closely Watched Trains*, contains the most nuanced and sustained critique of the trope. I will take it up in detail after a further consideration of the idea of anecdote.

CENTRAL EUROPE, THE ANECDOTE, AND THE PETTY HERO

In the titular essay of his collection *Troubles with History,* Kroutvor uses Hrabal and other Czech authors such as Kundera and Václav Havel to describe a distinction between the anecdote and History in his analysis of the trope of the petty hero. The essay has several significant flaws. As with other claims about Central Europe, the focus of Kroutvor's argument generally is on the writer's native country.[17] Certainly, some of his conclusions do apply elsewhere, and related perspectives on the value of small countries occur in the writings of other Central Europeans. And yet, the wider applicability of his thesis to the rest of (East-) Central Europe, would be indefensible without amendment. The term "Central Europe," on which Kroutvor builds his argument, comes with the caveat that his interpretation of the region depends primarily upon Czech history, literature, and views of history (and History). Additionally, the essay was written as a kind of provocation rather than as a purely academic work. As a result, it essentializes its subject matter. Despite these drawbacks, Kroutvor's distinction between an anecdotal and Historical event remains useful, and his views on History expressed in his essays can be considered primary documents for my investigation.

Kroutvor originally conceptualized History and the anecdote in the 1980s, when the term "Central Europe" was having a resurgence. Its proponents, such as Milan Kundera, Czesław Miłosz, and György Konrád, published articles describing Central Europe as the small states boxed in "by the Germans on the one side and the Russians on the other."[18] Kroutvor follows a similar principle, relating his understanding of Central Europe primarily to the former lands of the Habsburg Empire, including Austria, Czechoslovakia, Hungary, and Poland. Like Kundera, Konrád, and Miłosz, Kroutvor stresses the smallness of the Central European nations, their need for help from the West, and their reliance on each other.[19]

Kroutvor argues that by virtue of belonging to small nations, Central Europeans created a disjointed, anecdotal history to regain a sense of agency in the face of extrinsic, deterministic History. Kroutvor uses the distinction in Czech between the diminutive *historka* (anecdote, story, or a little history, and a synonym in his text for *anekdota*; here "anecdote" or "anecdotal history") and *historie* (history, especially academic, and a synonym in his text to *dějiny*; here "History") to emphasize the difference between the two types of temporalities. The origins of the term "anecdote," coming from Ancient Greek and meaning something outside the published History, demonstrate the fundamental difference of scale and focus between the two structures for Kroutvor.[20] History is fundamentally a published work, something that is constructed by, for, and about power; the anecdote, however, is developed from the elements omitted in the account of History. Because Central Europeans "are missing the right to their own History," they use anecdotes that need not be organized into a single overarching narrative to construct their sense of the past and the horizons of the future.[21]

The anecdote exists beside History, always in a dialogue with it. The greatest anecdotal writers, such as the three French authors Nicolas Chamfort, Voltaire, and Stendhal, as well as the German Romantic Novalis, developed the anecdote from something that accompanied Historical works to a more stand-alone form.[22] Chamfort and Voltaire used anecdotes to humanize great leaders, bringing court gossip to the cause. The anecdotes were of interest only because they provided another side to those in power, adding a more quotidian element to their existence and demonstrating their innate humanness. History still dominates anecdote in this example, because the anecdote only serves to fill in what History has omitted. Novalis, according to Kroutvor, began to understand the relationship between History and anecdote in the Central European way. Novalis, so fond of his philosophical fragments, claimed that History itself was one giant anecdote, leveling the distinction between the works of one great individual and a thousand smaller ones, and bringing History to the broader populace.

Anecdotes, in contrast to History, remain in the sphere of the oral, even if they are occasionally written down, creating an alternative to monologic History. Richard Coe writes, "[The anecdote] embodies one of the last surviving remnants of a pre-literary oral tradition."[23] Kroutvor cites Novalis in the remark that "the anecdote is a kind of dialogue."[24] Anecdotes are told and retold, to the point that Kroutvor claims that an anecdote needs not just two people, but rather three, since it is only through continued retelling that it truly comes into existence.[25] Relaying anecdotes establishes a community around them, but the community is distinctly unrelated to those that control the realm of power. History creates a civil society, but the anecdote produces a whole different kind of social order:

> For example, a Czech does not feel like a citizen, his everydayness is not civic, civil, but quotidian, banal, low. A Czech misses a civic consciousness, but still has a polished sense of the grotesque details of life, humor and human cunning. The truth of life is uncovered to the point of the absurdity of being, the disproportion of the paradox sparks with a joke.[26]

The everydayness of the Central European does not create civil society but rather stands in opposition to it.

The petty hero embodies the division between the anecdote and History because he exists only on the local level. The common trope of the little Czech (pejoratively *čecháček*) represents this petty hero in his or her small amount of agency. As Ladislav Holý claims, "The little Czech as the typical representative of the Czech nation is the embodiment of ordinariness and healthy common sense."[27] Kroutvor calls this figure the nation's mascot.[28] He—for such figures are usually male—rarely has any effect beyond the very local.[29] In the scheme of anecdote and History, the petty hero is clearly at home in the anecdote and can be understood as a character who reasserts a modicum of agency without having agency over the larger historical narrative.

The trope of the petty hero implies two conclusions: first, that those who are not heroes of the petty sort lack a fundamental respect for all human beings and, second, moving the scope out to the national level, that the small countries of Central Europe are more humane as well as humanistic by nature precisely due to their lack of Historical agency. Kroutvor argues that Central European authors "champion the humanity [*humanismus*] of the small person, the humorous truth, the humanity [*humanismus*] of Central Europe."[30] The term *humanismus* means both "humanity" and "humanism" in Czech, and Kroutvor means both at once in this sentence. If the petty hero champions the local, then the implication is that the non-petty hero ignores it; further, the non-petty hero, through ignoring the local, ignores the humanity of individuals in favor of the group. Kroutvor additionally argues that this point is a *moral* one, because the trope of the petty hero shows the value of each individual in those moments of agency, regardless of how significant or effectual they are.

It should already be clear why Hrabal resonated with Kroutvor: Hrma is the epitome of Kroutvor's construction of the petty hero, a small character who finds more meaning in the fundamentally human preoccupation with sex than with what might have been the most consequential war in European history. This inversion of importance demonstrates the Central European concern with subjectivity over politics, and Hrma becomes the hero of the story through his interest in the things right under his nose.

HRABAL AND THE PETTY ANTIHERO

Bohumil Hrabal consistently focused on the anecdote, writing about people who existed on the "trash heap of the epoch," those who had been tossed aside by the Historical narrative.[31] Beginning with *Closely Watched Trains* (1965), Hrabal published a series of works that dealt directly with Historical problems, from the Nazi occupation to the contemporaneous Socialist regime. Hrabal was never a dissident and did not actively oppose the regime, but his lack of direct support for the regime placed his works at the intersection of official and unofficial writings.

I Served the King of England covers more historical ground than any of Hrabal's other works.[32] A "joyful, picaresque story, which begins with Baron Munchausen–like adventures and ends in tears and solitude," traces its narrator Jan Dítě's journey from the interwar Czechoslovak Republic, through increasing nationalism and World War II, and then well into the Communist era.[33] Like in *Closely Watched Trains,* here History stands in the background, while Dítě's personal life emerges into the limelight. He safely survives each political change—not by dint of cunning, but simply by luck and obliviousness, in the tradition of Jaroslav Hašek's Švejk.

Although the novel is divided into five chronologically ordered sections, it does not have an overarching temporal structure. The Czech version of the work bears the subtitle *Povídky,* or "Short Stories," further disintegrating a sense of temporal completion and linking it to the anecdotal in Kroutvor's sense. Each section provides a personal history of Dítě as he changes jobs as a waiter in various hotels and restaurants across the country, making some adjustments to the changing political settings. He works his way up from a restaurant in a provincial town to the Prague outskirts, then to a fine restaurant in Prague, where he serves Haile Selassie, at that time emperor of Ethiopia. As World War II looms, Dítě becomes involved with a young Nazi woman in Prague, resulting in losing his job at a Czech restaurant only to end up in a *Lebensborn* camp, waiting on the young women chosen to bear the Nazi supermen. After the war, Dítě purchases, with ill-gotten gains, his own hotel, which is ultimately expropriated by the Communist government. The final chapters find Dítě performing various odd jobs for the Communist government in the forest at the Austrian border, where he sits down to compose his life story—in effect, the work that we read.

Unlike Hrma in *Closely Watched Trains,* Dítě cannot be described as an unimpeachable character. He is a cheat, a liar, a philanderer, a Nazi sympathizer, and a war profiteer. Like Hrma, he follows the tradition of being a small hero, and here I am using "hero" loosely. His name Dítě means "child" in Czech, but he engages in no act of petty heroism that could define him positively, at least not until the very end. Like the traditional petty hero, Dítě pays more attention to his immediate surroundings, without discovering their larger significance in terms of History. When he meets his future wife, he describes the pin she is wearing as "four F's arranged in a circle like a four-leaf clover," reimagining the heinous Nazi symbol in terms of the emblem for good luck, and thereby unwittingly playing on the Hindu origins of the swastika.[34]

Dítě's obliviousness to the political hues of the world around him underscores his ambivalent relationship to his sensory interpretation of this world. As a waiter, he had been taught to "see nothing and hear nothing" and simultaneously "see everything and hear everything" (1). Initially, the contradictory advice refers to keeping guest activities confidential while making sure that those same guests have everything they require. Dítě performs this task rather well and is able to anticipate the guests' appetites and desires before they can articulate them. Dítě should be able to see well beyond himself and his own understanding of the world, but because Dítě is such an extreme example of the petty hero, he is unable to apply his developing reason to his own case. This provides both an example and critique of Kroutvor's understanding of the separation of History and the anecdote. Dítě does not understand the meaning of the swastika. Incapable of making out the symbol's complex lineage, he acts within the local confines of the anecdote. His error, from the vantage point of Kroutvor's essay, would be only human. And yet cumulatively, erring achieves the contrary: it makes Dítě the amoral character that he is. Thus, turning a blind eye to the world, Dítě sells stamps stolen from deported Jews without a second thought: the stamps are now his, and their provenance matters little to him.

In the context of Kroutvor's insinuation that the countries of Central Europe have had no agency in History and thus can be blameless victims of its course, Dítě's immorality could be forgiven. Kroutvor's separation of the anecdotal and Historical allows for this reading and provides a rather convenient way of generally avoiding moral consequences. Dítě can be understood as someone who lacks agency because he certainly has little awareness, let alone control, over the Historical events occurring around him. Hrabal demonstrates, however, that Dítě cannot, and should not, be considered blameless. He does cooperate with the Nazis, he does use stolen stamps to buy a hotel and become a millionaire, and he does cheat people out of their money. His actions, although aimed at increasing his personal fortune, do have consequences on the larger scale, and Kroutvor's division between anecdotal history and History collapses.

Although Dítě may seem morally reprehensible in the first four parts of the novel, the final section makes him more aware of History and more capable of interpreting events in contexts large and small. Toward the end of the fourth section, Dítě finally turns his powers of observation upon himself, and "the sight made [him] sick" (154). Paradoxically, the protagonist's increasing separation from society in the final section of the novel connects him with this society's past and brings into view his own complicity in History's dark chapters. Dítě's awareness begins when History interferes with his own life, when he loses his potency to his wife's desire to create "the New Man" under Nazi ideological pressures, this is, when his quotidian sexual relations become subject to Nazi regulations (146–47).

Dítě's suffering from newly developed impotency reverses Hrma's situation in *Closely Watched Trains* just prior to becoming a petty hero. This also reveals a reversal of Hrabal's investment in petty heroism more generally. Hrma becomes sexually active only moments before bombing an incoming Nazi supply train, whereas Dítě's impotency occurs in tandem with his actions taking on larger significance. Dítě would also be acting in support of the Nazis, even as a Nazi petty hero. The small hero, just as the small nation, does not necessarily come from a morally justified position; the petty hero can just as easily be a petty antihero engaged in the anecdotal history of a less-than-humanist nation.

At the end of the story, Dítě finds himself close to the border with Germany, important in Kroutvor's essay due to its location between a country with History and one without, geographically representing the temporal disjuncture of the work. There Dítě dreams about his burial "in that graveyard on top of the little hill, at the highest point, with my coffin right on the divide, so that when what was left of me decomposed, it would be carried away by the rain in two different directions: part of me would wash down the streams that flow into Bohemia, and the other part of me down the other side, under the barbed wire of the border, through brooks and streams that feed the Danube" (229). Unlike Kroutvor's vision of the petty hero who operates merely in the realm of anecdotal history, Dítě wants to become a part of both topographies and chronologies, the Historical temporality of the German side and the anecdotal temporality of the Czech side. For Hrabal, then, the petty hero cannot be forgiven for being completely unaware of the two scopes of time. Rather, he must recognize overlaps between the two temporalities. Dítě's desire to be buried between the two countries demonstrates this recognition, as he ultimately wishes to live a synthesis of the two temporalities.

Further continuing the metaphor of water and time, Dítě finds that time is neither circular, as in the anecdote, nor linear, as in History, but rather a steady flow and a constant synthesis. Significantly, Dítě begins to collect mirrors and other artifacts from the old German villages along the border with Germany. One day, drinking from a nearby spring, he realizes:

> Just as a connoisseur of Bernkasteller Riesling can detect the smell of the hundreds of locomotives that pass by the vineyards each day, or of the little fires that the vintners make in the fields each day to heat their lunches, I too could taste the dead buried long ago in the graveyard up there. And I tasted them for the same reason I had got the mirrors, because the mirrors held the imprints of the Germans who had looked into them, who had departed years ago, leaving their smell behind in them, in the place I gazed into for a long time each day and where my double walked. (232)

Dítě experiences the past, not as the past, but rather as something still detectable in the present. The Germans are gone from the Sudetenland after their mass expulsion, but their presence is still palpable.

As he approaches his mortal end, Dítě finds traces of every human that lived before him in the water, soil, and artifacts that have been left behind. His humanism returns on a local scale, devoid of larger political ramifications on the one hand and filled with them on the other. He finds the traces of German inhabitants in the Sudetenland, but does not align them with any kind of ideology: "As with the departed in the drinking water, I rubbed shoulders with people who were invisible … I kept bumping into young girls in dirndls, into German furniture, into the ghosts of German families" (232). Instead of finding Germans only involved in acts belonging to the grand historical narrative, Dítě discovers their everydayness. The quotidian activities of the Germans demonstrate that they, too, are neither outside petty heroism nor outside the realm of the anecdotal.

Hrabal attempts to reconnect the temporal as well as geographical disjuncture in the Czech lands. The reconciliation between the anecdote and History does not always create a pretty picture, and Hrabal is well aware of the problems of the past. In his novel *Vita Nuova,* the second in an autobiographical trilogy narrated by his wife, she claims that "even in my dreams,

I would not have guessed that the past can be so living and wounding."[35] Hrabal's wife, Pipsi, was a Czech-speaking Sudeten German, someone who embodies the problems of both geography and time in Central Europe, and the past continued to haunt her throughout her life. Even as she tried to pay attention to the anecdotal, the more local and present life as she experienced it, the past in the form of other Czechs' unabating suspicion of her, returned again and again to bring her back to a Historical sense of the world. This troubling life in both forms, in both anecdotal and Historical, becomes the foundation for Hrabal's historical outlook, a synthesis between the two. The synthesis does not allow for greater Historical agency for most protagonists, but neither does it relieve anyone of responsibility for that which happens before them or because of them.

MORE TROUBLES WITH HISTORY

Hrabal's view of history and the anecdote reverses Kroutvor's claim that the anecdote is primary but also connected to History—it is not an either-or choice. Instead of believing that large nations, such as those of the Russians or Germans, have no anecdotal history, or at least justify the Czechs' superior understanding of the anecdote, Hrabal claims that the anecdote exists everywhere. Even at the end of his first historical novel, when Hrma destroys the Nazi train, one young Nazi dies right next to Hrma, calling out for his mother. The moment equates the two figures, one Czech and one German, in their anecdotal relationship to the world; both are ultimately caught up in the sweep of History, and neither has greater agency at this moment as they die side by side.

In synthesizing both anecdote and History, Hrabal counters the notion of either a continuous or discontinuous understanding of history. Hrabal opposes Kroutvor's conception of Central Europeans having no History or at least no agency in terms of it. The importance of this opposition lies in the problematic deployment of the lack of Historical agency, resulting in a discontinuous History, to justify retribution, such as in the postwar population transfers, or to absolve the small countries of Central Europe of all crimes, such as laying blame for the Communist persecutions at the feet of the Soviet Union instead of also accepting culpability.[36]

The issue of continuity or discontinuity emerges from self-determination, that Wilsonian concept that gave independence to the countries of Central Europe after World War I. If self-determination is a right for these countries, then discontinuity becomes a political statement about the rights of these groups. Kundera echoes the same idea in his latter essay "The Tragedy of Central Europe." Kundera claims that "the history of the Poles, the Czechs, the Slovaks, the Hungarians has been turbulent and fragmented. Their traditions of statehood have been weaker and less continuous than those of larger European nations."[37] The discontinuity in Kundera's estimation occurs due to Central Europe's geographical position between the Russians and Germans, implying, like Kroutvor, that Central Europeans are merely victims of outside oppression, who have not been allowed to define their own route, as they should have according to Wilson's concept of self-determination.

The discontinuity/continuity binary presented in Kroutvor and Kundera (and others) displays the traditional narrative time described by Benedict Anderson in *Imagined Communities*. Anderson claims that nations developed out of a change in the construction of temporality, from a form of simultaneous time to one "conceived as a solid community moving steadily down (or up) history."[38] Kroutvor and Kundera deem the discontinuity of History in Central Europe as negative, because this steady movement down history is positive, in its Enlightenment ideoscape form. In opposing Kroutvor, Hrabal undermines the binary of a continuous or discontinuous construction of history, and thus Hrabal undermines the fundamental temporal construction of the nation. If history for Hrabal is always already both continuous and discontinuous, then there can be no up or down movement along history. Instead, history is both continuous and discontinuous, not between them, but always already the constructed story of the anecdotal and the Historical.

Hrabal's view has not been accepted, as can be seen from the proliferation of the petty hero trope to the present day in the Czech Republic or Czechia. Even in the interpretation of Hrabal's own work, the trope of the petty hero has proved to be remarkably durable. In his 2006 film adaptation of Hrabal's *I Served the King of England* that was the Czech submission for the Academy Award for Best Film in a Foreign Language in 2007, Jiří Menzel used only the first four parts of the novel, ignoring the key fifth section in which Dítě becomes aware of his place in History. The film ends with a laughing Dítě who has become a millionaire as he had initially wanted and is imprisoned with the other millionaires. Unlike in the novel, Dítě has been accepted, not rejected, by the interwar bourgeois. Thus, in the film Dítě is a victim of History, more in line with the typical petty hero than with the troubling antihero who ultimately emerges from a careful reading of the novel.

Daniel W. Pratt is visiting assistant professor in the Department of Slavic and East European Languages and Cultures at the Ohio State University. He works on Polish, Czech, German, and Russian literature, culture, and intellectual history. He has published in *Comparative Literature Studies, Polish Review*, and *Rocznik Przemyski*. He is currently finishing the monograph *Aesthetic Selves: Non-Narrative Constructions of Personal and Historical Time*.

NOTES

I would like to thank the members of the Czech Studies community at the School of Slavic and East European Studies at University College London, who were so helpful in their comments on this paper.
1. Bohumil Hrabal, *Closely Watched Trains*, trans. Edith Pargeter (Evanston, IL: Northwestern University Press, 1995), 2.
2. Bohumil Hrabal, *Closely Watched Trains*, 7–8.
3. Bohumil Hrabal, *Closely Watched Trains*, vii.
4. For other examples, see Jan Hřebejk's other film *Pupendo* (2003), Michal Viewegh's *Báječná léta pod psa* (1992, film 1997), and to a certain degree, Karel Čapek's *War with the Newts* (1936). For more on the nostalgic version of the petty hero, see Veronika Pehe, "Drobné hrdinství: Vzdor jakožto předmět nostalgie v díle Petra Šabacha a Michala Viewegha," *Česká literatura* 63, no. 3 (2015), 419–34.
5. Josef Kroutvor, *Potíže s dějinami: Eseje* (Prague: Prostor, 1990), 62–63. The logic of capitalizing the word "History" in this chapter follows Kroutvor's approach.
6. Johann Gottfried Herder, *Ideen zur Philosophie der Geschichte der Menschheit* (Frankfurt am Main: Deutscher Klassiker Verlag, 1989), 696.
7. Bradley F. Abrams, *The Struggle for the Soul of the Nation: Czech Culture and the Rise of Communism* (Lanham, MD: Rowman & Littlefield, 2004), 109.
8. Laura Cashman, "Remembering 1948 and 1968: Two Pivotal Years in Czech and Slovak History," *Europe-Asia Studies* 60, no. 10 (December 2008): 1655.
9. "The Lisbon Conference on Literature: A Round Table of Central European and Russian Writers," *Cross Currents: A Yearbook of Central European Culture* 9 (1990): 92.
10. Milan Kundera, "The Tragedy of Central Europe," *New York Times Review of Books* 31, no. 7 (26 April 1984): 36.
11. Czesław Miłosz, "Central European Attitudes," *Cross Currents* 5 (1986): 101.
12. Arjun Appadurai, "Disjuncture and Difference in the Global Cultural Economy," *Theory, Culture & Society* 7 (1990): 299.
13. Benedict Anderson, *Imagined Communities: Reflections on the Origin and Spread of Nationalism* (London and New York: Verso, 2006), especially chapters 2–3.
14. Esterházy, Péter, "Dívat se a psát to přece je 'činnost', říká Péter Esterházy," *Lidové noviny*, 22 April 1999.
15. "The Lisbon Conference on Literature," 88.
16. "The Lisbon Conference on Literature," 89.
17. For more on this subject, see Michal Kopeček, "The Ups and Downs of Central Europe: Chapters from Czech Symbolic Geography," *The Weight of History in*

Central European Societies of the 20th Century, edited by Zora Hlavičková and Nicolas Maslowski (Prague: Central European Studies, 2005), 41–59.

18. Milan Kundera, "The Tragedy of Central Europe," 34. See also György Konrad, "Mitteleuropäische Meditationen an der Bruchlinie zweier Zivilisationen," *Dialog* 15, no. 2 (1989); and Czesław Miłosz, "Central European Attitudes," in *In Search of Central Europe,* ed. George Schöpflin and Nancy Wood (Oxford: Polity Press, 1981), 118–26.
19. Kroutvor never explicitly states that this is what he means, but judging from the list of typical Central European writers, it is fairly clear (Kroutvor, *Potíže s dějinami,* 55).
20. Kroutvor, *Potíže s dějinami,* 81.
21. Kroutvor, *Potíže s dějinami,* 66.
22. For more on the development of the anecdote as form, see Richard N. Coe, "The Anecdote and the Novel: A Brief Enquiry into the Origins of Stendhal's Technique," *Australian Journal of French Studies,* 1 January 1985, 3–25; and Joel Fineman, "The History of the Anecdote," in *The New Historicism,* ed. H. Aram Veeser (New York and London: Routledge, 1989), 57.
23. Coe, "The Anecdote and the Novel" 3.
24. Kroutvor, *Potíže s dějinami,* 85.
25. Kroutvor, *Potíže s dějinami,* 94.
26. Kroutvor, *Potíže s dějinami,* 64–65.
27. Ladislav Holy, *The Little Czech and the Great Czech Nation: National Identity and the Post-Communist Social Transformation* (Cambridge: Cambridge University Press, 1996), 72.
28. Kroutvor, *Potíže s dějinami,* 65.
29. For more on the "little Czech," see Holy, *The Little Czech,* 72–78; Petr Král, "Być Czechem," *Zeszyty Literackie* 2 (1983), 54–59; and Petra Hanáková, "The Construction of Normality: The Lineage of Male Figures in Contemporary Czech Cinema," in *Mediale Welten in Tschechien nach 1989: Genderprojektionen und Codes des Plebejismus,* ed. Jiřina van Leeuwen-Turnovcová and Nicole Richter (Munich: Kubon und Sagner, 2005).
30. Kroutvor, *Potíže s dějinami,* 55.
31. Bohumil Hrabal, *Sebrané spisy Bohumila Hrabala* (Pražská imaginace: Prague, 1995), 15:10.
32. Hrabal rarely provides an account of more than a few years in any of his stories, and *I Served the King of England* stands as a major exception to that rule.
33. James Wood, "Bohumil Hrabal," *London Review of Books* 23, no. 1 (4 January 2001), 15.
34. Hrabal, *I Served the King of England,* trans. Paul R. Wilson (New York: New Directions, 2007), 121–22. Further cited parenthetically.
35. Hrabal, *Sebrané spisy Bohumila Hrabala,* 11:306.
36. See for example, Eagle Glassheim's discussion in "National Mythologies and Ethnic Cleansing: The Expulsion of Czechoslovak Germans in 1945," *Central European History* 33, no. 4 (2000): 463–486.

37. Milan Kundera, "The Tragedy of Central Europe," *New York Review of Books*, 26 April 1984, 34.
38. Anderson, *Imagined Communities*, 26.

WORKS CITED

Abrams, Bradley F. *The Struggle for the Soul of the Nation: Czech Culture and the Rise of Communism*. Lanham, MD: Rowman & Littlefield, 2004.
Anderson, Benedict. *Imagined Communities: Reflections on the Origin and Spread of Nationalism*. London and New York: Verso, 2006.
Appadurai, Arjun. "Disjuncture and Difference in the Global Cultural Economy." *Theory, Culture & Society* 7 (1990): 295–310.
Cashman, Laura. "Remembering 1948 and 1968: Two Pivotal Years in Czech and Slovak History." *Europe-Asia Studies* 60, no. 10 (December 2008): 1645–658.
Coe, Richard. "The Anecdote and the Novel: A Brief Enquiry into the Origins of Stendhal's Technique." *Australian Journal of French Studies*, 1 January 1985, 3–25.
Esterházy, Péter. "Dívat se a psát to přece je 'činnost', říká Péter Esterházy." *Lidové noviny*, 22 April 1999. Accessed 22 December 2016. http://www.pwf.cz/archivy/texty/rozhovory/divat-se-a-psat-to-prece-je-cinnost-rika-madarsky-spisovatel-peter-esterhazy-v-rozhovoru-pro-lidove-noviny_2661.html.
Fineman, Joel. "The History of the Anecdote." In *The New Historicism*, edited by H. Aram Veeser, 49–76. New York and London: Routledge, 1989.
Glassheim, Eagle. "National Mythologies and Ethnic Cleansing: The Expulsion of Czechoslovak Germans in 1945." *Central European History* 33, no. 4 (2000): 463–86.
Hanáková, Petra. "The Construction of Normality: The Lineage of Male Figures in Contemporary Czech Cinema." In *Mediale Welten in Tschechien nach 1989: Genderprojektionen und Codes des Plebejismus*, edited by Jiřina van Leeuwen-Turnovcová and Nicole Richter. Munich: Kubon und Sagner, 2005.
Herder, Johann Gottfried. *Ideen zur Philosophie der Geschichte der Menschheit*. Frankfurt am Main: Deutscher Klassiker Verlag, 1989.
Holy, Ladislav. *The Little Czech and the Great Czech Nation: National Identity and the Post-Communist Social Transformation*. Cambridge: Cambridge University Press, 1996.
Hrabal, Bohumil, *Closely Watched Trains*. Translated by Edith Pargeter. Evanston, IL: Northwestern University Press, 1995.
———. *I Served the King of England*. Translated by Paul R. Wilson. New York: New Directions, 2007.
———. *Sebrané spisy Bohumila Hrabala*. Prague: Pražská imaginace, 1995.
Konrad, György. "Mitteleuropäische Meditationen an der Bruchlinie zweier Zivilisationen." *Dialog* 15, no. 2 (1989).
Kopeček, Michal. "The Ups and Downs of Central Europe: Chapters from Czech Symbolic Geography." *The Weight of History in Central European Societies of the 20th*

Century, edited by Zora Hlavičková and Nicolas Maslowski, 41–59. Prague: Central European Studies, 2005.

Král, Petr. "Być Czechem." *Zeszyty Literackie* 2 (1983): 45–9.

Kroutvor, Josef. *Potíže s dějinami: Eseje.* Prague: Prostor, 1990.

Kundera, Milan. "The Tragedy of Central Europe." *New York Times Review of Books* 31, no. 7 (26 April 1984): 33–38.

"The Lisbon Conference on Literature: A Round Table of Central European and Russian Writers." *Cross Currents: A Yearbook of Central European Culture* 9 (1990): 75–124.

Miłosz, Czesław. "Central European Attitudes." In *In Search of Central Europe*, edited by George Schöpflin and Nancy Wood, 118–26. Oxford: Polity Press, 1981.

———. "Central European Attitudes," *Cross Currents: A Yearbook of Central European Culture* 5 (1986): 101–108.

Pehe, Veronika. "Drobné hrdinství: Vzdor jakožto předmět nostalgie v díle Petra Šabacha a Michala Viewegha." *Česká literatura* 63, no. 3 (2015), 419–34.

Wood, James. "Bohumil Hrabal," *London Review of Books* 23, no. 1 (4 January 2001): 14–16.

Chapter Six

The Transnational Matrix of Post-Communist Spaces

Ioana Luca

Henri Lefebvre ponders the task of a social geographer: "How many maps ... might be needed to deal exhaustively with a given space, to code and decode all its meanings and contents? ... It is not only the codes [and] the maps' legend ... that are liable to change, but also the objects represented."[1] Elsewhere, Lefebvre denies the very possibility of any fruitful relationship between "mental or literary 'places'" and space "of a purely political and social kind."[2] Patricia Yaeger, in contrast, considers literature to be essential for sharpening the social geographer's traditional tools: maps, grids, statistics, or codes. According to Yaeger, "The layering that comes with the use of compound plots, points of view, tonality, atmosphere, and meter; and the dense range of figurative speech: each plaited literary device gives the weird, defamiliarizing treatment of cities a space-mapping advantage Lefebvre overlooks." Such space mapping, the literary critic suggests, implies a metropoetics that should describe "the flow of literature as it pours into and out of the life of the cities."[3] Yaeger's perspective amplifies geographer Doreen Massey's assertion that "the identity of places [in general] is very much bound up with the *histories* which are told of them, *how* those histories are told, and which history turns out to be dominant."[4]

Here I follow the scholars who view literary works as instrumental for spatial mapping and extend Andreas Huyssen's definition of the urban imaginary as "the cognitive and somatic image which we carry within us, of the places where we live, work and play" to space imaginaries in general.[5]

Such an image is an "embodied material fact" and not a "figment of one's imagination."[6] It shapes the reality of a place, into which fictive projections or imaginative geographies are at times incorporated as they conjure up and embody specific time-space coordinates and relations and thus encourage reflections about other worlds.

"Imaginative geographies," with reference to Eastern European spaces, have mostly been an Orientalist hallmark; they have often committed the double violence of canceling genuine difference and fabricating difference where it does not exist.[7] To go beyond their constraints, my essay examines the literary cartographies that transcend betweenness and contiguity (the two terms that, as the introduction to this volume summarizes, have underpinned discussions of Eastern Europe) and probes the role that the discontiguous plays in texts by the contemporary writers of Eastern European descent who publish in English and reside in the United States. More specifically, I am interested in the real and imaginary connections between the post-Communist and other, noncontiguous spaces (mostly US American). The nexus comes through especially forcefully in the work of Miroslav Penkov and Aleksandar Hemon, two writers of Bulgarian and Bosnian descent (respectively), who grew up under Communism and left in its aftermath.

Penkov's and Hemon's imaginings of their native countries offer a lens for reading Eastern European spaces as "transnationally constituted, embedded and influenced social arenas that interact with one another."[8] The transnational matrix that their texts propose reconfigures villages or cities as consisting of "multiple sets of dynamically overlapping and interacting transnational fields that create and shape seemingly bordered and bounded structures, actors, and processes."[9] The tradition of "geo-coding"[10] has been predicated on isomorphism between location and imaginary identification—a paradigm long unseated by critics of national approaches to literatures. For Paul Giles, who writes with an eye to American literature, "location ... might be said to provide a discursive rationale for imaginary identification, but it can no more be extended into a coherent theory for area studies than nineteenth century phrenologists could extend their observations ... into a theory of race."[11] In American studies there has been a sustained engagement with a "relational geography" that does not erase or invalidate local or national specificity "but allows other specificities to become visible."[12] As my chapter demonstrates, Penkov and Hemon unmap the Eastern European space in the aftermath of Communism by positing a relational geography with spaces beyond the region's borders, beyond geo-spatial limitations, or beyond historical contiguities. In this open-ended cartographic imaginary, distinct critical positions can be articulated, and new links, solidarities, and alternative potentialities can emerge.

The two writers insert themselves into a discussion of an Eastern European space that has frequently been exoticized and forced to comply with the mandates of more powerful countries or entities (spelled out, most recently, in the terms for joining the EU and NATO or in the conditions imposed by the IMF or World Bank). Scholars have demonstrated the gradual construction of Eastern Europe as "a work of cultural creation, of intellectual artifice, of ideological self-interest and self-promotion"[13] and have examined its imaginative geographies or literary mappings. At the same time, the Eastern European space as an object of public, political, and even academic discourse remains fraught. Post-1989 representations of Eastern Europe in American literature, for instance, led scholars to rightly state that in the "post-Communist [American] safari novel," the former Communist bloc is the playground of "sex, drunken debauchery," while the expat's foray into the region inevitably begets a "male narrative of conquest, submission and coming of age."[14] A quick overview of Eastern European exiles' or transnationals' writing in the early 1990s shows that even such writers as Eva Hoffman, Andrei Codrescu, or Slavenka Drakulić offer in their travelogues a preassigned generic path to their native region, depicting their own cultures as compliant with or dependent on the Western tradition in compelled or involuntary displays of self-exoticism.[15] At the same time, an increasing number of literary productions by writers born in the region but relocated elsewhere propose maps in motion and representations of post-Communist spaces predicated on discontiguous temporal and chronological scales.

MIROSLAV PENKOV: BULGARIAN CARTOGRAPHIES IN *EAST OF THE WEST*

Miroslav Penkov's *East of the West: A Country in Stories* (2011) offers one such example. His collection can be seen as belonging to the so-called literature of the "new arrival."[16] Yet, what clearly distinguishes Penkov within this genre is that his "soil of significance"[17] is always the dynamic palimpsest of the Eastern European space that his stories revisit. The title of the collection refers to Penkov's childhood memories and "the idea of the West" that he had received from his parents: "They had these fantasies that they're gonna go West, to the West. It didn't matter if it was Spain, Germany, it was one whole thing. That was your salvation: the West."[18] It also suggests a possible influence of and intertextual reference to Salman Rushdie's collection *East West* (1994), where the "East" (India) and the "West" (UK) come together and impact one another.[19] If Rushdie critically engages with and invalidates the Orientalist paradigm about the East, establishing dynamic and mutually reinforcing connections between India and the UK, Penkov builds an Eastern Europe (Bulgaria) in American literature that is no longer a foil, a psychological projection of political and ideological fears, or a phantasm. In fact, the writer derides the very existence of Eastern Europe as a whole. For him Eastern Europe "means nothing," and he calls his construction of Eastern Europe "an inversion of the idea that many Americans have."[20]

Penkov's book engages with imaginative geographies of Eastern Europe and examines reified positions or flattened signs about the region. The Bulgaria of his stories crosses historical, cultural, and geographical divides and disrupts expectations about the telltale "Balkan ghosts."[21] *East of the West* challenges the heavily "Balkanist" framework and numerous othering strategies employed by previous writers about Eastern Europe. It offers a complex textual representation of Bulgaria in particular in an attempt to put it on the map of American literature, creating the kind of discontiguity that involves excision and reinsertion.

My claims can be illustrated by the story that gives the title to the collection. It portrays a small Bulgarian village and reverses the perspective of "imagining" or "inventing Eastern Europe" by examining alternative images of the "West," past and present, articulated by the village inhabitants. In this way, the rural space and its community, whose members participate in and bear the effects of interactions with the "West," are revealed through a relational geography. The "East" is the Bulgarian side of the divided village, while the "West" is its other half, now the Serbian bank of the river. Dividing spatial metaphors and symbols such as the Berlin Wall or the Iron Curtain find their equivalent in the village river. What stands out in "East of the West" is the utter contingency of the "West" as a denominator, as it is *not* a Western European or a North American country but the socialist neighbor that is envisioned as its ostensible representative. The presence of the Serbian part of the village as the "West" is very much of a particular historical moment and place that can be traced to the circumstances of relative economic prosperity and slightly greater freedom that Yugoslavia enjoyed within the Eastern bloc. Penkov's depiction is in line with the imaginative geographies and hierarchies of Western-ness present within the former Eastern European bloc in socialist times.

Penkov redefines and relativizes the "West," which appears as an arbitrary and unstable geographical denominator meaningful only in its effects on people's lives. Yet the "East" is not favored and not offered as an alternative—neither during the Communist period nor the post-Communist era. The small village is anchored and examined in relation to World War I, when the border was drawn; the Cold War, when the border was severely militarized and people paid with their lives for transgressing it; and the post-1989 period, when crossing borders illegally is a question of the amount of money one can pay. This rural space—"Bulgarsko Selo" (Bulgarian Village), which appears in transliteration only, with no translation provided—becomes an embodiment of the shifting nature of descriptors such as "East" and "West," which Penkov empties out and reverses, thereby unsettling existing paradigms. The family history, the tonality and atmosphere of people's lives in the village in general are all artistically plaited, to borrow Yaeger's formulation, and this gives a defamiliarizing treatment to post-Communist spaces that adds in vital ways to their current understanding.

This is quite clear in the way Penkov's story unfolds. In the Communist 1980s, lovers commonly swim across the Cold War border. The narrator's sister plans to marry and run away to the "West," but she is shot dead by a border guard when trying to meet her lover from the "other side." The classic denouement of the Romeo and Juliet story, when set in Penkov's East, is marked by compelling historical circumstances. The sister's death is only the first tragic event in the story, and it sets in motion the destruction of nearly the entire family. The mother dies of grief right away, the father of alcoholism in the early 1990s—but not before urging his son to go west: "Go away. You can't have a life here. You must forget about your sister, about your mother, about me. Go west, get a job ... anywhere."[22] In 1999, the narrator follows his father's advice, disentangles himself from Bulgaria, saves money and goes west, to his first love, now in Belgrade. He arrives there only to find out that after having called him over, she is happily remarried. His going west does mean setting himself free from the small village, but his dreams and self-fulfillment are deferred. Moreover, given Bulgaria's support of the NATO forces during the bombing of Serbia, he receives a chilly welcome in Belgrade. There are only disillusionment, sadness, and loss. For his sister, the wish to go west resulted in tragic death in the 1980s; for him, the realization of this desire in the 1990s brings sorrow and almost hopelessness. "East of the West" challenges imaginative geographies of the West, dispels the specter of traditional imaginaries, and extracts the East from its proverbial role as a cursed or fateful location. In other words, it questions geographical determinism by interrupting the causation of individual crises. At the same time this reversed imaginative geography disrupts any regional geo-coding of Bulgaria and its neighbors. The spatial poetics that this story builds is one from which literature "pours in and out," to use Yaeger's words.

Elsewhere in the collection ("Makedonija," "The Night Horizon," "Devshirmeh"), multiple pasts and geographical erasures impinge on the present life of all protagonists, be they the aged grandfather in a sanatorium or the defiant daughter of Bulgarian Turks in a village under the Communist regime. Penkov masterfully distills and transforms both the histories and the lore of his places to render them in ways that point to the fluidity and dynamic nature of Eastern European spaces, past and present.

He highlights a complex flux of the Bulgarian spaces portrayed, dislodged from any preconceived understandings. The flux and dislodging in the stories are reinforced by the fact that the stories themselves are displaced from their original contexts, released as they are into the Anglophone literature sphere. This fluid and constantly questioned space gives way to transatlantic, even global, connections in stories such as "A Picture with Yuki," where another Bulgarian village is explored within the real or symbolic crossovers, negotiations or exchanges with the United States in the aftermath of the Cold War.

"A Picture with Yuki" portrays the return visit of a young Bulgarian immigrant to the places of his childhood. After having won the visa lottery, the narrator tries his luck in America,[23] where he works as a luggage loader at Chicago's O'Hare Airport. But it's "not really" nice in America, as he makes no money and has doubts about living there (119). The young immigrant then goes back to Bulgaria with his Japanese wife, Yuki, on a short vacation, in search of an inexpensive medical fertility treatment in Sofia. While glimpses of the capital are rare (the only significant reference that the reader gets pertains to his parents' effort to change the broken air conditioner), it is his grandparents' house and the visit to the village of his childhood that occupy center stage in this story.

The unnamed narrator eagerly revisits and shows his wife the house, where he had spent summers as a child. Here, the traumas of the family's past are revealed one by one. The gates of the house bear witness to the death of his great-grandfather, who was executed by the Communists when he refused to allow them to nationalize his property in 1944. As the couple takes pictures of monuments dedicated to the Communist heroes of the village, the narrator explains the meaning of 1944 to his wife, but he does *not* translate for her the inscription on the gate—*KULAK,* or "class enemy" (108). The protagonist-narrator preserves the silences in the family stories that he has inherited. The story of the execution of his great-grandfather, which his grandfather had to watch, together with the meaning of the word written on the house gate, is passed on only by his father, as Grandpa "never spoke of such things" (108). His own refusal to translate the inscription and thus explain his family past to his wife testifies to the impact that the traumatic history still has upon him. The legacy of Communism that this house bears is an open wound for the grandson, and distance neither in time nor in space can bring him closure. This painful legacy is not shared with his wife, and gaps in the family's narrative are destined to linger.

Yuki's presence in the small Bulgarian village allows Penkov to juxtapose and explore the global and the local in their points of contact, namely the narrator's current life and his family history, his return to the village and the welcoming rural community. Yuki is the subject of the villagers' gaze and constant inquiry. Racial hierarchies and racist stereotypes about distant others are all employed and exploded here. The narrator's mother grudgingly accepts a Japanese daughter-in-law—"at least she is not black" (107)—while the villagers' reactions when seeing her are "She is so tiny" and "*They* aren't that yellow" (101, emphasis mine). Yuki is taken as the yardstick for confirming or contradicting racial stereotypes. The villagers' curiosity and reification of the Japanese are counterpointed by the wife's own passionate interest in and imaginary construction of the village Roma: "she has always wanted to see real Gypsies, beautiful dark eyed enchantresses dancing barefooted around tall fires" (105). Ironically, only a Gypsy boy whom Yuki and her husband accidentally run over on the road sees her not through the lens of stereotype but rather just as "very pretty" (111).

A complex entanglement between two discontiguous kinds of otherness unfolds in the encounter between the Japanese wife and the Gypsy child. Instead of the reified standard against which racial stereotypes are tested, Yuki becomes a "pretty girl." A flesh-and-blood Gypsy child replaces the exotic specter in her imagination, but the substitution occurs in ways that fill her with burdening feelings of culpability for his subsequent death. The married couple runs over the child, who appears unharmed and returns home on his bike; the cause of his death, they are told, seems to be the beating he receives from his father the same evening. Two kinds of "other" meet in the Bulgarian village, with death, sadness, and self-blame enveloping the crossing of their fates.

The story ends with the couple, wracked with guilt, driving out of the village, but not before they are asked by the boy's father to "immortalize" him with their camera prior to the funeral. The returnee obliges and prepares for a confession about the accident, which, however, never takes place. The narrative masterfully renders this tense situation, with the juxtaposition of the couple's guilt with the Gypsy family's gratitude for the couple's kind help adding to the tension. It remains unclear if the couple later delivers the promised pictures.

The Bulgarian green card lottery winner returned to the spaces of his childhood both because of necessity (medical treatment in Sofia) and longing (visiting the house in which he spent his childhood vacations). Remorse and unconfessed guilt accrue to the return, with no closure in sight. The peaceful escape to his grandparents' house, and thus to his childhood, that he enjoys sharing with his wife is thwarted by his inability to communicate the past to her and further complicated by the death of the Gypsy boy. To put it otherwise, the incommunicable traumatic weight of the Communist legacy, embodied by the grandparents' house, clouds the return and thereby speaks the untranslatability of the painful past into the idiom of his present life with its concomitant inaccessibility to his Japanese wife. Similarly, his wife's facetious reaction—she jokingly calls him a "psycho" when he says he does not know the meaning of the inscription on the gate (109)—speaks about the impossibility of grasping the unsaid.

For numerous Cold War exiles, Communism was the prison they left behind so that their scars and wounds could gradually be healed and closure subsequently reached in the new country. Going into exile meant a "(re)turn to normality, overcoming the Communist handicap, acquiring one's own inner balance."[24] As the revisiting of his grandparents' house and the short stay in the village show, for the newer generation *both* the Communist legacy and the post-1989 transitions are times of uncertainty and unsolved conflicts. The childhood village enmeshes the narrator in a double bind: it stands for the painful Communist legacy of his family's past, as well as the unresolved present. All this is offset with glimpses of the United States and the protagonist's unfulfilled life there. The grandparents' house is no longer the Eden of his childhood but rather a physical reminder of the dark past. At the same time, his return route is imbricated with the present events in the village—the child's accident and the "immortalization" of the dead boy, which bear on him and his wife in ways that provide no solace. The village is thus a space inscribed not only by history, but also by the immigrant's fraught short visit and interaction with the Gypsy boy and his family. Life in the rural Bulgarian space is extracted from its contiguities and becomes entwined with the experience of global subjects, that is, the Japanese wife, as well as the visiting émigré. The recent history of the village resurfaces in memories, but the actual place is inscribed in the present and defined by its interaction with the American couple. In other words, the post-1989 village portrayed here is defined by its intersections with the world at large, while traditional borderlands and neighbors no longer provide significant crossing points.

Moreover, whatever their connection to the boy's death, the accident or his immortalization, Yuki is ready to leave the village only *after* she takes the bag of herbs that the Gypsy woman wanted to give them to make a pregnancy possible, "cradl[ing] it in her lap" (122). The villagers' encounter with the American couple foregrounds the real and symbolic intersections between Bulgaria and the United States or (given the wife's origins) even the world at large. There is a denial of his family's past and the impossibility to communicate it to Yuki. There is the wife's inability to sense the unsaid and read the silences in the husband's story. The present and the characters' connections to the village are highly ambiguous. The couple's implication in the boy's death is uncertain, as it is never clear if Yuki causes a life-threatening injury or if, regardless of this, the couple actually returns with the pictures of the dead boy that his family so desires. At the same time, as the ending of the story suggests, it is only the bag of herbs for the fertility treatment, given to Yuki by another Gypsy woman from the village, that is truly and fully significant for the recipient: "'It's all here,' she said, 'now we can go.'" The past and present of the remote Bulgarian village and its Roma community, the story suggests, thus become inseparable from the couple's future, just as the couple's intrusion earlier became inextricably entangled with the villagers' life. Bulgaria and the United States, these two discontiguous places that are nevertheless related through numerous layers of embeddedness and interaction, constantly define and redefine one another after 1989.

Penkov's village from "A Picture with Yuki" emerges fully only through its effect on the lives of its residents and outsiders. Its fluidity and dynamism are those of a space of encounters and metamorphoses. The short story's title also insinuates these multiple encounters. It can refer to the pictures that the protagonist took with his wife in the childhood village, thus suggesting the present inscription of the village on their life as well as of their presence in the village. But it may equally point to the pictures they took of the dead boy at the request of his family. Similarly, there is no preassigned meaning to the unnamed place that is the picture's background. Rather, there is a larger orbit where it is positioned, an orbit beyond geographical, linguistic, ethnic, or religious contiguities. The significance of the Bulgarian space of this story alternates between a place of the past (the house) and hope for the future (the pregnancy herbs). It is a place of historical trauma (the family's past) and present guilt (the boy's accident), but also of possible transcendence, bonds, memory work, and/or immortality (the picture of the dead boy who was photographed as if living).

There are multidirectional real and symbolic intersections between Bulgaria, the United States, and the world at large in "A Picture with Yuki"; they show the manifold embeddedness of a place and its changing significance across temporal and spatial coordinates. Penkov shakes off the constraining aspects of the Bulgarian village imaginary and highlights the possibilities of its transnational dimensions. These become analytical lenses and points of departure for enabling future connections. Taken together, Penkov's stories present us with reversed imaginative geographies, a critical inquiry into geographical determinism ("East of the West"), and the multiple intersections between Bulgaria and the United States, with their effects on people's lives ("A Picture with Yuki"). My next section shows how discontiguity and connections beyond the traditional geographical or historical borders acquire new meanings in Aleksandar Hemon's writing, thereby enabling a repositioning of the former Yugoslav space outside the more conventional mental or political maps. I will argue that distinct forms of "unmapping" Sarajevo, incisive frames of critique, and complex circles of convergence across a global orbit characterize Hemon's writing.

ALEKSANDAR HEMON: SARAJEVO'S IMAGINARIES

If generic (but highly evocative) rural spaces dominate Penkov's collection, Aleksandar Hemon's work can be seen as a chronicle and celebration of a city—Sarajevo. The Bosnian-born writer became stranded in Chicago in 1992, during his monthlong participation in a journalism program just as his hometown was coming under siege. Soon after, Hemon began publishing in English, authoring the short-story collections *The Question of Bruno* (2001) and *Love and Obstacles* (2009); novels *Nowhere Man* (2002), *The Lazarus Project* (2008), and *Zombie Wars* (2015); and a moving memoir, *The Book of My Lives* (2013), which together provide a collage of Sarajevan lives at home and abroad, lives saddled with the experience of waning socialism and Yugoslavia's disintegration.

His works also consistently depict convergences between Sarajevo and its people and numerous other places and peoples around the world, during pre-socialist times, during the Bosnian War, and in their wake. For instance, the juxtaposition of the "blank canvas of Socialist provincialism" with Kinshasa, "the hive of neocolonial pleasures," comes through in an adolescent Yugoslav boy's narrative in *Love and Obstacles*.[25] In *The Question of Bruno*, a young boy's apparently "vacant childhood" in the Yugoslavia of the 1970s is rendered both through mediated insights about cities in the Soviet Union (Baku, Moscow, and Leningrad) and through fantastic circles of convergences with the sites traveled by Richard Sorge, the well-known World War II spy, in Europe and Asia, presented in the intricate footnotes of the same story.[26] In the novels *Nowhere Man* and *The Lazarus Project*, the Sarajevan protagonists Pronek, Brik, and Rora envision their native city in constant dialogue with locations in present-day Ukraine, Romania, and the United States at the turn of the century. Such convergences of discontiguous places and epochs lend a wide range of meanings and understandings to the Eastern European sites that Hemon's fiction traverses. Without reducing the complexity of Hemon's writing, it is fair to say that both his fiction and nonfiction associate the former Yugoslavia with movement, change, and exchange with the world at large. In so doing, Hemon's work transforms the position of Eastern Europe within US American literature.

The pre- and post-socialist Yugoslav space in Hemon's writing has little to do with Sarajevo's images received in contemporary Anglo-American culture: images of the destroyed city, carnage and violence. Metaphors such as the "fault line," "tinder box," or "powder keg of Europe"[27] have recurred in public discourse about Sarajevo in the 1990s. In Hemon, the trope of the wounded, ruined city is definitely present, and the urbanicide of Sarajevo is poetically recorded. But the author also points to the life and beauty that hide in Sarajevo's scars. In "The Life of a Flâneur," the centerpiece of his memoir, mortar shell marks are "filled out with red paint," and the "people of Sarajevo now, incredibly, called them 'roses.'"[28] Previously published as "Mapping Home: Learning a New City, Remembering the Old," this autobiographical piece is joined in the *New Yorker* by an artistic visual representation of Hemon, a Gulliver-like figure, against images of the detritus of a possibly ruined apartment, a Sarajevo tram, and the iconic Chicago skyline. The story juxtaposes the two urban spaces with which the Bosnian-born author identifies, but I read no opposition between "the old" and "the new," as the *New Yorker* title might initially suggest. Instead, there is constant coexistence and overlay of apparently distinct urbanscapes.

A clear geographical de-territorialization of Sarajevo, "a new inscription" to a "new socius" in Deleuze and Guattari's term,[29] is present in Hemon's autobiographical representation, which differs significantly from earlier immigrant depictions of reconciliation or merging of the spaces bridged by protagonists or authors themselves.[30] Urbanscapes come together in Hemon's stories of "shiploads of Bosnians" arriving in the Edgewater neighborhood, of return journeys home, and of a visiting childhood friend. Not mnemonic or fictional re-creation but plotlines and situations conjoin them. The Sarajevo of Hemon's nonfiction is the lively city of his youth and the wounded city suffering in the Bosnian War, but it is also an increasingly scattered space that reaches him in Chicago by way of tourism, diaspora, and labor migration from former Yugoslavia. Hemon's two home cities are superimposed and coexist simultaneously by virtue of increased mobility and human flows—Appadurai's "ethnoscapes"[31]—during and after the Bosnian War.

The literary cartographies of Sarajevo go beyond tropes of the city as a carrier of memory, a nostalgic monumentalization of Sarajevo, or a memento of past times. The fictional mappings of the city (which is most often placed in numerous convergences with other places or extends beyond its physical borders) function as an analytical frame through which Hemon's affective and ethical commitment to his native country is voiced.[32] The tokens of discontiguity as an organizing principle vary significantly from text to text: we come across photography with its multiple significances, letter exchanges between correspondents in Bosnia and the United States, as well as Hemon's transatlantic explorations of spaces and the routes between them. These concrete and abstract manifestations of discontiguity shape a counterpoint to the region's conventional representations.

A common feature in Hemon's depictions of the former Yugoslavia is the role of the camera and the mass media as active agents in the creation and dissemination of images in international venues. The story of Sarajevo, particularly the siege of the city, is generally familiar from television news reports of the 1990s.[33] When Hemon takes us through Sarajevo under fire, the portrayals are mostly mediated: the narrators almost never experience the siege but rather read, watch, or hear stories about it. In *The Lazarus Project*, Brik, the aspiring writer of Bosnian descent in the United States, gets the story of wartime Sarajevo from Rora, his photographer friend who works for news agencies. In "Blind Joseph Pronek and Dead Souls," Pronek's experience of the conflict back home comes from television images: "Sarajevo was besieged [and] there were rumors of Serbian concentration camps, but [Pronek] only watched the images to recognize the people in them."[34] While Pronek looks for people and human faces, "friends shot by snipers or killed by shrapnel," and strongly feels that the conflict is not a distant abstraction, his housemates play TV games or watch pornography instead.

The characters' reactions in both *The Question of Bruno* and *Nowhere Man* align with Susan Sontag's view that "for all the voyeuristic lure" of the media, "it seems normal for people to fend off thinking about the ordeals of others."[35] By rendering Sarajevo via a host of scattered TV images, Hemon points to the indifference of the broader public to the Bosnian conflict. The sporadic images of Sarajevo that Pronek gets to watch become a means with which to criticize the trivialization of similar vignettes during any moment of violence and crisis, as Hemon's indictment extends beyond the reception of his hometown.[36] Many characters in the novel "fend off" the pain of others in Bosnia, but Hemon's nuanced explorations of their averted gaze, on the one hand, and the compulsive voyeurism equally prominent in war-torn Yugoslavia, on the other hand, make significant additions to US American literary images of Eastern Europe.

In the story "A Coin" (first published in 1997 in the *Chicago Review*), Hemon further explores the role of the camera, both in photography and video, in rendering images of the besieged city. Structured around the narrator's transatlantic correspondence with his friend Aida, caught in the siege, the story opens with Sarajevo as seen by a sniper. We learn that among the scattered and bullet-ridden objects on a Sarajevo street there is also a "dismembered videocassette."[37] Aida tours the city with her lover, Kevin, a US war correspondent, to take photographs because "the places on our tour were between being a memory and being reduced to nothing but a pile of rubble. The camera was recording the process of disappearance" (132). The camera records what is dear and lost and becomes the way of accessing the intimate and the familiar (Aida's school, the bars of her youth, the park, "now treeless"). The photograph that Aida sends the American narrator becomes a means of closing the chasm that separates him from her and Sarajevo from Chicago and then of registering the creation of a (new) gap between him and the world he had left behind through the war's destruction of all that was once familiar: he "could see holes that used to be windows, the pillars like scorched matches" (122).

Aida's job, as liaison for a pool of foreign journalists, is to edit footage and then send it out of the country to the journalists scattered across the globe. First she includes the "most telling images with … blood and bowels, stumps and child corpses" in order to "induce compassion" (122). But eventually, she ends up cutting out everything that was "horrid" (123). Instead of disseminating the gory footage, she archives it on a separate tape titled "Cinema Inferno" (a reversal of *Cinema Paradiso*, the Italian Oscar-winning movie she once watched). Then, Kevin, a senior correspondent, captures dismembered people "for a good five minutes, like fucking Tarkovsky" (126), instead of helping them, as Aida reproaches him. Kevin's attitude, the "'cameraman syndrome' always being a gaze away from the world" (125), symbolically stands for international inactivity with regard to the cataclysms in and around Sarajevo. Aida's or Kevin's footage reaches the narrator via *Headline News,* which he watches "waiting for a glimpse of Sarajevo" (124). For a Sarajevan in Chicago, images of destruction or carnage are the only means of connecting with the once familiar world and its people. Finally, Aida lives in a former TV studio, where old cameras always get in the way, "like ghosts recording us" (127). The locals under the media gaze, the affected subjects, the detached (or distant) observers are brought together through the ubiquity of the camera and its role in the production and dissemination of images. Camera tropes and Hemon's critical engagement with media representations of the Bosnian War render the question of proximity irrelevant, as non-contiguous spaces are just as connected to and significant for (mis)understanding the conflict. Through the nuanced depiction of the media and their critique, Hemon's story also shows that the ostensibly distant places play key roles in reframing the region within a geographically dynamic context.

A comment on media representations during the Bosnian War, Hemon's portrayal of Sarajevo also points to the ambivalent trajectories such images acquire. The camera offers a trace of Sarajevo and its people's past, the treasured and the familiar, while it captures what has been lost, as Aida's and the narrator's reactions illustrate. The edited or unedited footage that the camera archives does not simply record the conflict. Rather, it also participates in the conflict through the observer's inactivity and the possible aestheticization of pain (Kevin), the desire to induce compassion and the refusal to perpetuate violence through images of carnage (Aida). The camera also conjures up the future public of the recorded events in Sarajevo, with the reader of the story being positioned on the same receiving end. We are at the intersection of different image trajectories: the voyeuristic and detached gaze of the media, the frequently intimate connection of the natives to the captured scenes, and the sniper's gunsight. The camera image is not just a representation of faraway events but rather a field of action where affective ties and conflicting kinds of gaze intersect and interpolate one another. At the same time, the dismembered videocassette from the opening paragraph underscores the transient nature of all visual documentation.

Aida's letters reach the narrator in Chicago—and implicitly the reader—and consequently articulate the circulation of narratives outside the camera's purview. The correspondence between Aida and the narrator conveys the way distant sites become embedded on location. The exchange creates clear parallels: the narrator's apartment transforms itself during the exchange and metaphorically recalls Aida's Sarajevan realities. The narrator, in turn, assumes the position of the sharpshooter watching the cockroaches running at night and pondering the "horrible world," where "every living creature lives and dies in fear" (131). Or else, he is a possible target, reminded by the cobwebs of being "trapped" (133). If in "The Life of a Flâneur" the extension of Sarajevo to Chicago happens due to the ethnoscapes of the 1990s, there is an affective de-territorialization that takes place via the exchanged letters in "A Coin." The reality of Sarajevo becomes embedded in the narrator's life in Chicago, and thus distant and distinct geographical spaces undergo transatlantic convergence in the present. Another form of their convergence takes place symbolically through Kevin, who used to work as a war correspondent in Afghanistan, Lebanon, the Persian Gulf, and Africa. Kevin's perspective extracts Bosnia from the projections of barbarism onto Yugoslavia or the Balkans alone. Sarajevo under siege becomes a locus of violence and suffering among many, and the Bosnian War is positioned on a global map of conflicts.

In *The Lazarus Project*, the narrative of the Bosnian War is juxtaposed with the story of the US War on Terror and the turn-of-the-century antisemitism and xenophobia in Chicago, thus once again affecting a disjunction between spaces. When placed alongside other sites or periods of violence, the "powder keg of Europe" that the Balkans has come to represent in the

West is rendered irrelevant, devoid of its assumed inherent ethnic or national characteristics.

Cultural critics have pointed out that "the fate of European identity as a whole is being played out in Yugoslavia and more generally in the Balkans."[38] Referring to the constant resistance to a discourse that would meaningfully engage with the wars in former Yugoslavia, Étienne Balibar suggests that Europe has to "recognize in the Balkan situation not a monstrosity grafted to its breast, a pathological 'after-effect' of underdevelopment or of Communism, but rather an image ... of its own history, and ... undertake to confront it and resolve it and thus to put itself into question and transform itself."[39] Hemon offers a discursive frame for "com[ing] face to face"[40] with this history, while he also takes the latter out of the mutually exclusive discourses within the region. The many layers of critical cartographic imaginaries present in Hemon's fiction reclaim dialogue and open-endedness with reference to the former Yugoslav spaces, their history, and frequently biased worldwide circulation of their images.

The interaction with and de-territorialization of Sarajevo in other spaces near or far does not entail a flattening and homogenization of specific sites and historical conditions. Nor does it transpose Yugoslavia to yet another map of violence, nationalism, and backwardness. Instead, Hemon's multilayered post-socialist spaces move beyond the tired "Balkan ghosts" and Orientalizing topoi and, conversely, beyond many Eastern Europeans' reception of "America" as an unequivocal savior, riding in as a "shining knight" on a "white horse."[41] The Sarajevo of Hemon's fiction is no enclosed, bounded space between and betwixt. The new affiliations that Sarajevo's space poetics engender function as framework of critique against and dissent from contemporary media by resisting both political narrativization and victimhood. Sarajevo's new imaginary extends beyond geographical or temporal boundaries and informs and is informed by the understanding of sites elsewhere, be it Europe, North America, or Africa.

CODA: CRITICAL TRANSNATIONALISM

Eastern European spaces in Penkov's and Hemon's literary cartographies form a conjunction of interactions across time and space. Their rendering of these interactions is predicated on a transnational approach, namely a view or optic that "interrogate[s] the territorial breadth and scope of any social phenomenon without prior assumptions."[42] More specifically, their texts can be seen as embodiments of "critical transnationalism," namely a "method of inquiry" that serves to reveal regional formations and thus "hollow out their pressing, peremptory claims to legitimacy."[43] They help us interpret "more productively the interface between global and local, national and transnational,"[44] in connection with Eastern Europe, while they also move away from negating one approach in favor of the other. The literary cartographies of Hemon and Penkov also go beyond the predominant perspectives based on contiguity, to which eastern and southeastern parts of Europe have been subject. The cartographic imaginaries present in Penkov and Hemon offer multiple sets of dynamically overlapping and interacting geo-historical or geo-social fields that reshape what has been assumed to be the bordered and bounded structures or the categories typically chosen for their analysis. The literary mappings discussed here challenge the traditional imaginary constructions of Eastern European spaces and demystify these region's mistakenly naturalized affiliations as contingent and arbitrary. At interstices of times and places, the Eastern European space imaginaries presented in this chapter reflect the region's dynamism and its continued transformation.

The transnational matrix of such works bespeaks the multidirectional forces of globalization and the larger orbit in which Eastern Europe circulates. In the Anglo-American context, it breaks new ground by fleshing out new configurations and disjunctures of post-1989 Eastern European spaces on a worldwide scale. At the same time, neither Penkov nor Hemon puts forth a single paradigm or master narrative about spaces in Eastern Europe. As my analysis has shown, their texts scrutinize relational geographies to convey many varied discursive strategies and spatial poetics that exist in productive conversations with one another. They prefer to probe paradoxes, apparent contradictions, impossibilities, or the ambivalences of encounters, and in so doing they reorient readers away from traditional geographies of Eastern Europe toward complex circuits, relations, juxtapositions, and encounters with sites beyond geographical borders. They point to an Eastern Europe gone global, where identity is defined by the multiple and changing connections with places and times; an Eastern Europe as one of the many spots on a worldwide map characterized by moving vectors and innumerable dots that constantly define and redefine each other.

Ioana Luca, associate professor, National Taiwan Normal University, teaches courses in American studies, American literature, life writing, and memory studies. Her publications include articles in *Social Text, Rethinking History, Prose Studies, Biography, Journal of American Studies,* and *EJLW* and chapters in several edited volumes. She is the recipient of several fellowships (Fulbright, OSI/Chevening, HRC at ANU) as well as Academia Sinica's research award for junior scholars.

NOTES

This essay is the result of a research project supported by the Ministry of Science and Technology in Taiwan, grant 104-2410-H-003-038-MY2. I am very grateful to the editors of the volume for their valuable suggestions and kind support.

1. Henri Lefebvre, *The Production of Space* (Oxford: Blackwell, 1991), 85–86.
2. Lefebvre, *The Production of Space*, 288–89.
3. Patricia Yaeger, "Introduction: Dreaming of Infrastructure," *PMLA* 122 (2007): 21.
4. Doreen Massey, "Places and Their Pasts," *History Workshop Journal* 39 (1995): 186. Emphasis in the original.
5. Andreas Huyssen, *Other Cities, Other Worlds: Urban Imaginaries in a Globalizing Age* (Durham, NC: Duke University Press, 2009), 21.
6. Huyssen, *Other Cities, Other Worlds*, 3.
7. For the examination of the role of "imaginative geographies" with reference to Eastern Europe, see Larry Wolff, *Inventing Eastern Europe: The Map of Civilization on the Mind of the Enlightenment* (Stanford, CA: Stanford University Press, 1994); Maria Todorova, *Imagining the Balkans* (Oxford: Oxford University Press, 1997); Vesna Goldsworthy, *Inventing Ruritania: The Imperialism of the Imagination* (New Haven, CT: Yale University Press, 1998); Andrew Hammond, *The Debated Lands: British and American Representations of the Balkan* (Cardiff: University of Wales Press, 2007); Andrew Hammond, ed., *The Balkans and the West: Constructing the European Other, 1945–2003* (London: Ashgate, 2004); Dušan I. Bjelić and Obrad Savić, *Balkan as Metaphor between Globalization and Fragmentation* (Cambridge, MA: MIT Press, 2002).
8. Sanjeev Khagram and Peggy Levitt, "Constructing *Transnational Studies*," in *The Transnational Studies Reader: Intersections and Innovations* (New York: Routledge, 2008), 5.
9. Khagram and Levitt, "Constructing *Transnational Studies*," 5.
10. See Yuliya Komska's introduction to this volume.
11. Paul Giles, *Transnationalism in Practice: Essays on American Studies, Literature and Religion* (Edinburgh: Edinburgh University Press, 2010), 51.
12. Julia Leyda and Sheila Hones, "Geographies of American Studies," *American Quarterly* 57, no. 4 (2006): 1024.
13. Milica Bakić-Hayden, "Nesting Orientalisms: The Case of Former Yugoslavia," *Slavic Review* 54, no. 4 (1995): 917.
14. Eliot Borenstein, "Was It Sexy, or Just Soviet? The Post-Communist Expat Safari Novel Has Its Day," *Nation*, 16 January 2003, 33–34. Borenstein's comprehensive review includes Jonathan Franzen's *Corrections* (2001), Jonathan Safran Foer's *Everything is Illuminated* (2002), Paul Greenberg's *Leaving Katia* (2002), Arthur Phillips's *Prague* (2002), John Beckman's *The Winter Zoo* (2002), and Gary Shteyngart's *The Russian Debutante's Handbook* (2002).
15. See Ioana Luca, "Post-1989 Eastern European Itineraries with Eva Hoffman and Slavenka Drakulić," *Wenshan Review* 7, no. 2 (2014): 315–47.

16. Bharati Mukherjee, "Immigrant Writing: Changing the Contours of a National Literature," *American Literary History* 23, no. 3 (2011): 681.
17. Eva Hoffman, *Lost in Translation: A Life in a New Language* (New York: E. P. Dutton, 1989), 278.
18. Miroslav Penkov, "UNT's Miroslav Penkov Discusses *East of the West* and His Writing Process," *Dallas Observer*, 3 August 2011, accessed 5 July 2015, http://www.dallasobserver.com/arts/unts-miroslav-penkov-discusses-east-of-the-west-and-his-writing-process-7094182.
19. Such an intertextual connection might also be due to an earlier collaboration between Penkov and Rushdie, as one of Penkov's short stories, "Buying Lenin," was published in *The Best American Short Stories 2008* (Boston: Houghton Mifflin, 2008), edited by Rushdie.
20. Penkov, "UNT's Miroslav Penkov Discusses *East of the West*."
21. Robert D. Kaplan, *Balkan Ghosts: A Journey through History* (New York: Random House, 1993).
22. Miroslav Penkov, "East of the West," in *East of the West: A Country in Stories* (New York: Farrar, Straus and Giroux, 2011), 46.
23. Penkov, "A Picture with Yuki," in *East of the West*, 104. Further quoted parenthetically.
24. Monica Spiridon, "La vest de Eden" [West of Eden], *Secolul XX* 10–12 (1997–98): 225.
25. Aleksandar Hemon, "Stairway to Heaven," in *Love and Obstacles: Stories* (New York: Riverhead Books, 2009), 3. The intertextual connections that Hemon's short stories or novels establish with US or UK popular culture by way of titles further exemplify the transnational thrust of his work.
26. Aleksandar Hemon, "The Sorge Spy Ring," in *The Question of Bruno* (London: Vintage International, 2003), 73.
27. Bill Clinton, "Statement on Kosovo," Miller Center, 24 March 1999, accessed 29 October 2014, http://millercenter.org/president/speeches/detail/3932.
28. Aleksandar Hemon, *The Book of My Lives* (London: Macmillan, 2013), 105.
29. Gilles Deleuze and Félix Guattari, *Anti-Oedipus*, trans. Robert Hurley, Mark Seem, and Helen R. Lane (London: Continuum, 2004), 195.
30. See, for example, Mary Antin's *The Promised Land* (1912; New York: Penguin, 1997) or Eva Hoffman's *Lost in Translation* (1989).
31. Arjun Appadurai, *Modernity at Large: Cultural Dimensions of Globalization* (Minneapolis: University of Minnesota Press, 1996), 33.
32. Hemon's emphasis on the ethical role of storytelling is clearly expressed in interviews. For the most recent ones see Hemon, "A Little Blue Alien Helped Hemon Bear Witness to His 'Lives,'" *NPR*, 13 March 2013, accessed 5 July 2015, http://www.npr.org/2013/03/16/174202292/a-little-blue-alien-helped-hemon-bear-witness-to-his-lives; and Timothy Boswell, "The Audacity of Despair: An Interview with Aleksandar Hemon," *Studies in the Novel* 47, no. 2 (2015): 246–66.
33. For a succinct but insightful discussion of media images and representations of Sarajevo during and in the aftermath of the war, see Thomas Keenan, "Public-

ity and Indifference (Sarajevo on Television)," *PMLA* 117, no. 1 (2002): 104–16. A wider perspective on war images with a focus on Bosnia informs Branislav Jakovljevic, "Theater of Atrocities: Toward a Disreality Principle," *PMLA* 124, no. 5 (2009): 1813–19.
34. Hemon, *The Question of Bruno,* 187.
35. Susan Sontag, *Regarding the Pain of Others* (New York: Farrar, Straus and Giroux, 2003), 99.
36. *The Lazarus Project* is actually an Abu Ghraib novel, as it engages with the US War on Terror.
37. Hemon, *The Question of Bruno,* 119. In the following, quoted parenthetically.
38. Étienne Balibar, *We, the People of Europe? Reflections on Transnational Citizenship* (Princeton, NJ: Princeton University Press, 2009), 6.
39. Balibar, *We, the People of Europe?,* 6.
40. Balibar, *We, the People of Europe?,* 6.
41. Péter Esterházy, "How Big Is the European Dwarf?," in *Old Europe, New Europe, Core Europe: Transatlantic Relations after the Iraq War,* ed. Daniel Levy, Max Pensky, and John Torpey (London: Verso, 2005), 75.
42. Khagram and Levitt, "Constructing *Transnational Studies,*" 5.
43. Giles, *Transnationalism,* 45.
44. Will Higbee and Song Hwee Lim, "Concepts of Transnational Cinema: Towards a Critical Transnationalism in Film Studies," *Transnational Cinemas* 1, no. 1 (2010): 7–21. I draw on the concept of critical transnationalism as defined in connection to cultural studies by Will Higbee and Song Hwee Lim as well as by Ien Ang and Jon Stratton, "Asianing Australia: Notes toward a Critical Transnationalism in Cultural Studies," *Cultural Studies* 10, no. 1 (1996): 16–36. With reference to American literary history, see Giles, *Transnationalism.*

WORKS CITED

Ang, Ien, and Jon Stratton. "Asianing Australia: Notes toward a Critical Transnationalism in Cultural Studies." *Cultural Studies* 10, no. 1 (1996): 16–36.
Antin, Mary. *The Promised Land.* New York: Penguin, 1997 (1912).
Appadurai, Arjun. *Modernity at Large: Cultural Dimensions of Globalization.* Minneapolis: University of Minnesota Press, 1996.
Baker, Deborah, and Aleksandar Hemon. "Aleksandar Hemon: Interview." *BOMB Magazine,* 20 August 2008. Accessed 5 July 2015. http://bombsite.com/issues/999/articles/3175.
Bakić-Hayden, Milica. "Nesting Orientalisms: The Case of Former Yugoslavia." *Slavic Review* 54, no. 4 (1995): 917–31.
Balibar, Étienne. *We, the People of Europe? Reflections on Transnational Citizenship: Reflections on Transnational Citizenship.* Princeton, NJ: Princeton University Press, 2009.
Bjelić, Dušan I., and Obrad Savić. *Balkan as Metaphor between Globalization and Fragmentation.* Cambridge, MA: MIT Press, 2002.

Borenstein, Eliot. "Was It Sexy, or Just Soviet? The Post-Communist Expat Safari Novel Has Its Day." *Nation* 3 (2003): 33–36.
Boswell, Timothy. "The Audacity of Despair: An Interview with Aleksandar Hemon." *Studies in the Novel* 47, no. 2 (2015): 246–66.
Clinton, Bill. "Statement on Kosovo." Miller Center, 24 March 1999. Accessed 29 October 2014. http://millercenter.org/president/speeches/detail/3932.
Deleuze, Gilles, and Félix Guattari. *Anti-Oedipus*. Translated by Robert Hurley, Mark Seem, and Helen R. Lane. London and New York: Continuum, 2004 (1972).
Esterházy, Péter. "How Big Is the European Dwarf?" In *Old Europe, New Europe, Core Europe: Transatlantic Relations after the Iraq War*, edited by Daniel Levy, Max Pensky, and John Torpey, 74–80. London: Verso, 2005.
Giles, Paul. *Transnationalism in Practice: Essays on American Studies, Literature and Religion*. Edinburgh: Edinburgh University Press, 2010.
Goldsworthy, Vesna. *Inventing Ruritania: The Imperialism of the Imagination*. New Haven, CT: Yale University Press, 1998.
Hammond, Andrew. "'The Danger Zone of Europe' Balkanism between the Cold War and 9/11." *European Journal of Cultural Studies* 8, no. 2 (2005): 135–54.
Hammond, Andrew. *The Debated Lands: British and American Representations of the Balkans*. Cardiff: University of Wales Press, 2007.
Hammond, Andrew, ed. *The Balkans and the West: Constructing the European Other, 1945–2003*. London: Ashgate, 2004.
Hemon, Aleksandar. *The Book of My Lives*. London: Macmillan, 2013.
———. *The Lazarus Project*. New York: Riverhead Books, 2008.
———. "A Little Blue Alien Helped Hemon Bear Witness to His 'Lives.'" *NPR*, 13 March 2013. Accessed 5 July 2015. http://www.npr.org/2013/03/16/174202292/a-little-blue-alien-helped-hemon-bear-witness-to-his-lives
———. *Love and Obstacles: Stories*. New York: Riverhead Books, 2009.
———. *The Making of Zombie Wars*. London: Pan Macmillan, 2015.
———. "Mapping Home: Learning a New City, Remembering the Old." *New Yorker*, 5 December 2011. Accessed 25 August 2016. http://www.newyorker.com/reporting/2011/12/05/111205fa_fact_hemon.
———. *Nowhere Man*. London: Picador, 2003.
———. "The Sorge Spy Ring." In *The Question of Bruno*. 41–87. London: Vintage International, 2003.
———. "Stairway to Heaven." In *Love and Obstacles: Stories*. 1–37. New York: Riverhead Books, 2009.
———. *The Question of Bruno*. London: Vintage International, 2003.
Higbee, Will, and Song Hwee Lim. "Concepts of Transnational Cinema: Towards a Critical Transnationalism in Film Studies." *Transnational Cinemas* 1, no. 1 (2010): 7–21.
Hoffman, Eva. *Lost in Translation: A Life in a New Language*. New York: E. P. Dutton, 1989.
Huyssen, Andreas. *Other Cities, Other Worlds: Urban Imaginaries in a Globalizing Age*. Durham, NC: Duke University Press, 2009.

Jakovljevic, Branislav. "Theater of Atrocities: Toward a Disreality Principle." *PMLA* 124, no. 5 (2009): 1813–19.
Kaplan, Robert D. *Balkan Ghosts: A Journey through History.* New York: Random House, 1993.
Keenan, Thomas. "Publicity and Indifference (Sarajevo on Television)." *PMLA* 117, no. 1 (2002): 104–16.
Khagram, Sanjeev, and Peggy Levitt. *The Transnational Studies Reader: Intersections and Innovations.* New York: Routledge, 2008.
Kovačević, Nataša. *Narrating Post/Communism: Colonial Discourse and Europe's Borderline Civilization.* New York: Routledge, 2008.
Lefebvre, Henri. *The Production of Space.* Oxford: Blackwell, 1991.
Leyda, Julia, and Sheila Hones. "Geographies of American Studies." *American Quarterly* 57, no. 4 (2006): 1019–32.
Luca, Ioana. "Post-1989 Eastern European Itineraries with Eva Hoffman and Slavenka Drakulić." *Wenshan Review* 7, no. 2 (2014): 315–47.
Massey, Doreen. "Places and Their Pasts." *History Workshop Journal* 35 (Spring 1995): 182–92.
Mukherjee, Bharati. "Immigrant Writing: Changing the Contours of a National Literature." *American Literary History* 23, no. 3 (2011): 680–96.
Penkov, Miroslav. *East of the West: A Country in Stories.* New York: Farrar, Straus and Giroux, 2011.
———. "East of the West." In *East of the West: A Country in Stories,* 25–53. New York: Farrar, Straus and Giroux, 2011.
———. "A Picture with Yuki." In *East of the West: A Country in Stories,* 95–123. New York: Farrar, Straus and Giroux, 2011.
———. "UNT's Miroslav Penkov Discusses *East of the West* and His Writing Process." *Dallas Observer,* 3 August 2011. Accessed 25 August 2016. http://www.dallasobserver.com/arts/unts-miroslav-penkov-discusses-east-of-the-west-and-his-writing-process-7094182.
Rushdie, Salman. *East, West.* London: Jonathan Cape, 1994.
Sontag, Susan. *Regarding the Pain of Others.* New York: Farrar, Straus and Giroux, 2003.
Spiridon, Monica. "La vest de Eden" [West of Eden]. *Secolul XX* 10–12 (1997–98): 224–34.
Todorova, Maria. *Imagining the Balkans.* Oxford: Oxford University Press, 2009.
Wolff, Larry. *Inventing Eastern Europe: The Map of Civilization on the Mind of the Enlightenment.* Stanford, CA: Stanford University Press, 1994.
Yaeger, Patricia. "Introduction: Dreaming of Infrastructure." *PMLA* 122 (2007): 9–26.

Part IV

Appropriated Afterlives

What could seem more anchored in its immediate surroundings than a building? A synagogue, a *bet tahara* (a building for the ritual cleansing of corpses) with attached gatekeeper's house, a mural on a wall. We usually think of architectural heritage as a key component of local identity. And yet, the two essays in this section explore the seeming "disappearances" and "reappearances" of these constructions in the long wake of the cataclysms of the mid-twentieth century.

When entire segments of communities are made to disappear, as were Jewish populations in almost innumerable locations around Eastern Europe in the mid-twentieth century, the buildings they had erected for their use can be appropriated for different purposes. Alterations and new narratives can lead to the original purposes becoming obscured altogether. Historical contiguity can be ignored. Any new cataclysm can change once again communities' composition, daily and occasional needs with relation to built space, and of course the stories that those communities want to tell about themselves and where they live. In two of the cases discussed here, the (dead) Jewish others have posthumously become celebrities elsewhere and subsequently within the Gentile communities who had inherited the sites those individuals had created.

Sarah M. Schlachetzki contrasts the fates of buildings commissioned by the prewar Jewish communities of Olsztyn (Allenstein) and Poznań (Posen), a *bet tahara* and a new synagogue, respectively. While the current citizens of Olsztyn may want to reclaim a connection to Erich Mendelsohn (the building's famed architect) by saving his first commission, the citizens of Poznań hesitate to spend precious financial resources on the restoration of a synagogue, especially one that had been radically changed already during the

Nazi period and that since that time had been repurposed for secular uses. Schlachetzki lays out the two controversies to show how complicated the reclaiming of a building for cultural heritage can be. While Mendelsohn's subsequent fame could bring advantage (in the form of architectural tourism) to Olsztyn, restoring the Poznań synagogue would create undesirable physical reminders of a Poland not just "with Jews," but also under German domination, evident in the Prussian historicist style of the original building.

As for the nursery murals that Bruno Schulz had painted for a Gestapo officer's villa in Drohobych (now Ukraine), Adam Zachary Newton explains their rediscovery and spiriting out of this town in several fragments. Transported to Jerusalem's Yad Vashem with a portion left in situ, the murals now endure an uncannily ruptured afterlife in an unintended echo of what Schulz celebrated as "the migration of forms." That this fate also echoes a series of transpositions and appropriations undergone by the biographical figure of Schulz himself across the border of late twentieth- and early twenty-first-century prose fiction makes the episode especially uncanny. As Schlachetzki contrasts the fates of the two buildings, Newton juxtaposes the fate of the Schulz mural with the Emanuel Ringelblum *Oyneg Shabes* archive salvaged from ruins of the Warsaw Ghetto.

While the Nazis and their allies had created a profound social non-contiguity by slaughtering European Jews, agendas of current Israeli and Holocaust scholars add to the complexity of the resulting ruptures. By fleshing these out, both essays register the complicated process of appropriating heritage, be it the work of great visionaries like Mendelsohn and Schulz—or Ringelblum for that matter—or of lesser ones like the original (German) architects of Poznań's New Synagogue.

Chapter Seven

Appropriations of the Past
The New Synagogue in Poznań and Olsztyn's Bet Tahara

Sarah M. Schlachetzki

> This book is not a political one; but politics and economics are the vivid foundations of its architectonic cross section.... Juxtaposing "Russia—Europe—America," it touches upon a problem that is highly current, important, and crucial for our time.
> —Foreword to Erich Mendelsohn, *Russland—Europa—Amerika*[1]

In 1929, when he published his book *Russia–Europe–America,* Erich Mendelsohn was well established. He was one of the most successful German architects during the Weimar Republic, designing villas and department stores across the country, often for Jewish clients such as publisher Rudolf Mosse. Mosse Publishers also featured Mendelsohn's richly illustrated book on the architectural potential of the United States and Russia. Between the two powers of volition (*Willensmächte*), as Mendelsohn called them, lay Europe, Mendelsohn's homeland. From here, he appealed to the German-speaking readers to exchange "the explosives of political conflict ... for the conscience of European solidarity." The "encompassing technological spirit of a world being newly created" seemed to have placed within reach the dream of an architect of Mendelsohn's renown: *Neues Bauen* for a new world.[2] It all turned out differently. Modernism's belief in progress was shattered and Mendelsohn's life changed drastically with the National Socialists' rise to power and their destructive rule over parts of Europe in the ensuing years.

This chapter is a reflection on Mendelsohn's Europe—a land located between Russia and America, but actually a utopia, a non-place, an imaginary entity. Mendelsohn's early work will serve as a springboard for considering a European problem important today: what happens to Jewish architectural heritage that has been abandoned, at times virtually erased, rediscovered, questioned—specifically in a region that has experienced continuous shifts of borders? These sites testify to ruptures in contiguity and cohabitation. With the almost complete annihilation of the local Jewry, Central Europe's societies today are left with an abstract idea of someone "who had once been there." They struggle to include the often minuscule, sometimes growing, present Jewish communities in their self-identity as these societies' co-constitutive parts and not extrinsic next-door neighbors. After introducing my examples, I will address more precisely the fault lines of this "othering" and its relevance to debates on architectural remains.

The theoretical approach of this chapter is based on recent studies on Jewish culture in contemporary Poland. Several scholars, among them Ruth Gruber, Erica Lehrer, and Michael Meng, have become concerned with a pluralist perspective that eschews the focus on—and thereby co-construction of—the adversarial aspects of Polish-Jewish relations.[3] In line with the generally heightened interest in post-national, transnational, and local histories, their scholarship does not take sides in controversies. Rather, in openly addressing the ambiguities of historical evaluation, these researchers seek to do justice to the complexity of their politically and morally charged material.[4]

When we talk about architectural heritage, we usually talk about its stabilizing function within a local or national community. While times, politics, and societies change, architecture's permanence, we tend to assume, secures situated cultural identity by spanning generations.[5] Through the continuous rereading of cultural meaning ingrained in and projected upon our cities' fabric—and what is called their "heritage"—architecture provides a feeling of belonging that reaches well past its essential function to shelter.

Architecture can also become a site of struggle over meanings and values. The very term "heritage" is then contested: a place that is at best judged by its utility can become unwanted[6] or given up for demolition. Against the backdrop of the potential for conflict that is inherent in architecture, I will focus on two buildings, one in Poznań and the other in Olsztyn. The two sites exemplify different attitudes toward Jewish heritage in contemporary Poland. They are locally determined, historically anchored, and, most recently, reconsidered with an eye to a more or less inclusive local identity, depending on each case. The buildings in question are a former municipal swimming pool and a repository of the state archives. Put differently: they are Poznań's New Synagogue and Olsztyn's Bet Tahara.

Rather than focusing on the urban palimpsest, an entity legible from the bird's-eye view cartographically and diachronically, my point is that it is the debates about and actions taken for the two buildings that need to be scrutinized when considering how people deal with unwanted or appropriated heritage. My perspective on the matter harks back to Hannah Arendt's disambiguation of the polis as a discursive forum rather than as a material space. In this forum, cultural heritage—whether referred to as such or not—is conceptualized and sustained. In the case of Poland, this can happen by way of inclusion, that is, discussing the object in terms of *dziedzictwo* (heritage) or officially labeling it *zabytek nieruchomy* (immovable monument). But it can also remain exclusive, arguing over the future of something as "neutral" as *budynek* (building) or, as we shall see, *synagoga* or *bóżnica* (synagogue).[7]

NEUE SYNAGOGE—1907

Although architectural structures may count among the more lasting physical objects in the world (and "the worldliest" of them all, to quote Arendt), although they may outlast generations and gain relative independence from the ebbs and flows of human existence,[8] people still commission them, design them, and live with them. Along with building and tearing down, people create narratives about the affected sites. People suffer the losses; they are confronted with the mute and stubborn remnants of the past. Architecture's significance cannot be described without the human context. To understand the conflicts about the two buildings under scrutiny here, it is crucial to explore their history.

In 1900, Poznań (then German Posen), part of the Prussian empire since Poland's Second Partition in 1793, was a prosperous provincial city. Dominated by the Prussian annexationists, the province of Posen was inhabited by a Polish majority. Less than half of its inhabitants were Germans who had moved there following the colonizing logic of Prussia's long-term territorial expansion.[9] After Poland's disappearance from the map, Posen was located less than fifty miles from Prussia's border with the Russian Empire.

The first years of the twentieth century were particularly formative for Poznań's city planning, as its fortifications were torn down in 1902, and Hermann Josef Stübben, one of Prussia's most renowned urban planners, oversaw the construction of the Imperial Forum (Kaiserforum): the remodeling of a vast central part of the city, marked by the erection of the Kaiser Friedrich Museum in 1904, the Royal Academy (1905–10), the theater (1909–10) and, most important, the Residential Castle (Residenzschloss, 1905–13). The Imperial Forum was to epitomize the Prussian rule of the province and thereby demonstrate the German presence—and power—in the city.[10] The names of the architects who were involved in the city's architectural Germanization read like a register of Prussian building administration officials: Karl Hinckeldeyn, Eduard Fürstenau, Franz Heinrich Schwechten.

Shortly after the turn of the century, the Orthodox Jewish community of Poznań decided to build a new, prominent synagogue. By 1904 they had raised enough money to hold a competition and commission the construction of what became the Neue Synagoge (New Synagogue). The building was finished and solemnly dedicated in 1907.[11] Its architects, Wilhelm Cremer and Richard Wolffenstein, had been operating a thriving business, Cremer & Wolffenstein, in Berlin since 1882. They had built several department stores and apartment buildings and excelled in the design of synagogues. Among their works were Synagoge Lindenstrasse (1888–91; destroyed), Spandauer Vereinssynagoge (1894–95; destroyed), Synagoge Lützowstrasse (1897–98; destroyed), all in Berlin. But Cremer & Wolffenstein were also active outside the Prussian capital. In their typical historicist style, they constructed the Neue Synagoge in Königsberg (today Kaliningrad, Russia; 1893–96; destroyed). They won a prize in the competition to rebuild and enlarge Magdeburg's Alte Synagoge (1894; destroyed).[12] Finally, in the same year when they realized their ideas for Poznań, the synagogue in Dessau was built according to their plans (also destroyed).[13]

Poznań's New Synagogue can be regarded as representative of the enhanced self-image and improving urban integration of Jewish communities in Prussia—a mere thirty years before the nationwide outburst of lingering antisemitism and the attempted extermination of European Jewry. The building was located just a few meters north of the bustling Old Market Square. Impressive in size, it could host six hundred men and six hundred women. Instead of adhering to the Moorish-Oriental style seen in many synagogues at that time, Cremer & Wolffenstein opted for a neo-Romanesque rendition, as they had in their earlier sacred buildings. In times of eclectic historicism, this allowed for the architectural integration of a Jewish community building into its central setting (today Skwer Rabina Akiwy Egera), "a site of unprecedented prominence."[14] The new synagogue displayed the community's wealth and weight; its architecture also reflected the Jews' cultural affiliation with the Prussian Poznań. While the Prussian administration was waging its Kulturkampf against the (Catholic) Polish

Neuere Synagogen. Architekten: Cremer & Wolffenstein, kgl. Bauräte in Berlin. I. Die neue Synagoge in Posen.

Figure 7.1. Cremer & Wolffenstein, New Synagogue, Poznań, 1904–7. From "Die neue Synagoge in Posen," *Deutsche Bauzeitung* 43, no. 89 (6 November 1909), 613.

majority on several levels, and while the Germanization of the city was also architecturally manifested in the Imperial Forum, the Germans now "evidently considered the Jews to be allies in the face of ethnic Polish opposition to German rule."[15]

The majority of the Jewish community was German-speaking and economically successful. Against this background, Carol H. Krinsky even suggests a direct connection between the construction of the Prussian Residential Castle in Poznań and the New Synagogue, both built in the neo-Romanesque style, reinvented as the "German style" at that time and place.

On the periphery of the German Empire circa 1907, the construction of the New Synagogue marked the community's readiness to be a full-fledged actor in German society, some fifty years after it had received the same naturalization rights as Prussia's Christians.

ALLENSTEIN–1913

In 1913, Emperor Wilhelm II visited Poznań's Residential Castle, as the castle's chapel was finally completed and consecrated. At the same time, little more than two hundred miles northeast of Poznań, in his native town Allenstein (today Polish Olsztyn), young Erich Mendelsohn was given the chance to carry out his first building. Still a student at the Technical University in Munich, he was asked to design a *bet tahara,* a building for the ritual cleansing of the corpses, and a gatekeeper's house next to the Jewish cemetery. The sources are sparse about the actual circumstances of the commission and Mendelsohn's authorship. Among scholars it is undisputed, however, that it was Mendelsohn who designed the dome of the Bet Tahara along with the simple exterior of the two buildings at the cemetery.[16]

A close follower of Zionist ideas and member of the Zionist Union for Germany (Zionistische Vereinigung für Deutschland) during his early years in Munich,[17] Mendelsohn rarely mentioned his first commission in later life and never included it in his list of works. For a modernist architect, it was surely more attractive to begin his list of achievements with the famous expressionist Einstein Tower in Potsdam outside Berlin (begun in 1920), and not with a Jewish sacral building on Germany's periphery.[18]

In its center, the Bet Tahara included a little hall surmounted by a pyramidal dome. Pillars, architraves, and the dome itself were delicately ornamented with mosaic bands and patterns. The plastering was in violet, the ornamentation in blue, green, and gold.[19] While the Jewish community of Allenstein had not quite obtained "a real Mendelsohn"–that is, a building as recognizable as his streamlined architecture of the 1920s would be–its most prominent son did give his fellow townspeople a beautiful Jugendstil-infused work, its colors possibly inspired by Munich's avant-garde group the Blue Rider.[20] Mendelsohn would see little of his native town in his later life, as he went off to war and settled in Berlin in 1918 to begin his career, quickly becoming a leading modern architect of the twenties.

Rudolf Mosse, Mendelsohn's aforementioned publisher in the 1920s, can be considered a link between the two buildings for Jewish communities under consideration here, as his main office and publishing house in

Figure 7.2. Erich Mendelsohn, Bet Tahara, Olsztyn, 1911–13, contemporary interior view. Copyright Fondazione Bruno Zevi.

Berlin had also been built by Cremer & Wolffenstein. The Mossehaus was constructed on the corner of Jerusalemer Strasse and Schützenstrasse in the turn-of-the-century historicist style. After the Great War, the building was severely damaged during the Spartacist uprising in 1919,[21] and Mosse was looking for a state-of-the-art refurbishment. He therefore hired Mendelsohn, who modernized the edifice by adding three more stories and altering the corner section between 1922 and 1923. Mendelsohn, at the breakthrough of his career, grafted his budding futurist vision onto Cremer & Wolffenstein's Berlin premises.

Figure 7.3. Cremer & Wolffenstein and Erich Mendelsohn, Mossehaus, Berlin, 1923. Courtesy Deutsches Bundesarchiv, Koblenz, Bild 102-00182 / Georg Pahl.

REAPPEARANCES

After the collapse of Communist regimes in Eastern Europe, the two buildings considered in this essay had seemingly vanished. In the wake of the Nazi Judeocide, the Jewish communities of Olsztyn and Poznań no longer existed. Mendelsohn had fled Germany when the Nazis came to power—first to England, then to Palestine, and finally to the United States, where he died in 1953. The Jewish cemetery in Olsztyn was closed in 1955, ransacked in the 1960s, and finally bulldozed.[22] After the war there was little memory of the Jewish presence or its end in Catholic Poland, not least due to competing victimhood narratives, as both Jews and Poles were targets of Nazi atrocities. The People's Republic of Poland saw another outburst of antisemitism in 1968, as a result of which once again, several thousand Jews left the country.[23] Mendelsohn's first work in Olsztyn was seemingly forgotten.

The New Synagogue in Poznań, too, had disappeared—virtually. Only a few residents recalled that the building serving as the municipal swimming pool had once been the city's largest Jewish place of worship. By 1942, the German occupants, who had annexed Poznań again in 1939, had transformed the building into a center for convalescing Wehrmacht soldiers.[24] They had removed the dome and vaulted roofs, altered the large windows on the western façade, stripped the edifice bare, and remodeled the interior by inserting a pool in the former basement. After 1945, when Poland was liberated and rebuilt on war-damaged ground, the building continued to function as a pool. Above the four (originally six) windows at the front façade that had once been covered by a round arch, letters now read *Pływalnia Miejska* (Municipal Pool). It was not until after the fall of Communism that there finally was a rising awareness of this conversion.[25] Most people in Poznań, however, continued to ignore the origin of the building in which they—still in the 2000s—did their laps. The municipal pool was not closed until 2011.

From here, the story can be told in at least two ways. One can stress Poland's highly problematic attitude toward Jewish remains after the war. Or one can discuss its struggle with the incomparably more complex challenges than what is so easily painted in contrasting colors. This struggle concerns questions of contiguity, the "ghosts of others,"[26] as well as how to map the past. Neither Mendelsohn's Bet Tahara in Olsztyn nor Poznań's synagogue can be debated other than by recalling Jewish culture and past as parts of the Polish present. Beyond the positivistic sequence of "facts" to which the two architectonic structures were exposed, the recent developments around them are indicative of cultural politics and economic possibilities. They concern the loss of spatial familiarity and questions of ownership. And they crystallize in narratives and debates that are formative for and formed by local identities.

Poznań's New Synagogue mirrors the (Jewish) history of the city, the history of Poland, and also Poland's present. Reluctantly, the town gave up its most central pool. While the solidly built baths had been maintained for decades, the municipality now had little money to subsidize a fundamental refurbishment of the New Synagogue.[27] The recent history of the building—passing from *Pływalnia Miejska* to a padlocked *Synagoga Nowa,* equipped with commemorative plaques—demonstrates the city's decades of suppressed memories, as well as the current revival of Poznań's Jewish community and the struggle for its covetable real estate.[28] It is also a chronicle of how a community negotiates changing connotations of its built heritage.

While the former synagogue was restituted to the Union of Jewish Religious Communities in Poland (Związek Gmin Wyznaniowych Żydowskich w RP) in 2002,[29] vivid and at times fierce debates ensued about what to do with it. The central conflict revolved less around forthright financial matters. It concerned a more essential issue: what does the building stand for—and is it in any way part of Poznań's cultural heritage? "Ours," as opposed to "not ours," was the formulation more or less implicitly discussed in the press, while the actual term "heritage" (*dziedzictwo*) was rarely used.[30] The term's conspicuous absence, moreover, marked the building's public status. The dispute did not primarily focus on a former place of worship or on the building as part of the Polish city's heritage, but on the dilapidated swimming pool. With the Jewish community under constant pressure to raise money for a revitalization of the building and struggling to come up with financially feasible concepts, the verbal ammunition used by the extreme opposition against any restoration evoked the evil ghosts of the past.

The debate was fueled by Marcin Libicki, art historian and member of the European Parliament and of the national-conservative Law and Justice party. He argued that the "massive" synagogue building had been erected in unison with the Prussian Kulturkampf that had been waged against "Polish and Catholic influences in the city."[31] In his opinion, the synagogue could be torn down in order to set free the lot on which it had been built and reconstruct a segment of the city's historic fortifications. Libicki was referring to Poznań's urbanistic burden: the Prussian Imperial Forum that sprawls across large parts of the city center. The Imperial Forum's stylistic similarities to the neo-Romanesque design of the New Synagogue did little to dispel the impression that both buildings connoted Germanness and its hegemonic power over the Polish culture.

Yet Libicki's remark seems absurd on two levels. When he raised his voice in 2006, the synagogue had long lost the traces of its original neo-

Romanesque appearance, having been remodeled under the Nazi rule. More important, invoked were the German affinities of Poznań's Jewry in the early twentieth century. Since the city's Jews considered themselves culturally German, rather than Polish, went the argument, this affiliation was accordingly expressed in the neo-Romanesque appearance of their Orthodox synagogue. By equating the German-Jewish community with the German oppressor, however, Libicki's invectives fell short of the complexities of history, conjuring up ethnic and religious antagonisms and clichés. His focus was not on heritage, but on resolving the fate of the architectural remains of the unwanted other. His views condensed a hundred years of shifting alliances, cultural and political, to a single formulaic argument about what to do with undesirable stones.

Libicki's proposal to tear down the former synagogue represents only one extreme in this debate; it shows, however, just what was at stake. City mayor Ryszard Grobelny and other officials repudiated the argument, but Libicki's opinion had an afterlife in the press and in online platforms. Poznań's Jewish community and its spokeswoman Alicja Kobus, on the other hand, had long favored the idea of converting the restituted building into a center for intercultural dialogue. Yet this and similar projects were arrested in their initial stages of development and never evolved beyond rough drafts, visualizations, and proposals. After numerous futile attempts to raise enough money for the original "dream project," the Jewish community came

Figure 7.4. Cremer & Wolffenstein, New Synagogue, Poznań, 2015. Copyright Przemysław Królak, 2015. Digital photograph.

to an agreement with an investor in 2012. Together with the architect Stefan Bajer, the firm bs ARCHITEKCI developed plans according to which the building would be turned into a hotel.[32]

Giving its last remaining synagogue the cold shoulder, Poznań has continued its indecisive stance vis-à-vis the crumbling edifice; it has, so far, claimed it to be neither a meaningful nor an integral part of its history. In short, Poznań has yet to acknowledge the building as local heritage. The synagogue is not yet included on the city's Register of Immobile Monuments, which suggests that Jewish culture remains outside the "imagined community," that is, the Polish nation. Whether the present argument is linked to Prussia's historical animus toward Poland and Poles, or implicitly to the non-contiguous and untethered Jewish other, to fiscal reasons dictated by the municipality's budget, or, finally, to pressures from the Jewish owners themselves, for whom the status change would engender an even more challenging financial burden—the century-old edifice located within close range of the market square has not benefited from the same historical-preservationist attention that has been granted to other sites. The city's Residential Castle, for example, has recently been converted into a vast cultural venue with a movie theater and public galleries, in an effort to update Prussia's controversial legacy for the young and fashionable public. As such, the conversion exemplifies the flow of public money into projects of greater importance to the majority.[33]

BACK TO OLSZTYN

Polish-Jewish relations are most often viewed in the dichotomous terms ingrained in the very hyphenation of "Polish-Jewish." Jan T. Gross's books about postwar Polish antisemitism, *Neighbors* (2001) and *Fear* (2006), have had a lasting impact on the debate about Jewish culture in contemporary Poland. While Gross's studies have polarized the Polish public,[34] they have also brought to the fore questions of historical continuity and of generalizable statements concerning historical burdens, "collective responsibility,"[35] and "the Poles" as an entity. President Andrzej Duda's recent consideration to divest Gross of the national Order of Merit testifies to the instrumentalization of history for domestic affairs. All of these issues are central to this essay.

It remains difficult to index the overarching stance toward Jewish culture in postwar Poland in a differentiated way. One has to disentangle the overt antisemitic sentiments or covert resentments expressed by the Communist Party, the Catholic Church, or ordinary Poles, on the one hand, from the much more indeterminate attitudes of inhabitants of a country where the Holocaust has made it improbable for a Pole to actually meet a Jew, on the other hand. With few exceptions, Jewish history and life were essentially absent in Poland before the 1990s[36]—an absence that had also enfolded the German past of Olsztyn.

The Bet Tahara in Olsztyn is another case testifying to how this absence was manifested in the often frail yet abiding remains of Jewish culture in Poland. It is an epitome of architecture's ability to reflect varying stages of sociopolitical developments. Until the 1990s, Erich Mendelsohn's building at the Jewish cemetery had fallen into oblivion. Children played soccer on the former graveyard, now an abandoned lot, and no one asked about the traces of the region's Jewry, much less about the buildings that used to belong to a minority of close to five hundred souls.[37] Even to international scholars, Mendelsohn's first work was lost.[38]

After the fall of Communism, the political circumstances changed and private initiatives sprung up with new force. A small group of individuals gathered to broaden the local historical consciousness in a region that had experienced substantial population transfers and forced resettlements after 1945, first the expulsion of the area's substantial ethnic German populace and then the arrival of Poles and some Ukrainians from the Soviet Union's western borderlands. The activists were committed to shedding light on the suppressed memory of Olsztyn's multicultural history and specifically on the legacies of the German and Ukrainian communities.[39] They had also heard the rumor that a local state archive repository had been installed in Mendelsohn's mourners' chapel on what had once been the Jewish burial ground. The rumor was soon proved to be true.[40] In one of the two small bungalows at Zyndrama z Maszkowic Street, administrators of the state archives (Archiwum Państwowe w Olsztynie) had at some point inserted a suspended ceiling, altered the rooms, and painted the walls white.

For the newly formally established Borussia Foundation—partner of international volunteer services and active participant in educational transborder programs—the restoration of Mendelsohn's Bet Tahara became a priority project. The few permanent employees began to negotiate with the building's legal owner, the Foundation for the Preservation of Jewish Heritage in Poland (FPJH), to get permission for the restoration, subsequent lease, and use as a cultural venue. They raised money as well as support for the undertaking and ultimately received funding from the EU. The restoration of the architectural gem was begun in 2007, in parallel to the foundation's ongoing intercultural youth activities, and in October 2013 the building was formally re-inaugurated by its new tenant, the Borussia Foundation, in the presence of a representative of the Ministry of Culture and National Heritage.

Figure 7.5. Erich Mendelsohn, Bet Tahara, Olsztyn, view of the dome after restoration, 2013. Photo by author.

While the New Synagogue's revitalization in Poznań has been encumbered by substantial financial difficulties, activists involved in the restoration of the Bet Tahara did not encounter any considerable resistance. It seemed clear to everyone that without the foundation's engagement, Mendelsohn's chapel might simply have collapsed and vanished. Moreover, there seem never to have been any objections to the decision to call the former sacral Jewish structure simply Dom Mendelsohna (Mendelsohn's House) after the completion of the restoration.[41] This is how it was presented in the plan that was part of the lease agreement with the FPJH, and this is how it is promoted today.

The disappearance and subsequent reappearance of Mendelsohn's architectural debut echo Olsztyn's efforts to come to terms with its past. The little-known work of one of modernism's unabashed individualists merits not only rediscovery,[42] was the sentiment, but also positive reappraisal. By virtue of its presence, the long arm of built heritage demands a confrontation with, a discussion of, and a reaction to the suppressed history. Re-emergent, the Bet Tahara—by no means an epiphany, but rather the beneficiary of a few committed individuals—stands for the grassroots initiatives that are fundamental to the processes of historical reappraisal in Poland today.

This also means that Dom Mendelsohna is no longer—or not again—an exclusively Jewish place. It has become an architectural monument, a site of remembrance, a multipurpose structure. Linked to architectural modernity by the name of its draftsman, it attracts visitors specifically interested in Mendelsohn's oeuvre. Olsztyn's most famous historical resident besides Nicolaus Copernicus, Mendelsohn posthumously lends his name to disseminating the town's cultural heritage. In the very name Mendelsohn, Jewish and German histories meet. Dom Mendelsohna now makes him a part of Polish history, too.[43]

Given the absence of a Jewish community in Olsztyn today, Dom Mendelsohna is what Ruth Gruber calls a "virtually Jewish" space. She has aptly analyzed how Europe's onetime Jewish sites are often appropriated and maintained by Gentiles in a "process of 'creating' rather than 're-creating'"[44] a sense of Jewishness. Following scholars such as Gruber, Lehrer, and Meng, who have been interested in such places as "sites of pluralism,"[45] the Bet Tahara can be described as a propitious and inclusive example of appropriated and transformed local heritage. It is propitious in that also the FPJH has deliberately set a focus on co-operation with local (Gentile) partners in the struggle to restore—and maintain—numerous architectural objects in the country and particularly in places that lack Jewish practitioners. Erich Mendelsohn's renown as well as the local actors' connections certainly have been important factors in the building's transformation—unlike the so far less fortunate case of Poznań's much bigger synagogue, which has had no marketable architect's name to attract public funding and where conservationist interventions would have to be of incomparably larger scope.[46]

FRAMING THE PAST

While framing anew the past in Olsztyn and Poznań had been a political requisite in the People's Republic of Poland, a necessity for national cohesion, and an imperative after Poland as a whole was shifted westward in 1945, abrupt reframings may work by decree, but only as long as layers of paint and suspended ceilings veil what lies beneath. The re-appearance of the synagogue and the Jewish chapel has recently enforced the need to reconsider the official narrative.

The trauma of Poland's erasure from Europe's map following its eighteenth-century partitions and then its Nazi conquest, accompanied by border shifts, constitute as much a *lieu de mémoire* in the country as does the Holocaust. Dom Mendelsohna demonstrates how a fractured local identity may coalesce beyond the concept of victim nationhood, as has often been the case across Eastern and East Central Europe.[47] It is a place that symbolically asserts plurality where multiethnic history has been obscured for decades. In Poznań, on the contrary, the loss of spatial constants and locally fostered memory vectors has set up the New Synagogue for the conflation of Jewish heritage with its often negatively connoted German counterpart.

Far from reading the debates in Poznań as emblematic of Poland's latent antisemitism[48] or the Olsztyn case as an undiluted success story, I have aimed to contextualize the two divergent examples of Jewish heritage within the country shaken by long-term territorial segmentation in the hands of empires, shifting borders, ensuing nationalization, wartime German atrocities leading to the almost complete erasure of its Jewry, and subsequent decades of Communism.[49] Mendelsohn's foreword from 1929, cited in the epigraph to this essay, has not lost its relevance for this region. Lining up the three international giants, "Russia–Europe–America," he examines contiguity in terms that testify to his firm belief in European unity. With the imminent future of two opposing blocs, for Mendelsohn Europe as a whole became the "land between" that was not to be dissected into national fragments.[50] The problems to which he refers in 1929, "highly current, important, and crucial for [the] time,"[51]—rampant nationalism, cracks in the idea of Europe, and disastrous economic instability that would engulf not only his native Germany—would unleash what the architectonic cross-sections of Poznań's and Olsztyn's Jewish places emblematically disclose.

Propelled by formal concerns, like many other practitioners of his craft, Mendelsohn had a clear notion of the driving factors that enable or impede architectural creation: politics and economics. Politics and economics also play a vital role in Poland's current stance toward its architectural heritage. The national community today, inclusive or exclusive of remnants such as those in focus here, juggles political as well as financial issues in order to assure itself of its identity. It designates architectural objects as historic monuments (the Bet Tahara as early as 1988), or it defers such designations indefinitely (as is the case of Poznań New Synagogue, although the municipal conservator for monuments, Joanna Bielawska-Pałczyńska, has given her assent for the conversion of the building into a hotel).[52]

Europe as a whole is also a beacon for political and economic reasons. Without the co-funding from the European Regional Development Fund (ERDF) for Mendelsohn's Bet Tahara, its restoration and transformation into a center for intercultural dialogue would have been considerably more difficult, if not impossible. In Poznań, those eager to realize similar plans for the synagogue likewise hoped for EU funding, but their hopes never materialized. At the same time, more than a third of the costs for the revitalization of the Centrum Kultury Zamek, the cultural center in the former Prussian Residential Castle, totaling roughly $8.7 million, was covered by resources coming from the ERDF.[53]

Wherever the European project is not a mere rhetorical camouflage for economic interests, however, it has drawn from an imaginary beyond the bankroll. A Europeanization of memory culture may remain wishful thinking and a rhetorical abstraction in glossy EU brochures.[54] But the European project, as fragile as it is in view of some member countries' ready retreat into national contumacy and hubris, has been more than an economic playground. Mendelsohn's recently rediscovered and restored Bet Tahara in Olsztyn is an example of new categories within a Polish self-image.[55] In this single building, Jewish and German heritage have become facets of a pluralized local identity. The activities of the Borussia Foundation demonstrate how cultural heritage can be conceptualized and sustained as hybrid and inclusive.

Sociologist Sławomir Kapralski has pondered the importance of material substance and space for the debates about the present and future framings of Poland's past. He has argued that in nationwide intellectual deliberations it is precisely the lack of material and spatial frames capable of embracing new meanings that prevents the reintegration of a Jewish past into Poland's living memory.[56] The lukewarm stance of the local community toward Poznań's synagogue mirrors Kapralski's criticism. After years of ignoring the original function of the municipal pool, followed by the recent standoffs (or inaction) concerning its future, the central concern lies beyond formalist arguments and questions of historical contiguity. It inheres in the community's willingness to accept the formerly Jewish house of worship, its history as well as its owners, as part of their own imagined community, that is, the nation.

So far, Poznań's Jewish community feels compelled to advocate for a heritage that has little to do with any of the perceived Prussian Kulturkampf overtones that are ascribed to the building. And even if it is not confronted with the old logic that "Polish equals Catholic" or with antisemitic attitudes, the community remains at pains to justify its decision to sell the building to an investor with an eye to real estate and business models. Plans to reconstruct the synagogue's original massive dome in glass may prove to be, from the perspective of landmark preservation, an honest compromise vis-à-vis the impossible restoration of its old appearance. But a bitter aftertaste persists.[57]

Although Arjun Appadurai is primarily concerned with cultural flows in the era of globalization, his concept of ethnoscapes *and* ideoscapes—and more specifically his musings on the "production of locality"—provides another framework to conceptualize the case in point. "As groups migrate, regroup in new locations, reconstruct their histories, and reconfigure their ethnic projects, the *ethno* in ethnography now takes on a slippery, nonlocalized quality," he writes.[58] "Locality" is being so actively produced in Poznań or in Olsztyn today because Poles are, for good reasons, in many ways historically highly self-conscious but spatially bounded, unlike the communities that the anthropologist scrutinizes.[59] Appadurai's point is that in times of mass migration and cultural flows (and let us add: continuously shifting borders), locality and neighborhood are persistently being produced—and maintained. The examples of Poznań's synagogue and Olsztyn's Bet Tahara testify to neighborhoods' production in the face of ethnic politics. They also speak to de-territorialized -scapes, against which this local production as a cultural act is always taking place. Those who shape locality in confrontation with the material reminders of the past become part of an ideoscape that encompasses the nation-state as well as the counter-ideologies set in motion by the search for alternative narratives.

Heritage is something that has to be *declared*; it is *created* as something that is significant for the present and directed toward the future. To some, the debates about architectural remnants in Olsztyn and Poznań have revolved around meaningless piles of stone; in the eyes of others, they concern nationally meaningful architectural forms. In both cases, at stake is a specific kind of Jewish heritage: the German-Jewish kind. In Cracow and Warsaw, cities with extensive Polish-Jewish pasts, the question is resolved differently. Apart from the cities' sizes and considerable Jewish communities today, for historical reasons, revival and re-enactment of a Jewish past in Cracow and Warsaw do not inevitably touch on the past of Germans there.[60] Given this lack of contiguity with Germanness, it can be more readily incorporated into the local heritage.

With Poznań and Olsztyn, the case is different. The debates there are shaped by a twofold discontiguity of a Jewish presence. It is twofold in the sense that with the shift of borders and forced resettlements, the former Jewish neighbors had inhabited a different imagined community (in German Allenstein); and that the present Jewish community is no direct successor to the community that lived there earlier, prior to the end of World War I (in Poznań). A rereading of Mendelsohn's comments expands one's view of the tension between an a-topical Jewish memory and its local crystallization in Poland today. Mendelsohn—the German Jew, the Allensteiner, the Olsztynian, the cosmopolitan—concludes his allegedly apolitical book with a distinct expression of hope: "Between the two poles of volition, America and Russia, Europe will mediate, if it bethinks itself, [if it] practices moderation."[61] It is clearly a European imaginary that keeps Mendelsohn from mapping his standpoint nationally. The New Synagogue by Cremer & Wolffenstein and Mendelsohn's Bet Tahara, with their transnational, cosmopolitan Jewish order,[62] were later tragically remapped several times. It remains to be seen what role Europe can play as a consolidating factor for the Jewish architectural remains between (post-)national narratives, Jewish virtuality, and Jewish actuality.

Sarah M. Schlachetzki is assistant professor at the Department of History of Architecture at the University of Bern, Switzerland. She was visiting fellow at New York University for 2015–16. She studied art history, sociology, and French culture at the Universities of Trier, Leipzig, and Tours, pursued her doctoral research at the Swiss Federal Institute of Technology, and holds a PhD from the University of Zurich. Currently, she is working on a research project on Wrocław's architectural modernities.

NOTES

1. "Dieses Buch ist kein politisches; aber Politik und Wirtschaft sind die lebendigen Grundlagen seines architektonischen Querschnitts.... Mit der Gegenüberstellung 'Russland–Europa–Amerika,' berührt es ein höchst gegenwärtiges, zeitwichtiges und entscheidendes Problem." Foreword to Erich Mendelsohn, *Russland–Europa–Amerika: Ein architektonischer Querschnitt* (Berlin: Rudolf Mosse Buchverlag, 1929), 5. All translations are mine, unless indicated otherwise.
2. Mendelsohn, *Russland–Europa–Amerika,* 171.
3. Among her many publications, see Ruth Ellen Gruber, "Beyond Virtually Jewish ... Balancing the Real, the Surreal and Real Imaginary Places," in *Reclaiming Memory: Urban Regeneration in the Historic Jewish Quarters of Central Euro-*

pean Cities, ed. Monika Murzyn-Kupisz (Cracow: International Culture Center, 2009), 63–79; most recently, Erica Lehrer and Michael Meng, eds., *Jewish Space in Contemporary Poland* (Bloomington: Indiana University Press, 2015).

4. Lehrer and Meng, introduction to *Jewish Space in Contemporary Poland*, 1–15, especially 3–4.
5. In her contemplation upon "The Thing-Character of the World," Hannah Arendt highlights the function of homo faber's products, especially of art, to secure orientation in temporality and "give rise to the familiarity of the world." Hannah Arendt, *The Human Condition* (Chicago: University of Chicago Press, 1998 [1958]), 94. More in the German edition, *Vita activa oder Vom tätigen Leben* (Munich: Piper, 2014 [1958]), 201ff.
6. Lately scholars have used the term "unwanted heritage" to refer to architectural remains after historical ruptures. For the Polish or German context, see Agnieszka Wołodźko, ed., *Niechciane Dziedzictwo? Ungeliebtes Erbe? Unwanted Heritage?* (Gdańsk: Ryszard Ziarkiewicz, 2005); Matthew Rampley, ed., *Heritage, Ideology, and Identity in Central Eastern Europe: Contested Pasts, Contested Presents* (Woodbridge: Boydell Press, 2012). In the same vein on modernist heritage, see Aidan While and Michael Short, "Place Narratives and Heritage Management: The Modernist Legacy in Manchester," *Area* 43 (2011): 4–13.
7. Andreas Huyssen has promoted the now widespread metaphor of the palimpsestic character of cities. Huyssen, *Present Pasts: Urban Palimpsests and the Politics of Memory* (Stanford, CA: Stanford University Press, 2003). Arendt, *Human Condition*, 198.
8. Arendt, *Vita activa*, 202.
9. Anna Moskal, *Im Spannungsfeld von Region und Nation: Die Polonisierung der Stadt Posen nach 1918 und 1945* (Wiesbaden: Harrassowitz, 2013), 46.
10. Zenon Pałat, "Ostatnie Forum Cesarskie: Forma i symbolika urbanistyczno-architektoniczna założenia poznańskiego Ringu," *Artium Quaestiones* 2 (1983): 57–71.
11. See "Die Synagoge in Posen," *Deutsche Bauzeitung* 43 (1909): 609–13. On the background of the synagogue and its predecessor buildings, see Carol Herselle Krinsky, "The Synagogues of Poznań," in *Making Holocaust Memory*, ed. Gabriel N. Finder, Polin: Studies in Polish Jewry 20 (Oxford: Littman Library of Jewish Civilization, 2008), 439.
12. See "Konkurrenzen," *Schweizerische Bauzeitung* 23/24 (1894): 173.
13. Harold Hammer-Schenk, "Synagogen," in *Sakralbauten*, ed. Architekten- und Ingenieur-Verein zu Berlin, Berlin und seine Bauten 6 (Berlin: Ernst & Sohn, 1997), 282–88. The attribution of Charlottenburg Synagogue (1889; destroyed) to their oeuvre, mentioned in *Berliner Architekturwelt* in 1908, is not tenable according to Hammer-Schenk, "Synagogen," 286.
14. Krinsky, "Synagogues," 439.
15. Krinsky, "Synagogues," 439.
16. Bruno Zevi, *Erich Mendelsohn* (Bologna: Zanichelli, 1982), 6–7; Regina Stephan, "Wände wie der Blaue Reiter," *Frankfurter Allgemeine Zeitung*, 17 April 2008,

17; Ita Heinze-Greenberg, *Erich Mendelsohn: Olsztyn–Jerozolima–San Francisco* (Ostrava: Vydání první, 2012). It may have been Erich Mendelsohn's father David, a successful merchant in town, who helped secure the commission of the two new buildings for his son still in training. Stephan, "Wände," 17; also Rafał Bętkowski, *Olsztyn czasów Ericha Mendelsohna* (Olsztyn: Fundacja Borussia, 2013), 31. Mendelsohn later reported that he used sketches of the Bet Tahara for his coursework in Munich, handing them in as an exercise in "Renaissance style." Heinze-Greenberg, *Erich Mendelsohn,* citing a 1948 typescript by Mendelsohn.
17. See Regina Stephan, *Studien zu Waren- und Geschäftshäusern Erich Mendelsohns in Deutschland* (Munich: Tuduv, 1992), 22.
18. Heinze-Greenberg, *Erich Mendelsohn,* citing a 1948 typescript by Mendelsohn.
19. Julia Martino, municipal conservator, interview with author, Olsztyn, 16 June 2014.
20. See Stephan, "Wände," 17.
21. Achenbach cited in Stephan, *Studien,* 63.
22. Stephan, "Wände," 17.
23. As in many Eastern-bloc countries, in the People's Republic of Poland, its Jewish-Polish history remained mostly without any special emphasis. For decades, the history of Polish Jewry was implicitly folded into the narrative of Polish national losses under the Nazi occupation and was rarely mentioned independently. Michael C. Steinlauf, "Teaching about the Holocaust in Poland," in *Contested Memories: Poles and Jews during the Holocaust and Its Aftermath,* ed. Joshua D. Zimmerman (New Brunswick, NJ: Rutgers University Press, 2003). In worse cases, Polish antisemitism surfaced in persistent stereotypes and prejudices, both before and after the "anti-Zionist" campaign of 1968. See, for instance, Leszek W. Głuchowski and Antony Polonsky, eds., *1968: Forty Years After,* Polin: Studies in Polish Jewry 21 (Oxford: Littman Library of Jewish Civilization, 2009). Worst of all were the murders of Jews who came back to their towns right after the war, as documented in Jan Gross, *Fear: Anti-Semitism in Poland After Auschwitz: An Essay in Historical Interpretation* (New York: Random House), 2006.
24. See Krinsky, "Synagogues," 444.
25. Krinsky points out, however, that it seems to have been mostly foreigners who raised the issue. Krinsky, "Synagogues," 445.
26. Uilleam Blacker, "Living among the Ghosts of Others: Urban Postmemory in Eastern Europe," in *Memory and Theory in Eastern Europe,* ed. Uilleam Blacker et al. (New York: Palgrave Macmillan, 2013), 173–93.
27. Even in 2014, the tourist information office handed out city maps that indicated a pool where there should have been an icon with the Star of David.
28. The re-established community celebrated its fifteenth anniversary in 2014.
29. Krzysztof Kwiatkowski, e-mail communication with the author, 3 September 2014. See also Stanisław Tyszka, "Restitution of Communal Property and the Preservation of Jewish Heritage in Poland," in Lehrer and Meng, *Jewish Space in Contemporary Poland,* 59–60. In his excellent article on the legal process of resti-

tutions to Jewish interest groups in Poland, Tyszka briefly refers to the Poznań debate, albeit only until 2010.
30. Those who did use the term usually belonged to the Jewish community, like philosopher Seweryn Aszkenazi. See Elżbieta Podolska, "Aszkenazy oskarża poznańską gminę żydowską o chęć sprzedania synagogi," *Glos Wielkopolski,* 12 October 2012, accessed 23 May 2015, http://www.gloswielkopolski.pl/artykul/ 676425,aszkenazy-oskarza-poznanska-gmine-zydowska-o-chec-sprzedania-synag ogi,id,t.html. Also, Jakub Łukaszewski and Piotr Bojarski, "Synagoga w Poznaniu będzie hotelem. Z basenem i wielką kopułą," *Gazeta Wyborcza,* Poznań local edition, 10 March 2016, accessed 5 April 2016, http://poznan.wyborcza.pl/ poznan/1,36037,19743293,synagoga-bedzie-hotelem-z-basenem-i-wielka-kopula .html#.
31. His text "One has to buy it, one can tear it down" ("Trzeba odkupić, można wyburzyć") was published on *gazeta.pl Poznan,* 12 January 2006; cited: "Architektura i Urbanistyka," accessed 23 May 2015, http://www.skyscrapercity.com/ showthread.php?t=223754&page=6.
32. Alicja Kobus, interview with author, 4 January 2015. Only a small part of the edifice may now be consecrated to Jewish heritage, hosting a kosher restaurant and a little museum for the history of Jews in Wielkopolska Voivodeship. Even before this idea was made public, it provoked a wave of negative reactions. Krzysztof Kwiatkowski, e-mail message to author, 3 September 2014. See also "Szewach Weiss: Hotel w poznańskiej synagodze?," interview with Piotr Bojarski, *Domiporta.pl,* 18 January 2010, accessed 23 May 2015, http://porady.domi porta.pl/poradnik/1,127301,7468421,Szewach_Weiss__Hotel_w_poznanskiej_ synagodze_.html. The investor of the hotel project is the Poznań-based corporation Capital Budownictwo 2. Łukaszewski and Bojarski, "Synagoga."
33. For an overview over the renovation and its costs, see the website of the center, "Dofinansowanie z UE" http://www.zamek.poznan.pl/sub,pl,321,przebudo wa-2010-2012.html, accessed 23 December 2016.
34. Jan Tomasz Gross, *Neighbors: The Destruction of the Jewish Community in Jedwabne, Poland* (Princeton, NJ: Princeton University Press, 2001); and Gross, *Fear.* The Polish edition of *Neighbors* was published in 2000. The ensuing debate is captured in the afterword by Gross himself in the reprinted *Neighbors* (New York: Penguin, 2002) and in Magdalena Klimowicz, ed., *Difficult Postwar Years: Polish Voices in Debate over Jan T. Gross's Book* Fear (Warsaw: Polish Institute of International Affairs, 2006).
35. "Collective Responsibility" is the title of a chapter in Gross's *Neighbors.*
36. Exceptions include the commemoration of the Warsaw Ghetto Uprising and, since 1988, the Jewish Culture Festival in Cracow, itself a sign of an opening toward a multicultural heritage. Erica T. Lehrer, *Jewish Poland Revisited: Heritage Tourism in Unquiet Places* (Bloomington: Indiana University Press, 2013), 6; and Zvi Gitelman, "Collective Memory and Contemporary Polish-Jewish Relations," in Rampley, *Contested Pasts,* 271–90. Lehrer and Meng, nevertheless, question what they call the "widespread myth" of a veiled or absent Jewish

memory in Poland during the Cold War era; see Lehrer and Meng, introduction to *Jewish Space in Contemporary Poland*, 11.
37. See Bętkowski, *Olsztyn*, 17.
38. Regina Stephan, ed., *Erich Mendelsohn: Gebaute Welten: Architekt 1887–1953: Arbeiten für Europa, Palästina und Amerika* (Ostfildern-Ruit: Hatje, 1998), 316, note 32.
39. The Association Borussia, engaged in intercultural dialogue in the region Warmia and Masuria, formerly German East Prussia, was formed in 1990. In 2006, the newly established Borussia Foundation took over the association's cultural goals.
40. The building was added to the register of historic monuments of the Voivodeship Warmia-Masuria already in 1988. Barbara Maria Deja, "Renovation and Adaptation of the Historic Olsztyn Purification House Bet Tahara into a Public Utility Building," *Civil and Environmental Engineering Reports* 18 (2015): 24; and Kornelia Kurowska, director of Borussia Foundation, interview with author, 13 August 2014. I owe much of the following information to Ms. Kurowska.
41. Kornelia Kurowska, interview with author, 13 August 2014.
42. Henry-Russell Hitchcock, "Foreword to the 1966 Edition," in *The International Style*, ed. Henry-Russell Hitchcock and Philip Johnson (New York: W. W. Norton, 1966), xii.
43. According to Kurowska, "the renaming [of the place] was a symbolic act," and "Mendelsohn's House" was chosen to generate positive associations in any language. It remains open whether or not renaming the site may have been undertaken also to assuage the local community's alleged skepticism vis-à-vis a Jewish space, a *bet tahara*, in the neighborhood.
44. Gruber, "Beyond Virtually Jewish," 68.
45. Lehrer and Meng, introduction to *Jewish Space in Contemporary Poland*, 3.
46. On the history of restitutions in Poland, the policies of the FPJH, and associated financial and sociological questions, see the excellent overview in Tyszka, "Restitution," in Lehrer and Meng, *Jewish Space in Contemporary Poland*.
47. "The creation of an alternative, non-Soviet space by dissidents like Kundera was pursued precisely through underlining the distinctive memory culture of the victim nations of Central Europe that separated them from Russia." Uilleam Blacker and Alexander Etkind, introduction to *Memory and Theory in Eastern Europe*, 1.
48. This excludes, of course, comments by politicians like Marcin Libicki, quoted earlier in the text.
49. Today, the area around Poznań in particular has to be described in terms of its Germanization and its subsequent (re-)Polonization. On Poznań, see Moskal, *Im Spannungsfeld von Region und Nation*. On Allenstein/Olsztyn, see Robert Traba, *Wschodniopruskość: Tożsamość regionalna i narodowa w kulturze politycznej Niemiec* (Poznań: Wydawnictwo Poznańskiego Towarzystwa Przyjaciół Nauk, 2005).
50. On the concept of "betweenness" in this context, see Yuliya Komska's introduction to this volume.
51. Mendelsohn, *Russland–Europa–Amerika*, 5.

52. See Deja, "Renovation," 24; and Łukaszewski and Bojarski, "Synagoga."
53. "Dofinansowanie z UE," http://www.zamek.poznan.pl/sub,pl,321,przebudowa-2010-2012.html, accessed 23 December 2016.
54. According to Peter Loew, especially when Poland aspired to join the European Union (before and around 2004), the rhetoric of political and intellectual elites was rife with emphases on the country's European traditions and their connection to a "transnational historical discursive space." Peter Oliver Loew, "Helden oder Opfer? Erinnerungskulturen in Polen nach 1989," *Osteuropa* 58 (2008): 100.
55. For more on this topic, see Dirk Uffelmann, "Theory as Memory Practice: The Divided Discourse on Poland's Postcoloniality," in Blacker et al., *Memory and Theory in Eastern Europe*, 103–124.
56. Sławomir Kapralski, "(Mis)representations of the Jewish Past in Poland's Memoryscapes: Nationalism, Religion, and Political Economies of Commemoration," in *Curating Difficult Knowledge: Violent Pasts in Public Places*, ed. Erica T. Lehrer (Basingstoke: Palgrave Macmillan, 2011), 183.
57. It seems, however, that also as a hotel, the building cannot escape claims about its supposed dominance over Poznań's cityscape. See Łukaszewski and Bojarski, "Synagoga," quoting Poznań's municipal conservator Bielawska-Pałczyńska: "I gave my assent to the realization of this project [the conversion into a hotel], although I am aware that it could be received controversially. [In its prewar form, to which it will be restored by reconstructing the cupola, it] was an object that dominated the prewar city space."
58. Arjun Appadurai, *Modernity at Large: Cultural Dimensions of Globalization* (Minneapolis: University of Minnesota Press, 1996), 48.
59. Appadurai, *Modernity at Large*, 183.
60. See Gruber, "Beyond Virtually Jewish."
61. Mendelsohn, *Russland–Europa–Amerika*, 207.
62. On the concept of Jewish cosmopolitanism as opposed to universalism, see Natan Sznaider, *Jewish Memory and the Cosmopolitan Order: Hannah Arendt and the Jewish Condition* (Cambridge: Polity Press, 2011).

WORKS CITED

Anderson, Benedict. *Imagined Communities: Reflections on the Origin and Spread of Nationalism*. London: Verso, 1991.

Appadurai, Arjun. *Modernity at Large: Cultural Dimensions of Globalization*. Minneapolis: University of Minnesota Press, 1996.

"Architektura i Urbanistyka." Accessed 23 May 2015. http://www.skyscrapercity.com/showthread.php?t=223754&page=6.

Arendt, Hannah. *The Human Condition*. Chicago: University of Chicago Press, 1998.

———. *Vita activa oder Vom tätigen Leben*. Munich: Piper, 2014.

Bętkowski, Rafał. *Olsztyn czasów Ericha Mendelsohna*. Olsztyn: Fundacja Borussia 2013.

Blacker, Uilleam. "Living among the Ghosts of Others: Urban Postmemory in Eastern Europe." In *Memory and Theory in Eastern Europe,* edited by Uilleam Blacker et al., 173–93. New York: Palgrave Macmillan, 2013.

Blacker, Uilleam, and Alexander Etkind. Introduction to *Memory and Theory in Eastern Europe,* edited by Uilleam Blacker et al., 1–23. New York: Palgrave Macmillan, 2013.

Bojarski, Piotr. "Szewach Weiss: Hotel w poznańskiej synagodze?" *Domiporta.pl,* 18 January 2010. Accessed May 23, 2015. http://porady.domiporta.pl/poradnik/ 1,127301,7468421,Szewach_Weiss__Hotel_w_poznanskiej_synagodze_.html.

Cante, Markus, ed. *Sakralbauten.* Berlin und seine Bauten 6. Berlin: Ernst & Sohn, 1997.

Deja, Barbara Maria. "Renovation and Adaptation of the Historic Olsztyn Purification House Bet Tahara into a Public Utility Building." *Civil and Environmental Engineering Reports* 18 (2015): 23–32.

"Die Synagoge in Posen." *Deutsche Bauzeitung* 43 (1909): 609–13.

Gitelman, Zvi. "Collective Memory and Contemporary Polish-Jewish Relations." In *Contested Memories: Poles and Jews during the Holocaust and Its Aftermath,* edited by Joshua D. Zimmerman, 271–90. New Brunswick, NJ: Rutgers University Press, 2003.

Głuchowski, Leszek W., and Antony Polonsky, eds. *1968: Forty Years After.* Polin: Studies in Polish Jewry 21. Oxford: Littman Library of Jewish Civilization, 2009.

Gross, Jan Tomasz. *Fear: Anti-Semitism in Poland after Auschwitz: An Essay In Historical Interpretation.* New York: Random House, 2006.

———. *Neighbors: The Destruction of the Jewish Community in Jedwabne, Poland.* Princeton, NJ: Princeton University Press, 2001.

Gruber, Ruth Ellen. "Beyond Virtually Jewish ... Balancing the Real, the Surreal and Real Imaginary Places." In *Reclaiming Memory: Urban Regeneration in the Historic Jewish Quarters of Central European Cities,* ed. Monika Murzyn-Kupisz, 63–79. Cracow: International Culture Center, 2009.

Hammer-Schenk, Harold. "Synagogen." In *Sakralbauten,* Berlin und seine Bauten 6, edited by Architekten- und Ingenieur-Verein zu Berlin, 273–310. Berlin: Ernst & Sohn, 1997.

Heinze-Greenberg, Ita. *Erich Mendelsohn: Olsztyn–Jerozolima–San Francisco.* Ostrava: Vydání první, 2012.

Hitchcock, Henry-Russell. "Foreword to the 1966 Edition." In *The International Style,* edited by Henry-Russell Hitchcock and Philip Johnson, vii–xiii. New York: W. W. Norton, 1966.

Huyssen, Andreas. *Present Pasts: Urban Palimpsests and the Politics of Memory.* Stanford, CA: Stanford University Press, 2003.

Kapralski, Sławomir. "(Mis)representations of the Jewish Past in Poland's Memoryscapes: Nationalism, Religion, and Political Economies of Commemoration." In *Curating Difficult Knowledge: Violent Pasts in Public Places,* edited by Erica T. Lehrer, 179–92. Basingstoke: Palgrave Macmillan, 2011.

Klimowicz, Magdalena, ed. *Difficult Postwar Years: Polish Voices in Debate over Jan T. Gross's Book* Fear. Warsaw: Polish Institute of International Affairs, 2006.
"Konkurrenzen." *Schweizerische Bauzeitung* 23/24 (1894): 173.
Krinsky, Carol Herselle. "The Synagogues of Poznań." In *Making Holocaust Memory*, Polin: Studies in Polish Jewry 20, edited by Gabriel N. Finder, 431–45. Oxford: Littman Library of Jewish Civilization, 2008.
Lefebvre, Henri. *La production de l'espace*. Paris: Éditions Anthropos, 1974.
Lehrer, Erica T. *Jewish Poland Revisited: Heritage Tourism in Unquiet Places*. Bloomington: Indiana University Press, 2013.
Lehrer, Erica T., and Michael Meng, eds. *Jewish Space in Contemporary Poland*. Bloomington: Indiana University Press, 2015.
Loew, Peter Oliver. "Helden oder Opfer? Erinnerungskulturen in Polen nach 1989." *Osteuropa* 58 (2008): 85–102.
Łukaszewski, Jakub, and Piotr Bojarski. "Synagoga w Poznaniu będzie hotelem. Z basenem i wielką kopułą." *Gazeta Wyborcza,* Poznań local edition, 10 March 2016. Accessed 5 April 2016. http://poznan.wyborcza.pl/poznan/1,36037,19743293,synagoga-bedzie-hotelem-z-basenem-i-wielka-kopula.html#.
Mendelsohn, Erich. *Russland–Europa–Amerika: Ein architektonischer Querschnitt*. Berlin: Rudolf Mosse Buchverlag, 1929.
Moskal, Anna. *Im Spannungsfeld von Region und Nation: Die Polonisierung der Stadt Posen nach 1918 und 1945*. Wiesbaden: Harrassowitz, 2013.
Pałat, Zenon. "Ostatnie Forum Cesarskie: Forma i symbolika urbanistyczno-architektoniczna założenia poznańskiego Ringu." *Artium Quaestiones* 2 (1983): 57–71.
Podolska, Elżbieta. "Aszkenazy oskarża poznańską gminę żydowską o chęć sprzedania synagogi." *Głos Wielkopolski,* 12 October 2012. Accessed 23 May 2015. http://www.gloswielkopolski.pl/artykul/676425,aszkenazy-oskarza-poznanska-gmine-zydowska-o-chec-sprzedania-synagogi,id,t.html.
Rampley, Matthew, ed. *Heritage, Ideology, and Identity in Central Eastern Europe: Contested Pasts, Contested Presents*. Woodbridge: Boydell Press, 2012.
Steinlauf, Michael C. "Teaching about the Holocaust in Poland." In *Contested Memories: Poles and Jews during the Holocaust and Its Aftermath,* edited by Joshua D. Zimmerman, 262–70. New Brunswick, NJ: Rutgers University Press, 2003.
Stephan, Regina. *Studien zu Waren- und Geschäftshäusern Erich Mendelsohns in Deutschland*. Munich: Tuduv, 1992.
———, ed. *Erich Mendelsohn: Gebaute Welten. Architekt 1887–1953: Arbeiten für Europa, Palästina und Amerika*. Ostfildern-Ruit: Hatje, 1998.
———. "Wände wie der Blaue Reiter." *Frankfurter Allgemeine Zeitung,* 17 April 2008.
Sznaider, Natan. *Jewish Memory and the Cosmopolitan Order: Hannah Arendt and the Jewish Condition*. Cambridge: Polity Press, 2011.
Traba, Robert. *Wschodniopruskość: Tożsamość regionalna i narodowa w kulturze politycznej Niemiec*. Poznań: Wydawnictwo Poznańskiego Towarzystwa Przyjaciół Nauk, 2005.
Tyszka, Stanisław. "Restitution of Communal Property and the Preservation of Jewish Heritage in Poland." In *Jewish Space in Contemporary Poland,* edited by Erica

T. Lehrer and Michael Meng, 46–70. Bloomington: Indiana University Press, 2015.

Uffelmann, Dirk. "Theory as Memory Practice: The Divided Discourse on Poland's Postcoloniality." In *Memory and Theory in Eastern Europe,* edited by Uilleam Blacker et al., 103–24. New York: Palgrave Macmillan, 2013.

While, Aidan and Michael Short. "Place Narratives and Heritage Management: The Modernist Legacy in Manchester." *Area* 43 (2011): 4–13.

Wołodźko, Agnieszka, ed. *Niechciane Dziedzictwo? Ungeliebtes Erbe? Unwanted Heritage?* Gdańsk: Ryszard Ziarkiewicz, 2005.

Zevi, Bruno. *Erich Mendelsohn.* Bologna: Zanichelli, 1982.

Chapter Eight

Bruno Schulz's Murals, *Oyneg Shabes,* and the Migration of Forms
Seventeen Fragments and an Archive

Adam Zachary Newton

> Bruno Schulz, born an Austrian, lived as a Pole and died a Jew, missing the chance to become Russian.
> —Maurice Nadeau, ""Bruno Schulz," *Présences polonaises*

> The real subject matter, the ultimate raw material that I find in myself without any interference of will, is a certain dynamic state, completely "ineffabilis" and totally incommensurate with poetic means. Even so, it has a very definite atmosphere, indicating a specific kind of content that grows out of it and is layered upon it. The more this intangible nucleus is "ineffabilis" the greater its capacity, the sharper its tropism and the stronger the temptation to inject it into matter in which it could be realized.
> —Bruno Schulz, "Letter to *Wiadomości Literackie* [Literary News]," April 1939

> How, then, do "Literary Nodes of Political Time" work? Nodes of time are points (or "crossroads") at which various narrative strands come together without forming the heart or essence of an organic unit. Indeed, the political dates we chose tend to be moments of *dis*juncture, related to revolutions, wars, or flawed treaties that prepared the ground for new conflicts. Nodes are then simply historical moments (with a certain "thickness") that occasion short and incomplete transnational narratives that differ from the national perspectives on the events. Take, for example, the node "1848."
> —Marcel Cornis-Pope and John Neubauer, "Literary Nodes of Political Time," *History of the Literary Cultures of East-Central Europe Volume 1*

Or take the node "2001," for which the eleventh day of the ninth month in that fateful year now universally signals the crucial telescoping moment. But let us consider another node, one that fell several months earlier in May—a moment (or two) of more than abstract disjuncture. For this was the month that representatives from Yad Vashem, Israel's national memorial to the Shoah and world research center on the Holocaust, partially removed a set of wall paintings, the last-known artworks of Polish writer/artist Bruno Schulz (1892–1942) that, after six decades of oblivion, had been brought to light a scant three months earlier in a Drohobycz (Drohobych) apartment.

Unauthorized by Polish and Ukrainian ministers of culture and art conservators and through a hastily transacted arrangement with official authorities and the apartment's owners, the artifacts, described as "a queen, jesters, horse-and-carriage, and a self-portrait of Schulz as the driver,"[1] were semi-clandestinely salvaged from their recessed existence. Thence, they were spirited away to Yad Vashem's Museum of Holocaust Art on the western slope of Jerusalem's Mount Herzl. Curated now as "Wall Painting under Coercion," three fragments are finally on display, while a smaller portion (backgrounds, borders, and landscapes, fittingly) remains anchored, Schulz-like, in Drohobycz in the newly established Bruno Schulz Museum housed within the former Gymnasium—now Ivan Franko Pedagogical University—where Schulz taught art classes.

If, in one critic's astute formulation, "Schulz's entire universe is premised on the vitality of hidden life and encrypted purpose,"[2] the episode of the murals would seem concretely, if quasi-allegorically, to bear that principle out. For as Schulz himself will seem to have presaged, "certain strictly defined environments, such as old apartments [are] saturated with the emanations of numerous existences and events; used up atmospheres rich in the specific ingredients of human dreams."[3] Whether or not artists will or even should have the last word about their own work, contingency conspires here to throw its voice while configuring a plot of its own. The critical space it opens for us centers on the fate of objects and their resonance in and across time, on previously stranded objects (as the Germanist Eric Santner might say) that have become unexpectedly, albeit incompletely, recuperated. Such, to recall the Schulz epigraph, is the "dynamic state" of his orphaned fairy-tale murals.

The following essay will reflect on their strange afterlife by juxtaposing a descriptive chronicle on the one hand with a scaffold of selections from Schulz's prose on the other. This fugal counterpoint, on the model of the wall paintings themselves, will take the form of *fragments,* which taken together, comprise the exposition for this essay's first half. As in the modernist account of allegory's connection with ruin or remnant, apparent conjunctions or adjacencies should more properly be construed as syncopations.

Before the exposition formally commences, however, the epigraphs warrant a few words. While I do take a small liberty with Cornis-Pope and Neubauer's formulation, the posthumous episode of Schulz's wall paintings certainly lends itself to being regarded as a crossroads "at which various narrative strands come together." That the wall on which Schulz composed his paintings is itself no longer integral underscores the disjunctive character of the various transnational narrative strands spun by writers, politicians, and institutions in the wake of its discovery, which in their totality elude some synthetic, unifying weave.

Schulz himself uses the word "node" in his "Essay for S. I. Witkiewicz" (1935) when he describes the "basic material" of his imagination "as a kind of node [węzeł] to many receding series." In the passage quoted in the epigraph above (a reply written for the magazine *Wiadomości Literackie* in 1939), he returns to this idea, which seems to speak to the uncanny tension between whatever ineffable nucleus may still haunt the wall paintings on the one hand, and the various tropisms—political, moral, ethnic, national—to which they become subject on the other, now that their materiality, whatever Schulz's creative desires for them, has become so improbably "injected."

Maurice Nadeau's aperçu captures the fact that the Schulz myth itself—and not only biographically—resists amalgamation. As one very singular personification of the Galicia in which he spent almost the entirety of his fifty years, his is also a highly singular geopoetics. A kind of vertically non-contiguous self, Schulz became his own palimpsest, a process of overlay he and his murals were to undergo all over again, willy-nilly, in 2001. The juxtapositions in the next few pages mime this vertical discontiguity and in so doing produce, as Schulz already envisioned, another "kind of content ... layered upon it."

THE MURALS

Fragment 1: An Old Apartment

> "As you will no doubt know," said my father, "in old apartments there are rooms which are sometimes forgotten.... The doors, leading to them from some backstairs landing, have been overlooked by people living in the apartment for so long that they merge with the wall, grow into it, and all trace of them is obliterated in a complicated design of lines and cracks." ("Traktat o manekinach: Dokończenie," 1934)

With the help of Schulz's last living student, the wall paintings were found by a documentary film crew inside the kitchen pantry of an ex-party official's dwelling in post-Soviet East Galician Drohobycz, a town that, "in the last century or so, has changed hands eight times."[4]

Fragment 2: A Surprising Discovery

> Occasionally, one of those forgotten rooms was opened by chance and found to be empty; the occupant had moved out long ago, and in drawers left untouched for months, surprising discoveries were to be made. ("Nawiedzenie," 1934)

The apartment formed part of a larger building on what was then called Jana Street that, during the war, had served as the "Villa Landau," after the surname of Schulz's Viennese SIPO patron, Tischler-dilettante-brute SS Hauptscharführer Felix Landau. A member of the Sicherheitsdienst (the intelligence-gathering Security Service) in Radom who volunteered for Einsatzkommando service in 1941 and was transferred to Drohobycz, Landau had confiscated for himself the former police headquarters and commissioned Schulz to paint a set of Brothers Grimm figures in one of its converted rooms for his son's nursery.

Fragment 3: The Wearing Away of That Film

> ["The Book"] lay in its full glory on Father's desk, whilst he, silently engrossed in it, patiently rubbed with a licked finger its ridge of decals until the blank paper began to mist, to blur, and loom with blissful anticipation. Shreds of tissue paper suddenly began to peel away to disclose a mascaraed, peacock-eye rim, and my swooning gaze fell into a virgin dawn of godly colors, into wonderful dampness of the purest azures. Oh, the wearing away of that film! Oh, that invasion of splendor! ("Księga," 1937)

We see the moment in the documentary when the polychromes are painstakingly uncovered from behind a whitewash overlay to the gasps of the conservators and Schulz's last surviving student: the *frottage* of revelation, of anagnorisis.

Fragment 4: Bare Skeletons

> The books we read in childhood don't exist anymore; they sailed off with the wind, leaving bare skeletons behind. (Letter [57] "Do Romana Halpern," 5 December 1936)

The murals' belated discovery and subsequent re-disappearance (it took eight years until they were finally exhibited) also plucks a persistent Schulzian chord about the genealogical loss marked by the gradual recession of childhood. All discussions of them, polemical or otherwise, emphasize the irony of loss that will forever attach itself to artworks, which, having been lost, then found, were (in their wholeness) lost again. They exist now only as disjunctive and discontiguous fragments, scraps, and sections, veritable emblems of liminality—figures minus a background, recovered art objects rendered extraterritorial. If supplements are "pluses compensating for a minus in the origin,"[5] these particular supplements are stranded forever now *between* plus and minus.

Fragment 5: Chronotope

> Of all essences in the cosmos, matter is the most passive and most defenseless. Anyone may knead and shape it; it submits to all. All arrangements of matter are impermanent and loose, easy to reverse and to dissolve. ("Traktat o manekinach")

Traveling hundreds of kilometers farther than the writer ever did himself in his own lifetime (beyond brief trips in the early 1930s to Polish artistic centers, he got only as far as Vienna in 1917, a short cruise on the Baltic Sea for a day trip to Stockholm in 1936, and a regrettable summer sojourn in Paris in 1938), the wall murals do not merely lend themselves now to an allegory of scission. They seem to enact or embody that very condition.

> And then there is all this highly improper manipulation of time, these indecent dealings, sneaking into its mechanism at the back and tampering dangerously with its precarious secrets. ("Genialna epoka," 1937)

Their displacement also uncannily dovetails with a familiarly Schulzian account of time, less inexorable and more malleable than we might imagine. Like a railway, it accommodates multiple tracks and sidings while possessing a shadow side, a black market of branch lines, a "contraband of supernumerary events."[6]

Fragment 6: One Profile, One Hand, One Leg

> We are not concerned with long-winded creations, with long-term being. Our creatures will not be heroes of romances in many volumes. Their roles will be short, concise; their characters—without a background. Sometimes, for one gesture, for one word alone, we shall make the effort to bring them to life. We openly admit: we shall not insist either on durability or solidity of workmanship; our creations will be temporary, to serve for a single occasion. If they be human beings, we shall give them, for example, only one profile, one hand, one

leg, the one limb needed for their role. It would be pedantic to bother about the other, unnecessary, leg. Their backs can be made of canvas or simply whitewashed. ("Traktat o manekinach")

The double narrative the polychromes tell couples an improbable, posthumous variation on Schulzian poetics and a late appendix to the "haunted epilogue" of what, somewhat wistfully, has been called "Galicia after Galicia."[7] For Schulz's environs were themselves historically controlled by a succession of nation-states, rendering it vulnerable, in between, dangerously open to the politics of external reshaping and internal substitution. Schulz's creative instincts were not so different.

Fragment 7: Tandeta

"Who knows," he said, "how many suffering, crippled, fragmentary forms of life there are, such as the artificially created life of chests and tables quickly nailed together, crucified timbers, silent martyrs to cruel human inventiveness. The terrible transplantation of incompatible and hostile races of wood, their merging into one misbegotten personality ... Matter never makes jokes: it is always full of the tragically serious. Who dares to think that you can play with matter, that you can shape it for a joke, that the joke will not be built in, will not eat into it like fate, like destiny?" ("Traktat o manekinach: ciąg dalszy/Dokończenie")

Moreover, in their situational-compositional integrity, the artworks themselves suffered manifest damage, rents in their integrity. Ficowski's biography describes the portion that remained on the walls after being "plundered" as "rudiments, mutilated remnants of a whole no longer there—like Schulz's literature itself."[8] While that final phrase gestures in the direction of unfinished works like *Messiah* that have never been recovered, it is nevertheless a feature of "Schulz's literature itself" that rudiments and remnants play an ongoing role in its overarching poetics as theme, motif, even character and plot. Discontiguity ramifies.

But if we call Yad Vashem's rescue operation a botch, then also with a certain poetic justice, we find ourselves in the double-edged realm of *tandeta* ("tawdriness" or "trumpery"), that aesthetic mediator between Schulzian form and matter whereby, in Andreas Schönle's words, "the hitches of a careless execution redeem [a creative work or object] from standardization ... an incongruity which ensures that matter will be perceived as such, for its own qualities and identity."[9] Form acts as a way station, a temporary shelter for matter on its ever-mutable, migratory way. Unlike elevated, smoother kinds of creation, the coarse, unfinished, vernacular sort (say, a tailor's dummy as opposed to a wax-work figure) does not aspire to transcend its own materiality, leaving it all the more malleable. In its refusal of transparency, of lifelike mimesis and the fixed form, the derivative realm of *tandeta* (as in the fairy-tale murals) leaves space open for contingency as well as its own evolving agency.

> Demiurge, that great master and artist, made matter invisible, made it disappear under the surface of life. We, on the contrary, love its creaking, its resistance, its clumsiness. ("Traktat o manekinach: ciąg dalszy")

Say that the fairy-tale images incline partly toward kitsch (for Schulz was assuredly placating Landau's tastes even while subverting them). Even so, their fate six decades after composition uncannily falls in line with some of Schulz's own metapoetic principles. In the tripartite formula Schönle provides for the significance of the second-hand or the tacky in Schulzian aesthetics, *tandeta* gives precedence to matter over form, *tandeta* values fragmentariness, *tandeta* fosters ambivalence.[10] If, by entirely factoring out the creator (for Schulz personified little more than alienated labor in this instance), it thus "becomes the very paradigm of poetic story-telling," it also bestows on artworks their own life—even if they must be literally pried from their origins and damaged in the process. While the artist cannot obviously be indemnified against the breakage, the wall paintings' belated marring subserves the demiurgic imperative in his work, which exposes the artwork's fragility as it "casts a dubious light on the act of creation"[11] in the first place.

Fragment 8: Universal Masquerade

> Everything diffuses beyond its borders, remains in a given shape only momentarily, leaving this shape behind at the first opportunity. A principle of sorts appears in the habits, the modes of existence of this reality: universal masquerade. Reality takes on certain shapes merely for the sake of appearance, as a joke or form of play.... A certain extreme monism of the life substance is assumed here, for which specific objects are nothing more than masks. The life of the substance consists in the assuming and consuming of numberless masks. This migration of forms is the essence of life. ("Do Stanisława Ignacego Witkiewicza," 1935)

In the ensuing controversy over the murals and their rightful home—Ukrainian, Polish, Jewish, Israeli, international—claims to Schulz's art directly competed, ensuring they could not find mutual tangency. Unlike another of Cornis-Pope and Neubauer's constructs, the East Central European "marginocentric city" of shared boundaries, of hybridized social relations and cultural traditions, the agitated competition in this case spoke instead of appropriation and surrogacy, forced removal and usurpation, rescue and proprietary relocation. And thus the murals themselves migrated from obscure margin to conflicted foreground, tracing a small fable about boundaries and their overflow played out against the background of a European continent "always on the verge of becoming incontinent, of exceeding its limits ... constantly tending to go beyond itself, which is to say, beyond its given borders."[12]

Fragment 9: A Clown's Stuck-Out Tongue

> Thus an all-pervading aura of irony emanates from this substance. There is an ever-present atmosphere of the stage, of sets viewed from behind, where the actors make fun of the pathos of their parts after stripping off their costumes. The bare fact of separate individual existence holds an irony, a hoax, a clown's stuck-out tongue. ("Do Stanisława Ignacego Witkiewicza")

But while the wall paintings themselves may have retained a certain obscure sovereignty in those many years of concealment, the competing claims of ownership over them once they were exposed to view sought to efface one other through a politics of substitute inscription. As the site for vying national or territorial rights, the murals became palimpsestic (from Gr. παλίμψηστος, "scratched" or "scraped again"),[13] but not in a way Schulz's politically evacuated poetics would likely have licensed. Of course, he himself was a kind of layering, self-identity being the stuff of so many non-vertically integrated laminae: Jewish, Polish, Galician, Habsburgian.

Predictably, then, the migrated and transplanted murals prompted a regress of claims. Says Denise Powers, "Thus, the question, 'To whom does Schulz belong?'," as one [Polish] critic put it, "is prefigured by the deeper, more difficult question: 'Why do people want him?'"[14] Officially and damage notwithstanding, the international row has now been settled, the artworks, as the "cultural property of Ukraine" to be on "temporary loan at Yad Vashem," according to a 2008 press release.

Fragment 10: Angelicized Country and Chosen Land

> Here on a Warszawa pavement, on these turbulent, fiery, and stupefying days, my thoughts turn to the faraway town of my dreams. And my vision carries me over that low country, broad and folding like God's cloak thrown down in a mantle of colors at the very threshold of heaven.... Year by year, that country merges with the sky, blends in with the sunset, and is angelicized in reflexes of the vast atmosphere. ("Republika marzeń," 1936)

And yet, the narrative continues to generate epilogues, like the many vestigial elements that form another persistent motif in Schulz's literary imaginary. Ficowski's biography, for example, bestows the chapter title "The Last Fairy Tale of Bruno Schulz" on his account of the murals and their aftermath. No longer under Schulz's authorial control, the polychromes yet remain under the spell of Schulzian mimesis. Ironically or fittingly, that fate mimics the fate of East Galician Jews under the Habsburg imperium, whereby "a once cohesive community" became "irretrievably fragmented,"[15] a splitting that itself echoes the fate of Poland itself after the Three Partitions (*rozbióry*) of 1772, 1793, and 1795.

This applies in particular to what Poles call the *kresy* (borderlands) like East Galicia/Galicja/גאליציע (Galytsye), whose formal name under the Habsburgs was the fairy-tale-sounding "Kingdom of Galicia and Lodomeria." Schulz came of age during Józef Piłsudski's Second Polish Republic, with its multinational, state-assimilationist ethos that established at least temporary stability for Galician Jews. The Drohobycz of Jakub Schulz's generation, the one his son Bruno mythologized, lay nestled under both the Carpathian headland and the benign neglect of Emperor Franz Josef I. Toward the end of the nineteenth century, its anachronistic and rural-provincial character partly gave way to twentieth-century industrialization and cosmopolitan encroachment that followed in the wake of an oil-field discovery in nearby Borysław (now Boryslav, Ukraine). So it can be said, the wall murals acted likewise in their dormant, unexcavated state—until, disinterred, they were exported to a homeland never anticipated, a "homecoming" Schulz might well never have endorsed.[16] Still and with inadvertent clairvoyance, Schulz calls his republic of dreams a "chosen land ... beyond [whose] toll gates, the map of the country becomes nameless and cosmic, like Canaan."

Fragment 11: Peripeteias We Ourselves Had Instigated

> Above that forlorn, narrow strip of earth, a sky deeper and more expansive than anywhere else has opened up once more, an enormous sky like a many-storied and engulfing cupola, full of unfinished frescoes and improvisations, flying draperies and vehement Ascensions. How can I express it? While other towns were developing into economies, growing into statistical figures, numerical values, our town descended into its essentiality.... At every moment, something is decided here, exemplarily and for all time. ("Republika marzeń")

But while Drohobycz is certainly not Jerusalem, nor even *Yerushalayim de-Lita,* claims for similar essentiality and exemplarity have been a regular part of Zionist discourse from its earliest incarnations. And while they can be detected in the mainly Israeli-authored response in the *New York Times Review of Books* to the 29 November 2001 letter "Bruno Schulz's Wall Paintings," the land dreamt in Schulz's essay lay almost certainly not at the foot of Mount Herzl but of the Carpathians—a transcendentalized, demiurgic Drohobycz permeated by a "world republic of letters" *avant la lettre*.

> Here all the threads and fables would run in and out, as if hallucinated in its great and misty soul. Like Don Quixote, we wanted to open our lives to the channel of all histories and romances, and lay bare its edges to all the imbroglios, complications and peripeteias that strike up in the vast atmosphere, outbidding one another in fantasticality.... And at a certain point, an intrigue that pervaded these stories would break out of the framework of the narrative, and circulate among us—a sacrifice, alive and hungry, catching us all in its perilous whirlpool. We were overwhelmed, threatened by peripeteias that we ourselves had instigated. ("Republika marzeń")

Post-Austro-Hungarian Galicia was dreamable for Schulz because its provinciality and political congeniality—even after Galician Jewry found itself transformed at the turn of the twentieth century through the virtues of a superior Polish educational system and amidst differentially rising currents of Jewish nationalism, Marxism, and Yiddishism—resonated with his own atavistic character and in-betweenness, which he attributed to "a quietist and eudaemonic disposition"[17]—although, as Jaroslaw Anders reminds us, "The legend of his slavish attachment to Drohobycz—a kind of self-imprisonment in the Galician backwater—also has little support from the facts."[18]

Fragment 12: To Mature into Childhood

> You overrate the advantages of my situation in Drohobycz. What I miss here is quiet, my own quiet of the Muse, of a pendulum slowed to its own calm gravitational rhythm, marking a clean path undeformed by any alien pull. After all, the kind of art I care about is precisely a regression, childhood revisited. If it were possible to reverse development, to attain the state of childhood again, to have its abundance and limitlessness once more, that "age of genius," those "messianic times" promised and sworn to us by all mythologies, would come to pass. My ideal goal is to "mature" into childhood. (Letter [44] "Do Andrzeja Pleśniewicza," 4 March 1936)

Somewhat exceptionally for a member of the Galician Jewish intelligentsia, Schulz formally disaffiliated himself from his coreligionists. As Witold Gombrowicz insisted, any religiosity he evinced was always bound up with art—an acolyte's devotion that nevertheless situated him still ambivalently between avant-garde trends in international modernism on the one hand and a regressive mythologizing of childhood on the other.

Fragment 13: Director of Landscapes

> The works of man have the property that, once completed, they close in on themselves and become cut off from nature, stabilizing themselves on the basis of their own principle. ("Republika marzeń")

By contrast, the republic of dreams, which originates as an "anonymous virgin land that belonged to no one" and resides in phylogenetic youth, is still reclaimable but only by someone who proclaims and oversees it as "the sovereign territory of poetry," someone, however, who "is not an architect. Rather, he is a director—a director of landscapes and cosmic scenery." The oneiric landscape gorgeously evoked here, "that great theatre of the unconstrained atmosphere," verily traffics in the migration of forms, the overflowing of boundary and transformation of substance.

The distinction between these two realms, the dreamt and the mundane, the fantasy-republican and the prosaically quotidian, is eerily captured by the wall paintings themselves. By an admitted leap of the empathetic imagination, while their fairy-tale content might induce even the dreaming of children in the nursery of state-sponsored eliminators, their material forms (at least as far as Schulz intended and despite the subsequent institutionally engineered migration) were fated to close in on themselves. The distinction also may be applied to Schulz's afterlife in the hands of critics, acolytes, and fellow authors alike: those, like Jerzy Ficowski, who all but legendize Schulz in hypertrophic devotion (bearing out Gombrowicz's criticism of Schulz in his *Diary* as an idolatrous "fanatic of art, its slave"); and others, like Jaroslaw Anders or Cynthia Ozick, with less wide-eyed estimation.

Obviously, Poles, Jews (of various national allegiances), and Ukrainians are alternately susceptible or skeptical after their own fashion—especially against the background of current political and nationalist tensions.[19] According to Benjamin Paloff, Jewish life in twenty-first-century Ukrainian Drohobycz after Schulz, like that of Galicia after Jewish Galicia generally, "is something for cultural displays and historical exhibits, which helps explain why visitors to the innumerable souvenir shops can purchase wooden figurines of black-cloaked, bearded Jews, usually displayed somewhere between the witch puppet and the doll of the fairy princess." In other words, there, in Drohobycz, Schulz's last fairy tale possesses its own weird afterlife: "in the shape and semblance of a tailor's dummy."

Fragment 14: The Core Capital of Imagination

> The actual procedure of riding a carriage seemed to me full of gravity and hidden symbolism. Around the age of six or seven there constantly recurred in my

drawings the image of a carriage with its top up and lanterns lit coming out of the night forest. This image belongs to the core capital of my imagination; it is a node of many receding ranks. To this day I have not exhausted its metaphysical content. ("Do Stanisława Ignacego Witkiewicza")

In their content, the fairy-tale images Schulz painted for Hauptscharführer Landau reveal a set of all-too-familiar representations: the triangular Schulzian gęba (mug) that makes a regular appearance in so many of his Expressionist drawings and self-portraits, together with the recurrent motifs of horse and carriage and of a tall woman attended by dwarfish men (last iterated in the nursery of the Landau villa). As for Thomas De Quincey before him, the phenomenon of a horse and carriage was positively archetypal.

Fragment 15: Faces

> White spots appear in our biography-scented stigmata, the faded silvery imprints of the bare feet of angels, scattered footmarks on our nights and days— while the fullness of life waxes, incessantly supplements itself ... contained wholly and integrally in each of its crippled and fragmentary incarnations. ("Księga")

For one final time, Schulz inscribed his own repeatedly self-caricatured face, inserting it into the figure of the carriage driver. Could this, inadvertently perhaps, be what Schulz means when he writes, "The more this intangible nucleus is 'ineffabilis' the greater its capacity, the sharper its tropism and the stronger the temptation to inject it into matter in which it could be realized"? It is, doubtless, a Jewish face, thus confirming the opinion of a Gestapo officer who had adjudged Schulz's ceiling fresco in the nearby Gestapo officers' Villa Rajmund Jarosz, "*typische jüdische Malerei.*"[20] While the figures of Felix Landau on his horse along with his lover Gertrude and children were recognizable to Geissler, Ficowski quotes Schulz's former student, Emil Górski, on other particulars of the nursery-room images:

> And here Schulz remained somehow faithful to his creative principle: the characters of kings, knights, squires had the completely 'un-Aryan' features of the faces of people among whom Schulz lived at the time. Their similarity to the emaciated and tortured faces that Schulz had captured in memory was extraordinary.[21]

Curiously, although this account of a transposition to the Real accords with the rationale articulated by Aharon Appelfeld, A. B. Yehoshua, and the other Israeli signatories to the 22 May 2002 *New York Review of Books* letter that "Schulz's wall paintings are valuable Holocaust artifacts because they vividly and poignantly convey the exploitation of Jewish talent by the Nazis," it is Górski who actually makes good on their admonition that "one of the keys to understanding this terrible period in history is to recognize not only its universal, but its specific and particular characteristics."[22] Further:

> Here these tormented people—transported through Schulz's imagination from the world of tragic reality—found for themselves in paintings brilliant riches and pride; as kings on thrones in sable furs, with golden crowns on their heads, on beautiful white horses as knights in armor, with swords in their hands and surrounded by knights, seated like powerful lords in golden carriages.[23]

Fragment 16: Mere Legend

> How sad to think that at 30 Mazeppa Street, where I spent so many lovely hours, no one will be left, all of it will become mere legend. I don't know why I feel guilty towards myself, as if I had lost something and it was my own fault. (Letter [113] "Do Anny Płockier," 19 November 1941)

It is not uncommon among readings of Schulz, especially those of his latter-day fictionalizers, such as Cynthia Ozick, David Grossman, Amir Guttfreund, Maxim Biller, William Gass, Nicole Krauss, and Philip Roth, who turn biographical life to legendary afterlife, to position his imaginative vision as back-shadowed by the Holocaust that eventually consumed him. Certain passages can even seem to lend themselves to stroboscopic effect when read, however ill-advisedly, as pointers toward "foregone conclusion" (Michael André Bernstein) or foreshadows of "closed time" (Gary Saul Morson).

> There is no evil in reducing life to other and newer forms. Homicide is not a sin. It is sometimes a necessary violence on resistant and ossified forms of existence which have ceased to be amusing. In the interests of an important and fascinating experiment, it can even become meritorious. Here is the starting point of a new apologia for sadism. ("Traktat o manekinach")

The impulse to do so, however, suggests its own twist on the migration of forms. While Schulz's phantasmagoria can be made prophetic in this way, only some of his last letters (those that have survived) lay claim to any historical immediacy and, thus, foreboding or presaging. Schulz's vision is retrograde, his temperament fatally nostalgic; when he does have rare occasion to invoke the shadow of the state or its bureaucracy, it is under the sign of Austria-Hungary's monarchic doubled-headed eagle (well before the abdication of the last Habsburg monarch in 1918) and the figures of Emperor Franz Josef and Archduke Maximilian—the former conjured as "a powerful and sad demiurge" and the latter, "perhaps only invented ... in order to play out the symbolic drama." In the polarity between "be foreign forever" (Gombrowicz) and "wherever you are, you could never be an alien" (Czesław Miłosz) as one template for twentieth-century Polish vectors of belonging,[24] Schulz was stranded somewhere in the middle, or maybe in elliptical orbit around each—"mysteriously alien and wholly native."[25]

Fragment 17: Passing from One Face to Another

> The very term "human being" is a brilliant fiction whose beautiful and consoling lie covers all those abysses, those worlds, those hermetically sealed cosmoses that are individual human beings. There is no human being; there are only infinitely distant from each other sovereign ways of existence which cannot be contained in one coherent formula or reduced to a common denominator. Passing from one face to another we have to undergo a fundamental restructuring, we have to change all our measures and assumptions. (Letter [6] "Do Marii Kasprowicz," 25 January 1934)

As will certainly be noted long before this point, Bruno Schulz has thus far been conscripted in my essay to "comment" on a mimetic-migrational fate he could neither have predicted nor authorized. While it may have explored possibilities for infinite transformation, his writing, of course, never pronounced much upon discontiguity. Matter is endlessly fecund and, as Schulz proposes, therefore effectively monistic: "it overflows endlessly into itself." If a seam is introduced, if an area is bounded with a perimeter marked out, it is answered dialectically by metamorphosis, masquerade, migration, but categorically speaking, never rupture. "No Mexico is final," for "beyond each Mexico there opens another, even brighter one."[26]

Outside "regions of the great heresy," however, the question of specifically literary topographies becomes rather more freighted, notwithstanding the many critical pairings of Schulz with authorial others. Schulz's own neurasthenic personality provides a model here. As one critic astutely notes of the febrile correspondence, "an almost passionate entertaining of the idea of affinity is contradicted by an architecture of aversion" since "Schulz's fundamental response to the idea of sharing time and space with others on equal terms is one of allergic rejection."[27] Perhaps a less interpersonal, less obviously elective affinity may be more instructive.

THE *OYNEG SHABES* ARCHIVE

In that spirit, while still seeking to account for the supplementary meaning of whatever fable the fragmented wall paintings of Schulz's last fairy tale might convey, we conclude by juxtaposing them with a situationally analogous relic of inscription—a rather different assemblage in the lost-and-found department of twentieth-century Polish Jewry, at once more collectively costly and more collectively redemptive.

The artifact goes by the name *Oyneg Shabes* and denotes Emanuel Ringelblum's underground archive of sociohistorical documentation, artifacts, testimony, and personal memoir compiled in the Warsaw Ghetto, deposited just before it was liquidated in the spring of 1943. It was salvaged from under the debris of the Borochov School at Nowolipki 68, in separate portions contained in ten zinc/tin boxes and two large aluminum milk cans, in the not-quite-nodal years of 1946 and 1950. The name of the archive ("Sabbath Delight") was chosen because Ringelblum chose Sabbath afternoons as the meeting time for its executive committee. Fittingly enough in this Shulzian context, it is a choice that transposes or migrates the sense of spiritual refreshment to secular, cultural work.

YIVO historian Emanuel Ringelblum (1900–1944) also came from Jewish Galicia, 180 kilometers southeast from Drohobycz: the town of Buczacz (Bichuch, in Yiddish), made famous by *landsman* S. Y. Agnon. Unlike Schulz personally and yet in line with the workings of Schulzian plasticity, Ringelblum witnessed many of the transformations experienced by post-Habsburg Galician Jewry. He became a social historian, a disciple of Simon Dubnow, who in 1891 called upon Eastern European Jews to become the *zamlers* (collectors) of their own history and culture,[28] and later of Ber Borochov and the Labor Zionist Poalei Tsiyon, in a region that—again, in quasi-Schulzian fashion—all but proliferated Jewish historians: Meyer Balaban, Philip Friedman, Natan Gelber, Rafael Mahler, and perhaps most illustriously for the non-Galician West, Salo Baron. Unlike Schulz, and with profound consequence, he moved from Jewish Galicia to Warsaw in 1919 during its brief interwar period as a boomtown, where he remained until his death.

Ringelblum's enduring fame rests on the ethnographic archive over which he presided, unique in its scope and ambition to record Jewish everyday history among the totality of secreted material Eastern European Jews were determined to leave behind them in the face of extermination. The texts were written in Polish and Yiddish (German, Hebrew, and other languages, less frequently). The archive's contents ranged from the lofty-scholarly to the quotidian-mass cultural: "the underground press, documents, drawings, candy wrappers, tram tickets, ration cards, heater posters, invitations to concerts and lectures." It contained "copies of the convoluted doorbell codes for apartments housing dozens of tenants[,] restaurant menus advertising roast goose and fine wines, and an account of a starving mother who had eaten her dead child." It assembled official records, essays on vernacular culture (e.g., "Boots" and "Street Scenes"), shtetl monographs, guidelines for the study of various topics, postcards, poetry, songs, questionnaires, diaries, sketches, personal effects, and dozens of photographs.[29] All in all, more than thirty-five thousand pages were recovered.

As the collective corollary to the individual and restrictive case of Bruno Schulz, the *Oyneg Shabes* archive bespeaks its own extraordinary reservoirs of resilience and creativity, genius and industry of a distinctive sort. But where Schulz devoted himself to spiritual genealogy (his formulation from the luminous 1936 essay *Mityzacja rzeczywistości*) or "the impetuous regeneration of primordial myth," and the reclamation of childhood-as-imaginative fount, *Oyneg Shabes* represents a heroic effort to document—if it could not actually preserve—the lives of real children in extremis. At its height, the ghetto contained one hundred thousand of them. Through multiple kinds of documents including their own writings, the archive sought "to tell the story of the Jewish child in the Warsaw Ghetto."[30] In this respect, therefore, the archive represents not the counterpart to Schulz's wall paintings but rather its countertext: the world in which Warsaw's youth were soon to lose their lives had long since been estranged from the uses of enchantment even while Schulz's fairy-tale drawings found a use for the faces of his fellow Drohobyczers—commissioned to decorate the nursery of Nazi children, no less.

There are unexpected crosshatchings between these discontiguous relics of a Polish Jewish life lived under coercion. Perhaps the most resonant is the particular term that Emanuel Ringelblum employed to refer to the trove in a conversation with his coworker, the journalist Rachel Oyerbakh (Auerbach), who survived the war: *legend,* a "term historians used to indicate the description and location of a historical document. But it also meant 'legend.'"[31] Or if not that quintessentially Schulzian word (as in his letter to Anna Płockier quoted earlier or epitomizing his short essay "Powstają legendy," about Napoleon and Piłsudski), then this excerpt from a testimonial by the artist Gela Seksztajn, written two months before Bruno Schulz was shot twice in the head at the intersection of Czacki and Mickiewicz Streets by SS Scharführer Karl Günther:

> I think I am now the last surviving Jewish painter ... and perhaps one of the very few Jewish creative artists [writers, painters] who are left. In the future, I think, the Jewish people should not consist only of tailors, carpenters, and shoemakers. There should also be creative artists and cultural figures. Therefore it is important to save the Jewish artist so that (after the war) he'll be able to help rebuild the Jewish people with the help of the pen and the brush.... I ask for little. Just give me a chance to live so that I can keep Jewish art alive.[32]

These are Gela Seksztajn's words, of course, not those of Bruno Schulz. More or less like Schulz, she earned her living as an art teacher, but in a school that taught Zionism and Yiddish culture; she was famous for her portraits of children and was a protégé of I. J. Singer. Neither artist survived the Nazi onslaught, Seksztajn staving off the inevitable for only a few months longer than Schulz, disappearing shortly before the commencement of the Warsaw Ghetto uprising on 19 April 1943. To call both of them fellow Jews or even fellow Jewish Poles, let alone fellow Jewish artists, instantly risks presupposing affinities the two did not actually share, linguistically, religiously, familially, communally. According to one affronted defender of Schulz's claim on Jewish peoplehood (and vice versa), "Bruno Schulz did in fact write in Polish, but he was no Pole," and according to another, "Bruno Schulz lived as a Jew and died as a Jew."[33] This essay's epigraph from Maurice Nadeau makes the more nuanced case for these multiple filiations; Schulz's liminality nevertheless remains both idiosyncratic and extreme.

Of course, the story of Bruno Schulz's final moments in the "Czarny czwartek" (Black Thursday) *Aktion* of 19 November 1942, in which his Jewish fate effectively converges with Seksztajn's, has become iconic in its own way. Here is Henryk Grynberg's version, from his short story "Drohobycz, Drohobycz" (which, if not for its sheer horror, evokes the specter of Schulz's peer Gombrowicz, who specialized in dueling, reflexive vagaries of form):

> Schulz was seen for weeks on end on the scaffolding in the hall of the *Arbeitsamt* lying on his back under the ceiling like Michelangelo and painting at Felix Landau's command. He also painted in the Reithalle.... Jews trembled at the sight of Landau, but he was kindly disposed toward Schulz, toward his talent. He had him make his portraits and talked to him during the sessions. About aesthetics, of course. Unfortunately, he later had to burn all those interesting portraits. And Karl Günther's Jew was Hauptman, an artist-cabinetmaker, who created phenomenal marquetries, mosaics, panoramas of Drohobycz from various types of wood. Landau and Günther were the same age and competed in everything. When Landau noticed that Günther was sending the marquetries to the Reich, he called Günther's Jew aside and shot him in the nape of the neck. And for that Günther shot Schulz.[34]

Grynberg omits the grotesque tagline attributed to Scharführer Günther and invoked so often by Schulzologists and the secondary literature: "You shot my Jew: I shot yours."

Yet, it is also a matter of record that when he taught his art classes in the Władysław Jagiełło State Gymnasium, Schulz evidently joined with his students in Catholic prayer. In hopes of advancing a never to be realized marriage with his Catholic fiancée, Józefina Szelińska, Schulz publicly announced in Drohobycz's *Głos Drohobycko-Borysławski* in 1936 that he was thenceforward "without denomination" upon officially severing his connection with the Jewish religious community in Drohobycz. Ambitious efforts, especially in recent Polish criticism to recuperate Schulz's gnosticism in proximity to kabbalistic, biblical, and Hasidic tropes, nevertheless reveal an ambivalent, if (like Walter Benjamin's) porous, relationship to Jewish textual traditions.[35]

By contrast, here is the Jewishly saturated testament of Israel Lichtensztajn, Gela Seksztajn's husband, retrieved from one of the water-damaged tin boxes under Nowolipki 68 in 1946:

> I only wish to be remembered.... I wish my wife to be remembered, Gela Seksztajn.... I wish my little daughter to be remembered. Margalit is 20 months old today. She has fully mastered the Yiddish language and speaks it perfectly.... She too deserves to be remembered.[36]

Schulz left no such (deathbed) directive; if he did, it would doubtless not be that of a Jewish artist embedded in family and community. He did, however, make every effort to ensure that his writings would survive their imminent danger and his looming death (another not-so-surprising ligature with *Oyneg Shabes*), once he was forced to leave the house on Sklepy Floriańska in which he had spent three decades for the Drohobycz ghetto. His last surviving letter, dated exactly a year to the day before his murder, solicits its addressee, Anna Płockier, "to take me on as an adept of painting under your tutelage, to put me through a course in painting purged of the academic."[37] Purged of the academic or not, if the wall paintings themselves constitute some sort of inadvertent legacy, they signify yet another cleavage with *Oyneg Shabes,* the proprietary rights to which are entirely undisputed.[38]

If it can be claimed that Schulz's last creative works, certainly more than his writings, "'speak' of the Shoah,"[39] the documents assembled by Ringelblum and his colleagues *speak the Shoah* authoritatively and uncontestably. The rediscovered murals, exhumed sixty years after their creation under coercion, do indeed seem to belong to some branch track of time. Just as cleavage itself, discontiguity may be their most powerful and uncanny legacy: the difference they signal as *objects* (claimable by one party or another, displayable in one place or another) from a body of written work (putatively universal and ownerless) exposes the *cleft-that-is-also-a-cleaving* between realms aesthetic and political—realms unproblematically fused for Schulz in the Republic of Dreams. To cite Gombrowicz's trenchant analysis once again, "he shut himself in his form as in a fortress, or a prison."[40]

As this essay returns full circle, I once again transpose descriptive features of East Central Europe's marginocentric cities to the Schulz murals in their split state between Jerusalem and Drohobycz. If, as George G. Grabowicz observes of Lwów/Lviv, and Tomas Venclova, of Vilna/Vilnius, "their victories are temporary and contested, mixing the 'myth of division' with the 'mix of connection,'"[41] then the wall paintings now signify something analogous. From a pantry cul-de-sac, where Schulzian time and space, matter and form, are potentially at their most protean, to their now-fully visible, nominally fixed condition, the ruptured frescoes also function, differently than intended but perhaps no less transitively, as "topographic interfaces (crossroads, borderlands)."

Schulz declared about himself in his letter to the poet Stefan Szuman, "My concern was to be accepted into the family of creative spirits, to feel that my world borders on other worlds, that at those borders these worlds cross and interpenetrate, exchanging currents and ripples."[42] Accordingly, one might well ascribe parallel desires to Emanuel Ringelblum, Israel Lichtensztajn, Gela Seksztajn, and the many others whose commitment to the archive of cultural survival they assembled as both will and testament was ultimately affirmed. Both like *Oyneg Shabes* and wholly other, the final expressions of Schulz's creative spirit at last resurfaced into public view in accord with contingency's own mysterious logic. Their destiny, too, now lies in their brokenness.

Adam Zachary Newton, University Professor Emeritus at Yeshiva University, most recently Distinguished Visiting Professor at Emory University's Center for Humanistic Inquiry, has written and taught at the boundaries of several knowledge practices: literary studies, philosophy, and religion. His publications include *Narrative Ethics* (Harvard University Press, 1995), *Facing Black and Jew* (Cambridge University Press, 1998), *The Fence and the Neighbor* (SUNY Press, 2001), *The Elsewhere* (University of Wisconsin Press, 2005), and *To Make the Hands Impure: Art, Ethical Adventure, the Difficult and the Holy* (Fordham University Press, 2015), and the forthcoming *Jewish Studies as Counterlife: A Report to the Academy* (Fordham, 2018).

NOTES

For Miriam.
1. Denise V. Powers, "Fresco Fiasco: Narratives of National Identity and the Bruno Schulz Murals of Drogobych," *East European Politics and Societies* 17 (2003): 630. The polychromes are more accurately identified as depicting Cinderella and Snow White accompanied by five dwarves.
2. Rod Mengham, "The Folding Telescope and Many Other Virtues of Bruno Schulz," *Kenyon Review,* n.s., 33, no. 3 (Summer 2011): 154.

3. Bruno Schulz, *The Collected Works of Bruno Schulz*, ed. Jerzy Ficowski, trans. Celia Wienewska (New York: Picador, 1998), 32.
4. Natan Sznaider, *Jewish Memory and the Cosmopolitan Order* (Cambridge: Polity Press, 2011), 133.
5. Rodolphe Gasché, *The Tain of the Mirror: Derrida and the Philosophy of Reflection* (Cambridge, MA: Harvard University Press, 1986), 211.
6. Schulz, *Collected Works*, 112.
7. Larry Wolff, *The Idea of Galicia: History and Fantasy in Habsburg Political Culture* (Stanford, CA: Stanford University Press, 2010), 383.
8. Jerzy Ficowski, *Regions of the Great Heresy-Bruno Schulz: A Biographical Portrait*, trans. Theodosia Robertson (New York: W.W. Norton, 2002), 170–71.
9. Andreas Schönle, "Cinnamon Shops by Bruno Schulz: The Apology of Tandeta," *Polish Review* 36, no. 2 (1991): 131.
10. Schönle, "Cinnamon Shops by Bruno Schulz," 139.
11. Schönle, "Cinnamon Shops by Bruno Schulz," 131.
12. Samuel Weber, "Mind the *Cap*," in *Europe after Derrida: Crisis and Potentiality*, ed, Agnes Czajka and Bora Isyar (Edinburgh: Edinburgh University Press, 2014), 13.
13. This is the term Schulz himself uses in the stories "Noc wielkiego sezonu" and "Druga jesień," which compare days to pages of parchment.
14. Powers, "Fresco Fiasco," 624.
15. On Galician Jews' status after 1867 as a both de facto social-cultural-linguistic entity and de jure political nonentity, see Powers, "Fresco Fiasco," 627; and Wolff, *The Idea of Galicia*, chapters 5–6.
16. "Die Heimkehr," one of the lost manuscripts, was a German novella sent to Thomas Mann in 1938. See also Maxim Biller, *Im Kopf von Bruno Schulz* (Köln: Kiepenheuer & Witsch, 2013).
17. Schulz, *Collected Works*, 386.
18. Jaroslaw Anders, *Between Fire and Sleep: Essays on Modern Polish Poetry and Prose* (New Haven, CT: Yale University Press, 2009), 34.
19. See, for example, the articles by Anna Bikont and Jan-Werner Müller.
20. Ficowski, *Regions*, 168. The Villa Landau polychromes are not technically "frescoes," since the paint was applied to the wall without pigments merging with the plaster. On the particulars, especially the technique of *stacco a massello* (forcible removal), see Jukka Jokilehto, "Principles for the Preservation and Conservation-Restoration of Wall Paintings," ICOMOS, 2003, accessed 27 January 2017, www.icomos.org/charters/wallpaintings_e.pdf.
21. Ficowski, *Regions*, 166.
22. Ficowski, *Regions*, 167.
23. Ficowski, *Regions*, 167.
24. Ryszard Nycz, "'Every One of Us Is a Stranger': Patterns of Identity in Twentieth-Century Polish Literature," in *Framing the Polish Home: Postwar Constructions of Hearth, Nation, Self*, ed. Bożena Shallcross (Athens: Ohio State University Press, 2002), 14.

25. Benjamin Paloff, "Who Owns Bruno Schulz? Poland Stumbles over Its Jewish Past," *Boston Review*, 29, no. 6 (December 2004/January 2005), 22.
26. Schulz, *Collected Works*, 144.
27. Mengham, "The Folding Telescope," 161–62.
28. Robert Moses Shapiro and Tadeusz Epsztein, eds., *The Warsaw Ghetto Oyneg Shabes–Ringelblum Archive: Catalog and Guide* (Bloomington: Indiana University Press, 2009), xv.
29. Samuel D. Kassow, *Who Will Write History? Emanuel Ringelblum, the Warsaw Ghetto, and the Oyneg Shabes Archive* (Bloomington: Indiana University Press, 2007), 213.
30. Kassow, *Who Will Write History?*, 261.
31. Kassow, *Who Will Write History?*, 450.
32. Peter N. Miller, "'What We Know about Murdered Peoples,'" *New Republic*, 9 April 2008, 36; and Kassow, *Who Will Write History?*, 5.
33. Respectively, James R. Russell, "Harvard Death Fugue: On the Exploitation of Bruno Schulz," *Zeek Magazine* (January 2004), accessed 27 January 2017, http://www.zeek.net/art_0401.shtml, and Melvin Jules Bukiet, quoted in Dinitia Smith, "Debating Who Controls Holocaust Artifacts," *New York Times*, 18 July 2001, E6.
34. Henryk Grynberg, *Drohobycz, Drohobycz and Other Stories: True Tales from the Holocaust and Life After*, trans. Alicia Nitecki (New York: Penguin Books, 2002), 23–24. Ficowski adds more relevant detail in *Regions*, 165–68.
35. *Schulz/Forum 4* (Fundacja Terytoria Książk, 2014) is devoted to this topic. See also Monika Tokarzewska, "Bruno Schulz i Walter Benjamin. Między zachodnioeuropejską metropolią a środkowoeuropejską prowincją," *Przegląd Filozoficzno-Literacki Philosophical/Literary Review* 9, no. 3 (2010): 243–63.
36. Shapiro and Epsztein, *The Warsaw Ghetto Oyneg Shabes–Ringelblum Archive*.
37. Schulz, *Collected Works*, 465.
38. The archive ("RA," as it is formally known, or "Ringelblum I" and "Ringelblum II") is preserved in Warsaw's Jewish Historical Institute, and Stowarzyszenie Żydowskiego Instytutu Historycznego w Polsce is its legal owner. See Shapiro and Epsztein, *The Warsaw Ghetto Oyneg Shabes–Ringelblum Archive*, 1ff.
39. Gillian Banner, *Holocaust Literature: Schulz, Levi, Speigelman and the Memory of the Offense* (London and Portland, OR: Valentine Mitchell, 2000), 82.
40. Witold Gombrowicz, *Diary*, trans. Lillian Vallee (Evanston, IL: Northwestern University Press, 2012), 115.
41. In Marcel Cornis-Pope and John Neubauer, *Towards a History of the Literary Cultures in East-Central Europe: Theoretical Reflections*, ACLS Occasional Paper 52 (New York: American Council of Learned Societies, 2002), 27–28.
42. Schulz, *Collected Works*, 305.

WORKS CITED

Anders, Jaroslaw. *Between Fire and Sleep: Essays on Modern Polish Poetry and Prose*. New Haven, CT: Yale University Press, 2009.

Appelfeld, Aharon, et al. "Bruno Schulz's Wall Paintings: Reply." *New York Review of Books,* 23 May 2002.

Banner, Gillian. *Holocaust Literature: Schulz, Levi, Spiegelman and the Memory of the Offense.* London and Portland, OR: Valentine Mitchell, 2000.

Baranczak, Stanislaw. "The Face of Bruno Schulz." In *Breathing under Water and Other East European Essays,* 107–18. Cambridge, MA: Harvard University Press, 1990.

Bartal, Israel, and Antony Polonsky, eds. *Focusing on Galicia: Jews, Poles, and Ukrainians, 1772–1918.* Polin 12. London: Littman Library of Jewish Civilization, 1999.

Bartov, Omer. *Erased: Vanishing Traces of Jewish Galicia in Present-Day Ukraine.* Princeton, NJ: Princeton University Press, 2007.

Bernstein, Michael André. *Foregone Conclusions: Against Apocalyptic History.* Berkeley: University of California Press, 1994.

Białasiewicz, Luiza, and John O'Loughlin. "Re-ordering Europe's Eastern Frontier: Galician Identities and Political Cartographies on the Polish-Ukrainian Border." In *Boundaries and Place: European Borderlands in Geographical Context,* edited by David Kaplan and Jouni Häkli, 217–38. Lanham, MD: Rowman and Littlefield, 2003.

Bikont, Anna. "Jan Gross' Order of Merit." *Tablet,* 15 March 2016. Accessed 29 January 2017. http://www.tabletmag.com /jewish-arts-and-culture/books/198490/jan-gross-order-of-merit.

Biller, Maxim. *Im Kopf von Bruno Schulz.* Cologne: Kiepenheuer & Witsch, 2013.

Bohlen, Celestine. "Artwork by Holocaust Victim Is Focus of Dispute." *New York Times,* 20 June 2001.

Bronner, Ethan. "Behind Fairy Tale Drawings, Walls Talk of Unspeakable Cruelty." *New York Times,* 28 February 2009.

Brown, Russell E. *Myths and Relatives: Seven Essays on Bruno Schulz.* Munich: Verlag Otto Sagner, 1991.

Bruncevic, Merima. "The Lost Mural of Bruno Schulz: A Critical Legal Perspective on Control, Access to and Ownership of Art." *Law Critique* 22 (2011): 79–96.

Budurowycz, Bohdan. "Galicia in the Work of Bruno Schulz." *Canadian Slavonic Papers/Revue canadienne des Slavistes* 28, no. 4 (December 1986): 359–68.

Buszewicz, Maciej. *Bruno Schulz.* Lesko: Bosz, 2008.

Cornis-Pope, Marcel, and John Neubauer. *History of the Literary Cultures of East-Central Europe: Junctures and Disjunctures in the 19th and 20th Centuries.* Amsterdam: John Benjamins, 2004.

———. *Towards a History of the Literary Cultures in East-Central Europe: Theoretical Reflections.* ACLS Occasional Paper 52. New York: American Council of Learned Societies, 2002.

De Bruyn, Dieter, and Kris Van Heuckelom, eds. *Unmasking Bruno Schulz: New Combinations, Further Fragmentations, Ultimate Reintegrations.* Amsterdam: Rodopi, 2009.

Ficowski, Jerzy. *Listy, fragment, wspomnienia o pisarzu.* Cracow: Wydawnictwo Literackie, 1984.

———. *Regions of the Great Heresy: Bruno Schulz, a Biographical Portrait.* Translated by Theodosia Robertson. New York: W.W. Norton, 2002.

Franklin, Ruth. "The Lost: Searching for Bruno Schulz." *New Yorker,* 16 December 2002, 97–100.
Gasché, Rodolphe. *The Tain of the Mirror: Derrida and the Philosophy of Reflection.* Cambridge, MA: Harvard University Press, 1986.
Geissler, Benjamin. *Bilder Finden/Finding Pictures.* Germany, 2002.
——. "The Picture Chamber of Bruno Schulz—The Final Work of a Genius—Mobile Installation." Umweltbibliothek Großhennersdorf, 2011.
Goddard, Michael. *Gombrowicz, Polish Modernism, and the Subversion of Form.* West Lafayette, IN: Purdue University Press, 2010.
Goldfarb, David A. Appropriations of Bruno Schulz." *Jewish Quarterly* 218 (Summer 2011): 42–54.
——. "A Living Schulz: 'Noc wielkiego sezonu' ('The Night of the Great Season')." *Prooftexts—A Journal of Jewish Literary History* 14, no. 1 (1994): 25–47.
Gombrowicz, Witold. *Diary.* Translated by Lillian Vallee. Evanston, IL: Northwestern University Press, 2012.
——. *Polish Memories.* Translated by Bill Johnston. New Haven, CT: Yale University Press, 2011.
Gordon, Jaimy. "The Strange Afterlife of Bruno Schulz." *Michigan Quarterly Review* 43, no. 1 (Winter 2004): 1–36.
Grossman, David. "The Age of Genius: The Legend of Bruno Schulz." *New Yorker,* 8 June 2009: 66–77.
Grynberg, Henryk. *Drohobycz, Drohobycz and Other Stories: True Tales from the Holocaust and Life After.* Translated by Alicia Nitecki. New York: Penguin Books, 2002.
Iłłakowicz, Krystyna Lipińska. "Renegotiating the Provincial: Bruno Schulz—Local Space and Local Rhythms." *Polish Review* 49, no. 4 (2004): 1065–82.
Jenner, Lynn. *Lost and Gone Away.* Auckland: Auckland University Press, 2015.
Jokilehto, Jukka. "Principles for the Preservation and Conservation-Restoration of Wall Paintings." ICOMOS, 2003. Accessed 27 January 2017. www.icomos.org/charters/wallpaintings_e.pdf.
Kassow, Samuel D. *Who Will Write History? Emanuel Ringelblum, the Warsaw Ghetto, and the Oyneg Shabes Archive.* Bloomington: Indiana University Press, 2007.
Kenney, Padraic, et al. "Bruno Schulz's Wall Paintings: Reply." *New York Review of Books,* 23 May 2002.
Kitowska-Łysiak, Małgorzata. "Uwagi w sprawie kanonu. Brunona Schulza szkicownik młodzieńczy i freski w willi Landaua." In *Schulz/Forum 2,* 63–78. Gdańsk: Fundacja Terytoria Książk, 2013.
Kuprel, Diane. "Errant Events on the Branch Tracks of Time: Bruno Schulz and Mythical Consciousness." *Slavic and East European Journal* 40, no. 1 (Spring 1996): 100–117.
Kuryluk, Ewa. "Caterpillar Cat, or Bruno Schulz's Drive into the Future of the Past." In *The Drawings of Bruno Schulz,* edited by Jerzy Ficowski, 31–43. Evanston, IL: Northwestern University Press, 1990.
Landau, Felix. *Love Letters of a Nazi Murderer in Lemberg and Drohobycz.* Haifa: Institute of Documentation in Israel for the Investigation of Nazi War Crimes, 1987.

Latek, Stanisław, ed. *Bruno Schulz: New Readings, New Meanings.* Montreal: Polish Institute of Arts and Sciences in Canada, 2009.

Magocsi, Paul Robert. *Galicia: A Multicultured Land.* Toronto: University of Toronto Press, 2005.

Markovits, Andrei S., and Frank E. Sysyn. *Nationbuilding and the Politics of Nationalism: Essays on Austrian Galicia.* Cambridge, MA: Harvard University Press, 1982.

Maxwell, Alexander, et al. "Bruno Schulz's Frescoes." *New York Review of Books,* 29 November 2001.

Mengham, Rod. "The Folding Telescope and Many Other Virtues of Bruno Schulz." *Kenyon Review* 33, no. 3 (Summer 2011): 153–66.

Miller, Peter N. "'What We Know about Murdered Peoples.'" *New Republic,* 9 April 2008, 34–39.

Morson, Gary Saul. *Narrative and Freedom: The Shadows of Time.* New Haven, CT: Yale University Press, 1994.

Müller, Jan-Werner. "The Problem of Poland." *New York Review of Books,* 11 February 2016. Accessed 28 January 2017. http://www.nybooks.com/daily/2016/02/11/kaczynski-eu-problem-with-poland/.

Nadeau, Maurice. "Bruno Schulz (1892–1942)." *Présences polonaises. L'art vivant au musée de Lodz. Witkiewicz. Constructivisme, Les contemporains.* Paris: Centre Georges Pompidou, 1983.

Nycz, Ryszard. "'Every One of Us Is a Stranger': Patterns of Identity in Twentieth-Century Polish Literature." In *Framing the Polish Home: Postwar Constructions of Hearth, Nation, Self,* edited by Bożena Shallcross, 13–25. Athens: Ohio State University Press, 2002.

Ozick, Cynthia. "The Phantasmagoria of Bruno Schulz." 224-228. In *Art & Ardor: Essays.* New York: Knopf, 1983.

Pacewicz, Piotr, and Uri Huppert. "Czyj jest Schulz? Polemika w sprawie fresków z Drohobycza." *Gazeta Wyborcza,* 4 June 2001.

Paloff, Benjamin. "Who Owns Bruno Schulz? Poland Stumbles over Its Jewish Past." *Boston Review* 29, no. 6 (December 2004/January 2005): 22–27.

Panas, Władysław. *Bruno od Mesjasza: Rzecz o dwóch ekslibrisach oraz jednym obrazie i kilkudziesięciu rysunkach Brunona Schulza.* Lublin: Wydawn. Uniwersytetu Marii Curie-Skłodowskiej, 2001.

Powers, Denise V. "Fresco Fiasco: Narratives of National Identity and the Bruno Schulz Murals of Drogobych." *East European Politics and Societies* 17 (2003): 622–53.

Prokopczyk, Czeslaw Z. *Bruno Schulz New Documents and Interpretations.* New York: Peter Lang, 1999.

Prokop-Janiec, E. "Schultz and the Galicjan Melting Pot of Cultures." *Periphery* 3, nos. 1–2 (1997): 84–88.

Russell, James R. "Harvard Death Fugue: On the Exploitation of Bruno Schulz." *Zeek Magazine* (January 2004). Accessed 27 January 2017. http://www.zeek.net/art_0401.shtml.

Schönle, Andreas. "Cinnamon Shops by Bruno Schulz: The Apology of *Tandeta.*" *Polish Review* 36, no. 2 (1991): 127–44.

Schulz, Bruno. *Bruno Schulz's Stories and Other Writings*. Translated by John Curran. www.schulzian.net/.
——. *The Collected Works of Bruno Schulz*. Edited by Jerzy Ficowski. Translated by Celia Wienewska. New York: Picador, 1998.
——. *Księga Listów*. Edited by Jerzy Ficowski, Gdańsk: Słowo obraz/terytoria, 2002.
——. *Proza*. Cracow: Wydawnictwo Literackie, 1973.
Shapiro, Robert Moses, and Tadeusz Epsztein, eds. *The Warsaw Ghetto Oyneg Shabes–Ringelblum Archive: Catalog and Guide*. Bloomington: Indiana University Press, 2009.
Singer, Isaac Bashevis (Yiztkok Varshavsky). "A buch fun a polisher-yiddishn schrayber in English." *Der Forverts,* 3 December 1961.
Smith, Dinitia. "Debating Who Controls Holocaust Artifacts." *New York Times,* 18 July 2001.
Sznaider, Natan. *Jewish Memory and the Cosmopolitan Order*. Cambridge: Polity Press, 2011.
Tokarzewska, Monika. "Bruno Schulz i Walter Benjamin. *Między zachodnioeuropejską metropolią a środkowoeuropejską prowincją.*" *Przegląd Filozoficzno-Literacki Philosophical/Literary Review* 9, no. 3 (2010): 243–63.
Tuszynska, Agata. *La fiancée de Bruno Schulz: roman traduit du polonais par Isabelle Jannès-Kalinowski,* Paris: Grasset, 2015.
Underhill, Karen. "Bruno Schulz and Jewish Modernity." PhD diss., University of Chicago, 2011.
Weber, Samuel. "Mind the *Cap.*" In *Europe after Derrida: Crisis and Potentiality,* edited by Agnes Czajka and Bora Isyar, 9–29. Edinburgh: Edinburgh University Press, 2014.
Wolff, Larry. *The Idea of Galicia: History and Fantasy in Hapsburg Political Culture*. Stanford, CA: Stanford University Press, 2010.
Zemel, Carol. *Looking Jewish: Visual Culture and Modern Diaspora*. Bloomington: Indiana University Press, 2015.

Part V

Elective Affinities

Readers and scholars have debated for two centuries what Goethe really meant when he borrowed the concept of "elective affinity" from chemistry to title his great novel of marriage and infidelity (*Die Wahlverwandtschaften,* 1809, translated into English as "elective affinities" and also as "kindred by choice"). Did Goethe truly believe that human choice is determined by the laws of chemistry, or was he using the idea of elective affinities merely metaphorically and as a plot device? We editors selected the phrase for this section heading to underscore that time spent learning, thinking, and writing about Eastern Europe is a choice, an election. To state this in terms that Kacandes uses in her essay, "Can logic fully explain why two people like each other or why somebody gets interested in a person or a place?" Probably not. We like the idea of a chemical reaction because it implies that there's something factual to be examined, and yet that examination, at least as carried out in these two closing essays, cannot be conducted in a strictly scientific or academic fashion. Both contain personal narrative with a high level of self-consciousness about voice, appropriation, and motivation for the elected affinity.

In "The Balkan Notebooks," Ann Cvetkovich combines accounts of specific incidents and affects that she experienced during her trips to the former Yugoslavia with accounts of her readings of other writers on those spaces. While she evokes the idea of "rites of return" (Hirsch and Miller), she queries what one learns by making a trip. Cvetkovich treads carefully, acknowledging that her family spoke little about the places they'd come from, that family native informants were already deceased when she traveled, and that her own inability to speak the local language limits the types of contact she can have. Furthermore, whatever knowledge she will acquire by "going there," does not equate with "knowing there." Cvetkovich has long insisted on the value of writing as an activity, especially in the absence of archives. The writing she shares with us here bears testimony to her affective choice to connect with this place, its history, and its people.

Irene Kacandes's contribution might be said to involve the more tenuous connection, the even more "elected" affinity, so to speak. "Gratuitous" is one word she chooses. In "A Polish Childhood," Kacandes describes a friendship she cultivated with an older stranger who it turns out grew up in wartime Poland, a place and period Kacandes has studied professionally. When Kacandes reveals that her own interest in Poland started in childhood, triggered by learning of the exploits of Tadeusz Kościuszko in the American Revolution, we realize that the essay's title sets up an ambiguity: whose childhood is under discussion here? Could these childhoods and their "Polishnesses" be connected in some strange way? Ultimately the story of this friendship seems to disclose not so much answers to the questions that it raises as to bring our attention to the possibility that all affiliations are ultimately discontiguous and elected. This strikes us as a framework for a productive reconsideration of the topics raised in this anthology.

Chapter Nine

The Balkan Notebooks

Ann Cvetkovich

TRAVEL STORY 1: GRAČAC (2004)

When you travel in terrain for which you have very few pre-existing images, everything you see is of potential interest, and my first trip to Croatia in 2004 filled in blanks of many kinds. While on a teaching exchange in Paris for a semester, I was drawn to tourist ads in the Metro featuring the gorgeous beaches of the Dalmatian coast, which didn't quite fit my image of either genocidal war or drab post-Soviet culture. I wasn't just interested in resort vacations, though; as a theorist of trauma cultures, I was also curious to know about the aftermath of recovery from the region's wars and conflicts of the 1990s and wondered whether that history might still be visible alongside the re-emergent tourist culture. And I had a more personal motivation—I hoped to see the places my grandparents had left behind when they immigrated to Canada in the 1920s. My last name is often the only visible sign of my heritage, even to me, since, despite Canada's celebration of multicultural identities, I grew up having no idea what it meant to be Yugoslavian, or Croatian, or Serb—or which one I was. Even though my own connection to the region was effaced by migration and assimilation, as well as war and shifting maps, I still wanted to know where my family came from.

With my girlfriend, Gretchen, as my reluctant companion, we headed inland in a rental car on a day trip from Split to a town called Gračac, where, according to my aunt, my Serbian grandfather had come from. It wasn't much more than a name on a map close to the border with Bosnia, although I knew that the Krajina region, because it was predominantly Serb, had been the site of a lot of fighting during the war that led to Croatian independence in 1991. We had just spent an idyllic week island-hopping by cheap public ferry amidst a picturesque legacy of ancient and medieval cultures that made Croatia seem more like Italy than Eastern Europe. Old ladies met us at the ferry docks to offer *sobes* (rooms) in their houses with the backyard vegetable gardens and fig trees, we swam from rocky beaches in the clear blue waters of the Adriatic, and we ate Croatia's version of Mediterranean cuisine, fresh fish and *blitva* (potatoes and greens) grilled in homemade olive oil. Although there were signs of war in Dubrovnik—the ruins of a waterfront hotel, stories of guns being fired from the hills on the town below—there was enough rebuilding that you could ignore the evidence unless you were looking for it.

The steep roads through the mountains were good, but they required our full attention to navigate, and the dry rocky terrain seemed desolate, especially compared to the Dalmatian coast. On the other side, the terrain became greener, but we also began to see abandoned houses covered in bullet holes and graffiti, their missing roofs and walls suggesting they had been actively destroyed, not just neglected. Despite warnings about active land mines, we stopped to explore one. It looked like it had been left in a hurry—the twisted metal remnants of a stove, a table and chairs, and a sofa were still visible through the blasted-out windows, and broken dishes and rusted silverware were scattered on the ground. Along a pockmarked concrete wall, a pink rose bush was in full bloom, as poignant evidence of life's persistence, but the messy debris inside made it difficult to see the potential for regrowth and repair. We felt just a little too self-conscious and anxious to take in either the beauty or the wreckage, less from a fear of danger than a sense that we shouldn't be looking at the scars and remnants.

The town of Gračac was even more grim. The streets were lined with the gray concrete facades and broken and missing windows of abandoned buildings that might once have been industrial but were too far destroyed to identify. There was very little commercial activity in the center of town and certainly no provisions for tourists, but we did manage to find a little café where we could get a coffee and appear to have a reason for stopping other than impertinent voyeurism. People were not particularly welcoming and seemed to be watching us as much as we were watching them, and since we had only a few words in the language, we couldn't really communicate. We felt increasingly conspicuous, and although we would have liked to stroll around and take pictures, it felt awkward to turn the ethnographic gaze on a poor and still struggling community or to make a spectacle of their hardship.

Instead we drove a little beyond the town and turned into an empty field filled with abandoned cars, some of which had been crushed into colorful cubes of orange, red, and blue and stacked together in what looked like a sculpture installation. There were no people around, and it was a relief to finally pause and look without feeling awkward, to stare at these accidental works of art with their rusty crevassed surfaces and random foreign logos. Juxtaposed against the backdrop of the green and hilly landscape, they made for a familiar and picturesque ruin rather than one haunted by violence because so obviously connected to someone else's grief and loss. Calmed a bit, I also felt more able to linger at our next stop—a cemetery where I searched without success for the name Cvetkovich (or Cvetković), but was gratified at least to find names that seemed obviously Serbian, since it was still a novel discovery to me that there had been Serbs in Croatia. The crushed cars, however, remain one of the most vivid memories of the day, because we had been able to slow down long enough to actually see them.

There was nothing else we could think of to do so we turned around. On the trip back through the mountains along the steep and winding roads to the ocean, Gretchen was impatient about being stuck behind a truck and pulled out to pass, only to find herself in the path of an oncoming vehicle with no way to get back into our lane. Instead she crossed the road and came to an abrupt stop against a traffic barrier on the narrow shoulder—we were lucky that there was just enough room for the oncoming vehicle to pass by us. The fender of our car was mangled, but fortunately the damage was merely superficial, and despite being shaken, we pressed on.

Once we had safely returned to Split, Gretchen acknowledged that she had acted impulsively on the road because she was so rattled by what we had seen, especially the abandoned house. Later, in reading more about the area, I realized that the empty houses had probably been abandoned by Serbs and that the current inhabitants of Gračac were likely the Croats who remained or others who had taken over their properties. This wasn't quite what I expected—I thought the Serbs were the ones who had persecuted the Croats. I took some small comfort from the thought that even if much of what I observed was opaque to me, I had learned something from making the trip to see for myself.

WHERE ARE YOU FROM?—A RESEARCH QUESTION

This essay belongs to the increasingly common genre of narrative accounts of return to the homeland by first-, second-, and even third-generation children of immigrants seeking to learn about their heritage across the disruptions of diaspora, assimilation, and cultural loss. Marianne Hirsch and Nancy K. Miller have called such journeys "rites of return," in recognition of the way that they are affectively driven and yield uncertain results, with ritual sometimes a necessary substitute for the actual recovery of a lost homeland or people. The child of immigrants falls somewhere between insider and outsider, expert and amateur, perhaps begging the question of their differences, but nonetheless susceptible to distortions both factual and affective.

Some backstory, although a sketchy one. My grandparents came from what is now officially Croatia but what I knew growing up to be Yugoslavia, and what was at the time they left for Western Canada part of the Austro-Hungarian Empire (although I didn't know that until much later). Like many other Serbs, my grandfather immigrated during the upheavals of World War I to work in the mines, in places like Anyox, a copper-mining town in the remote north of British Columbia that is now a ghostly ruin, and Princeton, in the province's desert interior. My Croatian grandmother met and married him after leaving her family for Vancouver in the 1920s, but the marriage didn't last long, because my grandfather died of pneumonia when my father was only three. With three small children in tow (a fourth had died in infancy), my grandmother came to Vancouver, settling first in Strathcona, the East Vancouver neighborhood that was then home to immigrants from all over the world, including Scandinavia, Italy, and China. She married a Slovenian and had another child, and by the 1950s, they had enough financial stability to move, along with other upwardly mobile working-class immigrants, to a new neighborhood a little further out on the East Hastings artery. They were still there when I was growing up, and I saw that my grandmother had many "Slav" friends in the neighborhood, but I wasn't sure how they differed from the Italians, who were also prevalent. In my father's family, the emphasis was on assimilation, and by virtue of going to university, becoming a lawyer, and marrying my Anglo mother, he left his heritage behind. Although he spoke Serbo-Croatian with his mother, I didn't learn it, and I grew up with no sense of Slav or Croatian culture other than what I could glean indirectly. Because Yugoslavia was under Communist rule and had a language similar to that of Russians, Poles, and Czechs, it seemed to be Eastern European. But the rest was really quite vague. Over the years, I tried to piece together what I could from family stories, but my grandmother was always reluctant to talk about her past, and most of what I know comes second-hand from my father's older sister. One impulse for my trip to a newly independent Croatia was a desire to make up for the fact that my grandmother never returned there and my father and his siblings never visited.

This essay is a modest attempt to enter the terrain of rites of return from the vantage point of someone whose relation to the former Yugoslavia is shaped not only by the loss of language and culture that is often the result of immigration and assimilation, but also by the renewed prominence of the region in contemporary critical discussion of nationalism and imperialism.

Like Hirsch and Miller, I'm skeptical about roots tourism and nostalgia for origins that lends itself to conventional nationalisms, and as a scholar whose work has also been shaped by discourses of queer diaspora, my relation to home and return is a complicated one. Still, inspired by queer, feminist, and de-colonial histories of migration that emphasize affective affiliations across time and place, I wondered whether my personal lack of knowledge about the Balkans could be the point of departure for a more collective history. Rites of return, especially in the context of Holocaust or African diaspora, produce accounts of loss, seeking to explain the effects of absent memories rather than filling historical blanks. That the place from which my own family came was a flashpoint for contemporary discussions of nationalisms, ethnic cleansing, and human rights provided an opportunity for forms of scholarship and writing that combine the personal and the professional. My project was only partially about finding my ancestors' roots—I was also interested in whether a lack of cultural transmission could be traced not just to the immigrant's assimilation and willed forgetting, but also to the changes from Austro-Hungarian Empire, to the Kingdom of Serbs, Croats, and Slovenes, to Yugoslavia, to Croatia that professional historians and ordinary people were still laboring to explain.

The aims of my first trip were relatively modest—to learn more. But they were also meta-critical—to ask what it might be possible to learn through travel or direct experience, even without scholarly or cultural expertise, including language skills. In exploring where my people came from and what it means to ask that question, I draw upon multiple sources: travel-based observations from the streets and the museums, which offer both informal visible evidence and that which has been deliberately constructed, and research based on reading across a range of genres that encompass the scholarly and the popular, the fictional and the nonfictional. Trained to be wary of all of these sources, I am alert to how they supplement and contradict one another. And despite my critical awareness of the problems of both ethnographic and cultural roots tourism, I sought to see for myself. My method is in part that of Carolyn Dinshaw's "amateur," guided by passions that can be an important source of affective knowledge.[1] It is also that of the professional researcher insofar as I was taught, especially through my theoretical training, to see things differently. In particular I came with a conviction, under the influence of Walter Benjamin, that history can be embedded in the landscape and hence available to be felt or sensed in unpredictable and affective ways. Even as a casual tourist to Croatia's Dalmatian coast, it might be possible to learn something.

In drawing on personal forms of reading and observation, rather than conventional research, I seek to perform in my own way the unmapping process that Yuliya Komska calls for in the introduction to this collection. Sharing her reservations about geo-coding and metageographies, I try to come closer to specific places and locations in order to escape monolithic categories such as Eastern or Central Europe, which are so freighted with historical and conceptual baggage. I use the term "the Balkans" to describe former Yugoslavia and its successor states, but the difficulty of deciding what name to use already bespeaks the problem of efforts to both map and unmap the region. "Croatia" isn't quite right because it didn't exist when my grandparents immigrated and because its current terrain has included multiple groups, including Serbs. My working category of the Balkans seeks to displace these more directional categories, but it is also a placeholder in search of more precise descriptions. I often found myself working both with and against the maps, obsessively trying to match up the place names, routes, geographical contours, and histories of shifting borders with my own perceptions, and often failing to be able to reconcile them.

My solution has been to get local, to displace problematic archives with the evidence of my own experience, including the experience of critical reading. Although I appeal to landscape, trying to see what is in front of me, it is not a landscape that is essentialized or devoid of history. To the contrary, I look to geographies of all kinds as resolutely cultural and historical and approach the materiality of landscape and built environment as a site of layered histories that are often discontinuous with one another. Like Kacandes seeking to connect with Poland through elective affinity, I seek to understand the Balkans through what can only be a leap across time and space by means of an eclectic archive that assumes history to be constructed through personal and affective investment. The discontinuities of both geography and history yield forms of not knowing and disorientation that are often suppressed in conventional histories. Hence my turn toward the genre of creative nonfiction, and its incorporation of the literary and the memoir, as models for my own practice and for histories that can perform the work of unmapping. Although personal and affective histories may risk nostalgia or amateurism, when written from a place of critique, they can also be experiments in producing alternative maps.

TRAVEL STORY 2: LIKA (2005)

On my second trip to Croatia my entry point was Zagreb, where Gretchen and I braved another rental car to drive to Split for more vacation time on the Dalmatian coast via an overland route that would include Lika, the province my grandmother came from. This time the drive was very easy—over flat countryside with a stop along the way in a gorgeous national park with lush green forests, rushing rivers and waterfalls, and a historic old mill.

I had had a very hard time finding my grandmother's town on any maps and eventually came to the conclusion that the name might have changed or that it was too small to show up. So all we could do was head for the general area via the one small road heading west toward the coast from Gospić, Lika's main town. Although equally remote, the farmland dotted with small villages was more picturesque and less desolate than the bleak landscape of my grandfather's Krajina. Without much fanfare, we arrived in what I thought might be the spot. It was barely a village—just a church, a few houses, and a graveyard. There didn't seem to be many people around, but again I felt self-conscious and out of place.

As I stopped by the side of the road to take pictures of the landscape, an old man appeared beside us. Unlike the people in Gračac, he wanted to engage with us. But he spoke no English, and even though we had been trying to learn from the Croatian phrase books, we didn't yet have much more than *dobar dan* (good day) and *kako ste?* (how are you?). We happened upon German as a language of common ground, and I tried to ask if he knew anyone with my grandmother's maiden name. I couldn't really understand his answer, but he did seem to understand that my family had come from there. He wanted to know how old I was and if I was married and had children, and seemed perplexed by the fact that someone my age didn't have children. We soon exhausted our limited vocabulary, but there was the sense of goodwill that can mark exchanges between people who can't communicate verbally but want to connect. As we parted paths, he pressed a twenty-kuna note—about a dollar—upon me and insisted that we use it to buy *pivo* (beer). Although I was reluctant to take his money, I did so for the sake of the gift economy.

READING STORY 1: SLAVENKA DRAKULIĆ

I am the kind of traveler who reads en route, supplementing what I see with historical background and taking advantage of being on location to make reading that might otherwise seem more remote or abstract come to life. I know that I'm not alone, since even mainstream travel guides provide bibliographies, and bookstores that cater to tourists sell local authors in translation. But I also study this tourist book culture with the trained critical eye of scholar and literary critic, interested to see what genres, from fiction to history to personal essay, and what kinds of authors, both native and nonnative, do the job of making the region and its complicated history available to the casual visitor.

Once in Croatia, I found some books that were useful, but also many that were not. Mainstream histories designed for Western readers provide basic background information but can traffic in stereotypes, and they often don't provide the critical analysis I'm looking for to explain the historical timelines.[2] The more I dug, the more I needed to go back further—from the 1990s breakup of Yugoslavia to Communist Yugoslavia under Tito, to the World War II occupation by the Nazis, to the Balkan Wars and the infamous assassination in Sarajevo that inaugurated World War I, to the Austro-Hungarian, Ottoman, Venetian, Byzantine and Roman Empires.[3] A dizzying array of maps with shifting borders is necessary to get even the basic geographical facts in place, much less their significance. In the first phase of my reading, I gave up any simple dichotomy between Croats and Serbs, including the pull to make one good and the other bad, but often found myself with a plethora of historical and political details and no way to make sense of them.

For a more synthetic critical framework, I turned to scholarly books such as Maria Todorova's *Imagining the Balkans,* which outstrips most of the popular literature and history in offering a paradigm that both describes the Balkans in its local specificity and explains why it matters to other contexts.[4] As a Bulgarian scholar situated in the United States, Todorova also bridges the gap between books designed for outsiders and those who are area studies specialists, and she is helpful in explaining why many popular narratives, such as Robert Kaplan's *Balkan Ghosts,* are problematic: they perpetuate the idea of the Balkans as a backward place whose conflicts are the result of perennial ethnic differences.

While history may be the privileged source of expertise for scholars, literature remains important for general audiences, especially since writers are the native informants most likely to be translated. Moreover, as a form of world literature, including its Balkan versions, literary genres can serve the documentary functions assumed to belong to nonfiction genres, and the personal essay can be especially popular because it combines them. One of the most useful writers in my early explorations, especially because her publications were widely available in English in Croatia, was Slavenka Drakulić, whose collections of essays such as *Café Europa* and *They Wouldn't Hurt a Fly* combine historical and cultural expertise and a cosmopolitan political perspective with a personal voice.[5]

Drakulić's work is an example of how the essay form can provide a holistic knowledge that is subjective without compromising its authority. In my search for writing that can do justice to the complexity of the Balkans, and in my own effort here to write such an essay, I've been especially interested in hybrid forms that combine the personal and the general, the creative and the factual, the fictional and the nonfictional. Experimental use of form can help undo claims to a privileged perspective or vantage point, such as that of the expert (as opposed to the amateur), the insider (as opposed to the outsider), or a specific national or political position (such as that of the victims or losers as opposed to that of the perpetrators or winners). As has often been the case for my other scholarly projects, I have been driven to write because of an absent archive, because I can't find the book I am wanting to read and must instead invent a form that can register that difficulty, such as this essay's effort to combine personal travel narrative with multiple other sources.

Drakulić also provided me with one of the moments of shocking discovery that for me came as much from reading as from direct witnessing or travel. I happened to be reading her work at the same time that I was having trouble finding my grandmother's village in Lika on the available maps. While reading *They Wouldn't Hurt a Fly*, her collection of essays about war criminals and their trials in the Hague, I came across the name I had been looking for in the opening sentence of a chapter: "It was already late at night when a military truck stopped on the outskirts of Gospić, near a village called Pazarište." Drakulić proceeds to tell the story of the massacre of twelve Serbs, rounded up as part of a campaign of "ethnic cleansing" in Gospić, the major town in the province of Lika, under the direction of two Croats, Tihomir Orešković and Mirko Norac, who were part of a group that was tried in Rijeka in 2001–3. In the previous chapter, Drakulić tells the story of the murder in 2000 of Milan Levar by a bomb planted in the spare tire of his car at his mother's house. He had sought, often unsuccessfully, to bring attention to the murder of Serbs (and the destruction of their property) to which he had been a witness. It was startling to discover that the town that I hadn't been able to find anywhere on a map and that had seemed so nondescript when I visited was the site of a major massacre—and moreover, further complicating any simple categories of victims and perpetrators, a massacre of Serbs by Croats. I had expected that, as a Serbian town, Gračac might bear the traces of war, but if Lika was also marked, the sites of war were extensive and unpredictable. It was a reminder of how much I couldn't see or read in the apparently placid landscape.

TRAVEL STORY 3: SARAJEVO TO BELGRADE (2012)

My rite of return to the places from which my grandparents came had been revealing, but as much for what it didn't tell me as for what it did. My interest in the Balkans remained, shifting from direct inquiry into my own family to the larger context for what I had seen in Gračac and Lika. I wanted to go beyond Croatia to see this bigger picture, and I was longing to see both Sarajevo, the renowned site of Balkan cosmopolitanism including Bosnian Muslim culture, and Belgrade, the former capital of Yugoslavia and the center of a now suspect and stigmatized Serbian culture.

Although we made stops in Mostar, Sarajevo, and Belgrade, they were too brief to get more than a superficial impression, and the real point of the trip was the experience of getting from one country to the next by overland travel, to literally make the connections between Croatia and Bosnia and Serbia across borders that have been imposed politically and conceptually. The literal experience of travel was a surprise at every turn, since I didn't know what to expect of the landscape itself. I saw, for example, that Bosnia includes a tiny bit of Dalmatian coast, because the Neretva River flows into the sea there, and the route to Mostar, an ancient site of trade between East and West, follows its gentle valley through what are otherwise impenetrable mountains that come very close to the coast. Later I learn that Neum, the town at the mouth of the river, was an old Roman settlement, and I think about how the cultural and political geography sometimes follows the natural one. How was the Ottoman Empire's limit and the relative independence of the Dalmatian coast shaped by geography, and when are the borders merely arbitrary? And what about efforts to cross borders, as in Mostar's famous bridge across the Neretva River, which joins, but also separates, Christians from Muslims and was blown up during the war?

The difficulty of traveling from Sarajevo to Belgrade, even though they are not far apart, was especially revealing. There are fairly frequent buses that leave from the Serbian side of Sarajevo. Lured by the romance of train travel, we were curious to take the one train that leaves daily for Belgrade at 8 a.m., a service that had been revived only recently for the first time since the war. The route, involving many passport and ticket checks, is a circuitous one via Croatia in order to avoid a direct border crossing between Bosnia and Serbia. What could be a road trip of a few hours takes all day, especially since the train is extremely old and slow. At first the train is full of students on their way home to smaller towns from university, since it is the beginning of summer vacation. Gradually the locals peel off, and only a few foreigners turn out to be the ones actually going all the way to Serbia: a Japanese guy who is immersed in his screen for the entire trip, and a Canadian-Bosnian girl who is headed to Belgrade for a cousin's wedding.

I try to figure out where I am by watching the landscape from the window, as if that could explain borders past and present. In the mountains of Bosnia, the train hugs picturesque streams, whereas we make a straight shot through flat green fields when we finally get to Serbia. I feel a sense of ominousness as we approach Belgrade and pass what looks like a Roma camp in a garbage dump. As Gretchen says, we've come to the land of the perpetrators.

But it is not what I expected from the guidebook descriptions of a bleak post-Communist middle-European city. The geography is stunning—the old town is situated on a hill at the confluence of the Sava and Danube Rivers, with the fortress and park of Kalemegdan affording spectacular views. At the water level, there is a promenade lined with cafes and clubs in houseboats. The market is a real market, where old women bring fresh produce from the country; raspberries were in season and heaped on the tables in red jewel-like piles. We have only one day and it's not enough.

READING STORY 2: VLADISLAV BAJAC AND OTTOMAN BELGRADE

At the airport leaving Belgrade after our too brief visit, I happened upon a historical novel called *Hamam Balkania* on a table of Serbian books in English. It turned out to be a dream come true—a book about the history of Ottoman Serbia that isn't afraid to embrace Serbia's lengthy connections to Ottoman and Muslim culture rather than seeing them as an aberration to be disavowed and rejected, as Piro Rexhepi's essay details in chapter 2 in this volume. Vladislav Bajac writes a fictional account of the friendship, during the sixteenth-century reign of Suleiman the Magnificent, between the renowned Ottoman architect Sinan, who is depicted as Armenian, and the powerful vizier Mehmed Sokollu/Sokolović, who, like most of the viziers of this period, was a Serb raised in Bosnia. Although he can only speculate about their intimacy, Bajac's account is not entirely far-fetched, since he is drawing on actual historical evidence that the Ottomans made their colonized subjects central to their administrative structure by taking young boys from the provinces and training them to be their loyal servants. Central to Bajac's project is a psychic portrait of colonized identity that belies conventional notions of conversion, enslavement, and nationhood, in which the colonized retain the affective and subjective complexity of coexisting identities—Ottoman and Serb, Muslim and Christian, governed and governing. Sokolović must convert to Islam and display loyalty to the sultan ("submit or die"), yet also finds ways to retain his Serbian identity, if only in the intimacy of his own heart.

Mehmed Sokolović also preserves his Serbian identity more publicly, if covertly, by working with Sinan on building projects in Belgrade, thus directing the material resources of Constantinople to the provinces. Bajac devotes considerable attention to Belgrade's role as a crucial strategic center of military offense and defense for the Ottomans, the staging ground for Suleiman's ambition to conquer Budapest, Vienna, and Europe more generally. Belgrade's status as a cosmopolitan crossroads is of no interest to contemporary Serbian nationalisms that construct the Ottoman past as one of subservience.

Further consolidating the close ties between Constantinople and Belgrade are the geographical similarities between the two cities that Sinan points out to Sokolović: "I compared the positions of Belgrade and Istanbul on various maps, more precisely the parts of them known as Kalemegdan and the Golden Horn, and this is what I concluded: Belgrade has the River Sava on one side and the Danube on the other, while Istanbul has the Black Sea on one side and the Sea of Marmara on the other."[6] Like Sokolović in the novel, I was shocked by the affirmation of a connection that seems so taboo. For Belgrade to be able to claim the romance and mystique that was attached to Constantinople, with its geography of water and continents meeting, its mosques on the seven hills, and its rich cultural history, cuts against a tendency to cast it as another bland Central European city or a subsidiary capital. Reading Bajac helped me understand what I had also, like Sokolov, sensed intuitively but had had a hard time seeing through the haze of historical and political constructions—the beauty of Belgrade's location at the meeting of the Sava and Danube rivers, the spectacular overlook from the fortress at Kalemegdan, and the medieval streets and the riverside culture. That the link to Istanbul is topographic or natural cuts through the political and cultural divisions that have subsequently separated the two places.

Bajac further signals the intimacy of Belgrade and Constantinople/Istanbul by writing, in the contemporary narrative that is interspersed with the Ottoman story, about his friendship, which parallels that of Sinan and Mehmed, with Orhan Pamuk, whose own work focuses on the affective landscape of history in Istanbul.[7] Bajac dares to both resurrect and imagine Belgrade's Ottoman past, which has been so emphatically suppressed by Serbian nationalisms that have been defined in opposition to Ottoman conquest extending back to the mythic defeat at Kosovo in 1389. Perhaps the story of their linkage can only be ventured through an affective history, a wishful connection (or elective affinity) between past and present and between nations and cultures that have been severed. By writing between literature and history, and between past and present, Bajac, following Pamuk, constructs an affective and archival form of the historical novel that asserts connections that may not be present in the history books or the streets and museums, but can be projected onto the landscape of the city. Like Bajac, I want to see this Ottoman connection, but I'm not sure I can. I am alert to invisibilities and ghostly presences, especially because so much has vanished. Belgrade adds to my sense of the dividing line between Ottoman Empire and Europe, sometimes a geographical line such as the mountains between Croatia and Bosnia, sometimes a cultural line between Orthodox Serbs and Roman Catholic Croats. The obvious Muslim presence in Bosnia—the mosques and the old bazaar—is only one marker of this history of intimate entanglement.

TRAVEL STORY 4: BELGRADE'S MUSEUMS (2015)

Although walking the streets is a crucial way to see a place for yourself, I also like to see what the museums have to show about how the nation constructs itself and its history. Given the contested status of the "nation" in the former Yugoslavia, accessing the museum is difficult, often literally so. In Belgrade, the National Museum has been closed for over a decade for renovations, apparently delayed not only by lack of funding but also by disputes about the design. (Serbia is more interested in selling itself to the highest bidder, including plans for a giant tower on the water built with money from the United Arab Emirates.) I decide nonetheless to give it a try in hopes of at least seeing the building. The façade is completely obscured by scaffolding, but it does sit on an important open square across from the National Theatre, where ballet, theater, and opera continue to be offered on a regular basis, as one lasting legacy of the Austro-Hungarian presence and its version of national public culture.

We strike out. In a very gruff manner, the guard tells me that nothing is open and seems so hostile that we are afraid to even glance around the foyer. My cajoling skills are useless unless people speak some English, and we retreat defeated. I'm not sure where to go next so we head to the tourist office for a list of other museums, and I try to figure out which ones might be a good substitute. We wander a bit, passing the Hotel Moscow, a relic of Austro-Hungarian Serbia, where even in the morning a man in a tuxedo is playing piano for the people sitting in the faded splendor of the café. We take in the view of the National Assembly and the giant post office, with the Saint Marko cathedral beyond, and consider walking to the Sveti Sava cathedral visible in the distance.

Immediately in front of us I spot a giant museum exhibition poster displayed on the façade of a classical monolith of a building. It turns out to be the Museum of the History of Serbia—perfect—and there is a small exhibition of work by Franz Tittelbach, a Czech historian who became fascinated with Serbian culture in the late nineteenth century and documented its folkways in a variety of ethnographic genres, including writing, drawings and sketches, and collections of costumes. Although there are no English translations (another sign of lacking resources, even though it is presumptuous to expect this), the folk culture itself, as well as the fascination with it, provide visible evidence not only of efforts to construct the origins of Serbian nationalism but of the influence of Ottoman Turks. We have an extended conversation with the young man behind the counter, who is carefully trying to explain to two young German tourists, who are about the same age as he is, that there is no simple answer to their question about whether Serbia is better off independent or united with the rest of the former Yugoslavia. We learn that he has had a difficult time finding a job and that this one may only be temporary and pays a mere 200 euros a month, 100 of which goes to pay his rent.

Afterward, we go to the park around the corner and, quite unexpectedly, find ourselves both crying. What are these tears? Tears for the ordinary difficulty of a capable and eager young man struggling to eke out a life—a job, an apartment, and the chance to travel—and still expressing hope in the midst of precarity. Tears for the connections between present and past—between his foreclosed circumstances and the violence that has taken place here—and for how he, barely alive when it happened, continues to carry its burdens, and for how under other historical circumstances he might have been the perpetrator of violence.

Tears also for our feeble efforts to try to learn about this history here in the Museum of the History of Serbia, where the present and the not-so-distant past are part of a complex longer history of Serbian nationalism, world wars, Ottoman presence, and folk cultures whose documentation can be put to work as evidence of a coherent and singular Serbian nation but could also be evidence of multiple cultural traditions and influences. Even as I find the young German men's question—are you better off independent or united?—to be naively based in the assumption that some version of the nation will provide stability, I too wish I could ask this question and others that are equally blunt and simple: What happened here and how do you feel about it now? What museum of terrible acts are we blindly tracking through on the street? The tears may be sentimental, but they are also the product of frustrated inquiry—the desire for knowledge despite the inevitable failure of any museum to provide answers. They mark the crossroads of history where the touch of human encounter transmits both that which cannot be known and the persistent yearning to know.

READING STORY 3: REBECCA WEST

I resisted reading Rebecca West's massive tome *Black Lamb and Grey Falcon* for a long time, not just because the book is so fat and dense, but also because I was suspicious of the adulation for a woman who was only a short-term visitor. Still one of the most famous Anglophone books about the Balkans, it continues to be listed in the bibliographies for tourists and cited approvingly in many other sources. And in the end, I had to admit my own similarity to West as a casual visitor, albeit a strongly invested one, and I finally read her to see what, if anything, has changed for the non-specialist writer of the Balkans. Although I am wary of an epistemology of tourism that assumes that going there can be knowing there and that the traveler can explain a mysterious region for others, there may be no way to avoid that dilemma given the limits of my own position and my idiosyncratic and associative research practice. Taking up West has proved to be a strategy for exploring my self-consciousness about my own lack of knowledge and the possibility that this writing stages only my own failings rather than a shared and symptomatic ignorance.

As it turns out, reading West is a reminder that both subject position and genre are complicated and that the practice of writing can enable the performance of this complexity. West is no ordinary tourist—she is a modernist and feminist writer whose critical reputation still borders on neglect, and she wrote a sprawling volume that, while not always taken seriously as literature, has the bold ambition not just to explain the region but to ward off the threat of impending war. There is indeed much that is fascinating about West for the person who has just been to the Balkans. Although, unlike Drakulić and Bajac, she is not a native informant, like them, she is willing to write from a subjective position that actually strengthens rather than undermines her authority, and the writerliness of the book, even when overblown, is a reminder to read with care. Although I often disagree wildly with her judgments—she deplores the Ottoman influence, for example—I also appreciate how her love for the Serbs (and the nationalisms they import from Europe) runs against the grain of contemporary presumptions, and I recognize a version of my own romance with the past in her deeply affective relation to Byzantine culture. Her pronouncements, both positive and negative, are shot through with a sometimes outrageously essentializing primitivism that divides East and West along biological lines: "They have something we have not got.... A kind of nervous integrity, of muscular wisdom."[8]

But West's appreciation for Belgrade, for example, resembles that of Bajac, as she also finds Kalemegdan to be an exemplar of Belgrade's natural and cultural beauty and its promise, describing it as "one of the most beautiful parks in the world," whose "charm was separating us from everything outside it, as good parks should do," and whose wild flowers and greenery amidst the fortifications make it "the prettiest and most courageous piece of optimism I know" (466). For her, Kalemegdan is the heart of a Belgrade that has persisted in the face of oppression: "This was a very sacred Balkan village; the promontory on which it stood had been sanctified by the blood of men who had died making the simple demand that, since their kind had been created, it might have leave to live" (482). Indeed, West's sympathy for modern Serbian nationalism is dependent in part on its connections to a primitive peasant life that she also romanticizes as she observes how "the middle class in Yugoslavia is so near to its peasant origin," a point made vividly clear by the moment when the eponymous black lamb appears in the middle of a cosmopolitan hotel in the arms of a man looking like a Byzantine-era figure.

> That [the greeting of a newcomer at the bar] I might have seen in London or Paris or New York. But in none of those great cities have I seen hotel doors slowly swing open to admit, unhurried and at ease, a peasant holding a black lamb in his arms.... He stood still as a Byzantine king in a fresco, while the black lamb twisted and writhed in the firm cradle of his arms, its eyes sometimes catching the light as it turned and shining like small luminous plates. (483)

Indeed, West's fascination with peasant culture is especially evident in her section on Macedonia, which she constructs as the heart of traditional Slav culture. While she often critiques religion, her modernist secularism is crosshatched by enchantment with Orthodox Christianity and its Byzantine origins. In a church in Skopje at Easter, she sees a woman who for her represents Slav values that have persisted in the face of the long-term oppression exemplified by Ottoman rule: "All this we know with our minds, and with our minds only. But this woman knew it with all her being, because she knew nothing else. It was the medium in which she existed. Turkish misrule had deprived her of all benefit from Western culture; all she had to feed on was the sweetness spilled from the overturned cup of Constantinople" (639). Even as West expresses disdain for the Ottoman Turks, she reaches back to an earlier history in which Byzantine Constantinople spread its own version of imperial influence.

It is easy to critique West for her stereotypes, political sympathies, and her own elitist sense of what matters, but she also provides a cautionary note against too easily assuming one's ability to do it differently. The frequent outlandishness of her likes and dislikes—her blatant Orientalism and Balkanism—is also a model for an affective approach to writing about the Balkans. The aim is not to get it right but to learn from the place in unexpected ways. Perhaps *Black Lamb and Grey Falcon* remains one of the best guides to the Balkans because of its value in drawing attention to the problem of presuming to know a place or a culture.

CODA: MACEDONIA (2015)

We're sitting in Skopje's old town drinking Turkish coffee and eating rice pudding. The shop windows display elaborate party dresses designed for Albanian girls; just up the hill is an Orthodox church with an ornately carved wood iconostasis and a Virgin Mary whose silver hand both invites and withstands touch; also nearby are an old Ottoman hammam that is now the city museum and a number of historic mosques that remain in active use. As I watch men delivering trays of tea in small glasses to the businesses in the area, I'm reminded of old towns in Sarajevo and Istanbul, as well as Cairo, other cities I've visited at the confluence of multiple cultures and histories that continue to display a distinctively Ottoman influence. Skopje is far less symbolically freighted than Sarajevo, which has become the visible and symbolic site of the Muslim presence in the Balkans. It has an everyday cosmopolitanism, even as the overwrought statues of Alexander and his mother Olympia and the museums that proclaim Macedonian nationalism are also a short distance away, and the streets are about to erupt in violence that will barely appear in the global media. Efforts to construct a visible national history, which result in a false spectacle, are fraught here. My desire to resist them by looking for Byzantine and Ottoman histories that precede the modern nation-state could be an equally willful construction, as is my appreciation for the street's signs of cosmopolitanism. I try to see something else, to move between the visible and the invisible as icons and ruins both require, while also acknowledging my own ignorance and inability to see.

Ann Cvetkovich is the Ellen Clayton Garwood Centennial Professor of English and professor of women's and gender studies at the University of Texas at Austin. She is the author of *Mixed Feelings: Feminism, Mass Culture, and Victorian Sensationalism* (Rutgers University Press, 1992); *An Archive of Feelings: Trauma, Sexuality, and Lesbian Public Cultures* (Duke University Press, 2003); and *Depression: A Public Feeling* (Duke University Press, 2012).

NOTES

This essay would not exist without the generous encouragement and inspiration of Irene Kacandes across many years of conversations. For helpful readings, I wish to thank Lisa Moore, Aaron Sachs, and the members of the Toronto Writing Workshop, especially Elspeth Brown, Eva-Lynn Jagoe, Robyn Autry, Kevin Coleman, and our teacher Catherine Taylor. Much gratitude also to my traveling companion Gretchen Phillips.

1. For a discussion of the value of amateur knowledge, see Carolyn Dinshaw, *How Soon Is Now?* (Durham, NC: Duke University Press, 2013).
2. For one of the more prominent, and problematic, examples, see Robert Kaplan, *Balkan Ghosts* (New York: St. Martin's Press, 1993), which draws on the authority of his experience as a journalist in the region but promulgates the notion of irresolvable and permanent ethnic tensions. The editors of this collection also cite Kaplan's work as a significant example of geographical determinism.
3. Basic introductions include Mark Mazower, *The Balkans: A Short History* (New York: Modern Library, 2000); Misha Glenny, *The Balkans, 1804–1999* (London: Granta Books, 1999); Marcus Tanner, *Croatia: A Nation Forged in War* (New Haven, CT: Yale University Press, 1997, 2001); John R. Lampe, *Balkans into Southeastern Europe* (New York: Palgrave Macmillan, 2006). Most of the authoritative scholars are historians by training, who focus primarily on political history and nationalisms but offer less in the way of critical frameworks for understanding culture and everyday life.
4. In addition to Todorova's *Imagining the Balkans*, see also Dušan I. Bjelić and Obrad Savić, eds., *Balkan as Metaphor: Between Globalization and Fragmentation* (Cambridge, MA: MIT Press, 2002); and Radmila Gorup, ed., *After Yugoslavia: The Cultural Spaces of a Vanished Land* (Stanford, CA: Stanford University Press, 2013).
5. In addition to Drakulić's work, see personal narratives: Vesna Goldsworthy, *Chernobyl Strawberries: A Memoir* (London: Atlantic Books, 2005); Myrna Kostach, *Prodigal Daughter: A Journey to Byzantium* (Edmonton: University of Alberta Press, 2010); and Tony Fabijančić, *Bosnia: In the Footsteps of Gavrilo Princip* (Edmonton: University of Alberta Press, 2010). Like fiction writers, such as Bosnian Aleksandar Hemon and diasporic Serbian Tea Obreht, who have received important critical attention for their writings on the region, all of these writers live outside the Balkans, and very few writers currently living in the former Yugoslavia are translated, much less read widely.
6. Vladislav Bajac, *Hamam Balkania: A Novel and Other Stories,* trans. Randall A. Major (Belgrade: Geopoetika Publishing, 2009), 247.
7. See Orhan Pamuk, *Istanbul: Memories and the City* (New York: Knopf, 2005), a memoir about growing up in Istanbul; Pamuk, *The Museum of Innocence* (New York: Knopf, 2009), his novel; and Pamuk, *The Innocence of Objects: The Museum of Innocence* (New York: Abrams, 2012), about the museum (inspired by the novel) that Pamuk built in the historic neighborhood of Cihangir.
8. Rebecca West, *Black Lamb and Grey Falcon: A Journey through Yugoslavia* (originally published 1941; quoted from New York: Penguin, 1994), 661. Subsequent page references in text.

WORKS CITED

Bajac, Vladislav. *Hamam Balkania: A Novel and Other Stories.* Translated by Randall A. Major. Belgrade: Geopoetika Publishing, 2009.
Bjelić, Dušan I., and Obrad Savić, eds. *Balkan as Metaphor: Between Globalization and Fragmentation.* Cambridge, MA: MIT Press, 2002.
Dinshaw, Carolyn. *How Soon Is Now?* Durham, NC: Duke University Press, 2013.
Drakulić, Slavenka. *Café Europa: Life after Communism.* London: Abacus, 1996.
———. *They Would Never Hurt a Fly: War Criminals on Trial in the Hague.* New York: Viking, 2004.
Fabijančić, Tony. *Bosnia: In the Footsteps of Gavrilo Princip.* Edmonton: University of Alberta Press, 2010.
Glenny, Misha. *The Balkans, 1804–1999: Nationalism, War and the Great Powers.* London: Granta Books, 1999.
Goldsworthy, Vesna. *Chernobyl Strawberries: A Memoir.* London: Atlantic Books, 2005.
Gorup, Radmila, ed. *After Yugoslavia: The Cultural Spaces of a Vanished Land.* Stanford, CA: Stanford University Press, 2013.
Hirsch, Marianne, and Nancy K. Miller, eds. *Rites of Return: Diaspora Poetics and the Politics of Memory.* New York: Columbia University Press, 2011.
Kaplan, Robert D. *Balkan Ghosts: A Journey through History.* New York: St. Martin's Press, 1993.
Kostash, Myrna. *Prodigal Daughter: A Journey to Byzantium.* Edmonton: University of Alberta Press, 2010.
Lampe, John R. *Balkans into Southeastern Europe: A Century of War and Transition.* New York: Palgrave Macmillan, 2006.
Mazower, Mark. *The Balkans: A Short History.* New York: Modern Library, 2000.
Pamuk, Orhan. *The Innocence of Objects: The Museum of Innocence, Istanbul.* New York: Abrams, 2012.
———. *Istanbul: Memories and the City.* Translated by Maureen Freely. New York: Knopf, 2005.
———. *The Museum of Innocence.* Translated by Maureen Freely. New York: Knopf, 2009.
Tanner, Marcus. *Croatia: A Nation Forged in War.* New Haven, CT: Yale University Press, 1997, 2001.
Todorova, Maria. *Imagining the Balkans.* Oxford and New York: Oxford University Press, 1997.
West, Rebecca. *Black Lamb and Grey Falcon: A Journey through Yugoslavia* (1941). New York: Penguin, 1994.

Chapter Ten

A Polish Childhood

Irene Kacandes

It started in late April 2002. I'd been invited to speak at Cornell University. It's a long drive between Hanover, New Hampshire, and Ithaca, New York, and I hadn't been to Ithaca since attending a conference while in graduate school almost twenty years prior and before that since my childhood, when my parents took their kids to see the town where they'd met, fallen in love, and married. So, I decided to make it as special as I could, which meant, among other things, finally eating at the famed Moosewood Restaurant, which put out cookbooks I'd been using for years.

As a solitary diner, I was put at a small table that was next to another small table with a solitary diner. Also a woman. She was buried in a book. Reflex reaction to glance at the cover: *Die Glut,* a novel. I hadn't heard of it. If she was reading in German, she might only speak German. So I started the conversation in German. I'm not sure if she was more surprised by being addressed by a stranger or by hearing German. But it roused her curiosity, as she had roused mine. And off we went: How did I know German? How did she? She wasn't German, it turned out, but rather Polish. She'd been in Germany after the war and gone to German schools for a while. Fell in love with the language. And the literature. We certainly had that in common. What was that she was reading by the way? Oh, a German translation of a Hungarian novel by Sándor Márai. A writer I only vaguely remembered having heard of. It was good; she could recommend it. What was I doing in Ithaca? I'm a professor at Dartmouth, I found myself explaining. I've come to give a seminar to graduate students in the German department on a German-Jewish poet, Gertrud Kolmar, who had written a strange short novel in the early 1930s that seemed to presage the coming catastrophe.[1] Dartmouth, isn't that where the two professors were murdered? Weren't they Germans? Yes. Sorry. I don't want to talk about it.[2]

Back to literature, universities, 9/11, its horrendous aftermaths. Poland. I went there for the first time last year. The people were so interesting. Why do you think so? I am fascinated by their dilemma. They want to build a democracy. But they're not sure how. They know they don't have much experience with self-rule. A lot of their energy is (still) going into blaming the Russians for everything. Hard to build a democracy when one doesn't want to take responsibility for the present. Then again, it's hard to build a future when the past has been so inadequately accounted for. So many contradictions in what people told me. They were very articulate, even in English. I appreciated that they were willing to share their aspirations and their fears. That they could speak English well enough for us to have any kind of conversation. Given that I knew essentially no Polish.[3]

I myself had started conversations with many strangers before: in airplanes and trains, at conferences and parties. The conversation with Grazyna flowed like the best: effortlessly. Shall we stay in touch? May I write to you?

And write we have. In the fifteen plus intervening years, Grazyna G. and I have exchanged a couple of letters or so annually, more frequently in the last several years. Real letters. On paper. Mine usually handwritten; hers usually typed. Recently alternating with shorter e-mails. Like that first conversation, the letters often contain reports about what we've been reading and occasionally about films we've seen. Current events. Disastrous US policies. The weather. Our respective health challenges. The past. Poland. I've always loved receiving real letters—and writing them, too. Having a pen pal represented a certain amount of cultural capital when I was a child. But my desire to write to Grazyna was fervent. Her personality, her opinions, her past more than intrigued me; she quickly became part of the fabric of my own life. I've exchanged e-mail addresses or business cards with many strangers before. But this is the only time that the contact has lasted more than a couple of additional exchanges.

I ask myself here why.

That could seem unforgivably solipsistic. However, I think my relationship with Grazyna can serve readers of this volume as a kind of parable of discontiguous affiliation. Affiliate: from Medieval Latin, *affiliare*, "to adopt as a son." Discontiguous: "not touching or being next in sequence." So when I speak of a parable of discontiguous affiliation I mean a story about choosing to be in contact with, to make intimate precisely that which is not close, obvious, or logical. Elective affinities, for a more literary allusion and to connect with the title given this section.[4] On the one hand, and in their meaning in chemistry, elective affinities involve a process, a certain reaction that will occur under certain conditions. Those reactions can be observed and analyzed. On the other, when one thinks of the story that the genius Goethe spun out from that title or when one takes the two words on their own, this process seems to exceed the rational, involving both conscious choice (electing) and inexplicable attraction (affinity, kinship). Can logic fully explain why two people like each other or why somebody gets interested in a person or a place? My experiences with my own "polandophilia"[5] and with Grazyna have led me so far to answer this question negatively. In this sense, "elective affinity" also seems to describe my relationship to Eastern Europe. To Poland. I'm not a specialist and I have not tried to become one. But I am more than casually or accidentally interested. I'm deeply committed to trying to put myself in relation to.

What follows is not a research essay, then, but rather a series of observations about what Grazyna and I "did" with each other. In sharing these thoughts I hope that others will be able to mine what it might mean to opt to be in relationship to someone who is not like oneself. Someone who is not a neighbor. Someone who lives far away, geographically and temperamentally. This is a distinct if related task to what Ann Cvetkovich undertakes in relation to the former Yugoslavia, mainly because here I trace elective affinities for a person and only secondarily to a place, a culture, a history. What connects the two endeavors most importantly, I suggest, is the "election," the decision to put oneself in relationship to the unknown. In this regard, I see a similarity also to what Marianne Hirsch has called "postmemory": "a powerful and very particular form of memory precisely because its connection to its object or source is mediated not through [actual] recollection but through an imaginative investment and creation."[6]

Below readers will learn some things about Grazyna, about me, about what I learned about Poland and the war from her. However, personal narrative is not my goal. This essay falls, I suggest, into the genre of "paramemoir," a term I coined when I was trying to process and write about what had happened to my father in Occupied Greece and how those traumatic experiences affected the next generation.[7] What I created was "para"—a kind of *substitute* for a memoir he never wrote, itself going *beyond* the narrative restrictions of memoir and simultaneously working *against* the chronology or coherence of memoir. So that "paramemoir" was itself based on discontiguities, as is this "paraessay." It could seem obvious, yet I hope it is worth pointing out explicitly anyway, that I of course did not say to myself over the years of getting to know Grazyna: Oh, I'm building a discontiguous affiliation. Rather, the application of analysis to my set of experiences with Grazyna is very much a product of the same questions that Yuliya Komska and I put to the contributors to this volume: What comes into view when one asks oneself to unmap Eastern Europe? In what instances did so-called Eastern

Europeans choose to affiliate themselves with those peoples and countries not directly next to them but rather with groups, countries, cultures, histories that were not contiguous? Hence my first observation: by me writing first, I felt like I was choosing her, though of course correspondence does not work unless you trade places and the addressee writes back.

GRATUITOUSNESS

I suppose it's because it felt like a lark, like a bit of a transgression against my precious little free time for the academic writing that professors are supposed to be perpetually doing, that I purposely didn't keep track of our correspondence in those early years. Looking back on it now, I see that writing irregularly was a strategy to keep the activity of conducting the relationship voluntary and thus off my to-do list. When I think of those early exchanges, though, I realize too that there were little hooks in the mass of seemingly random topics that we chose to share, breadcrumbs in the forest, which kept me going. (Grazyna would send me short prose pieces about events from her wartime childhood.) Or, to use yet a different metaphor, little pearls that I eventually realized I was longing to see strung into a necklace. (I encouraged Grazyna to publish a memoir. And I still hope she will.) But Grazyna kept cutting the cord. (She didn't believe anyone would be interested in reading her stories.) Or I wasn't offering the right-quality silk thread. (My suggestion to try writing together was ignored.) Or I was not paying enough attention to the direction in which she was throwing the pearls. (When I reread the letters I did keep, I realized that there was a lot more information about her past shared there than I had remembered.) I decided I needed to go visit. In person. That long ride. Again. I wanted to do it. She wasn't sure.

> As for meeting sometime in spring, when would it be? I should warn you that I do not like to talk, writing is easier. It takes me a long time to warm up to people, I mean years. I write to you because we have similar interests. I assume that you know enough history to be able to follow the events I describe. When I throw in a German word, you know what it means. Also you are anonymous and that helps. I do not really know what you are like. Of course if we met, you could ask me questions that would depend on my answers. A more efficient way of communicating. (GG to IK, 15 February 2015)

Revealing what I am really like, stubborn, I did go. And it was lovely. I got to see her house. Meet her husband. Understand better her hobbies. Her serious commitment to animals. I can't say the communicating was more efficient or that I came away with a coherent story. I'm still not positive where she was born or exactly when. She did not want me to record our conversations. So I have to rely on my memory and sketchy notes I jotted down while we talked and in the breaks between our conversations.

Looking back on our relationship before my return to Ithaca, the visit, and our relationship after my visit, I note that initially Grazyna had found the distance between us and the time gap between our letters generative for communication itself. I liked what had been transpiring, too. Our relationship felt completely gratuitous in the sense that I had no obligation to write to her. Nor she to me. We weren't related. We weren't colleagues. We weren't the same generation. Our first contact had not even been that extensive. Still, at a certain point, that wasn't enough for me. I wanted to be right next to her. Now that I have been in her presence again, I feel like I know her profoundly better. The relationship is flourishing on its own terms, which is to say that we write even more frequently since that second visit of mine. In the spirit of Levinas, it seems to me that face-to-face encounters allow one to recognize the other's subjectivity in a way that mediated communication may not. Does the physical encounter with the spaces they touch play a parallel role to saying "thou," to allude to another genius of the twentieth century? How to describe the difference, I wonder.[8]

DIE GLUT, OR LANGUAGE AS THE BASIS OF AFFILIATION

I honestly don't remember whether Grazyna sent me her copy or whether I procured one myself. But I too read the German translation of Márai's novel. The Hungarian title, *A gyertyák csonkig égnek*, means literally "The Candles Burn Down to the Stump," whereas the German title means "Glowing Fire" or "Hot Coal" and could apply to my reading of it. I was totally engrossed and greedily consumed it. At least two elements captured my attention then: Márai's representation of a world that seemed very distant not just in time, but also in place and sensibilities, one that I truly only knew from books; and the quality and value attributed to the act of reflection, of careful thinking. I don't want to draw the parallels too closely. And yet, it's true that Grazyna grew up in a culture and at a time that I also knew only from reading books. I enjoyed from the start the quality of her reflections. Is that why I liked the novel? Or does that explain why I remember what I remember of the novel?

> I wonder how you will be deciding who the sages of Eastern Europe are when so little of East European writing is available to the general public [in the United States], not that it would be interested in it. (GG to IK, 24 August 2014)

What does it mean that two individuals living in America who are genuinely interested in Eastern Europe read one of its major works of literature in German translation? To be sure, human fate post-Babel means that we simply cannot read all languages. And Hungarian is reputed to be one of the more difficult. Nevertheless, don't we Americans need to hold ourselves accountable for the paltry number of Eastern European writers who have been translated into English? Márai for one was not widely translated until after his death in 1989, despite his prodigious output and his long career.

Returning to my own actions, I restate the obvious: I could have sought out the English translation. In point of fact, my general practice is to read books in languages I do not read myself in their English translation. When I chose to read *Die Glut* in German, was I using the German language to get closer somehow to the non-contiguous—which in this case would be the Hungarian world of the pre–Great War? The German (Second) Empire and the Austro-Hungarian Empire shared extensive borders. And the German language, after all, would be the "closer" language to Hungarian than English, in the sense of those shared borders as well as German and Hungarian being spoken in some of the same spaces. The German translation even followed the original publication in Hungarian much sooner than the English.[9]

With some kind of parallel and probably subconscious logic, was I trying to get closer to Grazyna by doing what she had done, that is, by reading the same translation she had read? How do we factor in that German is the language of my professional life and of Grazyna's schooling? Are discontiguous affiliations—either of our relationships to Hungarian and Márai—ultimately or necessarily enabled by contiguities, in this case, by our relationship to German? This brings me to reflect that when Grazyna and I first met, we conversed in German but then continued the relationship primarily in English, both in our correspondence and when we met again face-to-face. English is the mother tongue of neither of us, and yet because of where we have lived the longest periods of our respective lives, it has become the native tongue of both of us. That initial spark of curiosity about the stranger sitting next to me was caused at least in my own mind by seeing Grazyna with a German book. Ever since our initial acquaintance, it remains the case that when I read something in German I usually ask myself and sometimes then her if she would be interested in reading it too. I send her books almost as often as I send her letters.

NON-JEWISH POLES, OR AFFILIATION THROUGH THE FAMILIAR AND THE UNFAMILIAR

There's no doubt that one aspect of Grazyna's life that intrigued me from the start was that she'd experienced World War II as a non-Jewish Polish child. It seems to me now that that identity position offered me things to which I could relate and also raised questions. My father and mother had been children during the war in Greece. And I had studied the experiences of many Jewish children in wartime Poland. The position of a non-Jewish child there was unfamiliar to me at the time when I met Grazyna. The position of non-Jewish Poles in general. Because essentially every actual person whom I'd ever met with Polish roots was Jewish. I'm sure this would sound bizarre to a contemporary Polish citizen or, for that matter, to someone who grew up in the Polish Triangle of Chicago. But I grew up in White Plains, New York, the seat of Westchester County. While our immediate neighborhood was occupied mainly by Italian and Irish immigrant families, with a few leftover Anglo-Saxons and the odd Swiss or Dutch plus us, the one Greek family, once we were sent to junior high school, it was impossible to miss how many peers had roots in Eastern Europe, and they were all Jewish. I remember how it confused me, who thought of herself as "pure Greek," that someone could be Polish-Ukrainian-Russian. Despite how intelligent I thought my teenage self to be, I do not remember asking my friends about such a heritage or trying myself to learn about that part of the world and what their ancestors experienced there.

And yet, if I did not ask questions then, I certainly did later. Did those teenage relationships plant the seeds for my formal study of the Holocaust (mainly in graduate school) and eventual specialization in the catastrophes of mid-twentieth-century Europe?[10] In some respects such study only reinforced this connection I had in my head since youth between being Polish and being Jewish, because as I learned about the locations of European Jewish populations and of Nazi extermination camps, Poland loomed large. Of course I don't mean to imply that that early private association led me to ignore other aspects of the war like mass population transfers or the decimation of the Polish intelligentsia, aspects that Grazyna herself experienced and eventually shared with me.

How Grazyna expressed or qualified her identity as a Pole when we first met, I honestly do not remember. I mainly remember taking away the idea that though she was Polish and had lived through the war, she happily read and spoke German. Her identity as a non-Jewish Pole—I hesitate to say Christian or Catholic Pole, because even though her parents were nominally Catholic, as a child she entertained serious doubts about the existence of God—was a topic that came up frequently in our subsequent correspondence and conversations, often in unexpected ways. For instance, in one letter, Grazyna wrote:

> I make a poor specimen of a Pole. I left eastern Poland at the age of eight. At that time it must have been a very different country from western Poland where

I spent the war and, from today's perspective, felt like a refugee or an outsider. That my parents split up then did not help. There must have been a lot of Russian influence on the culture of eastern Poland but as a child I could not judge or even think about it. The picture I sent you [IK: of Wołożyn]—sorry about its poor quality—was described to me by a Swiss friend as something out of *Dr. Zhivago*. And since somehow I wandered off to *Dr. Zhivago*, I reread the book recently and appreciated it more than on the first reading. Some Russian fiction describes a way of life that seems very familiar to me, probably thanks to a place like Wolozyn. (GG to IK, 26 July 2012)

I like Grazyna's metaphor of "somehow wandering off." That seems like another good way to describe what we do with each other. It's as if we give each other permission to "wander." As for the wandering described above, it seems to me that one of the places where Grazyna grew up became accessible to her again as an adult not by visiting or conducting a "rite of return," as Marianne Hirsch and Nancy K. Miller (as well as Ann Cvetkovich, following them in this volume) have coined it and elaborated on it, but rather through a series of metonymies, discontiguities even: a fuzzy photo of a small part of the town downloaded from the Internet, comments about which led (back) to a work of Russian literature, the reading of which led to recollection of "a way of life that seems very familiar to me."

While I remember losing myself as a teenager in the atmosphere and plot of *Dr. Zhivago*, Grazyna's comments and the photo she sent did not lead me to reread the novel. They led me to reflect, rather, that though I knew the name of any number of concentration and extermination camps and larger cities in Poland, I was familiar with hardly any names of smaller towns like Wołożyn or Oszmiana, where Grazyna's father had first been posted as a judge before being assigned to a more prestigious position in Vilnius and before having to hide from the Soviets, who, it turned out, were as eager to kill off the Polish intelligentsia as the Nazis.[11]

I poked around on the Internet: Wołożyn or Volozhin or any number of other spellings. Now in Belarus. Part of Poland in the interwar period. Home to a famous yeshiva. And in 1942 the site of a major slaughter of its Jewish inhabitants.[12] I immediately thought to myself: maybe like those described by Christopher Browning in *Ordinary Men*, a book I have not just read, but studied and taught.[13] In the kind of self-examination I'm undertaking here, I realize that for me, this was the "click"; it was my learning of this genocidal massacre that most concretized the town Wołożyn for me. In juxtaposing these two anecdotes, I hasten to clarify immediately that Grazyna is a voracious and serious reader who probably knows as much about the Nazi Judeocide as I do. And she searches for the places of her childhood in any number of ways, of which I have mentioned only one here. Still, it's a feature of our relationship that I asked her about what I knew best about this part of the world and that I mainly processed what she shared with me through that lens too: antisemitism and genocidal massacres.

CAULDRONS OF HATRED

The phrase "cauldrons of hatred" popped into my mind one day when I was thinking about the world Grazyna described.[14] So, I asked her about signs of antisemitism while she was growing up, out of professional interest and also out of a desire to bring her world closer to mine, at least to a topic I thought I knew something about. She then shared with me some very striking anecdotes that reveal that children surely understand prejudice and discrimination even if they don't use the same terms for these phenomena as do adults.

Grazyna remembers hearing a landlord in Vilnius explain to her father that the rent was 90 złoty for Gentiles and 120 for Jews. She overheard another brag to her father that he encouraged his children to pick fights. He gave them money for doing so—and extra if the target was Jewish. There were lots of tensions in the period after the Soviets occupied Vilnius and before her family fled west. Grazyna's perception was that the Jews were put in positions of power by the occupiers and that the Poles and the Ukrainians resented them even more for those new positions. Some suspected—assumed, it seemed to Grazyna—that the Jews were denouncing members of the Polish army to the Soviets. And that that was how the Soviets managed to round up so many to slaughter at Katyn.[15] Grazyna remembers wondering if it wasn't the Jewish neighbors who were protecting her father while all her friends' fathers were disappearing; I took this as a sign of her ability to take in contradictory information and recognize that allegiances, hatreds, and rivalries weren't clear-cut or etched in stone.[16]

If a first spark of my admiration for Grazyna ignited from the banal fact that she wasn't afraid to eat in a restaurant alone—a fear of an embarrassing number of American women, in my view—it was fed by her powers of perception, her brutal honesty about her own feelings and prejudices, and her ability to step into others' shoes, even as a child. (Of course these abilities are only accessible to me through her adult reflections.)

The Ukrainians, to take another example, were clearly favored by the German occupiers in Cracow, where Grazyna eventually ended up spending the majority of the war with her mother after her parents had fled west with her and then separated. But she did not want to be identified with the Ukrainians:

> To make it brief, as far as I was concerned I was Polish—I had even asked my mother to make sure that my ration cards were not stamped UKR—and the Ukrainians were some kind of background distraction to make life more complicated. I do not know what I was to other people but assumed that they took me for Polish. No Ukrainian word ever passed through my lips. (GG to IK, 24 August 2014)

The Germans were clearly enemy number one. Grazyna recounts with a near-cavalier attitude the day she and her closest friend Renata were almost shot by German soldiers in Cracow after the girls had attempted to set on fire a German archive that was housed in the appropriated palace of her friend's family. If the girls were trespassing, it wouldn't seem remarkable that they were shot at. However, I was curious how Grazyna understood basic German attitudes toward Poles, because in all the reading I'd done, including of Hitler's *Mein Kampf,* the Poles were just one notch above the Jews at the bottom of the racialized cosmography.

> We knew; after the Jews, it's us. The worst part was being insulted. They think they're so much better than we are. And maybe they were. German kids were different. When I saw their clothes and that they were well-fed, I thought, maybe they were better ... (GG to IK, oral communication, 9 June 2015)

The present tense verbs jumped out at me, "They think they're so much better than we are"; it was as if Grazyna found herself right back there for a moment and hence could repeat what she had been thinking. Grazyna's comment also brought to my mind a bizarre book I'd read by Niklas Frank, youngest child of Hans Frank, Nazi head of the General Government, headquartered in Cracow, which I then told Grazyna about.[17] The book's thrust is toward Niklas's oldest sibling, his brother Norman. Most of it recounts Niklas reading to Norman document after document proving crimes of their father, with Niklas trying to get Norman to admit that he condemns their father for those crimes. But as the subtitle of the book makes clear, despite the myriad documents with which he is confronted, Norman is unable to do so: "Mein Vater war ein Naziverbrecher, aber ich liebe ihn" (My father was a Nazi criminal, but I love him). I consider Norman's own memories of wartime Cracow, of which he recounts quite a few to his younger brother, the inverse of Grazyna's. Norman was prince of the castle. Figuratively and almost literally. Grazyna wasn't allowed anywhere near it. Figuratively and literally. And her friend's family had been dispossessed of their castle.

Which brings me here to another social category that Grazyna picked up on as a child: class. Grazyna mentioned to me various escapades involving Renata, including the attempt to set archives on fire cited above.

Grazyna had found an article on the Internet shortly prior to my visit that discusses Renata's family's grand home, a neo-French Renaissance palace in Cracow, the same one that the Nazis had confiscated, that the Polish socialist state had continued to use, and that Renata's son regained possession of and renovated into a luxury hotel—with some effort after the opening of the Iron Curtain.[18]

> I think that the war made our friendship special and the palace and its surroundings—Renata lived in what the article calls "*oficyna*," a filthy, crumbling place—make me long for that piece of childhood when we lived in the moment, were sure that the future was going to be great and did not brood about it. (GG to IK, 21 December 2012)

Grazyna shared with me a "Christmas story," set in 1943:

> It is about five girls who meet for private lessons (*komplety,* in Polish) in wartime Poland when education beyond seventh grade was illegal. Jan Karski mentions *komplety* in his book *Story of a Secret State*. My story would tell you a lot about life in Generalgouvernement [General Government] and also about the relationship between the girls of different backgrounds. (GG to IK, 7 August 2015)

This story did indeed communicate richly about everyday wartime life in Cracow and about living in the moment. Since my sincere hope is that Grazyna will publish this story one day, I only point out some features here. Every girl had an escape route out of the space in the private home that the family was using for the lessons; no one took notes since there should be no evidence of school activities should one be caught; the current teacher could just stop showing up with no explanation received, no explanation expected. People disappeared. Often.

The high point of the plot concerns a Christmas tree decorated with candies that the girls are invited to taste. Renata cannot control herself and consumes candy after candy, leaving the tree almost completely bare. The other girls watch in horror and fascination, but say nothing. The denouement and the moral of the story concern, to my mind anyway, the negotiation of social class in wartime. In reaction to Renata's unacceptable behavior, the host mother—whose husband appears to provide for his family by exploiting Jews and others who had been kicked out of their homes or deported—does not berate her, but rather sends her home with precious provisions: sugar, flour, lard. Renata's mother, in turn, hungry though she may be, sends the provisions back with the message that they should be given to a family that needs them.

Grazyna referred repeatedly to herself and Renata as a pair of teenage hoodlums; that doesn't exactly fit their familial constellations, and yet it is clear to me from these and other anecdotes that the two enjoyed more freedom from adult supervision than girls their age or social classes would have been granted in peaceful times. In the midst of dangers, they obviously developed heightened allegiances to one another. Still, the war and paths to self-preservation thought up by adults dictated what actually happened.

In early 1945(?) Grazyna and her mother made a rather complicated escape from Cracow to Prague to Domažlice (Taus), eventually getting over the Czech border at Česká Kubice to Furth im Wald in Germany. So when the war in Europe ended, they were actually in Germany and came to live in a repurposed and renamed housing complex called the Ganghofersiedlung (previously the Hermann-Goering-Siedlung). From there she had the joy of going to school regularly in a nearby town, Cham.

> I liked Germany. But I didn't forget what the Germans had done. It was gut feelings, a kind of physical reaction. The Germans on the train I commuted to school in, they helped me out. They lent me books. Poles didn't do that. German school? I loved it. (GG to IK, oral communication, 9 June 2015)

In the next opportunity to converse, I asked Grazyna if she had had any personal experience with German attitudes toward Jews. Those nice Germans on the trains, Grazyna explained to me, expressed regret for losing the war and regret for the wartime slaughter of Jews. The latter not out of any philosemitism. Rather, "They shouldn't have killed the Jews," the natives told Grazyna, "because it gave Germany a bad name" (GG to IK, oral communication, 10 June 2015).

There it is. Another searing example of the contradictions and incongruities in personal behavior that Grazyna was able to register. Germans. Generous: loaning books when there are hardly any around. Unrepentant: if only we hadn't lost the war. Refusing personal responsibility: *they* shouldn't have killed the Jews. Self-interested: it gave Germany a bad name. The good. The bad. The ugly. People are complicated. Grazyna figured that out young. Wars tend to make children grow up fast. A bizarre concomitant: children can enjoy war too.

WRITING

Grazyna wrote down the anecdotes about her Polish wartime childhood in part because writing provided a way to return to happier times. Of course, her childhood did not consist of only happy times. The act of writing itself could also function for her as a kind of performative. She was doing something for herself *now* that the war had prevented her from doing *then*. In my earlier work on trauma in literature, I have called this "intrapsychic witnessing" or "witnessing to the self," where an individual (a character, in the case of literature) is able to bear witness to the self about personal experience.[19] When violent events result in psychic trauma, individuals are not able to carry out this psychic task; they are not able to integrate into their stored memories the experience they are having. Doing so at a later date usually involves a co-witness's assistance. However, one can also use writing to create, so to speak, this co-witness that helps the story of the trauma come into being. Without knowing anything about this part of my work, Grazyna put it to me this way:

> One of the reasons I need to write about people I knew as a child is because they disappeared suddenly in the war. In normal times people can grow apart gradually, as they change. One is not left then with a sense of loss or with the "what if?" question. (GG to IK, 18 May 2011)

I am not sure how many of Grazyna's important relationships were cut off prematurely. To be sure, her relationship to her father was, through no fault of her own. When Grazyna and I met for the second time in person in June 2015, I was able to ask her about a young Polish woman who had worked as a kind of general servant for her mother. She'd mentioned her to me in a letter, but as in so many of the letters I'd received, I didn't feel like I could place this particular person in time or space. I had written Grazyna once that "I get mad at myself when I can't keep names straight and I don't have a clue about correct pronunciations" (IK to GG, 2 February 2013).

Over the years, Grazyna had given me plenty of direct and indirect hints that her mother was a difficult person. Well, it seemed that despite how attached Grazyna was to this young woman servant, the latter ended up quitting and going to work for a German family with small children. Grazyna lost contact with her altogether.

> Then, on January first, 1944, I was returning from church. I heard a little voice next to me. "That's me. Josephine." She explained to me that she'd been working at a German officers' club. "See how well I'm dressed." I saw that. And more. How thin she was. The blood on her handkerchief. We agreed we would meet again several weeks later. But she didn't show. She had TB. I knew which hospital she was in. But I never went there.

I was confused. Why not? I asked.

> That way I could still think she was alive. She did a lot for me. (GG to IK, oral communication, 9 June 2015)

Of course! And so I found myself back where I'd begun, intellectually speaking. Trauma. I'd say it's both American and contemporary to think that it's always better to know. Always better to speak about things. To find out. To have the mystery solved.

However, for starters, there is often so much information missing. I'd learned from trying to put my father's war story together that no matter how much research you do or how many people you interview, there are always the archives that have been burned, the eyewitnesses who are already dead. In short: holes remain. There are so many things that will never be known about any of our pasts. About some of those, people do not actually want to know the historical "truth." And I get that. There was something about hearing this point from Grazyna's mouth that helped me take it in more easily than when I heard similar things from my father. Is that a kind of "more than bearable lightness of being" that derives from an elected affinity?

When I was working to understand what had happened to my own father during the war, especially at the beginning of the process, I had the feeling that I had "a right" to know his story, because he begat me and on some level—which I explore more critically in my book than I can do here now[20]—I felt that his traumas were passed on to me, and I was justified in trying to free myself from them. He owed it to me to help me do this, or so my silent logic initially went. With Grazyna, I didn't believe that I had any rights at all. I was opting to listen to her stories; she was opting to tell them. I was offering sometimes to help her write them up. But I never felt I could demand answers. As I wrote above, there are many things that I still do not know about her and her past. And there are a few things she has shared with me that I have not shared here because I consider it her decision, not mine, to put them into the public sphere. She read a draft of this essay. And I believe her reaction and my reaction to her reaction can help me put a point on discontiguous affiliations and elective affinities.

> I like the way you wrote it—there is suspense in it. What bothers me is that I am not a true specimen of a Pole but of someone who had the misfortune of growing up in Poland during the time of Polish independence after WWI. The towns I lived in are now in the Ukraine, Lithuania and Belarus. Some Poland it was. My father was a refugee from what is now Moldova where his family owned land, my mother was Ukrainian. (GG to IK, 12 August 2015)

What I wrote back to her can serve as my conclusion to this piece of writing:

> Thank you for reading my musings on Poland. Your reaction makes me realize that I need to make at least one point clearer: one of the reasons I'm fascinated

by Poland is because of the way its history shows at least two sides of nationalism. There is something I've observed that one could call "Polish pride": it involves a certain identifying with a certain place and a certain language. Maybe for some people a certain literature in the Polish language or a certain musical heritage. Clearly for some other people, it mainly involves certain foods, drinks, songs, and dances. But when you look at it: what is "Poland"? The political entity has changed configurations so many times—as you point out and as anyone who has even a casual knowledge of its history quickly discovers. So who really is Polish? As far as I can tell, you are as Polish as anyone else. What matters—maybe—is that you care about things that happened in certain places at certain times, things that happened to you and things that happened to others in those places.

That's the elective affinities part. In some ways it applies to you as much as it applies to me with regard to Poland.

If you know enough about history, you realize that that same logic applies to pretty much any nation-state. Certainly to Greece—a place, by the way, that I consider part of Eastern Europe—and to Greeks. I've told you that as a child I thought of myself as "pure Greek"; but what does that mean? Should others think of me differently when they find out that I speak Greek with an American accent? Does something change for me—about me?—when I'm told that my maternal grandmother spoke Arvanitika (a variety of Albanian) fluently? She certainly didn't learn it in school. (IK to GG, 13 August 2015)

There are so many things in life that we don't get to make a choice about. Not about when, where, or to whom we are born. Not usually about when or how we die. And for most of us ordinary mortals, not about starting or ending wars. Still, most humans experience a certain amount of conscious living, and in that period, we have choices. In choosing to be in relationship with Poland or with Grazyna, I have discovered yet again the wisdom in the distinction that Eve Kosofsky Sedgwick made about alliances, about the importance of identifying *with* rather than identifying *as*.[21] I wrote above that maybe the choice to care about Poland applies to Grazyna as much as it does to me. I'm not sure. I'm still thinking about that. About what difference it makes to go there, to have been there, to have grown up there. About what the limitations are, as Cvetkovich points out so effectively, between "going there" and "knowing there." Is there a "knowing there"? Is it not always a matter of degree?

POSTSCRIPT

I visited Poland a second time in 2013. Post first meeting with Grazyna. I felt almost intoxicated the whole time I was in Cracow, whereas I did not feel that way in Warsaw. It wasn't a completely comfortable feeling. It felt like I knew too much about the place, about the crimes committed there, even as I was more aware than ever of what I did not know about the place and its history. I was trying to see it through Grazyna's eyes and also through the eyes of some of the Holocaust survivors whose stories I had read, like Anita Lobel, who was five years old when German soldiers marched into her native Cracow. She and her younger brother survived by being hidden in the countryside, the ghetto, even a convent, before being arrested and deported.[22] Still, the intoxication wasn't only threatening either. I genuinely enjoyed being there. I learned for the first time of the artist Stanisław Wyspiański (1869–1907) and became fascinated with the art nouveau interior décor he'd designed for the Franciscan church.[23] I felt rather euphoric when I was in that space of architectural discontiguity, as I did sitting in cafés on Main Square (Rynek Główny) or walking through the National Museum encountering artist after artist I'd never heard of before. It felt important to me to witness to my own ignorance. To realize that there was a whole history depicted in those paintings that I knew little about. When I read current news about Poland, its present government's xenophobic and anti-democratic measures, my heart tightens. Does that sound pathetic? Maybe it is. Yet somehow, in this current world of ours where so many individuals are willing to act on the hate they feel for those who are not like them, it seems not insignificant to me to desire to know more about others. To care about distant others. To wish them well. To be anxious when they stumble.

The search goes on. For Grazyna. And for me.

"Sometimes," Grazyna wrote me, "I look on the web for people of Oszmiana, hoping to find a name I'll recognize and possibly find out what happened during the war when I was no longer there. So far I have not come up with much" (GG to IK, 21 December 2012).

After my 2015 visit to Grazyna, I found myself searching for signs of Oszmiana (now Ašmiany) and Wołożyn and making trees of Renata's family. Grazyna promised to send some stories I had not yet seen. I gobble them up as they arrive. One concerns being taken for a walk in Cracow in 1940 by a woman her family had known in eastern Poland prior to the outbreak of the war. As Grazyna stood staring at the toys miraculously still on display in a shop window, she explained to Mrs. B. the state of her personal finances and how the black market worked. Someone who had stopped behind them laughed and commented, "It's amazing what children know now" (GG to IK, 30 July 2016).

In the wake of that 2015 visit, I also spent hours reading about Tadeusz Kościuszko.[24] I had first learned about his contribution to the American Revolution as a Greek American immigrant kid in elementary school. I do not remember from what book the teacher read to us or many of the details of that first exposure to his exploits. But I do remember quite clearly becoming enthralled by the idea of this stranger showing up and helping the colonists free themselves from a tyrant that was not oppressing him or his country. I decided to read about him again in the hope of unearthing something I'd maybe learned in school and forgotten, some fact that might explain the quality of my enthusiasm then and what could at this stage in my life be labeled the launch of a fascination with Poland that would periodically resurface over decades.

As it turns out I have not unearthed such a fact yet. Kościuszko did not fight at the Battle of White Plains (my hometown), a battle I knew a lot about as a kid. I did learn or relearn that Kościuszko came fairly close to White Plains during the war.[25] Still, no sentence I've read has gotten my heart beating faster than another. I'm okay with that. Now I can say that Kościuszko had an elective affinity for young America. I have one for Poland. And for Grazyna.

This writing marks a certain moment in our relationship that is changed by it and by our continued interaction, for which I am profoundly grateful.

Irene Kacandes holds the Dartmouth Professorship in German Studies and Comparative Literature. She has authored or edited seven volumes, including an experimental paramemoir on generational trauma from World War II and the Holocaust, *Daddy's War* (University of Nebraska Press, 2009, paperback 2012). She edits the Interdisciplinary German Cultural Studies series at de Gruyter Verlag in Berlin and served as president of the German Studies Association in 2015 and 2016. In 2015, *Let's Talk about Death: Asking the Questions That Profoundly Change the Way We Live and Die,* her reflection on mortality (co-written with Steve Gordon), appeared with Prometheus Press.

NOTES

1. Gertrud Kolmar, *Eine jüdische Mutter. Eine Erzählung,* 2nd ed., afterword by Bernd Balzer (Frankfurt am Main: Ullstein, 1981; originally drafted in 1930–31 and first published posthumously in 1965). I have written about the novel several times. The publication closest to the talk I gave at Cornell is the following: Irene Kacandes, "Making the Stranger the Enemy: Gertrud Kolmar's *Eine jüdische Mutter,*" *Women in German Yearbook* 19 (2003): 99–116.
2. Susanne and Half Zantop were both professors at Dartmouth College when they were killed by two local teenagers looking to have an adventure. When I

met Grazyna, barely a year had passed since their deaths, and I was not ready to talk about it with people who did not know the Zantops. I have subsequently published my thoughts with regard to their deaths and to sudden death in general: Irene Kacandes, "9/11/01 = 1/27/01: The Changed Post-Traumatic Self," in *9/11: Trauma at Home,* ed. Judith Greenberg (Lincoln: University of Nebraska Press, 2002), 168–83; and Irene Kacandes and Steve Gordon, *Let's Talk about Death: Asking the Questions That Profoundly Change How We Live and Die* (New York: Prometheus Press, 2015).
3. On Eastern Europe's democracy learning curve and the eventual "export" of democracy, see Yuliya Komska's introduction to this volume.
4. I refer, of course, to Goethe's 1809 novel *Die Wahlverwandtschaften* (*Elective Affinities,* also translated into English as *Kindred by Choice*).
5. I was drawn to this term before my coeditor reminded me of the German *Vormärz* concept of *Polenbegeisterung,* something I must have learned about in graduate school, since I read many of the writers who supported the Poles and Polish campaigns for independence in 1830–31, but I didn't consciously remember learning it when she brought this up. A more intentional echo in my head was "philhellenism," since on some level, this elected affinity is triangulated by my own identity: Greek-American-Polish; or maybe it's a foursome with my professional identification with Germans—great philhellenes until recently, it bears noting.
6. Marianne Hirsch, *Family Frames: Photography, Narrative and Postmemory* (Cambridge, MA: Harvard University Press, 1997), 22.
7. Irene Kacandes, *Daddy's War: Greek American Stories; A Paramemoir* (Lincoln: University of Nebraska Press, 2009, 2012).
8. These questions are an obvious parallel to Ann Cvetkovich's about visiting places.
9. The Hungarian original appeared in 1942, the first German translation in 1954, and the first English translation came out in 1994.
10. Like Primo Levi, I use this term "'to be understood'" (as quoted in Giorgio Agamben, *Remnants of Auschwitz: The Witness and the Archives,* trans. Daniel Heller-Roazen [Cambridge, MA: Zone Books, 1999], 28), but I prefer the term "Nazi Judeocide," which attributes perpetration and purpose more accurately.
11. A particularly well-focused study on this period and problematic is *The Soviet Takeover of the Polish Eastern Provinces, 1939–41,* ed. Keith Sword (London: Macmillan Academic and Professional, 1991).
12. "Volozhin, also known as Valozhyn, Volozhy'N, Wolozyn, Volozine, Wolozine," accessed 4 August 2015, http://www.eilatgordinlevitan.com/volozhin/volozhin.html.
13. Christopher Browning, *Ordinary Men: Reserve Police Battalion 101 and the Final Solution in Poland* (New York: HarperCollins, 1992).
14. It was only later that I learned of a similar phrase that titles the powerful study by Norman M. Naimark: *Fires of Hatred: Ethnic Cleansing in Twentieth-Century Europe* (Cambridge, MA: Harvard University Press, 2001).

15. In addition to the extensive important older historical work on Katyn, such as Allen Paul's authoritative *Katyn: The Untold Story of Stalin's Polish Massacre* (New York: Charles Scribner's Sons, 1991), it seems important to note here that recent archival research has allowed for an even deeper understanding of the propagation of the myth of the omnipotent Jewish Bolshevik. See, for example, Waitman Wade Beorn, *Marching into Darkness: The Wehrmacht and the Holocaust in Belarus* (Cambridge, MA: Harvard University Press, 2014). See Norman Davies's *God's Playground: A History of Poland,* vol. 2 (Oxford: Oxford University Press, 2005), 331ff., for a concise account of Soviet treatment of Poles in newly occupied eastern Poland.
16. Grazyna's powers of reflection and deduction accord with the observations Susan R. Suleiman has made about what she terms "the 1.5 generation" of Holocaust survivors. Susan R. Suleiman, "The 1.5 Generation: Georges Perec's *W or the Memory of Childhood*," in *Teaching the Representation of the Holocaust,* ed. Marianne Hirsch and Irene Kacandes (New York: MLA, 2004), 372–85.
17. Niklas Frank, *Bruder Norman! "Mein Vater war ein Naziverbrecher, aber ich liebe ihn"* (Bonn: Dietz, 2013).
18. Grazyna sent me a photocopy of the article (in English) that she had found on the Internet, which is how I learned this history. However, I could not locate the URL for that article to write this note. I did find another site that reproduces a newspaper article (in Polish) that talks about the history of the palace in detail. See http://www.palac.pl/nowy_palac_pugetow/, accessed 25 July 2016.
19. Irene Kacandes, *Talk Fiction: Literature and the Talk Explosion* (Lincoln: University of Nebraska Press, 2001), 99–105.
20. Kacandes, *Daddy's War*.
21. Eve Kosofsky Sedgwick, *Epistemology of the Closet* (Berkeley: University of California Press, 1990), see especially 59–63.
22. Anita Lobel, *No Pretty Pictures: A Child of War* (1998; repr., New York: Greenwillow Books, 2008).
23. I was thrilled to locate a bilingual book about him so that I could learn more: Marta Romanowska, *Stanisław Wyspiański* (Cracow: Bosz, 2009).
24. Two older books published about him relatively shortly after his death in 1817 particularly captured my attention, I suppose because they were such good examples of hero worship and because he seemed to me to be a hero when I first learned about him as a child. See Marc-Antoine Jullien, *Notice biographique sur le général polonais Thaddée Kosciuszko* (Paris and London: C. L. F. Pancoucke, 1818); and Constantin Karl Falkenstein, *Thaddäus Kosciuszko nach seinem öffentlichen und häuslichen Leben geschildert* (Leipzig: Brockhaus, 1834).
25. The Battle of White Plains was fought in late October 1776 (the British are considered to have won it). The building George Washington used as his headquarters at the time of that battle was within walking distance of the house I grew up in; we siblings made frequent expeditions to it. Maybe having grown up in wartime Greece, our parents gave us more freedom to wander around alone than other neighborhood parents gave their kids. Kościuszko designed

and oversaw construction of numerous fortifications, including at West Point, another site of childhood excursions, though about forty miles away, thus reachable only by car and hence with our parents. When I mentioned this essay to my older sister, she spontaneously came out with "Thaddeus Kosciusko Bridge!" which she remembered seeing on family excursions north of our home. That brought to my mind a mental image of a sign with this impressive name on it. There is also a bridge in New York City named after Kościuszko, which we probably drove over numerous times. I was glad to see that the New York State Department of Transportation website includes information not only about its reconstruction, but also about the historical person (https://www.dot.ny.gov/kbridge/biography; accessed 17 August 2016). Despite these recent efforts, I still cannot say that I have found the madeleine for my commitment to Poland.

WORKS CITED

Agamben, Giorgio. *Remnants of Auschwitz: The Witness and the Archives*. Translated by Daniel Heller-Roazen. Cambridge, MA: Zone Books, 1999.

Beorn, Waitman Wade. *Marching into Darkness: The Wehrmacht and the Holocaust in Belarus*. Cambridge, MA: Harvard University Press, 2014.

Browning, Christopher. *Ordinary Men: Reserve Police Battalion 101 and the Final Solution in Poland*. New York: HarperCollins, 1992.

Davies, Norman. *God's Playground: A History of Poland*. Vol. 2. Oxford: Oxford University Press, 2005.

Falkenstein, Constantin Karl. *Thaddäus Kosciuszko nach seinem öffentlichen und häuslichen Leben geschildert*. Leipzig: Brockhaus, 1834.

Frank, Niklas. *Bruder Norman! "Mein Vater war ein Naziverbrecher, aber ich liebe ihn."* Bonn: Dietz, 2013.

Goethe, Johann Wolfgang. *Die Wahlverwandtschaften*. Frankfurt: Insel Verlag, 1972.

———. *Elective Affinities, a Novel*. Translated by James Anthony Froude and R. Dillon Boylan. New York: Frederick Ungar, 1962.

Hirsch, Marianne. *Family Frames: Photography, Narrative and Postmemory*. Cambridge, MA: Harvard University Press, 1997.

"Historia I nowe technologie w coraz piękniejszym paláacu Pugetów." Accessed 25 July 2016. http://www.palac.pl/nowy_palac_pugetow/.

Jullien, Marc-Antoine Jullien. *Notice biographique sur le général polonais Thaddée Kosciuszko*. Paris and London: C. L. F. Pancoucke, 1818.

Kacandes, Irene. *Daddy's War: Greek American Stories; A Paramemoir*. Lincoln: University of Nebraska Press, 2009, 2012.

———. "Making the Stranger the Enemy: Gertrud Kolmar's *Eine jüdische Mutter*." *Women in German Yearbook* 19 (2003): 99–116.

———. "9/11/01 = 1/27/01: The Changed Post-Traumatic Self." In *9/11: Trauma at Home*, edited by Judith Greenberg, 168–83. Lincoln: University of Nebraska Press, 2002.

———. *Talk Fiction: Literature and the Talk Explosion.* Lincoln: University of Nebraska Press, 2001.

Kacandes, Irene, and Steve Gordon. *Let's Talk about Death: Asking the Questions That Profoundly Change How We Live and Die.* New York: Prometheus Press, 2015.

Kolmar, Gertrud. *Eine jüdische Mutter. Eine Erzählung.* Afterword by Bernd Balzer. Frankfurt am Main: Ullstein, 1981.

Lobel, Anita. *No Pretty Pictures: A Child of War.* 1998. New York: Greenwillow Books, 2008.

Márai, Sándor. *Die Glut: Roman.* Translated by Christina Viragh. Munich: Piper Taschenbuch, 2001.

———. *Embers.* Translated by Carol Brown Janeway. New York: Vintage, 2002.

Naimark, Norman M. *Fires of Hatred: Ethnic Cleansing in Twentieth-Century Europe.* Cambridge, MA: Harvard University Press, 2001.

Paul, Allen. *Katyn: The Untold Story of Stalin's Polish Massacre.* New York: Charles Scribner's Sons, 1991.

Romanowska, Marta. *Stanisław Wyspiański.* Cracow: Bosz, 2009.

Sedgwick, Eve Kosofsky. *Epistemology of the Closet.* Berkeley: University of California Press, 1990.

Suleiman, Susan Rubin. "The 1.5 Generation: Georges Perec's *W or the Memory of Childhood.*" In *Teaching the Representation of the Holocaust,* edited by Marianne Hirsch and Irene Kacandes, 372–85. New York: MLA, 2004.

Sword, Keith, ed. *The Soviet Takeover of the Polish Eastern Provinces, 1939–41.* London: Macmillan Academic and Professional, 1991.

"Tadeusz Kosciuszko Biography." Accessed 17 August 2016. https://www.dot.ny.gov/kbridge/biography.

"Volozhin, also known as Valozhyn, Volozhy'N, Wolozyn, Volozine, Wolozine." Accessed 4 August 2015. http://www.eilatgordinlevitan.com/volozhin/volozhin.html.

Afterword/Afterward: Eastern Europe, Unmapped and Reborn

Vitaly Chernetsky

How does one imagine Eastern Europe? How can we responsibly alter the dominant strategies of its discursive production? What might be the most productive paths for addressing its past(s), present(s), and future(s) at the current nexus of global and local challenges? The contributors to this book have explored a wide variety of strategies to query and subvert the master narratives of betweenness and contiguity that have dominated the views of the region in the global sociocultural imagination. Instead, they have sought to uncover and reconstruct, and thereby encourage us to reimagine the diverse and often surprising linkages of this area to heterogeneous intellectual traditions, locales, and social movements. This tapestry of unexpected connections pushes us beyond the tired yet stubbornly persistent stereotypes of mystery and misery that are projected onto this region. Instead, it seeks to create a new periplus of the possible and the unexpected.

Do we recognize Eastern Europe as a palimpsest of ruins and traumas? Yes—but the same can be said with a fair degree of certainty of just about any region of our planet. Is it also a source of uncanny, paradoxical hope? Yes, that too. Ludwik Zamenhof's famous creation Esperanto is a testimony to this. Conceived and developed in Warsaw by a native of Białystok, it was envisioned as an attempt to bridge the many divides bedeviling humanity and to promote peaceful coexistence—hence the pseudonym by which Zamenhof signed his publication of the grammar of this new planned language, which means "Hopeful."

Yet hope went side by side with many setbacks. Zamenhof died in the middle of World War I, which fundamentally reshaped Eastern Europe. All his children perished in the Holocaust. Still, his vision and his project endures, as does his family legacy—his grandson was able to escape from the Warsaw Ghetto's *Umschlagplatz,* survive the war, and build a successful life and professional career—yet forced to emigrate from Poland in 1968, during a new wave of antisemitic pressure.

The twin factors of pressure and resilience, of which the above is but one of a myriad of instances, help us understand Eastern Europe as resistant to ongoing attempts at imposing external power/knowledge structures. With remarkable frequency, we find in Eastern Europe identity hallmarks built around surviving near-death experience, including notably the national anthems of both Poland and Ukraine. Even in the face of unimaginable horror, stories like that of the *Oyneg Shabes* archive, as Adam Zachary Newton reminds us, serve as a paradoxical testimony of survival.

Thinking through such testimonies, we find diverse new strategies of addressing and rebuilding historical memory. Products of such strategies, which hopefully push us to further action—intellectual, political, creative—can arise in the most unexpected places. As an instance of such a meeting of the utopian and the mundane, the in-your-face and the subversive, I offer the case of the Zamenhof monument in Odessa.

Figure 11.1. Mykola Blazhkov, monument to Ludwik Zamenhof in Odessa, 1959. Photo by Olga Lemann, 2015, Wikimedia Commons.

Odessa's monument to Zamenhof is one among several commemorating the hopeful doctor around the world; the network that they form is striking in the unexpected affinities that it builds—other statues of him can be found in such far-flung locales as Belo Horizonte, Brazil, and Prilep, Macedonia. However, the one in Odessa is remarkable also for its location within the city, inside the Mediterranean-style courtyard of a nineteenth-century building, on the site of a former rainwater cistern. Lovingly kept up by the residents, it is integrated in the fabric of their daily lives, shaded by grape vines, with linen hanging on the clothesline nearby and the nearly half-a-century-old cars parked behind it. It is an agent of situated knowledge, an active element of what Arjun Appadurai has called the production of locality.

It bears emphasizing that knowledge by and about Eastern Europe is indeed a situated knowledge that accounts for the agency of both the producer(s) of knowledge and the object(s) of study. As Linda Alcoff reminds us in her classic essay, we need to be consistently aware of the problem of speaking for others when one speaks about others; even when speaking for oneself, one is "participating in the creation and reproduction of discourses through which [one's] own and other selves are constituted."[1] In the era of cultural globalization, the discursive production of Eastern Europe, like that of other localities, is, as Appadurai has argued, "relational and contextual rather than scalar or spatial."[2]

In her introduction to this volume, Yuliya Komska critiques the tendency to "geo-code" knowledge about Eastern Europe at the expense of recognizing and pursuing the connections between this region (and its internal diversities and contradictions) and other spaces, real and symbolic. In lieu of this normative practice of geo-coding with its restrictive interpretive grid,[3] I offer an alternative project of cognitive mapping, understood both in its older psychological and in the more recent sociocultural and political sense. It is a kind of remapping that follows the unmapping for which this volume advocates. Cognitive mapping, as Fredric Jameson, the leading theorist of this concept in relation to contemporary culture, argues, "has ceased to be achievable by means of maps themselves."[4] It is, in fact, "a *process,* a way of *making* connections, of drawing networks and of situating ourselves as both individual and collective subjects within a particular spatial system."[5]

This process can at times feel extremely, yet productively, disorienting— as explored in Komska's reading of Yurii Andrukhovych's volume *Leksykon intymnykh mist* (*The Lexicon of Intimate Cities,* 2011). This more recent book is the culmination of a persistent impulse in the writer's work, as testified by the title of a collection of his essays from the 1990s, *Dezoriientatsiia na mistsevosti* (*Disorientation on Location,* 1999). In a key passage from that book, Andrukhovych asserts, "Location uses the person, his or her concentration and the state of optical melancholy. Similarly to a reflection in a mirror, location requires an outsider gaze in order to emerge and to betray oneself."[6]

The hybrid optics, the simultaneous perspectives of an insider and an outsider, witnessing self-emergence and self-betrayal, the emphatic emplacement in the local and the yearning for linkages with distant lands, are frequent attributes of Eastern European writing. The Book and the stamp album in the stories of Bruno Schulz, the father's *Bus, Ship, Rail and Air Travel Guide* in Danilo Kiš's *Garden, Ashes* are but a few famous examples among many.

This disorienting yet anchoring sense of locality is one of the crucial characteristics of Eastern European cultural imagination. In a telling instance of this paradox, Adam Mickiewicz, Poland's national poet, was born in what is now Belarus and addressed his most famous lines of patriotic poetry, the opening of his epic poem *Pan Tadeusz* (1834), to Lithuania:

> Litwo, Ojczyzno moja! ty jesteś jak zdrowie;
> Ile cię trzeba cenić, ten tylko się dowie,
> Kto cię stracił.
> [Lithuania, my country! You are as good health:
> How much one should prize you, only he can tell
> Who has lost you.][7]

Such slippage and fluidity of identification have long been associated with Eastern Europe. For Mickiewicz, the overlap of Polish/Lithuanian/Belarusian identities was not a contradiction; rather, his "Litwa" referred to the Grand Duchy of Lithuania, which from 1386 was in a dynastic union with the Kingdom of Poland, with the two states officially uniting into the Polish-Lithuanian Commonwealth from 1569 to 1795. Territorially, it encompassed most of modern-day Lithuania and all of modern-day Belarus, as well as a significant portion of Ukraine, and was characterized by great ethnic, linguistic, religious, and cultural diversity. Ethnic Lithuanians, ostensibly the titular population, were a minority within its borders. Linguistically and culturally, it was dominated for much of its history by the Eastern Slavs (future Belarusians and Ukrainians), which is why it forms a crucial part of the Belarusian national narrative. At the same time, the Grand Duchy of Lithuania was also home to a large Jewish community and a small yet prominent Muslim community of ethnic Tatars. Gradually, however, the Grand Duchy's elites were Polonized, both linguistically and culturally; in the final centuries of its existence, it was not uncommon for the local intellectuals to identify themselves with dual or triple attributions, such as *gente Ruthenes, natione Polonus* or *natione Polonus, gente Ruthenus, origine Judaeus*. When Mickiewicz wrote *Pan Tadeusz*, "Litwa," although no longer a political entity, retained its symbolic cultural value as an imagined space and an imagined community. Yet this was an imagined community of diverse and overlapping local identities, serving as inspiration both for Mickiewicz and, several generations later, for Zamenhof, another native of the historic Litwa. Its legacy can be seen as forming a bridge to the more recent Eastern European projects of exploring and reinventing identities, including religious ones, as discussed by Miriam Udel and Piro Rexhepi in their contributions to this volume.

For thinking of and through Eastern Europe's palimpsest of possible identifications, the concept of heterotopia—a space of otherness—might thus be of particular help. Since its introduction in theoretical discourse by Michel Foucault in the late 1960s, its uses have been very diverse in discussions of culture and society. Heterotopias, Foucault writes, are "something like counter-sites, a kind of effectively enacted utopia in which the real sites, all the other real sites that can be found within culture, are simultaneously represented, contested, and inverted"[8]—just like the elusive Lithuania/Poland/Belarus of Mickiewicz.

In "Of Other Spaces," Foucault sketches a typology of heterotopic sites within the "actually existing" space—boarding schools, prisons, mental hospitals, libraries, museums, fairs, brothels, ships; however, the concept itself is arrived at through a reading of a literary text, namely, a short story by Borges.[9] Heterotopias "are disturbing," Foucault writes, "because they secretly undermine language, because they make it impossible to name this *and* that, because they shatter or tangle common names, because they destroy 'syntax' in advance, and not only the syntax with which we construct sentences but also that less apparent syntax which causes words and things ... to 'hold together.'"[10] Recent studies, such as *Heterotopia and the City: Public Space in a Postcivil Society* and *Heterotopia: Alternative Pathways to Social Justice*, have sought to flesh out our understanding of the transformative social potential of an intellectual politics stemming from this concept.[11] At the same time, critical comparative investigations, to cite the example of Natalia Humeniuk's *Maidan Tahrir*, which links Ukraine's Euromaidan Revolution with the Arab Spring, focus precisely on the homologous nature of non-contiguous heterotopian spaces that emerge during such revolutionary struggles as well as on their long-term impact.[12]

The conceptual framework of heterotopia aids in our understanding of what made such projects as Jerzy Giedroyc's *Kultura*, explored in this volume by Jessie Labov, so powerful. Heterotopia as a model of literary discourse has been perhaps most eloquently posited by Cesare Casarino in his *Modernity at Sea: Melville, Marx, Conrad in Crisis*, which not only presents the modernist sea narratives as heterotopian. Crucially for our understanding of

Eastern Europe, it also places Joseph Conrad, Polish by ethnic background, Ukrainian by place of birth, and English by his choice of creative medium, at their center.[13] The related concept of "multidirectional memory," developed by Michael Rothberg and discussed in the introduction to this volume, enables radical linkages of global hybrid locales. Its logic could help us see a profound Eastern Europeanness of sites like Cape Town's District Six. One of the most ethnically and racially diverse neighborhoods in the world, it was deliberately destroyed and obliterated by South Africa's apartheid regime in the 1970s.[14] South Africa more broadly provides but one example of the still insufficiently explored destinations of Eastern Europe's intellectual influence.[15] On the other hand, the experience of post-apartheid South Africa, especially its Truth and Reconciliation Commission, lends crucial paradigms for restorative justice in the aftermath of crises, both recent and going as far back as World War II, in Eastern Europe itself.

In the work of numerous contemporary authors, Eastern Europe tends to be linked with indices of spatial instability, ranging from heterotopia to displacement. Intellectual exiles, jovial expats, anxious migrants and traumatized refugees spill over the pages of works by Eastern European authors, whether they are still based in the region or have left it. The titles of the works are often telling: *The Museum of Unconditional Surrender* (Dubravka Ugrešić); *Shards* (Ismet Prcic); *Panic in a Suitcase* (Yelena Akhtiorskaya); "The Berlin We Lost" (Serhiy Zhadan). The humor is usually dark, as in the works of Bohumil Hrabal discussed by Daniel Pratt; the overall tone, as evidenced by the title that Andzrej Stasiuk chose for one of his travelogues of hidden interstitial spaces within the region, *Fado*, is melancholy.

The boundaries of Eastern Europe as the site of creative authorial affinities are also subject to frequent change. To return to the example of Yurii Andrukhovych, in his earlier works from the 1980s and 1990s, Eastern Europe is coterminous with the Central Europe as imagined by Kundera and others in the 1980s. Yet later, Andrukhovych defaults to asserting that for the understanding of the region today, the former German Democratic Republic carries significantly more weight than Austria; the Habsburg nostalgia is banished from his sharp yet melancholy rethinking of Eastern Europe's "Soviet bloc" experience.[16] This radical shift of gears was completed in Andrukhovych's 2007 autobiographical quasi-novel *Taiemnytsia* (Secret), structured as a transcript of tape-recorded interviews given by the author to a fictional German journalist over a one-week period in Berlin. As the author claims in the introduction, these interviews were conducted during wanderings through the city in October 2005, and therefore meditations on personal and literary destiny are literally superimposed onto the geography of modern-day Berlin and its palimpsest of historical legacies.

The Berlin locales in *Taiemnytsia* highlight the heterogeneity of the city. The legacies of the Iron Curtain are at its core. The fictional interviewer lives in East Berlin, while the meetings with Andrukhovych start in a very specific place: a café in Stuttgarter Platz, in the Charlottenburg district of West Berlin. However, this specific locale becomes a starting point for a fragmentary journey through past experiences, in Ukraine, but also in Prague, in New York, in Moscow, elsewhere in Germany, and all over Europe—Western, Central and Eastern. Berlin re-emerges at the center of the narrative in the final chapter of the book, where rethinking the city's former division leads the author to explore the new divisions that have sprung up in contemporary Europe (such as the new *cordon sanitaire* separating Ukraine from the rest of Eastern Europe that is now part of the EU). Numerous Berlin locales are grafted onto a narrative reflecting on a possible utopian Eastern/Central Europe. However, the narrative becomes ever more frenetic, breathless, more and more Berlin street names flash before us, and then the text suddenly stops as if in midair, with a coda of a childhood memory of a train journey to Prague. Displacement to and within Berlin—an international city with an ambiguous inside/outside position within Eastern Europe, a palimpsest of cultures and histories—leads Andrukhovych to a powerful articulation of his desire for an alternative utopian vision of Europe and himself within it. This desire is undercut with doubt and despair, and in its tone *Taiemnytsia* is possibly the darkest of Andrukhovych's novels—yet the hopeful message in it does persist, seemingly against all odds.

Both self and place in Eastern Europe remain paradoxical, with the labyrinthine chronotope of Bruno Schulz's stories providing one of the most striking examples. Yet this does not preclude, indeed it very much encourages, quests in search of one's identity in relation to it. A particularly illuminating recent example is provided by Serhiy Zhadan's novel *Voroshylovhrad* (2010), which explores the motif of a return to one's place of origin, adding to it the painful and traumatic encounter with the palimpsest of the region's various legacies and the traumatic present-day warps in the fabric of Ukraine's eastern borderlands, then not yet ravaged by the horrors of war. Zhadan's book radically subverts the "journey home"—a classic narrative archetype—transforming it into a dramatic, anguished quest for the protagonist's own identity.

The author himself has described *Voroshylovhrad* as "a novel about memory, about the importance of memory, about the continuity of memory and about the fact that you must remember everything that happened to you— that's what lets you mold your future.... It is a novel about resistance."[17] The identity quest is occasioned by the disappearance of the protagonist's older brother, which, as Tamara Hundorova has suggested, could be read as an allegory for a parting with the Russian/Soviet dominance and a crisis of postcolonial self-identification. Moreover, the Soviet reality itself, accessed through imperfect fragmented memories, is coded in terms of nothingness or emptiness—certainly not a source for nostalgia. Zhadan, she argues, "offers an alternative paradigm of parting with the totalitarian past to simply a clean break or forgetting," an alternative that is neither nostalgic nor melancholic. Rather, one should speak here of "a call to live within the parameters of responsibility and remembering the past."[18]

The novel's chronotope is inextricably anchored in the transitional zone of Zhadan's native region (his place of birth, the town of Starobil's'k, and the northern part of the present-day Luhans'k Oblast). It would be tempting to transpose to this context the insights of the discourse on borderlands, including what has come to be known as decoloniality in Latino/a and Chicano/a studies and Gloria Anzaldúa's notion of *mestizaje*.[19] However, *Voroshylovhrad* is not strictly about life at the border, nor is it about a fusion of two languages and cultures; it is rather a thematization of the liminal, transitional nature of borderlands in a broader sense, of regions where the gravitational pull of state and ideological powers begin to break down and fade, where dominant geo-cultural hierarchies are challenged, and where one develops and nurtures a profoundly localized identity anchored in belonging to a community of non-belonging—becomes, to use the Belarusian term explored by Tatsiana Astrouskaya in this volume, a *"tuteishy."* In his novel, Zhadan specifically eschews stereotypes about the Ukrainian-Russian border that are numerous in Ukrainian, Russian, and international discourse; the world he builds has nothing to do with facile binaries. Its space is an emptiness that is simultaneously barren and pregnant with new possibilities—some hopeful, others terrifying. In the case of *Voroshylovhrad,* we are dealing with a work of magical realism that emerges as a triumph of cognitive mapping of a realm both utterly devastated and full of hope, where one is called to mobilize one's inner resources and work out a politics of solidarity based on critical remembrance and a sober look ahead.

This emphasis on hope in spite of multiple traumas is the leitmotif of Yurii Andrukhovych's essay provocatively titled "Europe That Still Hasn't Died" ("Shche ne vmerla Evropa," 2007), which puns on the opening line of Ukraine's national anthem, "Shche ne vmerla Ukraïny i slava, i volia" ("Ukraine's glory and freedom have not perished yet"). In it, the writer emphatically links Eastern Europe, and his native Ukraine within it, with a European project, but utopian rather than bureaucratic. The unmapping and cognitive remapping remains a work in progress. It combines sober and even bitter analysis with an undying utopian spirit of being and communication led by an inexhaustible principle of hope—even if this hope becomes tinged with irony as the investment in the utopian idea of a united Europe wanes in the EU itself but gains strength and symbolic significance at its margins, especially in Ukraine. Reflecting on this dilemma, Andrukhovych suggests:

> This is a really strange conflict, between Europe and Europe.
> Between the "pragmatic model" of the EU with its fears, self-enclosedness, and all other complexes of failed imperialists, and the "idealistic model" of United Europe with its organic need for growth and change, with its constantly shifting borders—borders that are not entirely geographic—in other words, with its openness, its unfinished structure, its vitality.
> For there probably is no task more exciting and more necessary than to unite Europe. At the very least in those places, along those lines where the EU structures have managed to disunite it.
> ... At the end, I come to the question "How can one unite Europe differently?"
> ... What should this alternative project be like?
> Should we perhaps start from the opposite end?
> Since the EU project is first and foremost bureaucratic, then this one should be anarchic?
> Or since the EU project is arrogantly puffed up and hierarchical, this one should be characterized by lightness, plasticity, and the carnivalesque spirit?
> Or since the EU project feigns democracy, this one would be openly liberal?
> In any case I have a name in mind. Let's give this project the name of a half-forgotten radio station: Free Europe. And let us place notices in all decent media outlets: "Seeking visionaries, ghost-catchers and reanimators. Seeking all those who are still looking for Europe."[20]

In this text, Andrukhovych anticipates the role the idea of Europe played in Ukraine's Euromaidan Revolution of 2013–14. This is a different vision of a postcolonial Europe (and of Eastern Europe within it)—the one that does not seek to "provincialize" it, to use Dipesh Chakrabarty's term, but rather to assert, in the face of the deep crisis that Europe now faces, its paradoxically persistent utopian potential. Andrukhovych challenges the dominant features of Europe's ethnoscape and ideoscape—to borrow from Appadurai's influential cluster of keywords[21]—and in the process, reinvigorates them. A productive parallel to Andrukhovych's vision can be seen in Paul Gilroy's use of the term "conviviality," radically different from the superficial nostalgic use of it by Robert Kaplan, deservedly critiqued by Komska in her introduction to this volume. Gilroy's "conviviality" is offered as an alternative path for thinking through the European project of multiculturalism and overcoming its recent deep crisis. "The radical openness that brings conviviality alive makes a nonsense of closed, fixed and reified identity and turns attention toward the always unpredictable mechanisms of identification."[22]

This radical openness is what ultimately makes unmapping Eastern Europe possible.

For sustaining such a project of unmapping, I propose we reimagine Franco Moretti's somewhat controversial concept of "distant reading,"[23] which is often understood as but a synonym for the digital humanities. Thanks to its unexpected evolutionary turns, in the long run Moretti's quest for understanding literature as a field of overlapping and competing factors has become more complicated than an "objective" organizing framework. In a similar vein, we can see inspiring examples of bold rethinking of our object of inquiry (Eastern Europe, in this case) at a distance. If bursts of the repressed onto the surface can destabilize, distant reading can ultimately heal, whereby the multiple potentialities of the future are cognizant of the past but no longer straightjacketed by it—a transformation associated with Gombrowicz's famous coinage "Filistria" (*synczyzna*) in *Trans-Atlantyk* and that novel's remarkable open ending.

Understood in this sense, distant reading is not opposed to closeness; nor does it preclude intimacy. On the contrary, works as intimate as Conrad's "Amy Foster," to which Edward Said returned throughout his scholarly career, provide insight into multiple spatialities and identities that underlie his theorization of the discourse on exile and of his politics of worldliness, a public intellectual's strategy designed to confront the crises of democracy and the resurgence of authoritarianism.[24] Conrad, argues Said, "made an aesthetic principle" out of the neuroses of his protagonist Yanko, a Carpathian mountaineer shipwrecked off the coast of England. "No one can understand or communicate in Conrad's world," notes Said, "but paradoxically this radical limitation on the possibilities of language doesn't inhibit elaborate efforts to communicate."[25] Sustaining those efforts, in hope that one day they breach the barriers to communication and overcome the chasms of intolerance that are now threatening both Eastern Europe and the world at large, is an urgent ethical imperative that emerges from this book.

Vitaly Chernetsky, a native of Ukraine, is associate professor of Slavic languages and literatures at the University of Kansas, where he is also director of the Center for Russian, East European & Eurasian Studies. He is the author of *Mapping Postcommunist Cultures: Russia and Ukraine in the Context of Globalization* (McGill-Queen's University Press, 2007) and of numerous articles on contemporary Russian and Ukrainian literature, culture, and society, where he seeks to highlight cross-regional and cross-disciplinary contexts. He is also a translator of poetry and fiction from Russian and Ukrainian into English.

NOTES

1. Linda Alcoff, "The Problem of Speaking for Others," *Cultural Critique* 20 (1991–92): 21.
2. Arjun Appadurai, *Modernity at Large: Cultural Dimensions of Globalization* (Minneapolis: University of Minnesota Press, 1996), 178.
3. For an example of such a normative strategy and the pitfalls that develop when it is applied to the cultural sphere, even if with the best of intentions, see Andrew Wachtel, *Remaining Relevant after Communism: The Role of the Writer in Eastern Europe* (Chicago: University of Chicago Press, 2006).
4. Fredric Jameson, *Postmodernism, or, The Cultural Logic of Late Capitalism* (Durham, NC: Duke University Press, 1990), 410.
5. Phillip E. Wegner, *Periodizing Jameson: Dialectics, the University, and the Desire for Narrative* (Evanston, IL: Northwestern University Press, 2014), 71–72 (author's emphasis).
6. Yurii Andrukhovych, *Dezoriientatsiia na mistsevosti: Sproby* (Ivano-Frankivs'k: Lileia-NV, 1999), 62. All translations are mine, unless otherwise indicated.
7. Adam Mickiewicz, *Pan Tadeusz*, trans. Marcel Weyland, book 1, lines 1–3, http://www.antoranz.net/BIBLIOTEKA/PT051225/PanTad-eng/PT-books/BOOK01.HTM, accessed 25 August 2016.
8. Michel Foucault, "Of Other Spaces," trans. Jay Miskowiec, *Diacritics* 16, no. 1 (1986): 24.
9. Foucault, *The Order of Things: An Archaeology of Human Sciences* (New York: Vintage, 1973), xv–xx.
10. Foucault, *The Order of Things*, xviii.
11. Michiel Dehaene and Lieven De Cauter, eds., *Heterotopia and the City: Public Space in a Postcivil Society* (New York: Routledge, 2008); Caroline Baillie, Jens Kabo, and John Reader, *Heterotopia: Alternative Pathways to Social Justice* (Winchester: Zero Books, 2012).
12. Natalia Humeniuk, *Maidan Takhrir: U poshukakh vtrachenoï revoliutsiï* (Kyiv: Politychna krytyka, 2015).
13. Cesare Casarino, *Modernity at Sea: Melville, Marx, Conrad in Crisis* (Minneapolis: University of Minnesota Press, 2002).
14. For more on this, see the website of the District Six Museum, opened in 1994, at http://www.districtsix.co.za/, accessed 20 August 2016.
15. This exploration was begun in a pioneering study by Monica Popescu, *South African Literature Beyond the Cold War* (New York: Palgrave Macmillan, 2010); see especially the introductory chapter, "Eastern Europe in the South African Cultural Imaginary."
16. Andrukhovych, "… no strannoi liubov'iu," in Andrukhovych, *Dyiavol khovaiet'sia v syri* (Kyiv: Krytyka, 2006), 79–90. See also Andzej Stasiuk's *Fado* (2006; trans. Bill Johnston [Champaign, IL: Dalkey Archive, 2009]) and *On the Road to Babadag: Travels in the Other Europe* (2004; trans. Michael Kandel [Boston: Houghton Mifflin Harcourt, 2011]), articulating a similar vision.

17. Serhii Zhadan, "*Voroshylovhrad*—roman pro zakhyst svoïkh pryntsypiv vid zovnishn'oho tysku," accessed 7 August 2016, http://gre4ka.info/kultura/111-68ser hii-zhadan-voroshylovohrad-roman-pro-zakhyst-svoikh-pryntsypiv-vid-zovnish noho-tysku. For an in-depth analysis of Zhadan's novel within the framework of memory studies, see Tanya Zaharchenko, "While the Ox Is Still Alive: Memory and Emptiness in Serhiy Zhadan's *Voroshylovhrad*." *Canadian Slavonic Papers* 55, nos. 1–2 (2013): 45–70.
18. Tamara Hundorova, "Voroshylovhrad i porozhnecha," accessed 7 August 2016, http://litakcent.com/2011/02/08/voroshylovhrad-i-porozhnecha/.
19. Gloria Anzaldúa, *Borderlands/La Frontera: The New Mestiza* (San Francisco: Spinsters/Aunt Lute, 1987); D. Emily Hicks, *Border Writing: The Multidimensional Text* (Minneapolis: University of Minnesota Press, 1991); Walter Mignolo, *Local Histories/Global Designs: Coloniality, Subaltern Knowledges, and Border Thinking* (Princeton, NJ: Princeton University Press, 2000).
20. Andrukhovych, "Shche ne vmerla Evropa," *Krytyka* 1–2 (2007). Accessed 7 August 2016. http://andruhovych.info/shhe-ne-vmerla-evropa/.
21. See Appadurai, *Modernity at Large*, 35–36.
22. Paul Gilroy, *Postcolonial Melancholia* (New York: Columbia University Press, 2004), xv.
23. Franco Moretti, *Distant Reading* (New York: Verso, 2013).
24. See Henry Giroux, "Edward Said and the Politics of Worldliness," *Cultural Studies, Critical Methodologies* 4, no. 3 (2004): 339–49.
25. Edward Said, *Reflections on Exile and Other Essays* (Cambridge, MA: Harvard University Press, 2000), 180.

WORKS CITED

Alcoff, Linda. "The Problem of Speaking for Others." *Cultural Critique* 20 (1991–92): 5–32.
Andrukhovych, Yurii. *Dezoriientatsiia na mistsevosti: Sproby*. Ivano-Frankivs'k: Lileia-NV, 1999.
———. *Dyiavol khovaiet'sia v syri*. Kyiv: Krytyka, 2006.
———. "Shche ne vmerla Evropa." *Krytyka* 1–2 (2007). Accessed 7 August 2016. http://andruhovych.info/shhe-ne-vmerla-evropa/.
———. *Taiemnytsia: Zamist' romanu*. Kharkiv: Folio, 2007.
Anzaldúa, Gloria. *Borderlands/La Frontera: The New Mestiza*. San Francisco: Spinsters/Aunt Lute, 1987.
Appadurai, Arjun. *Modernity at Large: Cultural Dimensions of Globalization*. Minneapolis: University of Minnesota Press, 1996.
Baillie, Caroline, Jens Kabo, and John Reader. *Heterotopia: Alternative Pathways to Social Justice*. Winchester: Zero Books, 2012.
Casarino, Cesare. *Modernity at Sea: Melville, Marx, Conrad in Crisis*. Minneapolis: University of Minnesota Press, 2002.

Dehaene, Michiel, and Lieven De Cauter, eds. *Heterotopia and the City: Public Space in a Postcivil Society.* New York: Routledge, 2008.
Gilroy, Paul. *Postcolonial Melancholia.* New York: Columbia University Press, 2004.
Giroux, Henry. "Edward Said and the Politics of Worldliness." *Cultural Studies, Critical Methodologies* 4, no. 3 (2004): 339–49.
Foucault, Michel. "Of Other Spaces." Translated by Jay Miskowiec. *Diacritics* 16, no. 1 (1986): 22–27.
———. *The Order of Things: An Archaeology of Human Sciences.* New York: Vintage, 1973.
Hicks, D. Emily. *Border Writing: The Multidimensional Text.* Minneapolis: University of Minnesota Press, 1991.
Humeniuk, Natalia. *Maidan Tahrir: U poshukakh vtrachenoï revoliutsiï.* Kyiv: Politychna krytyka, 2015.
Hundorova, Tamara. "Voroshylovhrad i porozhnecha." Accessed 7 August 2016. http://litakcent.com/2011/02/08/voroshylovhrad-i-porozhnecha/.
Jameson, Fredric. *Postmodernism, or, The Cultural Logic of Late Capitalism.* Durham, NC: Duke University Press, 1990.
Mickiewicz, Adam. *Pan Tadeusz.* Translated by Marcel Weyland. Accessed 25 August 2016. http://www.antoranz.net/BIBLIOTEKA/PT051225/PanTad-eng/PT-books/BOOK01.HTM.
Mignolo, Walter. *Local Histories/Global Designs: Coloniality, Subaltern Knowledges, and Border Thinking.* Princeton, NJ: Princeton University Press, 2000.
Moretti, Franco. *Distant Reading.* New York: Verso, 2013.
Popescu, Monica. *South African Literature beyond the Cold War.* New York: Palgrave Macmillan, 2010.
Said, Edward. *Reflections on Exile and Other Essays.* Cambridge, MA: Harvard University Press, 2000.
Stasiuk, Andrzej. *Fado.* Translated by Bill Johnston. Champaign, IL: Dalkey Archive, 2009.
———. *On the Road to Babadag: Travels in the Other Europe.* Translated by Michael Kandel. Boston: Houghton Mifflin Harcourt, 2011.
Wachtel, Andrew. *Remaining Relevant after Communism: The Role of the Writer in Eastern Europe.* Chicago: University of Chicago Press, 2006.
Wegner, Phillip E. *Periodizing Jameson: Dialectics, the University, and the Desire for Narrative.* Evanston, IL: Northwestern University Press, 2014.
Zaharchenko, Tanya. "While the Ox Is Still Alive: Memory and Emptiness in Serhiy Zhadan's *Voroshylovhrad.*" *Canadian Slavonic Papers* 55, nos. 1–2 (2013): 45–70.
Zhadan, Serhii. *Voroshilovgrad.* Translated by Reilly Costigan-Humes and Isaac Wheeler. Dallas: Deep Vellum, 2016.
———. "*Voroshylovhrad*—roman pro zakhyst svoïkh pryntsypiv vid zovnishn'oho tysku." Accessed 7 August 2016. http://gre4ka.info/kultura/111-68serhii-zhadan-voroshylovohrad-roman-pro-zakhyst-svoikh-pryntsypiv-vid-zovnishnoho-tysku.

Index

NOTE: page references with an f are figures.

A

activism, 13; Yiddish cultural activists, 45
Adelson, Leslie, 10
affiliate, definition of, 249
affiliation: language as basis of, 252–53; through the familiar and unfamiliar, 253–56
affinity, 250
African diaspora, 233
Ahamad, Jalal Al-E, 62
Akudovich, Valiantsin, 83
al-Albani, Muhammad Nasir-ud-Din, 54, 59, 66
Albania, 4, 58, 63; religions in, 30
Albanian expedition, 57
Alcoff, Linda, 271
Algerian War of Independence, 63
Ali and Nino (Said), 37
All-India Muslim League, 57
al-salaf al-salih (the pious ancestors), 67
American Revolutionary War, 5, 263–264
Anaclet II (Pope), 31, 35, 36
Anders, Jaroslaw, 211, 212
Anderson, Benedict, 137, 146
Andrukhovych, Yurii, 14, 15, 271, 274, 275, 276, 277
Andryczyk, Mark, 88

anecdotes: Central Europe, 138–41; Grazyna G., 259–62
Anzaldúa, Gloria, 276
Appadurai, Arjun, 4, 192, 271
Appelfeld, Aharon, 213
Aranauti, Abdul-Kader, 54, 59
Arazi Mirie (crown lands), 57
architectural heritage, 174, 175–80
Arnauti, Mahmud, 59
art, murals, 202–20
Ash, Timothy Garton, 11
Association of Polish Writers Abroad, 111
Association of Young Literati, 88
Astrouskaya, Tatsiana, 7
Austro-Hungarian Empire, 232, 233, 241
authoritarianism, 85, 91
authors of *Kultura* (journal), 112–18

B

Babkoŭ, Ihar, 85, 90–92, 93
Bahdanovich, Maksim, 83
Bajac, Vladislav, 239–41
Bajer, Stefan, 186
Bakunin, Mikhail, 5
Balkan Ghosts (Kaplan), 236
Balkans, Islam in, 53–68. *See also* Islam
Baron, Nick, 4
Bashevis Singer, Isaac, 29, 32, 38–40, 41, 42, 43, 44, 46

Battle of White Plains, 264
Beetroot *(Burachok)*, 88
Belarus, 79. *See also* Soviet Belarus; Babkoŭ, Ihar, 90–92; borders of, 83; Dubavets, Sjarhej, 88–90; intellectuals, 81–93; locals (Tuteishyia), 83–89; treaties, 1
Belarusian Communist Party, 86
Belarusian intelligentsia, 83–85
Belarusian Soviet Socialist Republic (BSSR). *See* Soviet Belarus
Benjamin, Walter, 233
bet tahara (a building for the ritual cleansing of corpses), 173
betweenness, 2, 269
Bhabha, Homi, 85, 92
Bielawska-Pałczyńska, Joanna, 191
Biller, Maxim, 214
Bjarozka (Little Birch), 87
Black Lamb and Grey Falcon (West), 242, 244
Błoński, Jan, 137
Blue Rider, 180
The Book of Hrabal (Błoński), 137
The Book of My Lives (Hemon), 160
borderlands, 3, 104; eastern borderlands *(kresy)*, 108
borders, 143; of Belarus, 83; Czechoslovakia, 259; open, 15
Borochov School, 216
Bosnia, 238; religions in, 30
boycotts of Polish publishing, 111
Braudel, Ferdinand, 105
Browning, Christopher, 255
Bruno Schulz Museum, 203. *See also* Schulz, Bruno
Bulgaria, 154, 158
Bulgarian Village (Bulgarsko Selo), 155
Bulhakaŭ, Valer, 90
Bunt Młodych (Youth Rebellion), 107, 108, 109
Burachok (Beetroot), 88
Burke III, Edmund, 56
Byzantine Constantinople, 244

C
Café Europa (Drakulić), 236
Café Ziemiańska, 107
Cafe Zodiak, 107
Canada, 229, 232
captive child, concept of, 35
cartograms. *See* maps
cartographic mandate, 1, 2, 6, 11–12
cartographies, fictional, 131–32
Casanova, Pascale, 113
Catholic Church, 186
Catholicism, 9, 29, 36
Catholic Poland, 183, 253–255
čecháček (little Czech), 140
Central Europe, 2, 15, 131, 275; anecdotes, 138–41; history of, 133–46; Hrabal, Bohumil, 141–45; petty heroes, 138–41; scope and meaning of, 11; troubles with history, 145–46
Christianity, 41
class enemy, 156
cleansing Europe of Islam, 54
Closely Watched Trains (Ostře sledované vlaky [Hrabal]), 133, 134, 138, 141, 142, 143
Codrescu, Andrei, 153
Coe, Richard, 139
cognitive mapping, 271
Cohen, Zeydl, 39
Cold War, 5, 6, 11, 13, 59, 60, 67, 106, 107, 113, 117, 154, 155, 156, 158
colonialism, 55
the Committee to Defend Workers (OR), 123
Communism, 111, 152. *See also* post-Communism; Belarusian Communist Party, 86; fall of, 83; legacy of, 156; post-Communism, 131; as prison, 158; transition from, 81; Yugoslavia, 232
Communist Party, 186
community of Muslims *(ummah)*, 54, 56–59, 68
Congress of Berlin, 53
Conrad, Joseph, 5, 274, 278

contiguity, 2, 3, 269
Copernicus, Nicolaus, 189
Cornell University, 248
correspondence with Grazyna G., 251–52
Cozy Dens (Pelíšky), 134
Cracow, Poland, 262–64. See also Poland
Cremer, Wilhelm, 178. See also New Synagogue (Poznań, Poland); Mossehaus (Berlin, Germany), 182*f*; New Synagogue (Poznań, Poland), 185*f*; Olsztyn's Bet Tahara (Poland), 181
Crimea, Russian annexation of, 9
crises, political, 12
critical transnationalism, 165–66
Croatia, 230, 232, 233, 234, 238; phrase books, 235
Croce, Benedetto, 110
Crossroads *(Perekrestki)*, 91
crown lands *(Arazi Mirie)*, 57
Čubrilović, Vasa, 58
Cvetkovich, Ann, 227, 250, 255, 262
Czapski, Josef, 108, 109, 110
Czechoslovakia: borders, 259; maritime commerce, 5; Soviet invasion of, 136
Czech Republic, 15; accession to European Union (EU), 8

D

DAESH, 66. See also ISIS
Daily Mirror *(Liustra Dzion)*, 88
Dalmatian coast, 229, 230, 234, 238
Dartmouth, 248
Daulatzai, Sohail, 56
decoloniality, 276
decolonization, 61, 68
democratization, 5
demons, 40
Department of Agitation and Propaganda, Soviet Belarus, 86
De Quincey, Thomas, 213
the devil, 40

Diary (Gombrowicz), 106
Die Glut (Márai), 252–53
Die Wahlverwandtschaften (Goethe), 227
Dingsdale, Alan, 7
Dinshaw, Carolyn, 233
discontiguity, 6
discontinuities, 6
dissent, 79
Dom Mendelsohna, 189, 190
Donskis, Leonidas, 86
Dovzhenko, Alexander, 2
Drakulić, Slavenka, 153, 235–37, 243
Dr. Zhivago (Pasternak), 255
Dubavets, Sjarhej, 88–90, 93
Duda, Andrzej, 186
Dynko, Andrej, 93
dziedzictwo (heritage), 177, 184; Jewish communities, 192

E

Earth (Dovzhenko), 2
East, definition of, 154; metageography, 2; and West, 8–9, 12
eastern borderlands *(kresy)*, 108
Eastern Europe, 10–11, 15, 250, 269–78; democratization, 5; designation of, 2; Gentile communities in, 173; history of, 1, 12; Jewish communities in, 173, 210; spaces, 152
East of the West: A Country in Stories (Penkov), 153–60
East West (Rushdie), 153
Einsatzkommando, 205
elective affinities, 227, 249–50, 262
el-Shabazz, el-Hajj Malik (Malcolm X), 60
émigré journals, 106. See also *Kultura* (journal)
Enlightenment, the, 2, 42
"Essay for S. I. Witkiewicz" (Schulz), 204
essays, 105. See also *Kultura* (journal); literature
Esterházy, Péter, 137

Estonia, 13; accession to European Union (EU), 8
Eurasia, ideology of, 9
European Regional Development Fund (ERDF), 191
European Union (EU), 82, 153, 277; accession to, 8
exiles, 43–46, 79; Cold War, 158
Expulsion of the Albanians (Čubrilović), 58
extraterritorial literature, 124–25

F
Feletti, Pier Gaetano, 36
Ficowski, Jerzy, 212
fiction, 6, 271, 272, 274
fictional: cartographies, 131–32
Filosov, Dmitri, 108
folk pan-Islamism, 61
Foucault, Michel, 91
Foundation for the Preservation of Jewish Heritage in Poland (FPJH), 186
Fragments *(Frahmenty* [Babkoŭ]*)*, 90–92
Frank, Hans, 257
Frank, Niklas, 257
Franz Josef I (Emperor), 210, 214
funders of *Kultura* (journal), 120–24

G
Galicia, Post-Austro-Hungarian, 211
Galician Jewry, 204, 205, 207, 210, 211, 216
Ganghofersiedlung housing complex, 259
Gass, William, 214
Gatrell, Peter, 4
Gavoçi, Vehbi Sulejman, 54, 59
Gentile communities in Eastern Europe, 43, 173
geo-coding, 152
geographical determinism, 2
German-Soviet Treaty of Friendship, Cooperation and Demarcation. *See* Molotov-Ribbentrop Pact (1939)

Giedroyc, Jerzy, 105, 107–12, 124, 273
Gilroy, Paul, 277
Glassheim, Eagle, 3
globalization, 7, 82
Głos Drohobycko-Borysławski (Drohobycz), 219
God, 40
Goethe, Johann Wolfgang von, 227, 250
Goldsworthy, Vesna, 4
Gombrowicz, Witold, 4, 105, 106–7, 211, 278
Gospodinov, Georgi, 13
Grabowicz, George G., 220
The Great Eastern Crisis, 53
Greece, 250, 262
Greek War of Independence, 53
Grobelny, Ryszard, 185
Gross, Jan T., 3
Grossman, David, 214
Gruber, Ruth, 176, 189
Grydzewski, Mieczysław, 107
Grynberg, Henryk, 218
Guttfreund, Amir, 214
Gypsies, 157, 158, 159

H
the hajj, 59–64
Hašek, Jaroslav, 136
Heart of Darkness (Conrad), 5
Hemon, Aleksandar, 131, 132, 152, 160–65, 166
Herder, Johann Gottfried, 2, 135
heritage *(dziedzictwo)*, 177, 184; Jewish communities, 192
Herling-Grudziński, Gustaw, 110
heterotopia, 273, 274
Hirsch, Marianne, 231, 233, 250, 255
Historiker und Herrschaft (Lindner), 82
History of Polish Literature (Miłosz), 108
Hitler, Adolf, 1, 9, 257
Hlobus, Adam, 87
Hoffman, Eva, 153
Holocaust, 44, 203, 233, 263, 270

Holý, Ladislav, 140
Holy Land, 43
homogenization of specific sites, 165
House of the Catechumens, 36
Hrabal, Bohumil, 131, 133–134, 137–138, 141, 144, 146, 274; petty heroes, 141–45
Hroch, Miroslav, 88
Hrytsak, Yaroslav, 4
Hundorova, Tamara, 275
Hungary, 12, 15; accession to European Union (EU), 8
Huyssen, Andreas, 151

I
Imagined Communities (Anderson), 146
Imagining the Balkans (Todorova), 236
immovable monument *(zabytek nieruchomy)*, 177
Imperial Forum, 178, 179, 184
imperialness *(mocarstwowość)*, 109
India, 153, 154
Innocent II (Pope), 35
intellectuals (Belarus), 81–93
International Monetary Fund (IMF), 153
Iran, 63; Islamic Revolution, 62
Iron Curtain, 81, 125, 258, 275
I Served the King of England (Hrabal), 141, 146
ISIS, 66
Islam, 7, 29, 30, 53–68; cleansing Europe of, 54; the hajj, 59–64; Hegel's conceptualization of, 53; scholarship of, 60; violence in Europe, 64–68
Islamic Association for the Defense of Justice, 59
Islamic Revolution (Iran), 62
Islamic State, 66
Islamophobia, 62, 63, 64
Israel, 203
Ivan Franko Pedagogical University, 203

J
Jameson, Fredric, 271
Jesus, 41
Jewish Baruch/Benedictus, 35
Jewish communities: in Allenstein, Poland, 180–82; in Eastern Europe, 173, 254, 256, 257; heritage, 192
Jewish identity *(yidishkeyt)*, 44
Jewish nationalism, 211
The Jewish Pope (Der yidisher poyps), 31; historical context of, 33–35; plot of, 32–33
Jewish religion, 29; cultural and ethnic plasticity, 31–46; exiles, 43–46; historical context of *The Jewish Pope*, 33–35; *lehavdl-loshn*, 40–43; Mortara, Edgardo, 35–37; Nussimbaum, Lev, 37–38; plot of *The Jewish Pope*, 32–33; "Zeydlus der ershter" ("Zeidlus the First"), 38–40
Jewish Weimar Republic, 37
journals, 106, 107. *See also Kultura* (journal)
Jugoslavska Muslimanska Organizacija, 59

K
Kacandes, Irene, 8, 227, 228, 234
Kaiser Friedrich Museum, 177–78
Kaplan, Robert, 236, 277
Kapralski, Sławomir, 191
Karski, Jan, 258
khalīfah (Ottoman sultan), 56, 57
Khvilinka (Babkoŭ), 93
kinship, 250
Klimkovich, Maksim, 87
Kobus, Alicja, 185
Kobylianska, Olha, 2
Koestler, Arthur, 5
Kołakowski, Leszek, 5, 11
Kolmar, Gertrud, 248
Komska, Yuliya, 82, 104, 135, 234, 250, 271
Konrád, György, 136, 138

KOR (the Committee to Defend Workers), 123
Korzeniowski, Józef Teodor Konrad. *See* Conrad, Joseph
Kościuszko, Tadeusz, 5, 228, 263, 264
Kosovo, 58, 68, 240; religions in, 30
Krajina region, 229
Krauss, Nicole, 214
kresy (eastern borderlands), 108
Krinsky, Carol H., 179
Kroutvor, Josef, 131, 135, 138, 139, 140, 141
Kultura (journal), 79, 80, 92, 104–25; authors of, 112–18; extraterritorial literature, 124–25; funders of, 120–24; Giedroyc, Jerzy, 107–12; Gombrowicz, Witold, 106–7; letter writers of, 117–20
Kundera, Milan, 6, 136, 138
Kupala, Yanka, 84

L

Labov, Jessie, 7, 79, 80, 92
Land (Kobylianska), 2
language (as basis of affiliation), 252–53
Latin America, 82
Latvia, accession to European Union (EU), 8
Law on Censorship (1990), 86
laws, Poland, 3
The Lazarus Project (Hemon), 160, 162, 164
Lebanon, 67
Lebensborn camp, 142
Lefebvre, Henri, 7, 151
lehavdl-loshn, 40–43
Lehrer, Erica, 176
Lem, Stanisław, 6
Leo IX (Pope), 35
Lerner, David Levine, 46
letter writers of *Kultura* (journal), 117–20
Lexicon of Intimate Cities (Andrukhovych), 14

Li Bai (Li Po), 88
Libicki, Marcin, 184, 185
Lichtensztajn, Israel, 220
limpieza de sangre (doctrine of racial purity), 36
Lindner, Rainer, 82
Literary News *(Wiadomości Literackie)*, 107, 109
Literary Weekly *(Tygodnik Literacki)*, 111
literature, 248, 249; extraterritorial, 124–25; *Kultura* (journal), 104–25 *(See also Kultura* (journal)); as social geographer's tool, 151
Lithuania: accession to European Union (EU), 8; treaties, 1
Little Birch *(Bjarozka)*, 87
little Czech *(čecháček)*, 140
liturgical poem *(piyyut)*, 34
Liustra Dzion (Daily Mirror), 88
Lobel, Anita, 263
locals (Tuteishyia), 79, 80, 82, 83–89, 91
lottery, 156, 157
Love and Obstacles (Hemon), 160
Luca, Ioana, 131, 132
Lukashenka, Aliaksandr, 81, 91
Lutsevich, Ivan. *See* Kupala, Yanka

M

Macedonia, 15, 244, 245
Magocsi, Paul, 4
Majalah al-Islam newspaper, 58
Maksimiuk, Jan, 88
Malcolm X, 60
Malraux, André, 110
The Man without Qualities (Musil), 11
maps, 2, 7, 8, 11, 14, 113–17; cartogram of *Kultura* authors by country (1947–49), 117*f*; cartogram of *Kultura* authors by country (1960–64), 117*f*; cartogram showing the proportional amount of funding by country (1955–63), 123*f*; cartogram showing the proportional amount of funding

by country (1974–81), 124*f*; *East of the West: A Country in Stories* (Penkov), 153–60; fictional cartographies, 131–32; graduated symbol map of *Kultura* authors by city (1947–89), 114*f*, 115*f*; graduated symbol map of *Kultura* authors by city–Europe (1954–63), 115*f*; graduated symbol map of *Kultura* authors by city–Europe (1974–81), 116*f*; graduated symbol map of *Kultura* authors by city–Europe (1982–89), 116*f*; graduated symbol map of *Kultura* funders by city (1947–89), 120; graduated symbol map of *Kultura* funders by city (1955–63), 121*f*; graduated symbol map of *Kultura* funders by city (1974–81), 121*f*; graduated symbol map of *Kultura* funders by city (1982–89), 122*f*; graduated symbol map of *Kultura* letter writers by city (1950–89), 118*f*; graduated symbol map of *Kultura* letter writers by city–Europe (1954–63), 119*f*; graduated symbol map of *Kultura* letter writers by city–Europe (1974–81), 119*f*; Sarajevo's imaginaries (Hemon), 160–65; transnational matrix of spaces, 151–66

Márai, Sándor, 248

Mark, Yudl, 31, 34, 35, 37, 38, 43, 44, 45. *See also The Jewish Pope (Der yidisher poyps)*

Marples, David, 85

Marxism, 124, 211

Mašeraŭ, Piotar, 86

Maximilian (Archduke), 214

Maxwell, Alexander, 10

Mayse bukh, 34

McMillin, Arnold, 87

Mehmeti, Halide, 60

Mein Kampf (Hitler), 257

Melâmî Sufi *tarqia* (school), 56

memory: postmemory, 250; wars, 3

Mendelsohn, Erich, 173, 174, 175, 176, 180, 183, 190; Mossehaus (Berlin, Germany), 182*f*; Olsztyn's Bet Tahara (Poland), 181, 186, 188*f*

Mendieta, Eduardo, 12

Meng, Michael, 176

Menzel, Jiří, 134

metageography, 2

Mickiewicz, Adam, 272, 273

Mieroszewski, Juliusz, 111

Miller, Hillis, 12

Miller, Nancy K., 231, 233, 255

Milošević, Slobodan, 62

Miłosz, Czesław, 6, 85, 106, 108, 136, 138

Minsk Party Committee, 86

Mirojević, Hidajeta, 54, 60

Mishkova, Dina, 105

Mishra, Pankaj, 56

Mladi Muslimani, 62

mocarstwowość (imperialness), 109

Molotov-Ribbentrop Pact (1939), 1

Montefiore, Moses, 36

Moretti, Franco, 113, 278

Morsi, Mohamed, 66

Mortara, Edgardo, 35–37

Mosse, Rudolf, 175, 180

Mossehaus (Berlin, Germany), 182*f*

Munich Accords (1938), 135

murals, 202–20; *Fragment 1: An Old Apartment*, 204–5; *Fragment 2: A Surprising Discovery*, 205; *Fragment 3: The Wearing Away of That Film*, 205; *Fragment 4: Bare Skeletons*, 205–6; *Fragment 5: Chronotope*, 206; *Fragment 6: One Profile, One Hand, One Leg*, 206–7; *Fragment 7: Tandeta*, 207–8; *Fragment 8: Universal Masquerade*, 208–9; *Fragment 9: A Clown's Stuck-Out Tongue*, 209; *Fragment 10: Angelicized Country and Chosen Land*, 209–10; *Fragment 11: Peripeteias We Ourselves Had Instigated*, 210–11; *Fragment 12: To Mature into Childhood*, 211;

Fragment 13: Director of Landscapes, 212; *Fragment 14: The Core Capital of Imagination,* 212–13; *Fragment 15: Faces,* 213–14; *Fragment 16: Mere Legend,* 214–15; *Fragment 17: Passing from One Face to Another,* 215
Museum of the History of Serbia, 242
Musil, Robert, 11
Muslim International, 59–64
Muslims, 29, 30. *See also* Islam; in the Balkans, 53–68; community of Muslims *(ummah),* 54, 56–59, 68; the hajj, 59–64; history of, 55
Myśl Mocarstwowa, 108

N
Nadeau, Maurice, 218
Napoleon III, 36
Nasha Niva (Our Field [Dubavets]), 88–90
National Identity Card (Občanský průkaz), 135
National Museum (Belgrade), 241
Native Realm (Miłosz), 85
NATO, 153, 155
Nazis, 36, 44, 134, 143, 174, 236, 255, 258
neighbors, 3
Neighbors (Gross), 186
Neue Synagoge. *See* New Synagogue (Poznań, Poland)
New Synagogue (Poznań, Poland), 174, 175–80, 179*f,* 185*f;* framing the past, 190–93; Jewish communities in Allenstein, Poland, 180–82; reappearance of, 183–86
Newton, Adam Zachary, 10, 174
New Yorker, 160
New York Review of Books, 213
non-Jewish Poles, 253–56
non-Slavic Muslims, 54. *See also* Muslims
North Africa, 56
Novi Pazar, 58

Nowhere Man (Hemon), 160
Nussimbaum, Lev, 37–38

O
Občanský průkaz (National Identity Card), 135
Occidentalism, 9
Olsztyn's Bet Tahara (Poland), 173, 177, 180, 181*f,* 186–89, 188*f. See also bet tahara;* framing the past, 190–93; reappearance of, 183–86
open borders, 15
Ordinary Men (Browning), 255
Orientalism, 9, 37, 152, 165, 244
Orthodox Christianity, 244
Orthodoxy, 9, 29
Orzeł Biały (journal), 106
Ostře sledované vlaky (Closely Watched Trains [Hrabel]), 133, 134, 138, 141, 142, 143
Ottoman Empire, 53, 54, 55, 58, 61, 239–41, 242, 243, 245; partitions from, 56
Ottoman sultan *(khalīfah),* 56, 57
Our Field *(Nasha Niva* [Dubavets]), 88–90
Oushakine, Serguei Alex., 7
Oyerbakh, Rachel, 217
Oyneg Shabes, 202, 215–20, 270
Ozick, Cynthia, 212, 214

P
Palestine, 43, 64
Paloff, Benjamin, 212
Pamuk, Orhan, 240
Pan Tadeusz (Mickiewicz), 272
Pelíšky (Cozy Dens), 134
Penkov, Miroslav, 131, 132, 152, 153–60, 165, 166
People's Republic of Poland, 183
Perekrestki (Crossroads), 91
Petrova, Tsveta, 13
petty heroes: Central Europe, 138–41; Hrabal, Bohumil, 141–45

phrase books (Croatian), 235
The Physics of Sorrow (Gospodinov), 13
Pickle, John, 2
Piłsudski, Józef, 210
the pious ancestors *(al-salaf al-salih)*, 67
Pius IX (Pope), 36
piyyut (liturgical poem), 34
Plaŭnik, Samuil, 84
Płockier, Anna, 217, 219
poems, 105. *See also Kultura* (journal); literature
Poland, 12, 210, 248–64; accession to European Union (EU), 8; anecdotes (Grazyna G.), 259–62; cauldrons of hatred, 256–59; correspondence with Grazyna G., 251–52; *Kultura* (journal), 79, 80, 92 (*See also Kultura*); language (as basis of affiliation), 252–53; laws, 3; non-Jewish Poles, 253–56; second visit to Cracow, 262–64; Stalin, Joseph, 4; treaties, 1; World War II experiences (Grazyna G.), 253–56
The Polish Imperial Idea *(Polska idea imperialna)*, 108
Polish-Lithuanian Commonwealth, 83
political crises, 12
Polityka, 107, 108
Polska idea imperialna (The Polish Imperial Idea), 108
popes of Jewish origin, 31, 32. *See also* Jewish religion
postcolonialism, 113
post-Communism, 131; critical transnationalism, 165–66; *East of the West: A Country in Stories* (Penkov), 153–60; Sarajevo's imaginaries (Hemon), 160–65; transnational matrix of spaces, 151–66
post-Habsburg Galician Jewry, 216
postmemory, 250
Potíže s dějinami (Troubles with History), 135
Powers, Denise, 209

Poznań's New Synagogue (Poland), 174, 175–80
Pratt, Daniel, 131
Prince Wied, 57
protest movements, 79

Q
Qamili, Sheikh Haxhi, 54, 56, 57
The Question of Bruno (Hemon), 160, 162
Qur'an, study of, 61. *See also* Islam

R
racial purity, doctrine of *(limpieza de sangre)*, 36
Ramet, Sabrina, 62
Ranstorp, Magnus, 65
Register of Immobile Monuments, 186
Reiss, Tom, 37, 38, 41
religions, 7, 9. *See also* specific religions; history of, 29–30
Republic of Belarus. *See* Belarus
Residential Castle (Residenzschloss), 178, 179
Residenzschloss (Residential Castle), 178, 179
Revel, Jacques, 105
Rexhepi, Piro, 7, 29, 30, 239, 273
Ringelblum, Emanuel, 216, 217, 220
rites of return, 231, 255
Roman Jewry, 36
Romantic heroism, 137
Rosh Hashanah, 34
Roskies, David, 40
Roth, Philip, 214
Rothberg, Michael, 3, 274
Rothschild, James, 36
Rothschild, Lionel, 36
Royal Academy, 178
Rushdie, Salman, 153
Russia, 4, 175; annexation of Crimea, 9
Russia–Europe–America (Mendelsohn), 175
Russian Revolution, 37

S
Said, Edward, 83, 278
Said, Khurban, 37
Salihbegović, Melika, 54, 62, 63
Santner, Eric, 203
Sarajevo Process of 1983, 62, 63
Schlachetzki, Sarah M., 173
Schulz, Bruno, 174, 202, 203–20, 272, 275; *Fragment 1: An Old Apartment*, 204–5; *Fragment 2: A Surprising Discovery*, 205; *Fragment 3: The Wearing Away of That Film*, 205; *Fragment 4: Bare Skeletons*, 205–6; *Fragment 5: Chronotope*, 206; *Fragment 6: One Profile, One Hand, One Leg*, 206–7; *Fragment 7: Tandeta*, 207–8; *Fragment 8: Universal Masquerade*, 208–9; *Fragment 9: A Clown's Stuck-Out Tongue*, 209; *Fragment 10: Angelicized Country and Chosen Land*, 209–10; *Fragment 11: Peripeteias We Ourselves Had Instigated*, 210–11; *Fragment 12: To Mature into Childhood*, 211; *Fragment 13: Director of Landscapes*, 212; *Fragment 14: The Core Capital of Imagination*, 212–13; *Fragment 15: Faces*, 213–14; *Fragment 16: Mere Legend*, 214–15; *Fragment 17: Passing from One Face to Another*, 215; *Oyneg Shabes*, 202, 215–20
Second Partition (1793), 177
Sedgwick, Eve Kosofsky, 262
Seegel, Steven, 11
Seksztajn, Gela, 218, 219, 220
Serbia, 238, 242, 243
Shajbak, Miraslaŭ, 87
Shariati, Ali, 62
Sherman, Joseph, 35, 41
Sicherheitsdienst, 205
Šiljak, Safija, 54, 60
Skamander (literary monthly), 107
Skurko, Andrej, 93
Škvorecký, Josef, 134
Slavic peoples, 2

Slovakia, accession to European Union (EU), 8
Slovenia, accession to European Union (EU), 8
Snyder, Timothy, 3, 5
Sokolović, Mehmed, 239, 240
Soviet Armenia, 4
Soviet Belarus, 79, 81, 85; protest movements, 79
Soviet Union, 186. *See also* Russia
Spivak, Gayatri, 92
Stalin, Josef, 1, 9, 86; Poland, 4
Story of a Secret State (Karski), 258
Stsiapan, Ŭladzimir, 87
Stübben, Hermann Josef, 177
Švejk, Jaroslav Hašek's, 141
Sys, Anatol, 87
Szelińska, Józefina, 218
Szuman, Stefan, 220

T
Talmudic period, 31
Tanoukhi, Nirvana, 104
terrorism, 64
The Ethnographic State: France and the Invention of Moroccan Islam (Burke), 56
"The Scale of World Literature" (Tanoukhi), 104
They Wouldn't Hurt a Fly (Drakulić), 236, 237
Tito, Broz, 7
Tittelbach, Franz, 241
Tlostanova, Madina, 6
Todorova, Maria, 2, 236
Toptani, Esad Pasha, 57
Trans-Atlantyk (Gombrowicz), 4
transnationalism, 165–66
Travel Story 1: Gračac (2004), 229–31
treaties, Molotov-Ribbentrop Pact (1939), 1
Troubles with History (Kroutvor), 138
Troubles with History (Potíže s dějinami), 135
Tuteishyia (Kupala), 84

Tuteishyia (locals), 79, 80, 82, 83–89, 91
Tygodnik Literacki (Literary Weekly), 111

U

Udel, Miriam, 29, 273
Ugrešić, Dubravka, 86
Ukraine, 1, 4, 82, 92, 277
ummah (community of Muslims), 54, 56–59, 68
Union of Jewish Religious Communities in Poland (Związek Gmin Wyznaniowych Żydowskichw RP), 184
United States, 152, 159, 175
Universal Declaration of Human Rights, 13
University of Medina, 67

V

Valéry, Paul, 110
Vita Nuova (Hrabel), 144
von Hagen, Mark, 105
von Kapos-Mére, Kajetan Mérey, 57

W

Wahhabis, 67
Waldstein, Maxim, 10
Wałęsa, Lech, 13
wars: American Revolutionary War, 5; Cold War (*See* Cold War); memory, 3; World War II (*See* World War II)
Warsaw Ghetto, 215, 216, 217
Weimar Republic, 37, 175
Weltanschauung (world view), 87
West, definition of, 154
West, Rebecca, 242–44
Western Europe, 4, 13, 37
Wiadomości Literackie (Literary News), 106, 107, 109, 204
Wilder, Gary, 56
Władysław Jagiełło State Gymnasium, 218
Wolff, Larry, 8

Wolffenstein, Richard, 178, 182*f*. *See also* New Synagogue (Poznań, Poland); New Synagogue (Poznań, Poland), 185*f*
World Bank, 153
world literature, 104. *See also* literature
World War I, 145, 154, 192, 236, 270
World War II, 1, 133, 141, 236, 253, 261

X

Xhudo, Gus, 65

Y

Yad Vashem, 174, 203
Yaeger, Patricia, 151
Yehoshua, A. B., 213
Yiddishism, 211
Der yidisher poyps (The Jewish Pope), 31; historical context of, 33–35; plot of, 32–33
yidishkeyt (Jewish identity), 44
Young Muslims, 59
Youth Rebellion *(Bunt Młodych)*, 107, 108, 109
Yugoslavia, 58, 62, 160, 162, 234, 244, 250; Communism, 232; disintegration of, 64; Islam in, 61
Yugoslav Muslim Organization, 59

Z

al-Zaatar, Tal, 63
zabytek nieruchomy (immovable monument), 177
Zamenhof, Ludwik, 269, 270, 271
Zamenhof monument in Odessa, 270*f*
"Zeydlus der ershter" ("Zeidlus the First"), 32, 38–40
Zhadan, Serhiy, 275, 276
Zionist Union for Germany (Zionistische Vereinigung für Deutschland), 180
Zombie Wars (Hemon), 160

www.ingramcontent.com/pod-product-compliance
Lightning Source LLC
Chambersburg PA
CBHW072146100526
44589CB00015B/2109